THE ART
OF PLANNING

Selected Essays of
Harvey S. Perloff

ENVIRONMENT, DEVELOPMENT, AND PUBLIC POLICY

A series of volumes under the general editorship of
Lawrence Susskind, *Massachusetts Institute of Technology*
Cambridge, Massachusetts

CITIES AND DEVELOPMENT

Series Editor: Lloyd Rodwin, *Massachusetts Institute of Technology*
Cambridge, Massachusetts

CITIES AND CITY PLANNING
Lloyd Rodwin

THINKING ABOUT DEVELOPMENT
Lisa Peattie

CONSERVING AMERICA'S NEIGHBORHOODS
Robert K. Yin

MAKING-WORK
Self-Created Jobs in Participatory Organizations
William Ronco and Lisa Peattie

CITIES OF THE MIND
Images and Themes of the City in the Social Sciences
Lloyd Rodwin and Robert M. Hollister

NEIGHBORHOODS, PEOPLE, AND COMMUNITY
Roger S. Ahlbrandt, Jr.

HERE THE PEOPLE RULE
Selected Essays
Edward C. Banfield

THE ART OF PLANNING
Selected Essays of Harvey S. Perloff
Edited by Leland S. Burns and John Friedmann

Other subseries:

ENVIRONMENTAL POLICY AND PLANNING
Series Editor: Lawrence Susskind, *Massachusetts Institute of Technology*
Cambridge, Massachusetts

PUBLIC POLICY AND SOCIAL SERVICES
Series Editor: Gary Marx, *Massachusetts Institute of Technolgoy*
Cambridge, Massachusetts

THE ART
OF PLANNING

Selected Essays of
Harvey S. Perloff

Edited by
Leland S. Burns

and

John Friedmann

Graduate School of Architecture and Urban Planning
University of California, Los Angeles
Los Angeles, California

PLENUM PRESS • NEW YORK AND LONDON

Library of Congress Cataloging in Publication Data

Perloff, Harvey S.
  The art of planning.

  (Environment, development, and public policy. Cities and development)
  Bibliography: p.
  Includes index.
  1. City planning—Addresses, essays, lectures. 2. Urban policy—Addresses, essays, lectures. 3. Urban economics—Addresses, essays, lectures. 4. Urban renewal—Addresses, essays, lectures. I. Burns, Leland Smith. II. Friedmann, John. III. Title. IV. Series.
HT166.P389   1985   307.1′2   85-12470
ISBN 0-306-42030-9

© 1985 Plenum Press, New York
·A Division of Plenum Publishing Corporation
233 Spring Street, New York, N.Y. 10013

Printed in the United States of America

HARVEY S. PERLOFF
(1915–1983)

Acknowledgments

The editors wish to thank the following for permission to reprint copyrighted materials in this book.

Chapter 1: From "New Towns Intown," in *Journal of the American Institute of Planners*, May 1966, Vol. 32, pp. 155–161. Reprinted by permission of the *Journal of the American Institute of Planners*.

Chapter 2: From "New-Towns-Intown in a National New-Communities Program," in *New Towns: Why—and for Whom?*, edited by Harvey S. Perloff and Neil C. Sandberg. New York: Praeger Publishers, 1973, pp. 159–178. Copyright © 1973, Praeger Publishers, Inc. Reprinted by permission of Praeger Publishers.

Chapter 3: From "The Central City in the Postindustrial Age," in *The Mature Metropolis*, edited by Charles L. Leven. Lexington, Mass.: Lexington Books, 1978, pp. 109–130. Reprinted by permission of Charles L. Leven and the publisher.

Chapter 4: From "Using the Arts to Improve Life in the City," in *Journal of Cultural Economics*, December 1979, Vol. 3, pp. 1–21. Reprinted by permission of the publisher.

Chapter 5: From "A Framework for Dealing with the Urban Environment: An Introductory Statement," in *The Quality of the Urban Environment*, edited by Harvey S. Perloff. Washington, D.C.: Resources for the Future, Inc., 1969, pp. 221–239. Reprinted by permission of the publisher.

Chapter 6: From "Urban Planning and the Quality of the Urban Environment," in *The Political Economy of Environmental Control*, edited by Joe S. Bain and Warren F. Ilchman. Berkeley, Calif.: Institute of Business and Economic Research, University of California, 1972, pp. 67–85. Reprinted by permission of the publisher.

Chapter 7: From "National Urban Policy: Stage I: Building the Foundation," in *Spatial, Regional and Populational Economics: Essays in Honor of Edgar Hoover*, edited by Mark Perlman, Charles J. Leven, and Benjamin Chinitz. New York: Gordon & Breach, 1972, pp. 311–331. Reprinted by permission of the editors and the publisher.

Chapter 8: From "Alternatives for Future Urban Land Policy," in *Modernizing Urban Land Policy*, edited by Marion Clawson. Baltimore: The Johns Hopkins Press for Resources for the Future, 1973, pp. 221–239. Reprinted by permission of the publisher.

Chapter 9: "Public Services and Social Priorities," in *Puerto Rico's Economic Future*. Chicago: The University of Chicago Press, 1950, pp. 378–394. Copyright 1950 by The University of Chicago. Reprinted by permission of the publisher.

Chapter 10: From "National Planning and Multinational Planning under the Alliance for Progress," with Raúl Saez, in *Organization, Planning, and Programming for Economic Development*. United States papers prepared for the United Nations Conference on the Application of Science and Technology for the Benefit of the Less Developed Areas. Washington, D.C.: U.S. Government Printing Office, 1962, pp. 47–54.

Chapter 11: From "Lagging Sectors and Regions of the American Economy," in *Papers and Proceedings, American Economic Association*, December 1959, pp. 223–230. Reprinted by permission of the publisher.

Chapter 12: From "Natural Resource Endowment and Regional Economic Growth," with Lowdon Wingo, Jr., in *Natural Resources and Economic Growth*, edited by Joseph J. Spengler. Washington, D.C.: Resources for the Future, Inc., 1961, pp. 191–212. Reprinted by permission of Lowdon Wingo, Jr., and the publisher.

Chapter 13: From "Relative Regional Economic Growth: An Approach to Regional Accounts," in *Design of Regional Accounts*, edited by Werner Hochwald. Baltimore: The Johns Hopkins Press for Resources for the Future, 1961, pp. 38–65. Reprinted by permission of the publisher.

Chapter 14: From "Key Features of Regional Planning," in *Journal of the American Institute of Planners*, May 1968, Vol. 34, pp. 153–159. Reprinted by permission of the *Journal of the American Institute of Planners*.

Chapter 15: From "Budgetary Symbolism and Fiscal Planning," in *Public Policy: A Yearbook of the Graduate School of Public Administration*, edited by C. J. Friedrich and Edward S. Mason. Cambridge, Mass.: Graduate School of Public Administration, Harvard University, 1941, pp. 36–62. Reprinted by permission of the John F. Kennedy School of Government, Harvard University.

Chapter 16: From "Fiscal Policy at the State and Local Levels," in *Postwar Economic Problems*, edited by Seymour E. Harris. New York: McGraw-Hill Book Co., 1943, pp. 221–238. Reprinted by permission of the publisher.

Chapter 17: From "Education of City Planners: Past, Present, and Future," in *Journal of the American Institute of Planners*, Fall 1956, Vol. 23, pp. 186–217. Reprinted by permission of the *Journal of the American Institute of Planners*.

Chapter 18: From "The Evolution of Planning Education," in *Planning in America: Learning from Turbulence*, edited by David R. Goldschalk. Washington, D.C.: American Institute of Planners, 1974, pp. 161–180. Reprinted by permission of David R. Goldschalk and the publisher.

Contents

Introduction

The work of Harvey S. Perloff stands as a landmark in the evolution of Anglo-American planning doctrine. It is impossible to fully capture the essence of the published work in a paragraph, page, or even an entire essay. Yet its highpoints can be identified. His work was innovative, reformist, comprehensive, and oriented toward the future. In emphasizing the greater importance of people compared to things, Perloff repeatedly prodded planners to be concerned with human needs and values. He was critical of the past. But inasmuch as he devoted more effort to envisioning what could lie ahead than in recalling the past, his work was markedly optimistic. He once admitted in writing to his "built-in weakness for expecting rational, socially oriented solutions ultimately to win out, no matter what the objective situation seems to be." To some the expectation may be seen as naive; to others, as a faith in the wisdom of humankind to take the best course. However received, Perloff's optimism served as a powerful stimulant to keep moving ahead for the best that would come of it.

Institutions and the ways they should be shaped and reshaped were of central concern, for institutions (though he rarely used the term) were the instruments through which "knowledge was translated into action." Perloff was constantly aware of the equity criterion as a norm against which decisions must be assessed; those whom society had passed over were very much in his mind and were central figures in his prescriptions for a better society.

Perloff's inventiveness manifested itself in many ways; innovations permeate his writing. Early on, there was the bold new experiment in planning education at the University of Chicago. As his autobiography recalls, "It must be remembered that this was the first effort to base planning on the social sciences and everything else was, in fact, invention." He was there to help structure experiments when so little was given: on occasions like this, he was at his very best. A review of his literary output uncovers other innovations as well: "New Towns in Town" and the concept of amenity resources, to cite from a long list. He invented the field of urban economics and was among the first to recognize the importance of environmental planning. The field of development economics owes him one of its pioneering studies. The list could easily be extended.

One can isolate many reasons why the future commanded Perloff's attention, but only speculate on which of these were determining. His formative years were lived during the Great Depression and World War II, two events that everyone hoped would never again be repeated. They left deep imprints that could not be erased, but only replaced by his faith in a brighter future for humanity.

What discipline is more deeply committed to envisioning the future than planning, a field that by necessity must look ahead? Perloff writes in unpublished materials, "it is the built-in feature of a search for 'a better future' in public planning that sets planning aside from other governmental activities."

Studies of the future can be dichotomized between those that predict what the future *will* be, in a deterministic or positivistic sense, and those that predict what it *should* be in a normative sense. Projections by futurists of the first mold are always subject to the criticism that reality fails to match expectations. This risk does not apply to futures work of the second type. The failure of society and its institutions to act along the lines desired by planners leaves the goals unsullied and intact. Perloff's work was of the second type.

It could be argued that the failure of history to comply with human goals and desires invalidates the vision. But on that reckoning, most visions would have to be scrapped, and we would be left groping blindly on the fringes of tomorrow. The facts of history are ineluctible, but the human spirit invariably seeks to transcend them. His unceasing efforts at transcendence rank as Perloff's greatest achievement.

His future rarely had a specific time horizon. It was not a program to be implemented but a general vision, or what Rexford Tugwell called "a directive in history." The pursuit of the vision itself was failsafe. Each setback would only lead to a redoubling of effort.

Some might see in this a Sysiphusian labor. And perhaps it was that. But as Albert Camus once allowed himself to speculate: what was it that Sysiphus thought as he pushed the heavy boulder, again and again, up that vast mountain slope from which it would inevitably roll down into the plains? Was he a man condemned or was he driven by hope that this once, surely, he would succeed, and the rock remain perched on its high precipice? Perloff clearly was inspired by such hope that inspired all who came within his orbit.

A major test of a work's importance in the policy sciences is its ability to address abiding social problems in ways that continue to be relevant years after it is written. On this test, Perloff's work does astoundingly well. Most policy studies compel momentary attention only to sink into early oblivion. But the problems of national, state, and local finance of which he wrote four decades ago remain with us, and Perloff's analysis of them, and his prescriptions, still carry a lesson. His prescriptions, based on a careful study of the requirements for industrial expansion in Puerto Rico, continue to be as valid today as they were in the early fifties when he drafted them. And planning educators gain inspiration from rereading his early essays on the education of planners. Perloff's acute insight into the role of the planning professional as a "generalist with a speciality," and his curricular innovation that introduced required core subjects into the study of planning continues to be the central pole of planning education in the United States.

Perloff's work is inclusive in a double sense. By embracing the uncertain future, it is inclusive in the direction of time, focussing on decisions. By being forthrightly interdisciplinary, his work is inclusive of other fields of knowledge.

In a period when most social scientists fretted over the possibilities of inter-disciplinary work (something that everyone recognized as important for a full understanding of social phenomena but few knew how to successfully inte-grate), Perloff in his own person combined the talents of the economist, political scientist, anthropologist, sociologist, and geographer. He refused to accept lim-its to knowledge and boldly asserted propositions that could only stem from his deep understanding of the social sciences.

The writings concern what needs to be done to improve the way that plan-ning is taught, learned, assessed, prescribed, practiced, or the way that plan-ning decisions are formulated, implemented and evaluated, or, more broadly yet, the way that we should think about cities and regions. Thus, it is the art of planning and the way the art is mastered, applied, and continually improved that runs throughout the articles—the constantly returning leitmotif that holds them together. The articles are filled with exhortations, though usually they are grounded in factual analysis and are carefully reasoned. In an academic perspec-tive, their theoretical underpinnings may appear to be a bit sketchy at times. But Perloff was a planner first and only then an economist or social scientist. He was concerned with influencing policy and practice. Abstract theorizing was foreign to his way of thinking.

This book is intended to serve as a collateral text for students of planning and allied fields, such as urban geography and economics. Aside from covering nearly all of the important issues that planners have confronted during the post-war era, and providing recipes for changes that could be the subject of consider-able discussion in advanced seminars, several of the essays succinctly review the history of the field in its several aspects. "Education of City Planners: Past, Present and Future" comprehensively tracks the development of planning prac-tice from its early days, and the parallel evolution of education for its practi-tioners; the two first articles in Part II, "Urban and Metropolitan Planning and Policy," furnish a critical narrative of the evolution of the environmental move-ment; the development of national policy for managing resources is covered in "National Urban Policy; Stage I: Building the Foundation." "Natural Resource Endowment and Regional Economic Growth" traces subnational development from 1850 to 1950, classifying it into growth stages that are determined by the dominant types of resources being exploited and developed. The first four chap-ters of Part I, read together, show how Perloff thinks about ideas starting from a very general and often quite ambiguous notion (the first chapter), refines it in light of new information (the second), defines it more precisely in terms of certain key causes and consequences (the third), and finally hones in on one particularly crucial aspect as an example of the type of solution that may be workable (the fourth).

The editors have contributed very little to the volume. Their task was to choose articles to reproduce from among materials appearing in 57 scholarly articles, 16 books, and 15 reports and brochures; to organize them substantively; and to furnish an introduction for each part. These prefaces attempt to establish the importance of the articles comprising chapters in each part by recalling the setting in which they were written, and to personalize them by describing the relation between that context and the author's intentions.

With a single exception, books were not excerpted, although selections were made from free-standing chapters that Perloff contributed to books edited by others. Just as symphonic movements were meant to be played as entities rather than separate pieces, the chapters of a book are meant to be read together. This rule required us to exclude some important work, such as *Regions, Resources and Economic Growth* (written with Edgar S. Dunn, Eric Lampard, and Richard W. Muth), a landmark in the area of regional economics but a book that simply cannot be reprinted satisfactorily in part. Still, three of the essays reproduced here (Chapters 11, 12, and 13), drawing extensively from materials in that book, capture much of its essence. The only exception to this rule is an excerpted chapter from *Puerto Rico's Economic Future*.

In 1981 Harvey Perloff began a comprehensive review of his own scholarly and professional work. The corpus was abstracted piece by piece and organized under six topical headings similar to those used in this volume. Introductions were written that set the stage by describing the circumstances that prompted his thinking. Drafts of the manuscript were circulated to his colleagues who recommended, instead, a more intimate autobiographical memoir. The suggestion was followed and the incomplete result, stopping at about 1970, concludes the collection.

The five categories for classifying the writings—Revitalizing Central Cities, Urban and Metropolitan Planning and Policy, Regional Planning and Analysis, Fiscal Policy and Planning, and Planning Education—cover fairly accurately the major topics tackled by this inordinately productive man and the range of his interests. Taken together, they describe the art of planning.

Mimi Perloff provided the editors with valuable insights and in many ways contributed, both knowingly and unknowingly, to the substance of the articles when they were first written. It is to her that this volume is dedicated.

Jeff Perloff who, as a member of the faculty of the Department of Natural Resources at the University of California, Berkeley, maintains his father's concerns for matters of resource development, has been dedicated to this project since its inception, and aided the editors in selecting materials for reproduction and annotation. Abstracts of each item in the complete corpus of work, written by Scott Edmondson, Richard Papel, and Bish Sanyal, assisted the editors in their task.

LELAND S. BURNS
JOHN FRIEDMANN

*Cambridge, England
and Los Angeles, California*

I

REVITALIZING CENTRAL CITIES

INTRODUCTION

The four papers comprising Part I, dealing with the difficulties confronting central cities and possible solutions, are arranged by their date of publication. Read as a group, they display in an orderly fashion the development of the author's thinking about strategies for addressing central city problems. The first piece proposes a solution that draws on the new towns experience, transferring the concept to the central city. The second essay, written after the proposals of the first were awkwardly and ineffectually incorporated into federal housing legislation, calls for a modified approach that concentrates more directly on the central city and its resident population. The third article examines the central city problem by focussing on shifts in employment structure at macroscale and assesses their consequences for central cities. Particularly emphasized is the rapid expansion of tertiary employment in areas previously dominated by, and dependent on, manufacturing activity, and the emergence of information-intensive activities and amenities. The potential for dealing with central city problems through the development of the arts industry is examined in the fourth essay. Taken together, the four pieces show the evolution of an idea.

Metropolitan areas boomed in the wake of World War II and during the following decades, but their overall growth masked the decline of central cities. Suburbanization, aided by implicit public policies, drained the cores of their population and economic life. Urban renewal offered the promise of stabilizing populations and renewing the dying centers. But the promise was not kept. Bulldozing was not the answer. It involved wholesale displacement of ghetto populations, destroyed capital assets of value, broke up fragile social networks of minority and elderly populations and, as the cleared land remained unbuilt for many years, failed to generate the expected windfalls for municipal treasuries. Alternatives were not apparent. The "New Towns Intown" idea (NTIT) attempted to fill the vacuum. It offered to solve central city problems without the disruptions caused by urban renewal. The solution could be read as physical, but the provisions of the proposal dealt more intimately with a reweaving of the community's social fabric.

The genesis of the NTIT idea was a proposal Harvey Perloff had put forth during the 1950s for the redevelopment of the Hyde Park neighborhood adjacent to the University of Chicago campus. New Towns Intown called for renewing the inner city as an "integral and harmonious whole," much like the new towns that had sprung up recently in Britain and on the European continent. The concept applies "the core principles of the new town . . . to already built-up sections of the metropolis." It called for mixed uses, selected community-oriented shops, a "lighted center," and high-use recreation in an urban park setting.

The proposals promised much—almost as much as urban renewal but without its unhappy consequences. Most importantly, under NTIT, renewal was to occur without displacing people and jobs. Neighborhoods would be upgraded *in situ* through economic development programs aimed at job creation and income generation. Services would be upgraded as well. Capital flight and disinvestment would be halted. Multiplier effects of new investment would generate additional spending, particularly of private resources.

Alas, the idea was poorly timed, and the NTIT legislation again illustrated that, like a law unenforced, a program unfunded has little impact. Perloff wrote pessimistically:

> The same inadequacies that had plagued the urban renewal and model cities program doomed the New Town Intown program to failure. The lack of federal planning meant a lack of clarity and consistency of objectives as well as inadequate authority and resources to get the assigned tasks accomplished.

The failure of a good idea neither discouraged Perloff nor dissuaded him of the significance of the central city problem and the possibilities for dealing with it. In "The Central City in the Post-Industrial Age" he pushed ahead by focussing more precisely on the socioeconomic transformation of the central city, and its consequences for policy, as the nation moved into the post-industrial age. At the heart of these changes was the shift in occupational mix from goods production to services and, within this trend, the emergence of information-intensive activities. The future economic viability of the central city in its new age will depend on a special form of innovation, said Perloff. He argued for "the development of organizational capacity and skill for encouraging the emergence and growth of those services that are particularly fitting to the future central city." Each offers opportunities for creating jobs for low-skilled workers as well as for infusing income and other forms of new life into the downtowns of large American cities. The appropriate services are communications-intensive activities, such as those of corporate head offices; tourism and recreation activities; health, education, and other social services; and the arts and cultural services.

The last-named group of services, arts and cultural activities, serve as a springboard to the last article in Part I. "Using the Arts to Improve Life in the City" summarizes the volume, *The Arts in the Economic Life of the City*. The arts, it is claimed, bolster urban economies not only by creating new jobs, including "backstage" employment for the low-skilled, but also by increasing the city's attractiveness for income-generating business activities. The article identifies potential impacts, but it stops short of measuring their magnitudes (perhaps they are unmeasureable). Nor does the article make the claim that stimulating the arts puts city centers on the optimal path to redevelopment. At the theoretical level, the article challenges the claim that the arts, as service activities, are parasitic in that they merely accommodate local markets rather than produce for export. On the contrary, arts activities can generate incomes through tourism. Moreover, by enriching urban life, they make cities more attractive for industries that export their product. The arguments apply with particular force to central cities, not only because of their pressing needs for redevelopment, but because they offer potentials for developing arts-based enterprises that give employment to their labor forces.

The other major contribution is a list of how-to-do-it methods for advancing the arts in central cities. On the list are hotel taxes to finance arts development and subsidize ticket prices; zoning law revisions to encourage artists' colonies in recycled, functionally obsolete structures; giving higher priority to education in elementary and secondary schools to train both performers and develop appreciative new audiences; local departments of cultural affairs to oversee public efforts; and inclusion of a cultural element in general plans. At least one American city, Los Angeles, has used the arts in this way to revitalize its center. Part of Los Angeles's recent renaissance is an object lesson of Perloff's theorizing about the city.

1

New Towns Intown

Many of the things we are trying to do in our cities—the modernization of the city plant, the provision of better housing and facilities, the elimination of poverty and disadvantage—can be greatly advanced by an overall, integrating concept. I would propose the *New Town Intown* as such a concept.

The idea of the new town has spread to many parts of the world as people have come to appreciate its advantages for building in the open outlying areas surrounding major metropolitan regions. The core principles of the new town can be applied equally well to the already built-up sections of the metropolis, granting the need for substantial modifications.

The heart of the new town idea is the creation of an urban community conceived as an integrated and harmonious whole. Starting from scratch in an open area, the new town can provide the most modern of facilities, whether schools, shopping, or parking. The ability to develop through an overall plan makes possible community amenities and aesthetic qualities normally not realized. Because people today have both rising income and expanding leisure time, recreation receives an important role in the new town plan. (Reston, Virginia, for example, has made a golf course, an artificial lake, riding stables and bridle paths, and other recreational facilities the very backbone of the community.) The more advanced new town makes an effort to provide a balance between workplaces and homes. It has a distinctive center with important functional and visual purposes. Highrise apartments as well as low-lying buildings and individual homes help to provide variety as well as a superior design for living.

With adequate imagination and purpose, the essence of all this can be applied to the older parts of the metropolis. Since replanning is much more difficult than starting from scratch, it will require particularly good planning—aimed at the same goals of harmony and balance. It will normally require some strategic rebuilding as well as rehabilitation for continuous improvement according to a plan. An essential element would be a working partnership in planned urban development between the people of the area, a variety of public agencies, and private enterprise. The aim should not be to create communities that are all alike; each should have its own special character, its own focal points, its own attractions.

The new town intown concept can greatly help in transforming the physical environment of the city in keeping with social objectives and human resources needs. It cannot *solve* the human problems of the city, nor even all the physical problems. It *can* provide a valuable lever for both. If we hope to achieve the objectives of the antipoverty and other social programs, it will be necessary, among other things, to transform the total environment of poverty—the physical aspects as well as the social, economic, and political. It is important to create an environment in which the community as well as the individual family are important.

Because of the limitations of our present concepts, we have almost abandoned the vast gray areas of our cities: the approach in the past can almost be characterized as complete demolition or nothing at all. The new town intown can provide form and structure to the amorphous mass of the gray areas, strong focal points of interest and improvement, and a new hopefulness. The aim is not to achieve stability in every area, to hold people where they happen to be. Certainly, some of the areas will tend to become more stable through a new towns intown program. But mobility of families is both inevitable and healthy— in some cases it should definitely be encouraged—and the replanning and rebuilding should be done with this very much in mind. Even the more transitory areas can gain greatly through the application of new town features in a program of gradual improvement.

There is urgent need for a new approach to urban development and city rebuilding. It is time to get away from the bits and pieces of renewal, rehabilitation, and public housing projects and the essentially negative approach involved in "removing the slums" or "doing something about run-down housing." A great deal is to be gained by evolving a *positive* communitywide approach which would undertake, stage by stage, to do all the things necessary to achieve a desirable environment within our intown communities, using all available urban development tools in concert.

The staging is particularly important. We might think of the task as one of rehabilitating our cities on the "installment plan." This would permit the application of a community system of priorities, based on human needs and the interrelationships among various kinds of changes. The process would not necessarily start, as now, through the removal of an almost accidental number of units which happen to have reached certain stages of decay, but would involve an attack on whatever problems required primary attention—whether these are more or better facilities, high-density housing to meet increased population needs, or additional places of work. Special priority would be given to those improvements which could stimulate additional building and rebuilding without the application of public funds or subsidies, that is, improvements to serve as levers or multipliers. For example, the rebuilding of the schools or the refurbishing of the commercial enterprises might often be more valuable in initiating a spirit of improvement than the building of some higher income housing units through an isolated redevelopment project.

All this suggests that the objectives would be set *not* in terms of clearing the slums or rehabilitating a certain number of housing units, but rather the creation, stage by stage, of attractive, viable communities which serve to meet the high priority needs of the people within that community as well as of the region as a whole.

Major objectives of staging are to minimize the dislocation of families and businesses and to meet the more pressing housing needs. A desirable approach to housing might well focus on the development of a metropolitanwide Housing Budget with housing needs, demands and supply carefully projected for individual communities so that the community plans can help meet the housing requirements realistically. This might mean in certain instances that residential density will have to be increased. The results, we know from experience, need not be negative as long as the public facilities and transportation network are upgraded to meet the increased burden.

CHOOSING COMMUNITIES FOR NEW-TOWN-INTOWN DEVELOPMENT

Throughout the build-up areas of every metropolis there are some communities with a distinctive character, a vital physical focal point—generally some interesting shopping streets, and often a name known to all (Georgetown in Washington, D.C.: Greenwich Village in New Work; Old Town in Chicago). These would lend themselves quite readily to New Town Intown development. Other sections of the city, which are more amorphous, are more difficult to develop as genuine communities. However, given the will and imagination, such areas can also be energized and brought up to satisfying levels by such development. The question of priorities is very important, since a city can undertake only one or two New Town developments at a time. While it is essential to be realistic about how much can be started at one time, it is also necessary to appreciate the fact that five or six community projects might well be initiated within a decade—given a genuine national push in this direction. Thus, even our older cities should be able to create a renewed environment throughout within a generation or so. In fact, the achievement of this objective in all of our cities by the (magic) year 2000 would be a logical goal for our national urban development policy.

In recognition of the crucial human resource problem we should reverse the pattern of the past which, as in the case of urban renewal, has emphasized the construction of higher income housing rather than the improvement of the environment of the poorer and more disadvantaged groups. By contrast, a new towns program should start in those very communities where a transformation of the environment is essential, where dramatic physical and public service improvement can be a valuable tool in racial integration and in the anti-poverty and other social programs. This is a much greater challenge than giving the final touches to a community, say, like Georgetown, which can achieve new town standards with a relatively small amount of replanning and reconstruction.

It is in the poorer areas that the new schools, the improved community facilities, the lighted center, and the other intown elements outlined here can help knit together various racial and income groups through common interest in community improvement. Highest priority, in fact, should be given to the communities that are beginning to achieve successful integration. The program in such instances might make all the difference in stabilizing and strengthening the community's efforts.

It is well to keep in mind that it is the *total* environment that matters, as well as the life of each family within the larger community. Thus, for example, it is not reasonable to provide little more than an isolated institutionalized public housing unit and expect favorable overall results. The focus must be the total environment and the totality of services and facilities provided, not the provision of cheap housing alone.

The question of the size of the community to be encompassed in an Intown development is important. While it is evident that the question would have to be studied in each specific instance, given the great difference in density and in the character of various communities, the main principle is that the community should be large enough to support a broad complement of shopping and public facilities and, in most instances, of industrial and service work places as well. Experience with new towns in outlying areas, as well as studies of public service areas, suggest that new towns intown could be expected most often to range from some 50,000 to 100,000 people (with lower or higher figures under special conditions).

The problems of definition here are complex and important. We have not yet settled on the meanings of terms like "community," "neighborhood," or "district," nor have we developed any clear concepts as to how much interaction among families is to be expected or called for within a community or neighborhood. In the present context, I am using the word *community* to refer to an intown, largely residential area in which the residents share certain common facilities and services—specifically, secondary and higher education, major shopping, places of work, major recreational facilities, and major transportation arteries. It is the sharing of such services and facilities which is taken to be central to the community concept rather than the standard of substantial communication among residents. The latter plays a somewhat more important role in individual neighborhoods which make up a community, although even here frequent communication among families is much more a function of ethnic background, social and economic class, and so forth, rather than an automatic result of proximity. In the cities today, even in the case of the smaller neighborhoods, the integrating features are the services and facilities and considerations of safety and convenience.

Nevertheless, the scale of planning and building—which is clearly different at the citywide, community, and neighborhood levels—and the opportunities for gradual improvements offered at each scale is most significant. The emphasis here is on the community scale.

Let me outline what I believe to be the major ingredients for the building of a more satisfying life to the city with the creation of new towns intown.

1. *Work places in town.* One of the traditional principles of city planning, the separation of work places and homes, was initiated at a time when almost all factories and other places of work were unpleasant neighbors. Under the banner of this principle, there has been a continuing drive to remove intown plants and even small work shops, increasingly to isolate homes from jobs. But this situation has now changed and many kinds of workplaces might well be intown. This is particularly important for the poorer and more disadvantaged groups; studies have shown that many strongly prefer working near home. In fact, when they

cannot, some are in reality excluded from the labor market. In the case of school-age youths, the availability of nearby jobs can make a large difference in the rate of drop-outs. The ability to add to family income has traditionally been an important factor in poorer areas of the city. Thus, even if the mixture of work and homes were not ideal from the purely physical standpoint, it could still be argued that it is more important to have jobs nearby than to achieve merely an ideal physical situation.

Under an Intown program, an effort should be made to develop compact industrial estates attractive for a variety of nonnoxious industries, warehouses, and services. Highrise plants renting space to many small industries might well be experimented with, substituting the efficiency of vertical transportation for the gains of one-floor operations. Urban renewal can be a major tool in provid-ing such facilities and thereby an important means for bringing more jobs into town. Equally important is the effort to make available relatively cheap loft space through the rehabilitation of older buildings, for new and experimental businesses.

The provision of space at low rentals for small businesses and for small group activities is a critical requirement for the creation of viable new towns intown. Today, the very small shop, the artisan, the music school, or the chil-dren's dance school generally survive only in the most rundown sections and buildings. They should not only be helped to obtain the necessary space but should be put at the very center of things where they can give diversity and color to urban life. Even more important, as we enter an era in which most people are employed in trade and service activities, is the need to give the little busi-nessmen every break and every encouragement so as to expand job oppor-tunities. A noteworthy start in this direction has been undertaken in Chicago by the Harper Court Foundation, a group which has been formed specifically to make it possible for the artisans and small businessmen to flourish in the Hyde Park area of southside Chicago. It has been created by a clever use of existing tools, including a bond flotation in the community and a government loan. However, new tools to help artisans and small businesses will be necessary to achieve the larger scale purposes of the New Town Intown.

2. *Community facilities and services.* New towns in the outlying areas are desired in large part because they can provide the most modern of public ser-vices and facilities. Now it is also time that we begin seriously to modernize the public facilities and services intown, where the people who most need such services and facilities tend to live. Hence, a New Town Intown program should work to bring community services and facilities up to the highest level manage-able, an effort which might well merit a number one priority for urban renewal.

We should be building the most modern schools, hospitals, libraries, cultur-al centers, and community centers precisely where incomes are low and density is high, in contrast to our present practice. There is nothing like a modern school with an adequate and attractive play area to give a new town feeling to a community.

Some exciting new possibilities in school plant and arrangements have been the subjects of experimentation in recent years. Some of these, such as the idea of a multiple-school campus, may well be ready for broader scale execution under appropriate circumstances. Many communities need junior colleges and these, combined with modern high schools, can play a large role in bringing new life to the run-down parts of the city. In other areas high schools can be combined with junior high schools and/or vocational schools. Obviously the quality of the education is more important than the excellence of the facilities, but the two in combination can provide the best results. In some of the poor communities, it would be appropriate to combine special places of work together with vocational schools in such multi-unit school campuses. Beyond such new facilities, a community plan would have to provide for *all* the local educational needs of the community and gradual improvements to meet changing conditions according to plan.

There are needs for other kinds of facilities as well. Performing groups in nearly every community need a place in which they can perform: the little theater groups, the jazz combos, the unusually successful high school play, the periodic visits of the symphony orchestra, or some of its members formed into a pop group—the possibilities are endless. These opportunities can be made available throughout the city by building cultural and community centers into the fabric of the intowns.

3. *Lighted center.* The very essence of urbanity is nighttime activity. Men and women work, children are at school during the day. The nighttime is when the family can be together, when the community can interact. Yet the nighttime American city, with only a few outstanding exceptions, is truly dismal. Physical development, if well conceived, can contribute importantly to the enhancement of community and family life.

The beginning of a new town plan and the very core of the new town, then, should be a *lighted center.* As the name suggests, it would be brightly illuminated—a place for fun and interchange. Shops, restaurants, ice cream parlors, movie theatres, coffee houses, and night clubs would be clustered together. Attractive leisure activities for all members of the family should be located here, including a community center with facilities for teenagers as well as older people. In some cases an outdoor market would add the right note to the lighted center. (The Farmers' Market in Los Angeles is a good example.)

There would be quite a bit of scope here for developing new forms of illumination: including lighted walls, ground illumination, and the like. We have a long way to go in the development of more effective and attractive lighting facilities.

4. *Intown parks.* Great possibilities for enhancing life in the city lie in a new conception of urban public parks. There has been little change in the basic notion of public parks over the past fifty years, save only the significant extension of active sport facilities. Essentially it is still tied to the idea of bringing something of the country into the city. While this is certainly desirable, and open space in densely built up areas is both a necessity and a great asset, the possibilities of creating standard parks in central city areas are extremely limited.

One potentially useful direction of change is in the creation, not of a park itself, but of a *public park setting* for urban recreation activities. This would combine commercial facilities with public facilities. Thus, an integral part of a lighted center might be a public park and gardens to provide facilities for evening, as well as daytime, recreation and to add beauty to an important focal point of community activities. The combination of public and private facilities would contribute to the attraction and value of each.

Other possibilities are the creation of public gardens and recreation facilities for intensive use (such as swimming pools), joined with shopping and other private activities, in closed-off streets and on large rooftop areas.

5. *From tower apartments to doll-sized homes: A variety of living patterns.* One of the great "discoveries" of the past decade is that various types of living can go well together—high-rise apartments can mix well with individual homes—as long as they are properly planned and overall density is controlled. The tower apartment in the older sections can not only provide new types of living but a visual lift of great importance; witness Chicago's Marina City, a fine example of what can be accomplished in modern living, even in a rundown part of a city. Self-contained city-within-a-city construction has tremendous possibilities in the new towns intown, particularly as part of a program of revitalization. Possibilities exist for various new forms of cooperative, as well as private, building, but government may have to give some additional boost to realize them.

6. *The neighborhood improvement program.* While New Towns Intown will require dramatic focal points of the type described above, they will be effective only to the extent that they can generate a continuous upgrading of the physical environment of the community. In the older sections of cities *either blight moves in or improvement spreads outward.* Thus intowns would need strong neighborhood programs, periodically adjusted, to carry on a continuous process of planning, rehabilitation, and general improvement. Community organizations will have to be developed that can work hand in glove with the city planning, social welfare, and anti-poverty agencies to evolve joint programs of physical *and* social improvement. Only thus can individual families be recruited for the vast job of rehabilitation that is called for in our cities. Concrete, visible, communitywide objectives provide an excellent focal point for community organization. What is involved here is that people are being asked to work together as a community on the very things they share as a community—the quality of their environment and the quality of the services and facilities available. Also, cooperation is more feasible when the people of the community set their own system of priorities in the planning.

The task of creating neighborhood improvement programs, within the broad outlines of a citywide or regionwide plan, implies a major overhaul of the whole planning process, with physical and social planning agencies working very closely together and with both of them being geared up to providing the technical assistance needed to make a success of such neighborhood improvement programs.

This would mean that the planning and rebuilding of cities would follow the needs and desires of residents of existing communities to a much larger extent than in the past. There is, however, a counterpart requirement of this proposed closer relationship between planning agencies and communities; that is, a process of educating people within the intown communities as to changes that must be brought about because of citywide or regionwide needs—as for a balanced transportation system, changes in densities, the taking of space for needed public facilities, and the like.

7. *Federal and local government tools for implementation.* Development and pro-

motion of a new towns intown program would be a fine, challenging task for the new Department of Housing and Urban Development, as well as for individual municipalities. To carry out the proposed program, the department would have to join forces with other federal agencies with direct urban responsibilities: including Health, Education and Welfare, Public Roads, Interior, the various anti-poverty groups, and so on. It will need not only new funds but also new tools to provide help for central cities and older suburbs and to encourage private enterprise. Thought should be given to the possibilities of providing federal technical and financial assistance to community development corporations, both profit and nonprofit, that might well be organized to spark and guide new town development. Such corporations would be needed to organize and, sometimes, to manage lighted centers, as well as to develop the intown industrial estates and other structures for small businesses.

The urban renewal and public facilities units of the Department of Housing and Urban Development would have to be given new guidelines to direct their efforts specifically towards the task of encouraging new towns intown. And, of course, the whole public housing activity needs to be strengthened far beyond the suggested improvements with regard to rent subsidies and the purchases of private homes for public housing purposes. For example, consideration would be given to the creation of new housing units and neighborhoods designed specifically to inspire and instruct families that have been living in poverty in the past, communities in which education and other public services facilities are at the very center of the design. The concentration on purely physical redevelopment and the mere provision of relatively cheap shelter as the key tool in providing better housing for the poor should become a thing of the past.

Here, then, is a central concept to enable us to reach out for the creation of truly great and beautiful cities, where humanistic values dominate and where full use is made of the evolving partnership in urban affairs between government and private enterprise. This is a fitting challenge for a great nation.

2

New Towns Intown in a National New-Communities Program

Given the predominant attitudes in the United States today—largely those of resistance to racial and class mixing—a major movement of new-community building could easily become the 1970s counterpart of the FHA-encouraged segregated suburban building of the post-World War II years. A further polarization of our society would be a high price to pay for the improvement in life styles that new communities could conceivably bring about for their residents. It is possible that those new communities that have been reliant upon federal government subsidies could be forced to provide a certain amount of racial and income-class mixing as the price for the subsidies, but a little arithmetic—combined with the logic of modern United States politics—suggests that the number of minority and poor families that are likely to gain in this way would be quite small.

We need a strategy that can balance improvements in the lives of minority and lower-income groups with the anticipated improvements in the lives of middle-class families that the new communities are expected to bring about. The new town intown concept, already part of the federal government's new-communities program, provides a valuable counterpart to new-community building in outlying areas. Those who are embarrassed by this kind of open *quid pro quo* strategy should remember that the most probable alternative under current social and political conditions is a gradual or even rapid abandonment of the inner city and its troubled (and troublesome) residents, while attention is shifted to so-called areas of future growth. Abandonment of the inner city by both private and public interests is already under way in various communities across the country, and the consequences are to make the human environment for many minority and lower-income families a thing of ugliness and terror.

Concern for both equity (or simple human decency) and quality of life requires more than merely highlighting the potential value of a major new-

I want to express my thanks to David Vetter for his valuable assistance in the preparation of this study. I am also grateful to a number of colleagues, associated with me in a new-towns-intown project in the School of Architecture and Urban Planning of the University of California at Los Angeles, for helping me develop some of the concepts included herein.

communities building program in the United States. It requires careful attention as to who is to be helped by such a program. Nor is it enough vaguely to suggest that "some" of the federal subsidy be directed to helping minority and lower-income families achieve a better living environment. Justice demands that the largest share of the federal government subsidy be directed to the revitalization of inner-city areas where the most undersatisfied human needs as well as the greatest danger to regional viability are to be found. Thus it seems to me that major emphasis on new towns intown within a federally subsidized new-communities building program makes both moral and political sense. Specifically the case for emphasis on *intown* new towns can be made on the basis of an analysis of the major goals generally associated with development of new towns. I take these goals to be (1) healthier national urban growth, (2) opportunities for innovation, (3) better opportunities for individual development and community development, (4) better opportunities for political participation, and (5) new and better opportunities for racial and income mixing.

Before launching into these, there is need for an explanation of the new-town-intown concept. It is well to note immediately that it is not a well-developed concept. Largely, it is today an empty box waiting to be filled. The Housing and Urban Development Act of 1970, which first introduced the concept into federal legislation, does not give much of a lead as to what it is all about; nor do the early efforts to launch developments in central cities called new towns intown, such as the Fort Lincoln project in Washington, D.C. In fact—and unfortunately—the concept does not have much more content than when I first introduced it as a strategy for the development of the area surrounding the University of Chicago in the early 1950s, or when I later proposed it as the base for a national program.[1] All I can do, then, is to spell out what the hope is.

The new town intown concept, as I see it, aims at substantial and continuing inner-city modernization and revitalization by bringing together in a single programmatic approach a variety of human-assistance and urban-development components of a character, scale, and combination that would maximize the chances for greatly improving the quality of environment and quality of life of inner-city residents. This definition itself needs explanation. Through the many urban programs that have been tried, we have learned some useful things about the social, economic, and physical development of the inner city. This knowledge has not come easily or cheaply. We have learned from our mistakes—mistakes that have been costly in both human and economic terms. Basically, the new town intown concept channels what we have learned into programmatic ideas (with, it is to be hoped, inherent logic) aimed at improving the quality of life of people in the inner city. It differs from existing urban programs in important ways.

OBJECTIVES OF A NEW-TOWN-INTOWN PROGRAM

Many of the existing governmental urban programs, we have learned from experience, suffer from certain common ills. They are more place- or territory-

---

[1]See Chapter 1.

oriented than people-oriented; they tend to deal more with outer symptoms than with underlying causes; they tend to be largely static in nature rather than dynamic (that is, they do not deal with fundamental urban development processes); and their human objectives are far from clear. The provisions for new towns intown in the federal government's 1970 new-communities act do not indicate at all clearly what the objectives of such a program are to be, nor how the other common ills of the existing inner-city programs are to be avoided.

Against the background of conditions in American cities today, new towns intown should aim at achieving two interrelated objectives.

The first objective should be *to enhance opportunities for the disadvantaged people of the inner city to live better lives.* This has been an objective of several federal government programs, including the public housing and Model Cities programs, but the approach and scale of these have been inadequate. The term *disadvantaged people* is taken to encompass individuals and families from minority groups and/or having incomes below the poverty level. This is not a particularly felicitous term, but there is no fully satisfactory way to identify people whose living and environmental choices are far more limited than those of the majority. The disadvantaged in the inner city are taken as the target population, rather than all disadvantaged wherever they may be located, because a new town intown program can provide special (and additional) place-oriented improvement opportunities not provided by nonplace programs (such as minimum income, rent subsidies, and education supports). In other words it is assumed that the new town intown program will build on the nonplace programs and open new possibilities beyond. Also, the inner-city areas, because of the territorial concentration of poverty and minority groups, have substantial political clout of the kind needed to carry out development programs. At the same time this concentration provides a good base for popular participation; that is, a base for involving poor and minority persons in the planning and execution of plans. It is hard to organize this kind of participation if the populations are scattered.

Enhancement of "opportunities . . . to live better lives" can be taken to require the following:

1. More and better jobs (and therefore higher incomes), as well as training for these jobs; more broadly conceived this means *economic development.*
2. Improved public and private services, and more personal security.
3. Improved housing (higher quality, more varied choices, more accessibility to jobs and other activities, or lower prices).
4. Improved environment (i.e., better neighborhood conditions).

While each of these supports the others in various ways, and ideally all should be included, it is essential that there be a priority ordering—given the inevitable limitation on resources—with the greatest effort directed to the higher-priority items. Economic development should receive the greatest attention and serve as the main base for the other elements. If programs are too ambitious and try to be comprehensive from the beginning, they may well suffer the fate of most other federal urban programs that have been too ambitious in terms of the funds made available. This is not to imply that the planning should not be very broad from the beginning; rather, it is to stress the necessity for building one

program element on another so that important, even if modest, gains can be
realized if program funds fall short of those needed for large efforts. Our experience with housing and urban-development programs over the last three decades
demonstrates the importance of the so-called building-block strategy. Funds
have just not been available to carry through the kinds of comprehensive programs initially planned. The Model Cities program is an excellent example of
what can happen. As Kaitz and Hyman put it, "The design of Model Cities is
grand, the objectives laudable, and the resources negligible."[2] The operational
strategy for new towns intown should permit meaningful (and greatly multiplied) returns from whatever resources are devoted to this program.

In addition to "enhancing opportunities . . . to live better lives," as the
second objective new towns intown programs should aim to strengthen the
processes of central-city modernization and revitalization. The latter term is not
used to suggest the reestablishment of old central-city functions, but rather the
establishment of new functions and activities appropriate to central locations.

We have remarkably little understanding of what is involved in maintaining
the efficient functioning of core-city areas and their continued vitality. Our
urban-renewal experience suggests that it probably does not involve reestablish-
ing the commercial dominance of the downtown area or substituting isolated
new middle-class neighborhoods for former slum neighborhoods, scattering the
former slum dwellers to wherever housing can be found for them. Nor does it
seem to demand the construction of inner-city superhighways or freeways to
bring hordes of suburbanites to jobs in the city for a few hours a day. For in this
process lies the continuing decline of even larger areas than can possibly be
cleared by urban renewal and an undermining of the sound functioning of the
central city. It is far less clear as to what is essential to central-city modernization. I would suggest that at a minimum it calls for strengthening—in economic,
political, and human terms—the inner-city communities where the disadvantaged families live.

In the past, the city in the United States has always functioned as a "human
upgrading factory," preparing workers for the jobs that needed doing and preparing families for effective urban living. It was the place where the new entrepreneurs and the new ideas could be launched. In the process, capital as well
as human skills would be put to work, and continuing change (or modernization) would result. The opposite is the case when the city becomes simply a
dumping ground and the place from which capital and skills flee.

Revitalization in such human terms is clearly compatible with the first proposed objective (i.e., providing better living opportunities for disadvantaged

---

[2]Edwin M. Kaitz and Herbert Harvey Hyman, *Urban Planning for Social Welfare: A Model
Cities Approach* (Washington: Praeger Publishers, 1970), p. 36. For a short history of the
development of the Model Cities concept and an evaluation of the program to 1970, see
Judson Lehman James, "Evaluation Report on the Model Cities Program," in *Papers*
submitted to Subcommittee on Housing Panels, Committee on Banking and Currency,
U.S. House of Representatives, 92d Congress, 1st Session, June 1971. For an evaluation
and history of efforts to plan for Model Cities see *The Model Cities Program: A Comparative
Analysis of The Planning Process in Eleven Cities*, U.S. Department of Housing and Urban
Development (Washington, D.C., 1970).

families). Such a modernization and revitalization objective is a key reason for bringing the inherent vitality of new towns to the inner city. The inner city more than any other place needs the powerful leverage that coordinated overall planning and development can bring. In the case of the inner city, this means specifically (1) reversing the outflow of capital, and (2) creating a linked set of resource-and-opportunity developmental areas throughout the metropolitan region to support the core new town intown. Both of these require explanation.

Most of our present intown programs founder on the rock of capital disinvestment in inner-city areas. In the face of expanding housing needs, many existing housing units in our downtown areas are either being abandoned or are not being properly maintained. As Sternlieb points out: "Abandonment is a process, a reflection of a much deeper seated and extensive phenomenon—the disinvestment of private capital in the cores of our cities."[3]

An important aim of new towns intown would be to stem this flight of capital. What happens now is that institutional lenders abandon the inner city due to fear of neighborhood decline. Unfortunately, institutional lenders acting individually to protect themselves from neighborhood decay often accelerate the very blight they fear. At the first sign of deterioration the lender will often refuse to make loans in the neighborhood. This in itself causes neighborhood decline. And such decline is reinforced by the fear of businessmen to build commercial and industrial establishments in declining areas. Thus the vitality that new economic activities tend to bring is lost.

A new town intown effort would seek to halt neighborhood decline and to organize lenders so that they could act collectively to provide the steady flow of capital so vital to neighborhood maintenance and improvement. It would proceed on the notion that just as decline and disinvestment make up a process building on itself, so does investment and improvement. Whether, and to what extent, higher-income persons and particularly higher-income whites have to be attracted back to the city for this investment-and-improvement process to take hold firmly will probably not be known until a number of new towns intown have been under way for some time. Under a substantial new towns intown program, there are strong reasons to assume that, at a very minimum, the spread of blight can be halted, entrepreneurship encouraged, and activities that normally function most effectively in the core-city areas encouraged to return to the central city or to set up shop there anew. There are strong favorable forces to be built on, including the slowdown in in-migration from the poor rural areas and the continuing increases in nonwhite family incomes.

Stemming the flight of capital is by itself clearly not enough. A strong forward thrust must be initiated. The latter calls for an areawide developmental approach. As I see it, what is needed is not too far removed from what is involved in broad-scale regional development programs both here and overseas. In both cases a key objective is to find the most critical leverage points for change in desired direction, looking to such things as investment in human upgrading,

---

[3]George Sternlieb, "Abandonment and Rehabilitation: What is to be Done," in *Papers* submitted to Subcommittee on Housing Panels, Committee on Banking and Currency, U.S. House of Representatives, 92d Congress, 1st Session, June 1971, p. 315.

finding of new and expanding economic opportunities, and the construction and improvement of infrastructure that would provide a base and framework for public and private efforts—and all of this within a territory specifically designated to encompass opportunity and not the problems alone. This is true for the present-day American city as much as for Appalachia or other so-called problem regions. Opportunity has to be found and leveraged, whether in growth centers or in the encouragement of activities that promise good returns.

The Model Cities experience provides some suggestive lessons. The legislation requires that Model Cities areas encompass the worst slums and problem areas, the city counterpart of the unhappy "worst first" strategy of the Economic Development Administration of the U.S. Department of Commerce in rural and small-town areas. The way the Model Cities program was designed made it impossible to do the kind of planning originally advocated:

> Planning difficulties arose out of the relation of the target neighborhood to the rest of the city, especially since the ghetto was the most dependent and least viable part of any city's economic and social structure. On the other hand, the dilution of effort with larger boundaries would be fatal to the program given the modest level of funding.[4]

The ghetto may be the least viable part of the city economically, but it does not follow that larger boundaries would dilute the resources available. In fact, by increasing the size of the target area, the total amount of resources may be increased. By encompassing economically and socially stronger areas and providing more leverage for investment, more private capital may be attracted, so that every dollar of federal funding could conceivably attract additional flows of funds into the target area. Under the present nondevelopmental approach, almost all of the funding must come from the federal government and can easily be absorbed into programs with only a temporary impact. It is typical of the present approach that only by accident would the urban economic development program sponsored by the Economic Development Administration coincide with a Model Cities program. Nor do Model Cities programs have any special priority with regard to federally sponsored manpower-training programs or any other programs that could conceivably increase the economic or social viability of the target area.

A particularly important consideration of an inner-city program (as of other developmental programs) is its multiplier impact. Spending in any part of the urban system normally generates spending in other parts of the system. The amount of additional spending generated by each dollar spent is called the multiplier. A key indicator of the success of a new town intown program is the amount of public and private investment induced by the initial government expenditures. One often-ignored characteristic of the multiplier is that it works both ways. A given decrease in spending will also be multiplied to accelerate the decline of an area (as already noted). The size of the multiplier will depend to an important extent on the ways in which the government investments are linked to the private sector. For example, functional deficiencies within the inner city

---

[4]Judson Lehman James, *op. cit.*, pp. 847–48.

may make it quite unprofitable for existing firms to expand or new firms to move in. There may be inadequate transportation, parking, or personal security, and it may be difficult to secure land. Thus there is a strong forward linkage between the strengthening of the infrastructure of the inner city and other investments in the private sector. These developmental considerations must be among the dominant ones in defining the size and scope of new town intown programs.

TERRITORIAL EXTENT

A key aspect of the new-town-intown concept is to view physical development as a "tool" for achieving human objectives. Thus, the territorial extent of a new town intown is not to be determined by the physical condition of structures (as in urban renewal). Nor is it to be determined by extremely bad social conditions within a given neighborhood (as in the Model Cities program). Rather it is to be determined on the basis of future community viability. The boundaries of urban-renewal projects have been set by the extent of physical "blight"—blight defined strictly in terms of the condition of physical structures. In the Model Cities program the definition of blight was broadened to include social factors; however, not only were the boundaries of the target area restricted to a single residential neighborhood, but also the choice of area was to be dominated by how bad social conditions were. At least a major part of the neighborhood had to be "hard-core slum in which low-income families are concentrated."[5]

The territorial extent of a new town intown project would have to be determined, case by case, by certain principles aiming at long-term community viability and the ability of a developmental agency to turn things around so that a strong sense of improvement can be generated and sustained throughout the area. I appreciate how difficult it will be to designate areas on such broad principles with any sense of assurance. At the very least this approach would let down territorial barriers that now condemn most in-city projects to failure.

Probably three factors will have to be brought into play in the designation of territorial extent of a new-town-intown program: (1) large scale, (2) the configuration of certain key physical and nonphysical features, and (3) noncontiguous character. These are all interrelated. It can be expected that in most cities there would be at least one core or primary new town intown in the inner city covering a substantial territory—that is, at town scale—as an important element in achieving the major objectives of a new town intown program. It would encompass a territory much larger than either the typical urban-renewal project or Model Cities neighborhood. It would include commercial, industrial, and recreational areas as well as residential areas, stable neighborhoods as well as declining and slum neighborhoods. Territorial designation would be based on (1) the extent of the public-service delivery systems and the location of public facilities, (2) present and future economic possibilities, (3) the configuration of transporta-

---

[5]*Improving the Quality of Urban Life: A Program Guide to Model Neighborhoods in Demonstration Cities,* U.S. Department of Housing and Urban Development (Washington, D.C., 1967), pp. 6–7.

tion networks, and (4) and the extent of community awareness and community institutions.

It seems unlikely in most large cities that one such concentrated new town intown will be able to go a long way by itself in achieving the major objectives. It is more likely that the optimal arrangement will need to involve, in addition to the core area, several different territories designated within a new town intown *program* as linked resource-and-opportunity developmental areas throughout the metropolitan region. These would be areas in which particularly attractive employment opportunities could be developed (say, an underdeveloped port area or an open area near the core new town intown where an industrial estate could be established). It may also involve an open area outside the built-up metropolitan zone that could be developed as a paired outlying new town with strong links to the intown new town.[6] Such areas could be referred to as resource-and-opportunity areas, to suggest that they are included in the new towns intown program because they provide new opportunities for the inner-city target population—mainly new opportunities for jobs, improved services, and housing.

The important point to appreciate is that inner-city areas should not be developed in isolation—that is, aside from the larger regional considerations. Clearly, as Vietorisz and Harrison argue so convincingly in their thoughtful study of the economic development of Harlem, "The major symptom of underlying economic and social distress—pervasive employment and income deficits—could not be dealt with exclusively within the confines of the ghetto."[7]

Relating inner-city development to broad regional considerations imposes three requirements that largely have been lacking in previous inner-city programs.[8] In fact the ultimate success of a new-town-intown program, given its human-welfare and quality-of-life objectives, would depend on how thoroughly these requirements can be met.

One requirement is to make it much easier than at present for ghetto residents to get to jobs in every part of the region. For the lesser-skilled workers, who tend also to be those who shift jobs most frequently, an inner-city location close to transportation hubs is a decided advantage. But it takes effort to fully exploit this advantage. There is need for the development of means by which inner-city workers can get to jobs throughout the region with greater ease and at lower cost than in the past. Training for jobs wherever they may be located is an even more important need.

A second requirement is to encourage the new town intown local economy to become essentially a human-development and human-convenience economy.

---

[6]For a specific proposal for the building of paired new towns in both inner-city and outlying areas, see Metropolitan Fund, Inc., *Regional New-Town Design: A Paired Community for Southeast Michigan* (Detroit: Metropolitan Fund, February 1971).

[7]Thomas Vietorisz and Bennett Harrison, *The Economic Development of Harlem* (New York: Praeger Publishers, 1970).

[8]These are aside from the requirement of enabling minority workers to find housing near jobs in the suburbs and other outlying areas. See Harvey S. Perloff, "What Economic Future for the Inner City Ghetto?" presented to the Committee on Science and Astronautics, U.S. House of Representatives, 91st Congress, 1st Session, February 5, 1969.

The aim would not be, as it supposedly is in large outlying new towns, to create enough jobs for most of the local residents. Economic development in inner-city areas has to have several different elements.

There could be, and should be, a major effort to exploit all of the economic advantages that an inner-city area may have because of both its location within the region and its special labor supply. Thus industrial land could be made available at various high-accessibility points, but not necessarily within the ghetto or slum itself. These sites would have to be competitive with other sites in the metropolitan economy, as well as accessible to the work force in the new town intown core area. Some subsidy may be required to make these sites fully competitive, but at the edges of the area such subsidy would probably not be as high as that required to locate and maintain industry in the heart of the ghetto. Such subsidy for land-cost write-down would surely be more justifiable than the write-down in the typical urban-renewal project in the past, which removed slum dwellers in favor of middle-class residents.

In addition to new economic activities for the more-or-less established labor force in the inner-city areas, there may be need for what Vietorisz and Harrison call "greenhouse industries"—that is, heavily subsidized industries intended primarily to raise the caliber of the work force in the ghetto. This is an admittedly tricky business, and it could be argued that it is better to subsidize established business to take on the job of raising the caliber of the work force than to bring in special industries for this purpose. Subsidizing already established business for training purposes could well be the backbone of a manpower-upgrading program. Experience with all sorts of upgrading programs, however, suggests the importance of nearby location in the case of some of the workers—in fact of those who need the most assistance. The geographic range of their movements tends to be restricted, and nearness is a helpful factor. Subsidizing such industries would be an interim step, certainly not a final solution, in the integration of minority and untrained workers into the regional economy.

A third requirement relates to the character of the surrounding environment. Economic upgrading and economic integration of ghetto workers into the mainstream undoubtedly depend—to an unknown but surely significant degree—on self-image, and this in turn is intimately related to the quality of the environment and the quality of life that an individual experiences. Vietorisz and Harrison put it well when they point to the idiocy of a situation in which a worker is "exiled every night to a rat-infested, overcrowded, personally hazardous, and miserably serviced environment while being expected to deliver a high degree of productivity on the job."[9]

We now know—particularly after our experience with public housing and findings of the Coleman Report—that physical improvement, and even spanking newness, can make little difference in the life and performance of disadvantaged persons when other socially helpful conditions are not also available. But surely we also know that a degrading and insecure environment and way of life make it inordinately hard for individuals to pull themselves up by their bootstraps.

---

[9]Vietorisz and Harrison, *op. cit.*, p. 59.

Beyond the question of self-image there is the more direct matter of the close relationship between environmental adequacy and ability to achieve economic and social betterment goals. Even minimal economic improvement goals require a relatively efficient and safe environment, while social improvement goals call for substantial improvement in public facilities and services. I read past experience to say, not that physical improvement is unimportant, but that either the forces of decline—human *and* physical—are stopped and turned around, with forces for improvement encouraged along a broad spectrum, or else human progress will be painfully slow in the ghetto.

CENTRALIZED MANAGEMENT

One of the key features of a new town intown should be the centralized management of all federal and state assistance monies and related activities for the given area, as well as certain of the municipal government's funds, through a strong development corporation. It seems to me, therefore, that all of the following should be managed through the development corporation:

1. Economic-development activities and funds
2. Manpower-training activities and funds
3. Special education-planning and experimentation grants
4. Special health-planning and experimentation grants
5. All housing assistance
6. Facilities grants
7. Urban renewal (of a new type, geared to the specific objectives of new towns intown)
8. Other human resources funds (including poverty, Model Cities, and similar funds where available) and
9. Funds specifically made available for new towns intown and related activities

If the corporation is to manage such funds and related activities, it would have to be public in nature or of a mixed public and private variety. In addition to having control of such funds, it would be necessary for the corporation to have powers of eminent domain, as well as related powers needed for land development and rehabilitation. What this says in effect is that the intown modernization and revitalization job can be carried out only if there is a developmental unit strong enough and well enough funded to do it.

Can such development corporations be established under present conditions characterized by extreme fragmentation of governmental activities and little tradition in public-private administrative cooperation? My guess is that such corporations will be established only if the federal government ties its financial assistance to given areas to the requirement that such corporations be established. This is a logical enough requirement, since the chances for successful inner-city improvement on town scale are slim without such a strong agency to manage it.

While such an agency with public powers may be needed to direct the public-oriented activities, it does not follow that it must necessarily carry out the developmental (building and rehabilitation) tasks itself—although it may choose to do so. It may well turn over these developmental tasks to a private developer under contract, or to a number of private developers. This may be needed to mobilize both the necessary funds and the necessary skills for large-scale development. In fact the few new town intown projects already underway are being carried out by private developers working closely with urban renewal and housing agencies. What are lacking now are institutions capable of coordinating and channeling the public funds and activities so that the projects can achieve the kinds of objectives discussed above.

If inner-city residents are to gain from new town intown projects, it is also essential that development corporations be controlled by such residents—that is, by the target population whose welfare is the raison d'être of the corporation. The problems of achieving such resident control while maintaining effective centralized management of a complex program should not be underestimated. No formula has yet been discovered to achieve this dual objective, but we do have some useful experience to go on.[10] I interpret this experience to suggest that the following deserve special attention:

1. Major emphasis should be placed on a sound system of representation, with a reasonable balance between resident and nonresident members of the board of the corporation, and with the residents members elected in such a way that the community feels it is effectively represented.

2. Opportunities should be provided to enable community members and minority entrepreneurs and minority organizations to acquire equity holdings in the corporation and its developmental arms, so that the community feels it has a stake in the enterprise on this score as well. This type of equity arrangement has already been worked out in the Fort Lincoln new town intown being developed through a private development corporation. It should be even simpler in the case of projects directed by public or mixed public-and-private corporations.

ADJUSTMENT TO INNER-CITY POPULATIONS

There is yet another characteristic of new towns intown, at least as I conceive them. Such towns are intended to serve a highly varied and highly mobile intown population. In the past, urban-development programs have either largely disregarded inner-city residents (as in urban renewal) or treated them simply as "problem families" or problem situations (as in the public housing and Model Cities program). But if we view the inner city broadly, and not just in

---

[10]For a discussion of this problem, see Charles E. Olken, "Economic Development in the Model Cities Program," *Law and Contemporary Problems*, Vol. 36 (Spring 1972), pp. 205–26. Methods through which development corporations are currently controlled are discussed in *CDC's: New Hope for the Inner City*, Report of the Twentieth Century Fund Task Force on Community Development Corporations (New York: The Twentieth Century Fund, 1971), with background paper by Geoffrey Faux.

terms of the poorest, most run-down and crime-ridden sections, certain formerly invisible people become visible, and certain needs not normally associated
with the inner city appear. The needs of the following groups should be
considered:

1. Families currently in a lower-income status, often recent in-migrants,
who are upwardly mobile and are concerned about education and job opportunities for themselves and even more for their children.

2. Individuals and families in the lower-income class who have limited
income because of physical disability, age, or the like, who are much concerned
about the quality of certain public services and recreation facilities. They also
greatly value nearby opportunities for earning extra income.

3. Middle-class minority families who prefer to live with their own racial
and ethnic group, but want better housing, better shopping, and better public
services (particularly better schooling), as well as greater personal safety.

4. White and minority families who like being in a highly urbanized environment, where "the action is," but who also want better housing (or lower-
cost housing), better services, and a safer and more attractive environment.

An intown program must be fully sensitive to these varying needs and
situations. Thus a new town intown program should not be viewed as some sort
of upgrading abstraction, as was generally true for urban renewal in the past,
but rather as a program seeking to understand and to meet the needs and
aspirations of specified groups of people with specific characteristics. Again, this
highlights the requirement for the kind and scale of planning, building, and
rehabilitation typical of a *town* rather than a neighborhood, and covering not
only housing, localized services, and shopping but the full spectrum of human
concerns viewed at the town scale—including particularly jobs and income,
personal safety, and different kinds of services and facilities for a wide variety of
population groups.

A new town intown would seek to incorporate the concept of broad-scale
planning and carefully planned building sequences (here also, rebuilding and
rehabilitation) central to most thinking about new-community development. But
other features would be very different. Thus the planning in a new town intown
would be for and with population groups already in the area, not for a future
population with characteristics dictated largely by market considerations. Jobs
would be given top priority so that workplaces would be located in whatever
part of the community to which they could be attracted, consistent with overall
town efficiency. A so-called lighted center would be a dominant feature of a new
town intown to achieve a number of objectives—such as to enlarge the scope for
jobs and income, bring excitement and urbanity to the inner city (as well as
spenders), and enhance personal safety.[11] Physical features in general would be
incorporated in a new town intown to achieve specific developmental objectives,
aiming for the greatest returns *in human terms* for a given expenditure, rather
than to achieve a predetermined aesthetic and tone, as in most thinking about
outlying new towns.

---

[11]The Lighted Center idea is discussed in Perloff, "New Towns Intown," see Chapter 1.

ACHIEVING NEW-COMMUNITY GOALS

As suggested at the beginning of this study, new towns intown can contribute significantly to the objectives or gains that are normally associated with new-community development. In fact it can be argued that, for most of the objectives, new towns intown can make an even larger contribution than outlying new communities. It is worth examining some of the gains associated with new communities in general.

Healthier National Urban Growth

The widespread concern over the unhealthy growth of the present giant metropolises is closely associated with the endless urban scatteration and the growth of so-called slurbs. But the latter are themselves closely related to the decline in the attractiveness of the central city. Clearly the pressures on the outlying areas will be reduced by greatly increasing the attractiveness of the core city through new town intown programs. More generally, it seems to me that healthy urban growth implies a wide choice among many satisfying forms of urban living. Today one of the most important of these choices is being denied to many people—that of living well and safely in the core city. Finally, and most importantly, healthy national urban growth should imply that various racial and income groups gain fairly from the unique opportunities that urban life provides. This can be achieved only if the inner-city populations are helped to achieve better lives and environments.

Opportunities for Innovation

The major urban problems, at least in the United States, are associated with the difficulties arising in the human, social, political, and economic realms (and probably in that order). This is evident in any list of the top-priority problems of American urban communities—a list that must include the relatively poor educational performance of many minority children, the extent to which crime and self-destructive abuses (such as drug abuse) are associated with poverty clustering, the financial difficulties of central cities and suburban areas, and the governmental problems of dealing with region-wide matters. Clearly here are the areas where innovation is most urgently needed, not in the areas usually mentioned in connection with experimentation in new-communities development—the delivery of garbage, water, and sewerage services or in transportation and communications, or even in the provision of health, education, and recreation services. Moreover probably little that is innovated in an isolated, brand-new community can be carried over even to most of the established suburban communities, much less to the central city.

Much that is innovative in human, socioeconomic, and political terms could conceivably be tried in outlying new towns, but the probabilities are against it. There are no really significant pressures to take the kind of risks that are involved in genuine nontechnical innovation. The average builder feels that it is tough enough to sell and rent housing and industrial land without worrying about encouraging social experiments. And anyway, people are not interested in innovation when they are not in trouble. Mostly they want a nice, simple, clean life—without the old urban problems.

The creation of new towns intown, by contrast, demands innovation in these very areas. People associated with a new town intown development will have very strong incentives to innovate, since they know that the old methods do not work; new methods are the key to success.

In an outlying new town the developer can make anything look like innovation by simply doing traditional things well, particularly since he has the advantage of not being forced to cope with the really difficult urban problems; he can keep most of them out by a careful choice of business units and selective choice of buyers and renters. The new town intown developer is in the opposite camp; his task is to cope directly with the major urban problems. Here, making even simple things work calls for genuine innovation. For example, the use of a basic organizational tool such as a strong development corporation with substantial power for coordinated action—certainly no big deal in the construction of an outlying new town—would be a major innovation in the central city. In the same light, racial, ethnic, and income mixing in outlying new communities will surely involve nothing more startling than figuring out the largest number of minority and poor families that will be acceptable to the predominant middle-class residents. In the inner city, however, the issue of mixing is quite another matter, and it involves such complex questions as the possible loss of minority-group political control and the kinds of incentives that can induce white middle-class families to return to the inner city.

More Opportunities for Individual and Community Development

Although it tends to be discussed more seriously overseas than in the United States, even here progressively inclined people think of this goal as one of the more appealing of a new-town program.

While human development as such is of importance to all groups in all strata of society, the major human-development problems in the United States are strongly class-oriented. The middle-class individual already has many advantages and options. The most severe difficulties arise in the case of the poor and minority populations. These are stated powerfully in the findings of the Coleman Report, which highlights the difficulty in overcoming through educational inputs the educational disadvantages imposed on children growing up in poverty surroundings. These findings pose what I take to be one of our most critical challenges. Mixing of social groups evidently helps to some extent, but surely it is at least as important to try to turn the family and community surroundings of the poor, minority child into less of a personal-development disadvantage. Outlying new towns could certainly contribute to such an effort, and socially helpful environments could be created, but here we have to face the conflict between such a goal and the fact that private new-town developers find it economically attractive to sell escape and safety to white middle-class families. Also, *numbers* are important. I suspect that during the next two decades at least, we can do very much more in the central city for the disadvantaged children taken as a whole than in outlying new towns. In the latter the rate of absorption of poor, minority families into middle-class communities must be relied upon, and, for the reason stated above, this is likely to be limited. Almost by definition the new town intown effort makes the creation of more helpful environments for poor, minority children a central goal, and it must do this for all such children living within its territorial boundary.

Community development is closely associated with individual development as a new-town objective, particularly in the sense that one of the major goals of community development is to provide new sources of support for the individual and new strengths for self-development. Clearly the question of individual and group self-image is important here. So is the possibility of finding community means for overcoming certain of the developmental limitations growing out of disadvantaged home lives. Also, as is discussed in the next section, the development of new and greater minority leverage in urban politics can be a significant force in eliminating some of the personally destructive features associated with a sense of utter powerlessness. Community development in a new town intown, unlike the situation one expects to find in an outlying new community, is not a matter of absorbing new neighbors and colleagues into established white middle-class institutions and community arrangements. Rather it is a matter of developing stronger and more viable communities with their own character, institutions, and arrangements—some where nonwhite families are in the majority, alongside others that are blended, with nonwhites making up a substantial, rather than an unimportant, minority. While the existing suburbs and already built new towns provide ample opportunity for testing the effects on individual development of absorption of poor and minority families into white middle-class communities, only a concentration of major effort in the central city can begin to test the possibilities of building on minority cultures and/or a strongly blended situation.

More Opportunities for Political Participation

As Robert Wood has suggested, the present white middle-class suburban community is a model of active political participation.[12] Of course such participation is often directed at promoting the isolationist feelings of the white middle-class, as witness the active support of exclusionary zoning. Surely the major problem in the realm of political participation arises from the present powerlessness of poor and minority groups and the lack of a regional politics— that is, a politics that can support needed regionwide planning and regionwide service activities. On the first of these, there is no question as to the advantages of new town intown development. On the issue of regional politics, I am afraid that neither intown nor outling new towns will contribute much, if anything.

Providing More Opportunities for Racial and Income Mixing

Events of the past decade have provided important new insights to the issue of integration and have posed new questions.[13] Earlier it was easy to assume

---

[12]Robert C. Wood, *Suburbia* (Boston: Houghton Mifflin, 1959).
[13]Anthony Downs, *Urban Problems and Prospects*. (Chicago: Markham, 1970), pp. 27–74. Note particularly his discussion of the integrated-core strategy in his "alternative futures for the ghetto."

that the answer lay entirely in the mixing of racial and income groups. The problem was one of opening up formerly segregated areas to minority groups. It was a matter of providing free choice for everyone.

I still think that it is indecent and socially harmful to exclude individuals and families from any spot in the country because of race (or religion, or national origin, or whatever). But I now appreciate that this is a necessary but not sufficient condition to achieve anything resembling an equitable and socially healthy situation. The latter requires more choices for nonwhites than simply the choice of either being a minority member in a relatively pleasant but white-dominated community or a resident of a hand-me-down area already totally nonwhite or always threatening to become so. The problem would not be so difficult if nonwhite incomes were more or less comparable to those of white families. Then the equity issue would depend on genuine enforcement of antidiscrimination laws on the racial side, and greater income distribution efforts on the income side. These three—rapid equalization of nonwhite and white income, genuine enforcement of antidiscrimination laws (and stronger laws), and a rapid narrowing of the income gap between rich and poor—seem to me to deserve the highest priority in any national political agenda.

While at a lower priority than the above, new towns intown can make a significant contribution to the equity goal. Some of their advantages have already been identified. They would enable minority members (those who so preferred) to live in all-black or other minority communities while enjoying a good level of public services and an improving rather than a declining environment. Alternately they could live in stable communities in which they are a substantial minority or a small minority, again depending on choice and income. This assumes, and it is an important assumption, that substantial and imaginative investment in the inner city—based on the many attractions that a new town intown can contribute to urban living—will provide a strong element of stability to all-minority and to already mixed neighborhoods, and will serve to attract white families back to the city. Outlying new communities as such simply cannot make this kind of contribution to the welfare of nonwhite and poorer families. The important thing they can do is to provide housing for minority and poorer families close to major new employment centers. (Unless the centers are large, such families may soon find themselves stranded when the employment situation changes, since being on the margin of the job market they tend to have to change jobs fairly frequently.)

CONCLUDING NOTE

What is suggested here, then, is the logic of directing the great bulk of federally subsidy for new-town development to the central city, since development of the inner city along new-town lines is the key to achieving the major objectives associated with new-community building. I am convinced that the decision by the federal government to do so or not to do so will have a great deal to do with whether the polarization of our society will be increased or diminished within the next decade or two.

3

The Central City in the Postindustrial Age

Some of the major economic trends—particularly the continuing growth of the service industries—would seem to favor large central cities. Services provide many jobs of the kind that fit the characteristics of the segment of the labor force that is most unemployment-prone: unskilled or semiskilled work, often part-time, frequently calling for interests and talents found among groups living in the central cities. But there is a catch-22 situation here. Public service jobs have a definite ceiling imposed by fiscal restraints; in fact, resistance to increased public outlays is growing. Private service jobs are in an underdeveloped state. And therein lies a tale, a tale which is all tied up with the socioeconomic transformation on which we are embarked.[1]

SOCIOECONOMIC CHANGES UNDER WAY

There is broad agreement that the United States is going through a major transformation, entering on a postindustrial age. As the vagueness of the term "postindustrial" suggests, there is not the same agreement as to what the nature of the new era is, but two features of the postindustrial era emerge as particularly significant and are widely accepted as central to the concept. One is the growing importance of the service industries, as contrasted to the goods-producing industries. The other is the importance of information, or knowledge, technology and of a technical and professional class, or what Daniel Bell calls a "knowledge class."

It is interesting to note that the centrality of these notions was identified as early as 1935 by Allan G. B. Fisher, a British economist.

> The transfers (to service employments) are being made, but they are not being made with sufficient speed, and they are made in the face of wide-spread feeling that the new types of work are wasteful and unproductive. If

[1]Leland Burns, Richard Kirwan, Peter Marris, Donald Shoup, and Martin Wachs made valuable suggestions on an earlier version of this "tale" and Lee Lashway assisted in a literature review and data collection.

our argument is sound, poetry and philosophy are significant not only on account of their own intrinsic value, but also because their organization on an economic base is an essential condition for stability in a progressive economy. . . . It is essential that steadily increasing attention should be paid to the production of the amenities of life, of things which poorer communities have been in the habit of regarding as luxuries. . . .

When we reach a level of wealth where the provision of personal services becomes economically important, the importance of the limitations of physical natural resources in the narrow sense steadily diminishes. We are then much more concerned with the exploitation of human capacity (which is also perfectly "natural"), and the maintenance of a moving equilibrium in a progressive economy comes to depend more and more upon the effective organization and education of human capacity.[2]

In 1940 Clark established the fact of the shifting importance of the primary, secondary, and tertiary (service) sectors as an economy develops and incomes grow.[3] Both Clark and Fisher stressed sector differences in income elasticity of demand and changes in productivity as responsible for the growth of services. People want just so many things and, above certain income levels, buy more and more services. At the same time, goods-producing industries enjoy higher productivity than service industries, thus releasing workers for nongoods production.

In the United States, in the decades since these writings by Fisher and Clark, agricultural and manufacturing employment have indeed decreased in relative importance and service employment has grown steadily, until today about two out of every three workers in the country are engaged in service industries.[4] At the same time, knowledge technology has achieved ever-greater importance, and professional and technical employment (normally, jobs that require relatively high levels of education) has grown tremendously: from 3.9 million in 1940 to 11 million in 1970, making it one of the largest of the census occupational categories, second only to the 13.5 million in clerical and kindred workers.

The impact on the central cities of these and related changes has, not unexpectedly, been enormous. The related changes are themselves of no small significance. These include the flood of migrants (mostly poor and relatively uneducated) from the countryside and small towns to the central cities as agricultural jobs disappeared and the location of manufacturing changed. They also include the increasing footlooseness of manufacturing industries as mechanization and automation progressed and as communication technology reduced

---

[2]A. G. B. Fisher, *The Clash of Progress and Security* (London: Macmillan, 1935).
[3]Colin Clark, *The Conditions of Economic Progress* (London: Macmillan, 1940), pp. 31 and 38.
[4]Here the figures for employment in services are based on the census concept of nongoods-producing industries. A different figure would be appropriate if "service jobs" are related to occupations, so that managers and clerks in manufacturing, agriculture, and other goods-producing industries were encompassed. The concept of services is still a very fuzzy one, but this is not the place to try to put the concept on a sturdy foundation. That remains for later research, but here it should be noted that the conventional definitions we are using, if anything, understate the shift to services.

the importance of face-to-face contacts and permitted the separation of various processes in manufacturing.

Actually, the rapid growth of manufacturing which characterized the period between the Civil War and World War II, and which accompanied the decline in resources industries, continued past the midpoint of the twentieth century, stimulated to no small degree by the military demands of World War II and the Korean war and by postwar filling of delayed consumer demand. But it soon became apparent that manufacturing employment was declining in relative terms. Manufacturing employees as a percentage of employees in non-agricultural establishments fell from 34 percent in 1950 to 26 percent in 1974, while service employment rose from 59 percent to 69 percent.[5] In the not-too-distant future even absolute numbers in manufacturing might flatten out or decline, leaving all employment expansions to be filled by service activities.

The first major impact of the changes under way was felt in the older cities of the Northeast in which manufactures had long been important. Boston, New York, Detroit, Pittsburgh, Cleveland, St. Louis, and other giants of the Northeast and Midwest manufacturing belt found themselves facing problems of economic decline and resultant fiscal difficulties in the public sector. Important insights into what was going on were provided by large in-depth studies of New York and Pittsburgh at the end of the 1950s and the early 1960s as well as by a number of detailed national studies.[6] It was noted that the flattening out of overall industrial employment, as in the earlier cases of agriculture and mining, were accompanied by large interregional and interindustry shifts. Some industries and regions were hard-hit while others were experiencing expansion. Manufacturing industries, particularly where production processes had become routinized, as in textiles, were beginning to move away from the older high-cost areas and were locating in areas that had cheaper labor or pleasant climate and other amenities. The so-called Sunbelt was increasingly becoming a favored section of the country.

In addition, the various studies noted, economic activities were becoming more footloose, and this helped not only to explain the differential growth of employment and population among the various regions of the country but also their location in outlying parts of the large metropolitan regions. With flexible truck and automobile transportation, a firm could locate anywhere within the metropolitan region or beyond, and still take advantage of agglomeration economies and economies of scale in the specialized services and labor skills provided by a large metropolis, yet achieve the desired amenities for its managers and workers in the pleasanter, more protected outlying sections of the metropolis.

Whatever hopefulness was to be found in the situation of the central city was associated with the services industries. The studies of the 1950s and early

---

[5]*The Statistical Abstract of the U.S., 1975* (Washington: Government Printing Office, 1975), Table No. 563, p. 345.

[6]See particularly Raymond Vernon, *Metropolis 1985: An Interpretation of the Findings of the New York Metropolitan Region Study.* (Cambridge, Mass.: Harvard University Press, 1960); and Pittsburgh Regional Planning Association, Economic Study of the Pittsburgh Region. Vol. 3, *Region with a Future*, (Pittsburgh: University of Pittsburgh Press, 1963).

1960s stressed the fact that while the cities had grown as they did in order to accommodate the industrial expansion of the earlier years, and were in fact the products of the industrial age, they were also the natural habitat of the rapidly expanding service sectors of the economy. The service sectors were in fact more subject to economies of agglomeration through clustering than were the manufacturing industries, as verified by Healy, based on the 1963 national input–output table.[7]

Also, these various studies suggested that services growth in the cities might well be bolstered by the growth of *new* manufacturing and service industries since the large cities were the source of much of the invention and innovation which were key to an expanding economy, so that while some industries were being lost, other industries were germinating in the cities and providing new sources of employment. Jacobs argued that the decline and growth of cities are directly tied to the relative vigor of their innovative activities.[8] Economic expansion, she suggested, results from the unpredictable growth of innumerable offshoots that break away from established businesses. Interestingly enough, almost all the examples she gave referred to manufacturing activities.

IS A TURNAROUND LIKELY?

Now, as we review the figures of population decreases in such a high proportion of the larger central cities in the recent past, and employment decreases in some of them, we have to cope with the question of whether we are merely seeing a temporary phenomenon, and can expect future continued growth of the central cities by way of expansion of existing industries, or are observing a long-term change in urban structure, despite the fact that over half of the large central cities (those with a population of a half million or more) lost population between 1960 and 1975.

My own view is that we can eliminate the possibilities of a substantial turnabout in the forces that have brought about a leveling off in manufacturing employment nationally and that are encouraging the move of manufacturing firms away from the central city. Automation continues unabated and is likely to have the same impact in the future as in the past, in the face of increasing labor costs and of improved techniques of quality control. Increased manufacturing footlooseness also seems assured with the continued automation of production, the greater possibilities for separation of the different manufacturing processes, increasing miniaturization, and the improvements in communications. Manufacturing firms can be expected to continue to seek out locations where wages are lower and unionization limited, or the appropriate labor force is available.

So strong are these forces that one can assume that even if the city was to continue to be an important source of invention and innovation in manufacturing, actual production and employment in the manufacturing realm resulting from this entrepreneurship would still take place largely in the outlying areas of

---

[7]Robert Healy, *Agglomeration and Footlooseness: The Distribution of Economic Activities among Metropolitan Areas*, Ph.D. dissertation, UCLA, 1972 (unpublished).
[8]Jane Jacobs, *The Economy of Cities*. (New York: Random House, 1969).

the metropolis and in communities beyond the metropolis.[9] Thus, the economic future of the central city would seem to depend on the growth of service activities within the city. What can we anticipate, then, in the critically important services realm?

First, we should note that the service sector is merely a convenient catchall category for the many kinds of activities other than goods production. It is made up of wholesale and retail trade, business services, consumer services, and government, and each of these is composed of a wide variety of activities which can be classified in many different ways, depending on the purpose of the classification. A useful way of looking at this sector, in trying to get at the dynamics affecting the future of the central city, is in terms of, first, locational propensies and, second, organizational characteristics.

By looking at locational propensities of the various traditional services, we can see readily that the play of agglomeration economies does *not* serve to cluster these different services *together*, except in limited instances, but rather tends to relate the services to people and to manufacturing industry.

In the trade category, retail trade is, of course, associated with household numbers and income, and both of these factors have dictated, and will continue to dictate, a continued move to the suburbs and beyond. Wholesale trade has also been moving outward (1) because the new technologies (such as mechanized and automatic loading) generally call for substantially increased space, which can more easily be had in outlying areas, (2) because of the wholesaling's close association to manufacturing, and (3) because the flexibility of trucking makes outlying locations attractive and feasible. The trend is clearly outward, without any reason to expect a turnabout.

In the business service category, such as transportation and repairs, a substantial proportion of the activities are related to manufacturing and wholesaling, so that further decentralization can be expected. The development of major activity centers throughout the metropolitan region and beyond is of significance, since the needed amount of clustering (for example, to be sure of nearby financial and legal services) can be achieved in many centers rather than necessarily downtown. Only where the services are provided over a very wide area and substantial face-to-face contacts are involved does the hold of the central city continue to be strong. This has been the situation in the case of the so-called FIRE (finance, insurance, and real estate) group, but even here it is not at all certain the decentralization may not be found attractive and feasible in the future.

In general, the agglomeration that was traditionally associated with the downtown area, and which gave the central city as a whole its economic vitality, can now be achieved in a variety of activity, or employment, centers spotted around the metropolitan field, over a very large area.[10] It is difficult to conceive

---

[9]See several articles in Parts I and II of George Sternlieb and James W. Hughes, eds., *Post-Industrial America: Metropolitan Decline and Inter-Regional Job Shifts.* (New Brunswick, N.J.: Center for Urban Policy Research, Rutgers, 1975).

[10]In 1960, 413 of the 500 largest industrial corporations had their corporate head offices—activities which are information intensive and are supported by agglomeration econo-

any strong reasons why the present forces behind the trend lines would change and create conditions for a return of the various services discussed so far— which have been the dominant services of the past industrial era—to the central city.

Among the services, the most substantial employment growth in the central cities, aside from FIRE, has been in government and in the medical and education services, private as well as public. Here the locational propensity is different in nature than in the case of most of the other service categories. Agglomeration economies play only a limited role. The services tend to be subject to political pressures and to the evolving situation which categorizes the new era we are entering. This is particularly so in the case of public employment; a number of factors seem to be at work here. One is the generally higher demands for the services supplied by city governments in both quantity and quality.[11] A second is the service requirements imposed on the central city by the concentration of poor persons and the continued in-migration of poor families, particularly in welfare, health, education, and police protection. A third, and critically important, feature is the political pressure for the absorption of otherwise unemployed individuals into government employment. As poor and minority persons become an increasing proportion of the total population in the central city, the provision of jobs in government for these groups becomes a political imperative. This, however, is a self-limiting solution to the problems of employment in the central city, since a brake is inevitably applied by the increasingly serious fiscal difficulties the city faces as private jobs and higher-income taxpayers leave the city.

The picture that emerges from this view of service employment is quite different from one where the focus is limited to the relatively high growth of the service category *as a whole* and when the phenomenon of agglomeration economies is interpreted in terms of the situation that characterized the services *in the past.*

ARE NEW SERVICES IN THE OFFING?

Some insight into the new and the more rapidly evolving services is provided through a review of the census occupation statistics (the service and nonservice categories are not as clearly differentiated as would have been desired). For the two decades between 1950 and 1970, the largest increase by far has been in the professional and technical category: an increase of 121 percent as

---

mies—in central cities. That number had declined by twenty-two by 1970. An even larger relative change was registered for the home offices of retail firms, where 10 percent suburbanized between 1960 and 1970. However, there was virtually no change in the concentration in central cities of corporate home offices of commercial banks and life insurance companies. Leland S. Burns, "The Location of the Headquarters of Industrial Companies," *Urban Studies* (June 1977.)

[11]See George E. Peterson, "Finance," in William Gorham and Nathan Glazer, eds., *The Urban Predicament* (Washington, D.C.: Urban Institute, 1976).

against a total labor force growth of 37 percent for the two decades. Most striking is the increase in the "knowledge class" categories, a substantial proportion of which were not even listed in the 1950 census (e.g., computer specialists, mathematical specialists, operations and systems researchers and analysts, and vocational and educational counselors). Also striking is the increase in the number of "technologists and technicians," many of a paraprofessional character. Thus, while physicians, dentists, and related practitioners increased 31 percent in numbers, registered nurses, dietitians, and therapists increased by 125 percent, and health technologists and technicians grew by 238 percent. Also impressive is the growth of engineering and science technicians, a category not listed in 1950, to a total of 828,000.

Less recognized is the fact that there has been a relatively small increase in the managers and administrative category. The only substantial increases were in health administrators, public officials, school administrators, and in the FIRE group, particularly bank officers and financial managers. There has been a major decrease in the self-employed category, from 2,248,000 in 1950 to 913,000 in 1970.

In the large clerical category, the greatest increases were in the following well-established groups: bank tellers, bookkeepers, cashiers, secretaries, library attendants, and office machine operators; the last of these grew from 146,000 in 1950 to 572,000 in 1970, up 292 percent. More interesting are the new categories not separately identified in 1950: teacher aides, enumerators and interviewers, estimators and investigators, and expediters and production controllers. In the "service worker" category the largest increases and the new groups are in health services (particularly nursing aides, orderlies and attendants, and other health aides), cleaning service workers (outside the household), protective service workers, and in such new categories as child care workers (outside the household).[12]

WHAT IS NEW ABOUT THE NEW AGE?

The question about *new* services raises the basic question of what might be new about the emerging postindustrial period and what services might be particularly appropriate to this period. Further, can such new services develop on their own to help overcome the problems of the declining large central cities, or will they need special assistance to come into being or to expand. The discussion in this chapter will make the case that, to an important degree, the future economic viability of the large central city can be expected to depend on a special kind of invention and innovation—the development of *organizational capacity and skill* for encouraging the emergence and growth of those services which are particularly fitting to the future central city. The traditional kinds of invention and innovation—those associated with private R&D (research and develop-

---

[12]A confusion in terminology could result because of the different meanings attached to the word *service*. Here it covers cleaning service workers, food service workers, health service workers, personal service workers (barbers and hairdressers, child care workers, etc.), and protective service workers (guards, firemen, policemen, etc.).

ment) activities and private business risk taking—by themselves, may well not be adequate to the evolving new situation. In an oft-quoted comment, Thompson has noted:

> The long-range viability of any area must rest ultimately on its capacity to invent and/or innovate or otherwise acquire new export bases.
> The economic base of the larger metropolitan area is, then, the creativity of its universities and research parks, the sophistication of its engineering firms and financial institutions, the persuasiveness of its public relations and advertising agencies, the flexibility of its transportation network and utility systems, and all the other dimensions of infrastructure that facilitate the quick and orderly transfer from old dying bases to new growing ones.[13]

The new postindustrial era may well call for invention and innovation of a kind not contemplated by Thompson.

Against this background, what services *are* appropriate to the emerging period? To arrive at some notion of what such services might be, we cannot avoid conjecture on the characteristics of the age we are anticipating. Daniel Bell, who has written extensively on the postindustrial concept, puts the major emphasis on the centrality of theoretical knowledge, involving increasing dependence on science as the means of innovating and organizing technological change. "Most of the industrial societies," he has written, "are highly sensitive to the need for access to scientific knowledge, the organization of research, and the increasing importance of information as the strategic resource in the society."[14]

The importance of knowledge and information certainly seems key to everything else. But there are other forces at work as well which are likely to have a profound impact on the nature of future society in the United States. These include

1. Increasing importance of transnational and international economic (and other) activities: there are many forces making for increasing interdependence among nations and for investment, production, and sales of resources, goods, and services and transmission of information across national boundaries.

2. Increasing leisure and leisure-time activities: both actual events—such as the emphasis on vacations and other free time and of early retirement in Gallup, Harris, and other polls suggest that activities related to leisure can be expected to gain in significance in the future, even though some of us may be uncomfortable with this idea in a period when "lowered expectations" are asked for.

3. Increasing emphasis on the arts and on culture in all aspects of American life: this may be associated with rising incomes and greater leisure time, but may also be related to a reaction or resistance to the increasing role of science and technology in our lives.

4. Increasing concern with self (self-awareness and mental and physical

---

[13]Wilbur R. Thompson, "Internal and External Factors in the Development of Urban Economies," in Harvey S. Perloff and Lowdon Wingo, Jr., eds., *Issues in Urban Economics* (Baltimore: Johns Hopkins Press, 1968), p. 53.

[14]Foreword to the 1976 edition of *The Coming of Post-Industrial Society* (New York: Basic Books, 1976), p. xix.

health) and with quality of life: again, probably associated at least in part with rising incomes and greater leisure time and with the creation of a counterforce to the powerful technological and economic developments under way and to the power of the organizations directing these developments.

These tendencies are not easy to pin down (certainly not in traditional measurement and conceptual terms), and it is difficult to judge whether they are likely to be basic long-term forces or are temporary (fashionable?) features of current life. For the time being, at least, they seem very real and quite powerful and are likely to have a significant impact on the middle-term future, say, the next two decades or to the magic year 2000.

For our purposes, these tendencies, taken with the two central features—growth of service industries and of knowledge technology—provide a suggestive base for thinking about the service activities that could conceivably evolve as important employment outlets in a postindustrial era. Thus, there are a number of candidate services that should be considered as potentially significant in the future life of the city.

Head Office and Knowledge–Technology Activities

The management and administration of economic and other societal activities are often organized into separate offices, removed from the operations they direct. Hoover and Vernon stress the importance to central offices of being near a host of specialized services. "Face-to-face interchange is the only adequate means of communication for much of the executives' work. . . . Delicate negotiations and subtle, complex ideas are not easily entrusted to the telephone or the letter." They suggest that the other factors that favor central-city location are mass transit, the better opportunities for after-hours recreation, lunch-hour shopping (or window shopping), and "the greater opportunities for husband hunting," on the part of the young women who make up the largest part of the office workers.[15] These "headquarter" activities have grown rapidly in recent decades and are expected to continue to expand. Substantial numbers of them have located in central cities because of the advantages of face-to-face contacts both with others in the same industry and with persons and groups performing a wide variety of specialized services.[16] Increasingly, headquarter services employ knowledge technology to substantial degrees. It is interesting in this connection to note that computer specialists increased from some 12,000 in 1960 to 258,000 in 1970; there was no such census category in 1950.

Certain trends in these activities are likely to have a major influence on their future location, particularly the fact that they are increasingly national and international in scope. Thus, convenience in regard to transportation, particularly air transport, and movement between suburbs and central city, already significant,

---

[15]E. Hoover and R. Vernon, *Anatomy of Metropolis* (Cambridge, Mass.: Harvard University Press, 1960), p. 102.

[16]For a useful analysis of the location of headquarter offices of large firms, see Leland Burns and Wing Ning Pang, "Big Business in the Big City: Corporate Headquarters in the CBD," *Urban Affairs Quarterly* (September 1977).

will be even more important in the future. The effectiveness with which transportation is organized in central cities will undoubtedly play a large role in the location of these activities.

The growing international scope of central-office activities is particularly intriguing. The likelihood of large foreign investments in the United States suggests the counterpart of foreign office employment here and substantial back-and-forth movement of foreign business and government officials. The existence of ethnic enclaves in many of our major cities could conceivably turn out to be an advantage in locational terms with regard to some countries (such as Japan) *if* these enclaves are themselves satisfying places for visiting, work, living, and recreation. In a more general sense, the relative attractiveness of the city as a place in which to live and work will probably have a more substantial impact on the location of this set of activities than any of the other service categories.

Recreation and Tourism

While these are already significant in present-day cities, if we look ahead to the likely pattern of life in the postindustrial era, we can begin to appreciate the tremendous scope for enlargement and elaboration of recreation and tourism into major service industries. Reasonable projections of family expenditures for recreation in the future suggest a large demand for such services *overall*, but the form of these outlays will be determining of the share that will provide employment opportunities in central cities. While there is a temptation to assume that if there is demand for a service, supply will be forthcoming, the fact is that there have been very few creative, imaginative private investments in recreation in the cities. The concentrated urban form of Disneyland and Disneyworld have yet to be invented; and Disneyland, it should be noted, attracts 20 million paying customers a year. Nor have any U.S. cities yet developed an attraction to match Tivoli Gardens in Copenhagen.

Sports are only now being organized as sizable businesses, but most recreation is still in the horse-and-buggy stage. In the public realm, "parks and recreation" activities in most places provide a primitive attempt to cope with the new demands. It seems likely that quite new kinds of agencies, sponsored and supported by local governments but possibly private or mixed in form, will have to go into the recreation-development business if the necessary physical facilities are to be created which fit the scale of recreation and leisure-time activities appropriate to the postindustrial period. Such agencies will have to stop being squeamish about charging for the use of recreational facilities if they are to be built at the scale and with the quality and imagination to make them economically successful.

Tourism is already a major central-city industry, but it, too, has a long way to go. Certain trends are particularly suggestive. Thus, tourism tends to be combined with conferencing and other activities as there is a greater tendency to combine work and play. Also, the "package deal" is becoming the heart of the tourism industry and this means that expert marketing is key to tourist dollars. To date, there has been remarkably little imaginative planning in cities of this key service and the facilities required, though private groups have invested large sums in the business end of the services (in hotels particularly), and governments have lent a hand in a limited way through the building of convention centers and other facilities. While outlying areas have advantages in the space available for tourism activities, cities also have certain advantages which come with clustering and urbanity. However, both the facility and service elements have not been planned and developed as yet in a form fully to exploit these advantages.

Arts and Cultural Services

As outlets for employment and income generation, the performing, graphic, and other arts present even more of a problem in the organizational realm than do recreation and tourism; and the latter are difficult enough. One can readily see the arts and cultural activities as a dominant feature of the future urban scene, if appropriate organizational (including financing) forms and techniques can be developed.

Certain of the popular performing arts are just now beginning to be organized as major business activities (e.g., rock and jazz concerts and the giant record industry), but the employment and income-generating potentials are hardly being scratched. Also, a revival of the crafts that seems to be under way may have some potential. Substantial numbers of potters, leather workers, stained glass workers, photographers, furniture makers, and other craftsmen and artists appear in large numbers at street fairs in major cities around the country. It is intriguing to speculate whether American cities, in the most advanced industrial nation, might begin to develop the kind of informal sector which accounts for so much of urban employment in the Third World, as suggested by Peter Marris in discussion with the author. This development could be encouraged by relaxing zoning restrictions and by a willingness to preserve old, cheap, small-scale facilities suitable for craft workshops rather than redevelop them out of existence. This is a counterpart to the plea made by Vernon in his New York study twenty-five years ago not to destroy the old lofts which are important for small businesses just getting started.

Aside from their direct contribution to employment, the arts in various forms may turn out to be as much an element in the future infrastructure of the city to support its economic base as is transportation or other traditional infrastructure elements. But its potential contribution to the economic base should not be underestimated; the backward linkages in the arts, particularly the performing arts, are substantial, with backstage employment opportunities providing semiskilled and low-skilled persons over and above the front-stage professionals. Special efforts in training paraprofessionals can help expand the role of such workers.

A city flourishing in the arts can be expected to attract tourism, office employment, and other activities. Providing appropriate public facilities, sensitivity in the preservation of old buildings and facilities that can be useful for the arts, provision of tax breaks for performing groups, adjusting regulations building by building rather than zoning in large blocks in certain sections of the city, sponsorship of art fairs and changing those regulations that hinder them, and many other kinds of assistance can help meet the special needs of the arts if they are to comprise a substantial service component in the city of the future.

Health, Learning, and Other Personal Services

There are at least three considerations in this area of service. First, a major expansion of the more-or-less traditional medical and educational services in the cities will depend on new forms of national financing and organization, such as the creation of a national health service, adoption of national health insurance, or substantial national support of community and junior college education. For example, as the medical care for local people is more and more often paid from state or national governments, health insurance plans, or other sources external to local communities, the health industry takes on the character of an export activity contributing to the local economic base. Traditionally, manufacturing generated the "foreign" income which triggered the local employment multiplier; now services which are paid for externally do the same. Hence, a regional hospital may stimulate local economic growth, through generating "foreign exchange" just as a manufacturer of, say, optical goods did in the past. The possibilities involved in this type of development have been so widely discussed in recent years that no further elaboration is needed here.

Less widely discussed have been the newly developing health and learning services, as contrasted with conventional medical and educational services. These may be of special interest to the central city. On the health side, there has been a proliferation of health-related activities, such as the health spas and clubs, exercise studios, yoga centers, body-beautifying salons, hair care centers, reducing parlors and other nutrition-related activities, and a wide variety of similar activities. Particularly profuse—and intriguing—are the activities broadly related to mental health and emotional stability, for a fee. Somewhat associated are psychological types of activities, including self-awareness and consciousness-raising activities. Some religious types of activities relate to these various elements.

On the learning side, new services—both private and public—are being created which extend beyond traditional schooling, for example, which offer to help parents in the development of their children in the supposedly critical early years of life, which train skills of every conceivable type from the martial arts to rapid reading, and which offer child-sitting service in a supposedly educational environment.

Related to both health and learning services are activities associated with child care, care of the aged, and the care of others who need continuing attention. While some of these services are already well established (e.g., nursing homes), it seems evident that personal care is at an early stage of development and has a long way to go, including the probable development of such features as interage care and the creation of various forms of communal living which involve extended family characteristics.

All of these developing activities are of interest here because they involve employment and income-generation features of potential importance for central cities as well, of course, as for suburbs and outlying communities. Unless there is something quite special about our own period which has given birth to many new activities noted above, so that they can be expected to peter out over time, we can expect a substantial growth of such activities and their development as regular service *industries*. Substantial portions of the employment and income generation from these services could conceivably be in the central cities.

A third consideration is the fact that the future scope for these services will depend in no small part on how the delivery of the services is organized. It is in this light that the reorganization of these services to permit the use of less-skilled and more readily available labor achieves importance for the future. An indication of the potentialities here is the development of paraprofessionals in the medical field that has taken place in recent years, which permits the use of semiskilled labor and the conserving of the rarer and more expensive skills of the doctor and specialist. There has been some interesting work on the portion of a physician's tasks judged by physicians to be appropriate for delegation. It turns out that even physicians think that substantial portions can be turned over to "physician extenders."[17]

Another useful and appropriate response to the needs in the medical field has been the development of emergency services, particularly associated with fire departments. This is clearly only a beginning and in the future many paraprofessionals and nonprofessionals will have to be employed and many non-hospital facilities used for medical and public health purposes if medicine is to achieve its full service potential.

The same holds for education. Experiments have been carried out to encourage the use of less-skilled and lower-cost personnel in education as well, but there has been substantial resistance among educators because of the fear that trained teachers will lose their jobs or suffer a decrease in salary levels. Given the tremendous needs for education in the future, to enable urbanites to live and work well in the highly complex and interdependent environment of the postindustrial era, there is clearly need for a vast array of paraprofessionals and nonprofessionals in the education field as well as in medicine. As pointed out long ago, however,

> Barriers are maintained or raised to limit entry into the professions and similar "tertiary" types of work. In a poor community few people can be spared for work of these kinds. In a wealthy community it is inevitable and desirable that the number of workers in these departments should increase, but fearful lest the quasi-monopolistic privileges which they have been in the habit of enjoying should be destroyed, those who are already at work there raise the cry that "the professions are overcrowded."[18]

Thus, our ability to make appropriate use of such personnel and thereby enlarge the job as well as service-delivery possibilities of these important services in the

---

[17]See Gary L. Appel and Aaron Lowin, *Appendices to Physician Extenders: An Evaluation of Policy-Related Research*, Final Report, January 1975, Interstudy (123 East Grant Street, Minneapolis, Minnesota 55403).
[18]A. G. B. Fisher, *Progress and Security*, p. 64.

postindustrial period will depend on organizational inventiveness, involving, in many cases, a major departure from present practices.

Neighborhood, Preservation, and Rehabilitation Services

Preservation and rehabilitation to maintain, modernize, and enrich the tremendous social overhead in our cities have only just begun; the scope for the service components of these activities has been severely limited. But they fit evolving tendencies and have characteristics which suggest that they *could* achieve importance in a future period. These activities are closely related to the construction industry, but they have been a construction "step child," moving along in a disorganized, isolated, sporadic fashion, which, of course, means a highly costly fashion. If they were to proceed on an economically viable scale, there would be need for substantial innovation in learning how to do the job, the support of craftsmanship related to these activities, and a greatly improved legal and fiscal framework to encourage such efforts.

Similar considerations hold for what might in total be referred to as *neighborhood services,* ranging from the encouragement of "sweat equity" (individuals gaining assets through their own work) and of tenants furnishing housing services as a way of paying rent to the *collective* provision of security services, education services, rehabilitation activities, and the like. While such services might involve less money exchange than in the traditional patterns of providing services, they could add substantially to *real* local income and product, make life in the postindustrial era more community oriented than in the past, or reduce the high cost of living in cities. The further development of neighborhood cooperative food stores, lending operations, and related cooperative activities is in the same category.

There are other services that may well play a significant role in the life of the city in the future. There may be substantial employment possibilities in the many newer types of communication services that are already beginning to develop, for example, as well as in newer types of privately organized and community-organized protective services; there were almost a million protective service workers in 1970, reflecting the widespread concern for safety in response to growing crime rates. And, of course, there will be other opportunities, but they are likely to have many of the same basic characteristics as those described above.

HOW IS A PROPER FIT TO BE ACHIEVED?

Central cities, as indicated earlier, are facing severe economic problems arising from the clustering of the poorer families and the unemployed and the mismatch of jobs and low-income people in metropolitan areas. Some 90 percent of the labor force in central-city poverty areas and an equal percentage of the long-term unemployed are in occupational categories other than high-skilled professional and managerial workers. Yet 100 percent of the net new male-held jobs created in central cities in the 1960s were professional and managerial jobs, not at all suited to the skill level of central-city poor and unemployed. Even in the best of times economically, the unemployment rate for minority youths ran as high as 15 to 20 percent; during the recession in the mid-1970s it was over 50 percent in some areas. The fact that many persons cannot get jobs when they want to, and particularly those first entering the labor market, is a personal and social tragedy of the greatest dimension.

As we review the economic activities that *can* be expected to grow in volume and in the provision of job opportunities that *might* be located in the central city in the future, we find that they have certain special characteristics in almost every case which pose serious problems from the standpoint of providing needed central city employment:

1. Many of them, *as now organized*—the arts and cultural activities, recreation, and preservation and rehabilitation activities, for example—are likely to require large amounts of public financial support and sponsorship if they are to expand substantially
2. Many of them, *as now organized*, call for a relatively high level of skills.
3. Many of them provide a high proportion of part-time jobs and relatively low wages and salaries.
4. Most of them, to achieve much greater economic importance and service-industry status (i.e., a highly organized, sustained, exchange and employment-provision system) would need provision of substantial social overhead—for example, improved transportation, appropriate facilities, various public supports, helpful legal arrangements, and improvements in residential quality.

In general, a close look at the most promising services for the postindustrial age suggests that if they are to become important features of central-city life, they will require *substantial reorganization* in the forms in which they are provided and financed and will require a very close public-private partnership as well as sophisticated planning and provision of appropriate infrastructure.

At this point, a pessimist would say that the population and job decreases of the recent past, the fiscal difficulties, and the planning inadequacies of the large central city signal not only a culmination of the environmental and organizational mess left by the retreating industrial age but also signal an inadequate preparation for the coming postindustrial age, with its unique and different requirements and possibilities. In fact, he might say that what has emerged here is a perfect catch-22 situation. The only way the city can achieve rejuvenation, in the face of the powerful, well-established trends, is by a very substantial reorganization of service activities by governments and other institutions that today are unprepared and ill-equipped to lead such reorganization. Thus, we can expect the continuing decline of the central city for some time to come, with increasing social tensions and increased reliance on inadequate welfare solutions, the "city as sandbox," as Sternlieb has called it.[19]

---

[19]George Sternlieb, "The City as Sandbox," Part I in George Sternlieb and Norton Long, "Is the Inner City Doomed?," *The Public Interest* (Fall 1971).

On the opposite side, an optimist might point to the fact that it took a very long period of time before private industry organized itself for the industrial era, and at least as long for the necessary infrastructure and other public supports for industry to be forthcoming; the adjustment to the postindustrial era, at worst, is likely to be much shorter. What is now most needed is the development of a new outlook that can enable us better to cope with the requirements of the new era, together with intensive and sustained study about these requirements and social experiments to learn to deal with them effectively. Taking this optimistic view as reflecting, at a minimum, a possible socially beneficial speeding up of what can be expected to happen anyway over time, we can draw on what has been described above to outline the kind of approach that seems to be called for.

First, decision makers and the general public will have to be convinced of the probability that, in the middle-term future, the present economic system will have difficulty in providing the number and kinds of jobs needed and that a conscious effort to develop ane encourage the kind of new era services discussed here will have to be made. The price system should, supposedly, be able to guide the necessary adjustments if there is indeed greater and greater demand for services as compared to goods. But we have powerful institutional barriers. The minimum wage law, particularly as it impacts the employment of young persons in services, is one of them. The governmental requirements for preservation and building reconstruction and the controls with regard to construction crafts employment are another. The economic system is still largely geared to goods production, distribution, and consumption, and that extends from lending practices to the character of sales outlets.

Second, in-depth studies of the locational propensities of the various service industries are needed, so that cities can gear themselves to attract the most promising ones—that is, those that can conceivably gain from being located in the central cities. Trying to attract manufacturing firms seems to be misplaced effort. The cities must try to adjust to the economics of the evolving new era.

Third, given the nature of present unemployment in central cities, particular efforts will have to be made in promoting the new services to extend the scope for employing substantial numbers of workers from the poverty and minority communities as well as others who have found it difficult to enter the employment mainstream. What has been done to develop paramedical personnel and other paraprofessionals is in the right direction, but a very small drop in the bucket so far. Special efforts will have to be made to open up the scope for many new talents and skills as well as many jobs that are essentially unskilled. Some of the services, as in the case of neighborhood and rehabilitation services, are community oriented (or they can be) and can be geared specifically to help workers from within specific communities. Even the services that demand certain advanced skills, as in the case of most of the personal services, would, if appropriately organized, provide many jobs for workers in presently disadvantaged communities.

Fourth, many of the jobs in service industries today are part-time in nature and often poorly paid relative to the average wages and salaries in the nonser-

vice industries.[20] It is quite possible that these characteristics will be as important in service occupations in the future, and maybe even more so. This is a two-
edged proposition, however. While the disadvantages are obvious, there are
also some advantages in terms of many women and young persons who are
already in the labor force or who would like to enter it. A 1977 Labor Department
survey showed that while only 15.6 million families continued to rely on one
breadwinner, some 26.9 million families had two or more wage earners—nearly
22.3 million with both husbands and wives working, but with many of the wives
working on a part-time basis only. Moonlighting, part-time jobs, and multiple
family earners may well characterize the postindustrial age. Again, our laws and
regulations may well have to be adjusted to make this a positive force in people's
lives rather than largely a negative one.

Fifth, it seems inconceivable that there can be a "grand strategy" for promoting postindustrial era services, a strategy that can fit all the many different
kinds of services, the various needs for physical infrastructure and other social
overhead, and the wide variety of situations in which the different central cities
find themselves. A variety of approaches will undoubtedly have to be worked
out and all sorts of special situations provided for. Here is where the next phase
of invention and innovation is needed; we cannot rely on the traditional sources
of invention and innovation in this regard. We will need more public R&D than
we have had in the past, including central-city organizations that can initiate and
carry out social experiments. We need experiments on how to make services
more *self-supporting*, when traditionally they have been publicly supported.
Given the anticipated growth in service demands, public funds will otherwise be
stretched thinner and thinner. We need experiments on the development of
neighborhood services and preservation and rehabilitation services, on the extension of recreational and cultural services, on child care and care of the aged
and on interage care services, on enhancing the attraction of ethnic enclaves,
and similar developmental possibilities. Also, R&D approaches need to be applied to the development of central-city transportation and other infrastructure
geared to the requirements of the new era. And we will need a much more
flexible and sophisticated type of central-city planning than we have had to date.
Such planning will have to be much more concerned with economic, social, and
fiscal considerations than has been true to date, as well as with the new physical
requirements of the emerging postindustrial age. However, while a grand strategy of the type envisaged in the national urban renewal, model cities, or pover-
ty-program efforts in the past, seems inappropriate, that is not to say that central
cities can meet future requirements entirely on their own. They will need federal
financial support, given their own fiscal limitations. Central-city governments
will also have to find ways to relate to sources of income and organizational
strength in the remainder of the metropolitan region, so that the move-out of
persons and industries is not as economically and fiscally damaging as in the
past.

---

[20]See discussion in Victor R. Fuchs, *The Growing Importance of the Service Industries*,
Occasional Paper 96 (New York: National Bureau of Economic Research, 1965).

Finally, at least some of the older large cities will have to learn how to adjust to a situation of population and job decrease (or steady state) and how to grow old gracefully. Here, there is much to be learned from the experience of European cities.[21] The difficulties, however, should not be underestimated. Most of our institutions and our thinking are adjusted to expectation of continuing growth. We have never learned the art of diminution. Now that art has to be learned, and quickly. That seems essential if population and job decreases are to be levers in achieving a higher quality of life rather than the kind of unhelpful decline and abandonment that older sections of the older cities are now experiencing.

---

[21]See Peter Hall and David Metcalf, "The Declining Metropolis: Patterns, Problems, and Policies in Britain and Mainland Europe," and Piotr Korcelli, "Metropolitan Development in Poland and Implications for America," Part III in Charles L. Leven (ed.), *The Mature Metropolis* (Lexington, Mass.: Lesington Books, 1978).

4

Using the Arts to Improve Life in the City

One can imagine an arts enthusiast saying to the worried mayor of a large city which is suffering substantial unemployment:

> "I know of an 'industry' that can supply many jobs for the unemployed of the city and strengthen the city's economy. Oddly enough, this 'industry' itself suffers from a great deal of unemployment. It is largely unorganized; in fact, it is hardly an 'industry' in the usual economic meaning of the term. It is the *laissez-faire* economist's dream of an open labor market. Everyone can enter the industry and many, many do. The more job opportunities that appear, the more additional workers are drawn in and declare themselves as unemployed in it."

The question of strengthening the local economy would probably be of the greatest concern to the mayor if his was among the majority of large cities losing population, facing a job drain to the suburbs, and suffering fiscal difficulties. Yet the mayor would probably think the arts advocate mad—unless the mayor was himself closely associated with the arts, in which case the whole thing would have a familiar ring.

It is not easy to make sense out of the seeming contradictions when the economics of the arts are considered: How, indeed, can a field suffering high unemployment come to the aid of an economically troubled city? There is need for a model of the arts (essentially a systemic picture) that can explain where economics fits in, that can, in fact, characterize the whole set of activities known as "the arts" and provide a framework for making cooperative and public plans and policies with regard to this set of activities. There are a number of elements that fit into such a model of the arts.

DUAL OBJECTIVES

First and foremost is the fact of our society's dual objectives—rather than a single one—for the arts: the achievement of artistic excellence *and* community contribution. Not only are there *dual* objectives, but these encompass expanding

47

concepts. Thus, the search for excellence extends not only to the traditional "high" arts, but to an ever-growing set of activities that are each generation's view of the arts: not only the traditional arts of symphony, opera, theater, ballet, literature, architecture, painting and sculpture, but also modern musical forms, movies, radio, and TV, and a very wide spectrum of crafts and of graphic activities from photography to silk-screening. Artistry is the common thread, and time and means to create are essentials. And just as the concept of artistry expands, so, too, does the concept of the contribution that the arts are expected to make to the society at large. The arts have always been seen as the essence of culture, of the world at large and of the concerned community. They have also traditionally been seen as contributing to community and ethnic pride and therefore as a force in community cohesion. More recently, people have begun to look to the arts to help in educating "the whole person" and the hard-to-educate. They have been seen as potentially playing a role in neighborhood revitalization, a modern version of contributing to community cohesion. And the arts are being increasingly viewed as actually and potentially contributing to the strengthening of local economies, the last still being a relatively new and uncertain attribute of the arts' contribution to the community.

The full import of the fact that, in the arts, we are dealing with a wide range of disparate activities and with continually expanding concepts comes to life when one tries to categorize "the arts." The Census constantly gets itself in trouble in trying to report what is happening in the arts. While continuous change is an ingrained characteristic of the U.S. economy in general, nowhere does the Census have more trouble in reporting on the most basic of statistics— reports on employment and unemployment and on the life and death of enterprises—than in the arts. The arts categories are totally different from the censuses of population, occupations, industry and business, and within these censuses, the categories and definitions differ substantially from decade to decade. Thus, the major *occupational* grouping is "Writers, Artists and Entertainers": the major *industrial* category is "Entertainment and Recreational Services," and the key categories in the *Survey of Current Business* are "Motion Pictures" and "Other Amusements." Clearly, all of these categories are inadequate to report on what is happening in the arts.

The Arts System

It is hard to understand what is going on in the arts, or to grasp the future potentialities of the arts in the economic life of the city, without taking hold of the totality, or the arts "system" (or "network" or "industry" or whatever collective term is preferred). There are clearly many ways of categorizing a substantial set of activities and institutions of a collectivity like the arts, depending on the purpose at hand. For our own limited purposes, we can categorize the arts—largely to appreciate the breadth of their reach and to highlight the areas about which one needs to be concerned.

Three main elements are identified: (1) the artists and other participants; (2) the supportive institutions, and (3) the community, or even broader, the encompassing social and physical environment.

The *artists* (in the broadest sense of the term) are, of course, central to the whole system, more so than are the key persons in almost any other set of activities in our nation. They make the arts system "go," they give life to it. The quality, as well as the quantity, of what they create says a great deal not only about their own excellence but about the effectiveness of the other participants and the supporting institutions. It is important to appreciate the essential roles that the *other participants* (the managers, agents, administrators, technicians, teachers and volunteers) and the *supporting institutions* (articles, technical financial and job-and-income support) play in both of the objectives set for the arts— artistic excellence and community contribution. These two major categories are complicated enough, but they have been much discussed in the literature and in the concerns of the National Endowment for the Arts (if not so much in practical affairs), so there is some appreciation of their roles and importance. There is much less understanding and appreciation of the third of the three major categories—*the community and the social and physical environment*. This category encompasses the society as a whole and its physical setting, both of which are very much involved with the arts. The encompassing society, or community, is involved as actual and potential audiences, as well as in the form of community, neighborhood, and governmental support arrangements and organizations. The physical environment encompasses the public and private facilities that are or can be employed for the arts and the arts setting—that part of the physical environment that is actually and potentially supportive of the arts (as in the case of parks or downtown areas that are used for arts activities or in the case of outdoor murals and sculpture).

ENTER "THE DISMAL SCIENCE"

The arts model that will help us frame and come to grips with the actual and potential contribution of the arts to the economic life of the city must inevitably use the language and concepts of economics.But here we discover something disturbing. The economic studies that have been carried out to date have been exceedingly limited in scope and, indeed, have tended to put the arts in rather an unfavorable light. Three kinds of studies (and concerns) have been dominant:

1. The income gap, or Baumol's Disease (named after the economist who first highlighted the pervasiveness of an income gap in arts organizations)[1]
2. The high unemployment in the arts; and
3. The economic impacts of the arts, including the so-called "ripple effect"

The first makes the arts appear as a failed activity against the normal economic model of a productive, money-making industry or well-supported not-for-profit activity. The second underlines what seems like economic failure and makes one

---

[1]W. J. Baumol and W. G. Bowen, *Performing Arts: The Economic Dilemma* (New York: The Twentieth Century Fund, 1966).

feel sorry for the artists. The third simply puts the arts in the same mold as every other activity that involves various rounds of expenditures ("my expenditures create as many money ripples as your expenditures").[2]

A different picture emerges if one asks the question about the role of the arts in the economic future of the central city. A very brief overview shows the following: most of the large central cities all over the country—from New York and New Haven to San Francisco and Los Angeles—have serious economic problems. Economic activities are moving out of the cities to the suburbs and outlying areas beyond. Manufacturing is particularly on the move outward, since manufacturing technology frequently calls for fast horizontal movement of materials for mass-production processes, so that large spaces are needed, and transportation is increasingly by truck. Middle-class residents are also moving to the suburbs and beyond, while poor and minority families move into the city. Wholesale and retail trade activities also move out as manufacturing and middle-class families relocate themselves. As a result of these moves, cities often face financial difficulties through the diminution of the tax base and the increase in public service costs associated with poor families.

In the future, cities will have to rely on service industries for jobs, even more than they do today.[3] Already over 70 percent of total employment in the United States is in services, and the percentage is going up each decade. Some people are much disturbed by the increasing importance to the city of service employment, seeing this largely as a situation of "taking in your own washing." This is associated with the economic principle that a healthy, growing economy requires a large and growing "export base"; that is, industries that earn money by shipping goods outside the community, money that can then be used to buy service activities internally (activities like domestic and business services). But many of the service industries in a city today (and probably even more so in the future) are of an "export" variety; that is, they are sold outside the community or are sold to persons who have earned their income elsewhere and come to the city to buy these services. That is true of many specialized services (as in the case of finance and insurance services or major hospitals and universities). It is also true of many present-day arts activities and can be even more so in the future. Also, economic developments in the past years suggest that we may indeed be "taking in more of each other's laundry." Just as the economy can continue to grow with a declining proportion of employment in the goods-producing activities (agriculture, mining, construction, and manufacturing), so the economy seems to have been able to expand gross national product and national income while increasing the amount of "internal" service employment.

This is not to suggest that these directions are all that firmly established and that we really can be sure that the economy will flourish as goods-producing

---

[2]These topics are all discussed in the various papers reproduced in Mark Blaug, editor, *The Economics of the Arts* (London: Martin Robertson & Company, 1976). Some rarely discussed subjects are also touched on in these papers. This is probably the broadest treatment of the economics of the arts to date.

[3]See Harvey S. Perloff, "The Central City in the Post-Industrial Age," in Charles L. Leven, ed., *The Mature Metropolis* (New York: Lexington Books, 1978).

activities grow less and less important. However, until we do know more about what makes for a healthy national and local economy, we have to assume that from the standpoint of the central city—now suffering from a declining economic base—the strengthening of service employment is all to the good.

We also have to note that, of the services, the arts have special importance for the central city (1) because of their potential for employing many workers who would otherwise have difficulty in getting jobs, and (2) because of the contribution the arts can make to the attractiveness of the city and therefore to its economic viability. On the first score, the arts are valuable because they can absorb talents and skills that are to be found in the various individuals and groups who live in the city. The contribution the arts can make to the economic viability of the city is equally important and intriguing. These days, the economic future of any area or community is tied to how attractive a place it is for living and working. The arts can and do make a big contribution on that score. They can draw in many tourists and local persons. The major impacts are not the more direct ones (the ones that are normally measured through impact analysis), but the indirect ones, the economic stimulus that results, for example, when an area is redeveloped with arts at the center. (An example of the latter is the French Quarter in New Orleans.) But before we get into the more general concepts we need to take note of the special character of employment and unemployment in the arts, and here, too, we can make use of the economists' concepts and tools. Of particular value are the supply/demand concepts.

SUPPLY

Supply in the arts emerges as that part of the labor force that is associated with arts activities. But here some peculiarities appear: the labor force acts differently than it does in most other economic activities. Thus, an individual may declare himself to be an unemployed actor to his labor union and to the Census or Department of Labor interviewer, yet work as a real estate agent, or he may insist that he is an unemployed artist while working either part-time or full time in a printing shop or a shoe store. Census and Department of Labor statistics gives us only a small inkling of what is going on. It would take a probing search to figure out what actually is going on in the arts labor force. To provide a rounded picture from the standpoint of those who associate themselves with the arts, the following categories must have data attached to them:

1. Persons employed full-time in the arts
2. Persons employed part-time in the arts
3. Persons employed part-time in the arts, and part-time in another industry
4. Persons who are unemployed
5. Persons unemployed in the arts but employed full-time in another industry; and
6. Persons unemployed in the arts, but employed part-time in another industry

In general in the United States economy, when things are slow in their own industries, some workers will take a job elsewhere if available. Then usually they declare themselves as workers in the industry that has given them employment. The attachment to the arts is quite special. It is intriguing to find that performing arts unions in Los Angeles reported that over three-quarters of their registered members were unemployed at the end of 1977 when the city's unemployment rate as a whole was around 7%. Performing artists normally work only part time, so that at any one time, the union's "unemployment" roles will cover highly-paid actors and actresses who appear frequently—but intermittently—in theatres, movies, and TV, as well as those who have not had an acting job during the past 12 months and are only marginally "in" the arts at best. Similarly, how does one calculate the employment of a world-famous author who sells an article now and then? In addition, in the arts, to which people are emotionally devoted, more than in most activities, the dividing line between the "volunteer" and the "worker" is very thin indeed; the volunteer is often a worker who is not being paid because the arts agency is simply out of funds. Here we see that supply (employed and unemployed labor force) is related to demand as in all economic activities, but that supply is much more persistent and erratic in the arts than elsewhere.

Not surprisingly, given the background of disorganization in the arts industry, individual labor unions, mostly formed around skill groups, such as actors, musicians, writers, announcers, back-stage technicians, and others (in some cases organized around a medium, such as TV or movies) have come to play a strong and very special role on the supply side. They have given some stability and security for at least the established members of the various arts professions. But the ties among the individual unions are tenuous, and collective strength, even within a given medium, can rarely, if ever, be applied. The substantial unemployment and the vast differences among the various arts activities makes organization across large segments of the industry extremely difficult. Yet the unions are important in the economic life of the city in influencing employment and income of persons in the arts. They determine, through the rules which they set, the extent to which certain kinds of activities, such as community (neighborhood) arts activities and experimental arts efforts (as in the theatre) can be carried out with performers receiving less than the established hourly rates of pay. The unions face a delicate balancing act in this predominantly unorganized industry between protecting the gains already won and helping to push the arts into realms that can also open up new possibilities for economic returns in the future.

DEMAND

The demand factor in the arts is equally unusual. For most products and services, *demand* emerges as simply the amount of the product or service that consumers are willing to acquire either through individual purchases (out of their pocketbooks) or through collective purchases (by way of taxation). The number of workers in the industry—supply—is then determined by the number needed to produce that particular product or service. But the arts fall within a limited category of services—medicine and education are among them—where the direct payments for the service make up only a part of the funds available to cover the costs of supplying the service. Such services are deemed to be of such societal value as to have a special claim on the community's wealth and income.

Thus, in addition to the income that is provided through individual purchases of the service (in the case of the arts, in the form of tickets to performances and displays and acquisition of works of art), there are governmental grants, foundation grants, individual philanthropy and corporate philanthropy directed at supporting these highly regarded activities.

Here, however, the arts depart from medicine and education. Whereas medicine and education are substantially organized and the rationale for public support has long been established, in the case of the arts the rationale for consistent, substantial support by private and public wealth in the United States has not yet been developed fully or accepted widely. Art organizations, as already noted, consistently suffer from *Baumol's disease*. The result is a chaotic demand situation. If the "worried mayor" mentioned at the beginning wanted to figure out how much the arts industry might conceivably contribute to the city economy, he would be forced to make some pretty wild guesses, since he would have very little firm data available on either the supply side or the demand side to go on. The situation in the United States is different from that in Europe where public support for the arts is firmly established.

Not only is governmental and philanthropic support for the arts less certain than in the case of medicine and education, but individual "purchases" do not provide as broad a base, at least in the case of the more traditional art forms. Here there is an interesting split between the highly commercialized more modern art forms, such as movies, TV, radio, records, and popular concerts, and the traditional forms of live theatre, symphony, opera and the like. The economic view of the arts naturally raises the issue of whether certain of the methods for increasing audiences employed in the former could not well be employed in the traditional areas, as well as new methods that might be particularly appropriate for the traditional forms.

Community Arts

There are additional features that are quite special to the arts and that give a particular character to the supply and demand situation. Looming large among them is the development of what has come to be called "community or neighborhood arts." Artists and art groups that have associated themselves with particular communities and/or ethnic groups have developed innovative art forms, independent of but often related to the more traditional forms, which contribute importantly to community cohesion. This has been part of the American rediscovery of the values of ethnic diversity, of neighborhood and neighboring, and of the great artistry to be found in popular culture and native forms. One has the sense that there may be here the beginnings of a significant movement important in quantitative as well as qualitative terms. There is now a national organization established to work with and assist such community art groups, of which thousands are already in existence. Neighborhood arts organizations have pioneered the use of C.E.T.A. (the federal government's Comprehensive Employment and Training Act) funds to employ community-based artists and organizers. They are introducing a new dimension into even the most traditional of the art forms, such as theatre, and are using established forms, such as mural painting, in a quite new way. It is hard to grasp the full potential of this evolving movement but our worried mayor would be certain to be intrigued by the possibilities of this development in quite practical supply-and-demand terms.

DISORGANIZATION AND ORGANIZATION

What emerges from this overview of supply and demand in the arts is a picture of a disparate, largely unorganized set of activities that fall under the arts rubric, but, nevertheless, activities that have great actual, and even greater potential, economic significance. These features which distinguish the arts industry from other industries include the following:

1. There are many part-time workers, a large proportion of whom actually prefer working only part-time (normally taken to be under 35 hours per week).

2. Many persons declare themselves to be unemployed even though they may be only marginally related to the arts, because of strong attachment to arts activities. In addition, of course, many of those declaring themselves to be unemployed do have a substantial employment background in arts activities.

3. Strong labor unions are important in individual arts activities, but are able to influence labor conditions for only a small proportion of those actually involved in such individual activities. There are only tenuous relationships among the different arts unions.

4. There is a relatively narrow base of support through individual purchases of arts services and products in the traditional arts areas and an erratic support of the more modern areas (essentially varying with each "output") as with movies, TV, and popular concerts.

5. There is an equally uncertain support of arts activities through governmental and philanthropic sources, based on no agreed-upon quantitative or qualitative principles.

6. There is only minimal cooperation and coordination of the different arts activities, with limited national organization of individual activities and even less across-the-board local organization in most communities. Arts organization in general is, obviously, at a very early stage of development.

It seems clear that the fact of disorganization is at the heart of the problem of trying to understand what the arts might contribute to the economic life of the city, and that *organization* must be at the heart of any policy or program that looks towards greatly enlarging the contribution of the arts to local economies. What form such organization may, and should, take is a matter of concern throughout this report, probing as it does, the *economic potential* of the arts, in the face of the serious economic difficulties of so many of our cities. Thus, in effect, we are looking towards the change from a current model of the arts which is largely characterized by disorganization to an evolving model characterized by substantially increased organization.

This is not necessarily a costless solution. The present difficulties—of unemployment and the rest—and the limited contribution to the economic life of the city could easily be traded for a much more *certain* situation for the arts but with more constraints on freedom and innovation. Freedom in artistic creation has long been the most precious ingredient of the arts. The challenge is to evolve organization that can strengthen the second of the dual objectives for the arts—contribution to the community—without jeopardizing the freedom that has long been a key factor in the first objective—artistic excellence.

Organization, particularly when viewed in the context of enlarging the contribution of the arts to the economic life of the city, is not alone a matter of better management of arts activities, more cooperation, coordination and planning among them, or a more effective organizational infrastructure—although it *is* all of these. Organization in the present context must be seen also as encompassing widely understood and firmly established sets of relationships with city and regional governments and with private enterprise (both supporters of the arts and investors in the city).

The greatest demands on *organization* emerge particularly when it becomes evident that arts activities should become an integral part of the physical development of the city and region. The current model of the arts would encompass this element as a relatively minor item, referring only to the activities of preservation and restoration and to the construction and maintenance of a limited number of arts facilities, public and private. The potential is another matter entirely. For the arts—including one of the most traditional of the arts, architecture—can make a special and highly significant contribution to the physical development of the city and region in such a way as to have substantial economic pay-offs. Thus, they can contribute importantly to the economic revitalization of downtown areas and older neighborhoods of the city and region; to the enlargement of tourism, the convention trade, and other attractions to visitors (and their expenditures); and, in general, to the economic viability of urban communities.

Organization, as encompassing widely understood and firmly established sets of relationships with the city and regional governments, must extend also to the role of the arts in the provision of the many public services that are part of the life of the modern American city. This includes the role of the arts in education, health activities, parks and recreation, transportation and other public works, public and assisted housing, law enforcement and, of course, city beautification. The arts currently have only tenuous relationships to each of these, even education, recreation, and city beautification, since they have traditionally been seen as add-ons in public services and facilities and in public life in general. When the economic potential of the arts is considered, this facet of the arts must be of central concern.

One final item under the rubric of organization must be mentioned: the contribution to the economic life of the city through special events. Festivals and other special events have been associated with the arts from the beginning of recorded history. Celebrations have always *naturally* centered around the arts. It does not detract from the full glory of the arts as community celebration to note that such celebrations can and do have an economic component. If we are not to rely only on the wealthy to make community celebration possible, as has often been the case in the past, then the ability to pay for such celebrations—and to have them contribute to the economic life of the community—is of no small moment.

USING THE SUGGESTED MODEL OF THE ARTS

The very simple model which has been suggested as helpful in describing the arts system as it is and might become, by providing a logical and consistent framework for inventorying and analyzing arts activities, can also be used as a framework for discussing strategy and tactics for bringing about improvements. Thus, strategy for change might be thought of in terms of approaches for achieving general goals for employment and income for artists and other participants, for more sharply defining the role of the supporting institutions, and for specifying the changes needed in the social and physical environment if the arts are to contribute importantly to the economic life of the city. The lack of data and the present limited state of knowledge about the arts (as well as the limitation of funds and time of our own study) prevents us from carrying such an analysis very far. Without relatively complete data on employment and unemployment in the arts, it is hard to discuss measures that might be employed to attempt to achieve a *specific* level of employment (aside from other difficulties in such an analysis). We are also far from the time when *specific* levels of public and private support of arts institutions and planned changes in the social and physical environment can be related to specific levels of employment and specific levels of contribution to the economic growth of a given city. However, the model does suggest where to look for blockages to improvements and the direction and scope of improvements called for if the more general goals are to be achieved. This has led us to look closely at changes in organization that are called for and the kinds of public policies that would serve substantially to enhance the contribution of the arts to the economic life of the city.

What to Do

City governments and private business and labor interests, as well as artists and art organizations, have to learn how to join forces to turn joy and beauty into practical economic advantage—while enjoying the arts and art creation for their own sake.

Marketing. A logical starting point for expanding the economic scope of the arts is to concentrate on methods for increasing the size of audiences. Sound marketing requires, first, effective *dissemination of information.* There are advanced media and other techniques to be learned and more personal methods to be employed. (When the San Francisco Ballet came close to extinction a few years ago, the dancers took to the streets, ballet shoes in hand, to solicit funds. The company gained notice of its product and stimulated a new interested audience.) Ties to tourism are important, as are the use of special events. Arts organizations spend 5–8 percent of their operating expenditures for promotion, where a figure of 10–15 percent is thought to be needed. Subscriptions sales are critically important. Cooperative, or umbrella, marketing agencies offer significant possibilities for the future.

Stimulating desire for the arts by education is key. Awareness and appreciation of the arts must begin early in life to ensure future "consumption." How to prevent public school funds for art and music instruction from being cut (they are usually the first to be cut) should become a matter of concern for all arts organizations. Ancillary institutions for arts learning have been established and should be expanded.

Voucher ticket sales (through which the consumer purchases a block of tickets to a variety of events) may be general or limited to special audiences. Booths for the sale at a reduced rate of unsold theater tickets (pioneered in New York) is an innovation with great potential.

Financing. If the arts are to play their proper role in the economy and culture of our cities, *access to the arts must be available to the broad public.* This requires a fundamental rethinking about economic support of the arts and the responsibility that government bears toward artistic enterprise. The key is to rationalize the market exchanges of four interrelated sectors: (1) government, (2) for-profit enterprises, (3) nonprofit sector, and (4) the individual, as organization member and as consumer.

The present rules of the game prevent all these sectors from being as supportive of the arts as they might be. Scarcity as the explanation of price setting is based on a model of man which asserts that he receives economic value not only from the consumption of goods and services, but also by excluding others from doing the same. Scarcity in reality then becomes a brute-force mechanism for establishing prices, which insures that the wealthy get served first. However, the principle of scarcity runs counter to the principle of broad *access* to the arts. When the demand curve (as a graphic presentation of a complex reality) is looked at as representative of individual behavior, it can show that different people and institutions are willing to pay different amounts for the consumption of the same good. If the arts are able to develop other ways to get consumers to express their full economic valuing of artistic goods and services, scarcity can be discarded as the sole mechanism and access to the arts can be more fully realized.

For the non-profit sector, public service budgets can permit a more appropriate kind of accounting than the present concentration on the bottom line of an organization's financial statement. Residual exclusivity would be reduced.

Government subsidy provides for the delivery of arts goods or services which could not otherwise be afforded by the public. It represents the fee-for-public-service cost, which must go with any claim by government that it is assuring access to the arts. Beyond that, to foster or preserve the arts for future generations, government must provide additional resources.

Part of the cost is appropriately covered by wealthy individuals in the community, as well as the private and semi-private collectivities, the corporations and foundations. This is the area in which these individuals and collectivities can exhibit their sense of social responsibility, the desire to increase the quality of life of their community, as well as the judgment that the value associated with support of the arts is greater than the cost incurred.

Also, along the same principles, this analysis calls for local governments to return to the arts a reasonable share of the hotel tax (or similar levy) equal to the contribution of the arts in attracting visitors and their capital to the city.

Federal Government Support.   The national government supports the arts in a variety of forms. Except for the highly important support provided by the National Endowment for the Arts, federal financial assistance is related to other, non-art purposes, such as generating employment, providing training for the unemployed, education, transportation, and the like. This turns out to be a two-edged knife. It significantly broadens the total government assistance provided the arts but, at the same time, puts the arts in a Procrustean-bed situation, where they are stretched or cut to fit some pre-ordained general purpose. In each of the federal programs, there are not-unreasonable adjustments to existing rules of the game that can be enormously helpful to the arts without subverting the overall purposes of the federal grants and programs. CETA is used as an example of how this might be done. Similar principles would apply to other federal programs.

The proposal for the creation of an Office of Cultural Affairs in the Executive Office of the President, to increase the visibility of the arts and to provide a continuing overview of federal programs touching on the arts, deserves support.

Unions.   Unions can play a significant role in enhancing the strength of the arts within the economy. Currently, unions help stabilize the arts industry and serve to control the labor market. In collective bargaining, unions have to act as an adversary against employers and managers. With the expansion of financing by government and other collectives, future collective bargaining might logically be between management and unions on one side confronting the sources of funding on the other.

With the shifting of fund-raising to collectivities, the union leader should be encouraged to play a larger role in obtaining funds, increasing audience support, and perhaps even making financial contributions to the arts organization in the interest of enhancing arts employment.

The encouragement of additional employment opportunities for actors and related professionals by the Actors Equity 99-seat waiver plan (a waiving of its own work rules in theaters of 99 seats or less) in Los Angeles and San Francisco, in effect since 1972, has had enough success to suggest that other arts unions might well follow Equity's example.

Another strategy for increasing employment in the arts is the establishment of a Performing Arts Trust Fund, a concept pioneered by the American Federation of Musicians. The fund provides a self-circulating financial mechanism which not only benefits the community, but also helps to maintain the livelihood of many artists. There are numerous avenues for financing a trust fund: an agreed-upon proportion of royalties, programs sold at arts performances, parking fees, and various forms of residuals.

A United Arts Fund Drive could be an effective means of generating support for all the arts organizations of a community.

Beautifying, Restoring, and Revitalizing the City. The arts can serve in many ways to vitalize the city. In a truly foundational sense, architects and architecture can help create an environment which is not only well organized, but poetic and symbolic as well. Buildings and clusters of buildings—like other major works of art—help attract people to city areas, at times providing the welcome net additions to sections lacking the pedestrian traffic necessary for increased business activity.

Preserving and adapting historic buildings are in many instances economically more feasible than new construction and can provide a significant job market (because of their labor-intensive nature) for craftspeople and architects.

Existing enlightened support for architecture and building from the corporate sector (in one case encompassing programs to encourage minority builders, help displaced tenants, and provide funds for city improvement and restoration) might well be emulated. But it is the broadening of public support on which the future contribution of architecture to the economic and cultural life of the city will depend. This should cover (1) the reservation of land for future community use, (2) expansion of support for public facilities and housing, (3) tax incentives for town-scale projects, (4) revisions of property-tax systems and of zoning and building codes to encourage city development, (5) establishment of trust funds for community redevelopment, (6) creation of a national development corporation (already proposed by President Carter), (7) special zoning and codes for cultural facilities and historic restoration, and (8) provision of design services for construction in government grants. Also, critically important is the establishment of "1% funding" to support art work associated with new building and to provide art in public places.

Many of the larger older cities are obsolete in large sections because they are the product of the previous industrial age and have not adapted to the post-industrial period. They are presently not the ideal sites for either manufacturing or the new service industries, nor for middle and upper income families. The population is responding to this obsolescence by settling in outlying areas. The central cities can stop the (net) out-migration of people by becoming a good place in which to live and work. This requires that the amenities unique to the older areas become the basis for effectively competing with the younger outlying employment centers. These amenities include the centralized location of downtown and the assets and charms of the older buildings and spaces—and the arts.

The redevelopment process and the state laws regulating it are receptive to the financing of cultural facilities in the city. However, to be eligible for tax-increment financing (which is key to financing redevelopment), cultural-facility investments must prove to contribute to the economic viability of the city and not just "the quality of life." Under such terms of reference, measuring the economic benefit of cultural facilities requires consideration of other factors than projected gross revenues from ticket sales. It requires inclusion of a broadly defined economic multiplier effect. Experiences in various cities suggest that arts facilities and activities, when imaginatively developed to attract a maximum of local and tourist visitors, can be a major economic asset to the local economy. The multiplier measurement should be able to capture that. There are significant possibilities, as demonstrated in various cities across the country, in mixed-use facilities, the use of public spaces for cultural activities, historic restoration, and the use of special opportunities to revitalize the city.

Public regulations dealing with land use and structures can be changed in certain instances to have a favorable impact on the expansion of the arts. Examples are changes in the current zoning laws to accommodate artists in parts of the city where the mixing of studios and living accommodations are now prohibited. Such changes can encourage the development of artist colonies—which might well become an important symbol of the post-industrial city.

Community Arts. Neighborhood arts must play a key role in the revitalization of our central cities. This is particularly important because they are associated with minority cultures that represent a majority or near-majority of the population in most large cities. By stimulating a more general interest in and appreciation of the arts in a variety of forms, a decentralized arts program could have a long-run impact upon patronage of the arts in both the nonprofit and profitmaking sectors.

A public organization that can speak for all the neighborhood arts in the city is needed. Private nonprofit arts organizations can retain their individual and independent identities, but receive financial and technical assistance from such an agency.

For the neighborhood arts programs to develop in the long run, there must be educational programs to build future community involvement with the arts. Creative skills may be related to a range of career occupations, including many which are outside the arts field, and educational research might well focus on new instructional and counseling techniques for identification and development of this relationship.

Universities in urban areas have the potential capacity to serve artistic needs in minority communities, but, with few exceptions, this potential remains undeveloped.

Neighborhood recreation and cultural centers need to be developed and/or expanded for local residents, as a locus for arts events and education. Parks and playgrounds, child day-care facilities, shopping malls, work places, post offices and other public buildings, housing projects, and other such facilities can serve as conduits for both the performing and visual arts. Musical instruments, art supplies, and other equipment should be available for use by residents, especially by young people, in classes and workshops. Construction, staffing, and programming of such neighborhood facilities should be a specific element in urban redevelopment planning and in the general plan for the total community.

The problem of security might be diminished through the proper planning of programs and facilities so as to minimize risks of crime; for example, shopping malls and other centers which are well lit and well policed, with adequate and secure parking areas, are ideal locations for artistic events. Consideration should also be given to the establishment of "cultural parks," akin to industrial parks (indeed, in some areas cultural and industrial parks might occupy the same space and facilities), which can encompass these security measures as an element in their planning and construction.

All of these elements should be the responsibility of a Neighborhood Arts Program, which might well be along the lines of the San Francisco model.

Department of Cultural Affairs. Large cities need a public agency that can not only provide specific cultural services and programs, but can coordinate the city's arts activities, foster its overall cultural development, and create a comprehensive policy for the city.

A new Department of Cultural Affairs would combine the major existing departments providing arts services and programs. It should take leadership in developing and articulating a comprehensive cultural policy for the city and have the power to implement it. It would stimulate the development of the arts by (1) supervising city aid to cultural institutions, (2) helping determine funding allocations, (3) administering fee programs to the public, (4) providing technical services to cultural organizations, groups, and individual artists, and (5) coordinating the efforts of the other city agencies that affect cultural activities, and cooperating with the county. The agency should also be allowed to play an active role in the development of historical districts and redevelopment projects. Also, the Department should work closely with such agencies as the City Planning Department and the Community Redevelopment Agency in overall planning efforts to encourage the arts component in development strategies.

The Department should have a division to foster the development of community arts organizations. Guidance and assistance should run from securing permits for community arts festivals to obtaining major funding for innovative programs. It should explore opportunities for cooperative partnerships in projects of mutual benefit between the city and community art groups.

The Department should take an active interest in nurturing the development of for-profit arts activities. There are helpful public regulations that can be sponsored to meet needs of these industries (such as the "one-stop" permit arrangement for using public streets and facilities in movie-making in Los Angeles). Also, the city can help provide useful information on available training facilities to youthful unemployed workers, and press for-profit arts employers on "affirmative action" hiring.

Arts in Economic Development Efforts. The post-industrial city must depend on service activities, rather than manufacturing and trade as formerly, as the mainstay of its economy. But service activities have different requirements than traditional manufacturing or trade activities, and this should be reflected in economic development (promotion) efforts by city agencies. Just as public-private task forces are organized to try to hold on to a garment industry or jewelry exchange, so task forces need to be organized to increase employment in the arts and to help magnify the economic impact of the arts. City efforts in this regard would be greatly enhanced if the federal government's grants for economic development (through HUD and EDA) made specific provision for the arts in relation to their economic development grants.

Corporations contributing to the arts, and interested in the economic viability of the central city, might well consider the economic dimensions of the arts in making decisions on grants and sponsored art shows and performances. Their knowledge about economic stimulus should be sought by city agencies in evolving programs to attract tourists and private investment to the city.

Cultural Planning.   Planning is required if the arts are to achieve the objectives which have been set for them, including a major contribution to the local economy. This can be done by introducing a Cultural Element in the General Plan (prepared in almost every city in the country), which can serve as a framework for specific governmental decisions.

A cultural element should do the following: (1) provide basic information about the arts activities in the city and the people involved in them (a constantly maintained inventory of the arts); (2) make plans for broader and more flexible use of public (and, to some extent, private) facilities for arts activities, experimental arts groups, and arts education efforts; (3) probe for ways in which the arts might be tied into various private activities and public services in order to enlarge the scope of arts employment and income; and (4) make plans for the fuller use of the arts in urban development and redevelopment.

II

URBAN AND METROPOLITAN
PLANNING AND POLICY

INTRODUCTION

In unpublished materials written in 1982, Harvey Perloff set out his view of how the nation should plan in the years ahead. That included, first, strategic national economic planning to deal with currently "weak and fractionated economic management"; second, preparation by the Executive Branch of "cost-conscious national development plans, encompassing time- and site-specific programs"; third, establishment of a multi-year capital budget for federal investment; fourth, federal guidance of urban development and renewal; and finally, coherent national programs in the realm of human resources.

Two themes, central to all of these proposals, are the necessity for coordinating public programs and developing long-range goals to guide policy. These themes also run through his publications on urban and metropolitan planning. Their importance was underscored by the chaos that for many decades had bedeviled public policy and its implementation.

Disarray characterized the federal approach to guiding urban affairs through the programs and policies innaugurated during the postwar era. With a proliferation of federally sponsored urban activities, but no clear guidelines for what it was that the program were meant to do, conflicts and unsatisfied ambitions were inevitable. The Model Cities Program, the centerpiece of Lyndon Johnson's Great Society, channeled resources into the inner cities. So did other activities under the poverty program. Federal support for highway construction and mortgage finance, on the other hand, furthered suburban growth at the expense of central cities.

The reaction to the smouldering frustrations of minorities, and to the conditions and areas in which they lived, were highlighted by the urban riots of 1965–66 and 1968. The response was the National Urban Policy Act that required the President to prepare a biennial report, to confront urban problems systematically, and to try to reconcile conflicting federal policies. The Act was intended to insure coherence in national urban policy and the purpose of the report was to provide a framework for those federal activities that substantially impacted urban communities.

The laudable intents of the legislation were not to be realized. The effort was scuttled when a new Administration assumed power. Nixon maintained that urban problems were outside the domain of federal action. Local initiative, aided by revenue sharing (the "New Federalism"), provided a better answer. The view that the federal government should keep hands off local matters persisted until the Carter administration, in its 1978 report, returned to the position that the federal government should have an explicit urban policy stance and take an active role in urban affairs. That report (and its later 1980 edition) was intended to legitimate the shift in federal policy toward targetting programs to distressed groups and places. With the return of a Republican administration in 1980, the government once again turned away from the city. And that is where matters stand now.

Perloff's papers on urban and metropolitan planning, written during this period of turmoil and uncertainty regarding the proper federal posture for urban policy, range broadly from concerns for the variety of resources that planning should encompass a ways for improving land policy.

Despite the comprehensiveness assumed in the meaning of urban planning, the field has defined its concern for the environment in narrow terms, focussing on land use and zoning. Because its major thrust has been one of protecting property values rather than the total environment, planning has remained only a potentially useful tool for improving environmental quality. "A Framework for Dealing with the Urban Environment" attempts to expand the planner's vision into the realm of "new resources in an urban age." The urban environment, as a system connecting natural and man-made elements, provides the setting for the discussion.

Resources include natural amenities—the juxtaposition of features such as climate, land, coastline, and water—that increasingly govern the location of economic activities and the quality of life; open spaces that offer breathing space and recreation possibilities; and "three-dimensional space resources" consisting of airway space, radio spectrum space, underground space. Depending on the ways they are used, these resources confer either welfare or "illfare" on society.

Linking urban systems with resources, including all of the types embraced by the broadened definition of resources, is facilitated by an expanded concept of indicators and accounts that provides a framework for identifying relationships and interactions. Social indicators could become the basis for annual state-of-the-region reports. The article lists the types of indicators such a document might include. A new urban ecology, not dissimilar in concept from the one Kenneth Boulding envisions in his concept of "spaceship earth," is called for where human settlement is understood to interpenetrate with a natural environmental "envelope."

During the 1960s, a major preoccupation of liberal social scientists was the confection of "social indicators and reports" that would allow central planners to assess the current situation nationally as well as regionally and to propose scientifically based solutions. Buttressed with statistics, social reports would focus the attention of decision makers on key problems. They would permit the public monitoring of the success (or failure) of government programs, and they would encourage the formation of an enlightened and informed public opinion. Perloff was an ardent champion of these ideas, and his essay, published in 1969, was an attempt to set out an indicators framework for metropolitan regions. Despite the years of research following his original formulation of the idea, not much came of it. Politicians were not particularly eager to be informed by social scientists, nor did they care for "monitoring" public programs or for an "informed public opinion." Besides, in the wake of the Viet Nam disaster, there was little support for the kind of central planning Perloff envisioned.

Such setbacks, however, never stopped Perloff for very long. In 1972, he was among the first to champion "quality of environment" ideas. In the essay reprinted here as Chapter 6, he specifies those features of the urban environment with which planners, he thought, should be concerned. The essay starts with a paradox. "The quality of the urban environment," Perloff writes, "has been the raison d'être of city planning for more than three-quarters of a century. . . . Yet if there has been any gain in popularity or in support or in influence of city planning, it is hardly discernible. . . . One reason is that planning, instead of leading the vanguard of issue-identification, has been following the changes in fashion rather than leading the way." Another reason is that planners equate environmental quality with planned land uses controlled by zoning regulations. A narrow construction of the proper role for public intervention, limited to preventing or managing external effects of private decisions, has also hamstrung the planners' purview. The article proposes broadening planning powers to embrace regional assets, those vital features of metropolitan regions that sustain and support urban functions. Once they are defined, it becomes the planner's task to enhance urban environmental quality "by policy and action aimed at preserving and improving regional assets" and specifically to prevent

(1) damaging mixes, (2) a density or intensity of use that exceeds capacity (as in the case of air pollution and natural recreation resources), (3) damaging and costly deterioration or decline, and (4) lower rather than higher returns on the use of the regional assets—but always from the overall regional standpoint rather than from the standpoint of property protection in highly limited zones.

In "National Urban Policy; Stage I, Building the Foundation," Perloff blames urban problems on "our national socioeconomic system and way of doing things." The problems can be confronted effectively only when urban development is guided by *national* policy that addresses certain equity and quality of life objectives, and the enhancement of individual welfare. As background, Perloff traces the historical evolution of United States development through its agricultural, industrial, and post-industrial stages, and of policy responses at each stage. Filling the policy gaps requires, first, developing a sharply focussed and well-financed national policy aimed at accelerating the development of human resources, particularly of the most disadvantaged, to meet the needs of the post-industrial era. The second requirement involves increasing the capacity of states and localities for carrying out critical developmental activities. And third, it calls for urban R & D to design effective urban policies and programs.

Land use controls, particularly zoning, have discriminatory effects that exclude minority and low-income families from ready access to urban housing. Reforming land use controls presents formidable, but not insuperable, obstacles. So begins "Alternatives for Future Urban Land Policy." The primary focus of land use controls is physical. "This is not to imply that they are lacking in social consequences, but social objectives are not the primary aim." Perloff and his colleague at Resources for the Future, Marion Clawson, propose revising land use controls, particularly to eliminate their bias favoring housing discrimination. They advocate other reforms as well. Procedural reforms are required to make existing controls work more effectively, more democratically, and less parochially. Substantive reforms, as new measures to replace old ones, consist of requiring residential developers to include provisions for low-income and/or racial, minority populations (inclusionary zoning). Specific alternatives advocated include the public purchase and holding of land, control of speculation, and devices encouraging private renewal.

Reading through these articles, one has a sense of scanning the limits of science in relation to public policy. Here surely is the best of social-scientific thinking about cities in a context of public policy and action. Because now for the first time in the history of humankind planners can model the metropolis as a "system," planning can be comprehensive. Perloff lays out the concepts and tools for such planning.

But the American people distrusted these models. They preferred politics-as-usual, even if it meant a quality of urban life that appeared to be diminishing from year to year. Whether they will eventually put their trust in the mechanics of a scientific planning, or whether they will choose a different direction, remains to be seen. In either case, we can be grateful to Harvey Perloff for having raised the issue in the strongest possible terms.

5

A Framework for Dealing with the Urban Environment

The current interest in the quality of the urban environment is in large part a convergence of two other evolving public concerns. One is a concern with the quality of the natural environment—the quality of air, water, land, wilderness areas, and other resources. The other is a concern with the development of our urban communities—with all the matters coming under the rubric of more traditional city planning, but recently refocused to a special concern for the human beings in the city. The quality of life of all the people who are clustering into urban communities is clearly influenced by what happens to both the natural and the man-made environments in direct interrelationship with each other.

Our capacity to deal effectively with the enormously complex problems of the urban environment—problems that become more complex with each passing year—will certainly be much increased if we can sharpen our concepts, clarify the nature of the problems, improve our measurement tools (including the measurement of alternative proposed solutions), and be inventive about new institutional arrangements to cope with new situations. The present paper merely points, in an introductory vein, to some conceptual and measurement issues that deserve attention within such a policy-oriented probing of the subject.

We know from experience that it is difficult to make much progress in the realm of public policy and coordinated public-private action unless there is fairly substantial common ground of understanding and agreement as to just what the public interest is and why group action is called for. This is true whether we are talking about cleaning up the rivers, improving mass transportation, or eliminating slums (or, for that matter, providing financial aid overseas). The importance of such common ground is particularly great where most proposed solutions involve governmental restraints on the use of private property and the making of profits, or the imposition of extra costs on private groups, or the expenditure of large sums of public money. In spite of the fact that some people see the

This paper owes a great deal to the valuable comments made by Irving Hoch on earlier drafts. I am also indebted to Stuart Chapin, Mancur Olson, and Benjamin H. Stevens for their suggestions.

United States as increasingly subject to creeping or galloping socialism, it takes quite a bit of doing to get the necessary public backing to enable a governmental agency to impose limitations on private activities.[1]

The rationale on which public action is based—and the breadth and depth of its acceptance—thus has a great deal to do with the ability of governments to carry out a coherent set of policies over a substantial period of time. This normally calls for rather broad social concepts which in their very essence point to the objectives involved, the nature of the problems of difficulties, and the kinds of solutions which would seem to follow logically. Concepts of this type are sometimes rather vague and at times might even have contradictory elements within them. They can also linger long after the situation has changed. But whatever the difficulties and dangers, such broad social concepts tend to play an important role in providing a foundation for public policy and action in given matters.[2]

In dealing with problems that are as numerous, diverse, and complex as those involved in the quality of the urban environment, there is a clear gain if we can have concepts that serve simultaneously a simplifying and unifying role, since they contribute to the development of a common ground of understanding.

I would like to suggest two concepts that can play such a simplifying and unifying role with regard to the quality of the urban environment. One is an extension of the meaning and scope of natural resources, to encompass what I have called "new resources in an urban age." The other is a view of the urban environment as a contained (but not closed), highly interrelated system (or subsystem) of natural and man-made elements in various mixes.

EXTENDING THE CONCEPT OF RESOURCES

For a very long time—in fact, for many centuries—natural resources have been thought of essentially as the elements of the natural environment needed for the production of certain basic commodities (farm, forestry, fishing, water, and mineral *products*) and, to a much lesser extent, of certain services (especially

---

[1] A good example is the difficulty that state agencies have experienced in carrying out existing water pollution control legislation. The private interests in such a situation—the polluting industries—are specific and known (restrictions by a state pollution control agency can be very costly indeed for a specific firm), while the public interest is much more diffuse and vague. Not surprisingly, the energy that the state agency will normally exert will be more or less in direct proportion to the interest that the public, or representatives of the public, take in the matter. Matthew Holden, Jr. (1966) suggests, in an interesting monograph, that the whole matter of degree of application of state pollution legislation is the subject of *negotiation* between the agencies and the polluting industries.

[2] In an earlier period, for example, one thinks of the role of the concept centering on "the settlement of the West," encompassing notions of national stature, new opportunity, and the individual farmer as the backbone of democracy—all of which provided a base for governmental action "in the general interest" over a substantial period of time. In a more recent period, we have observed the role that the concept of full employment has played as a basis for public action in coping with problems of the business cycle and economic growth.

recreation and water transportation). My colleagues and I have described elsewhere (Perloff & Wingo, 1961; Perloff, Dunn, Lampard, & Muth, 1960), the slowly changing meaning of natural resources ('the resources that matter') as the nation's economy has evolved from an agricultural to an industrial base and, more recently, as tertiary activities have grown in importance. The ever greater capacity for substitution among natural resource commodities (through developments in science and technology), the increasing elaboration of commodities so that the economic value of the first stage is a small part of the total value added, and the fabulous growth in the demand for services have all joined to reduce the relative importance of natural resources commodities. The extent of this reduction is suggested by the fact that contribution of the so-called natural resources industries to GNP has declined from a third of the total in 1870 to some 11 percent roughly a hundred years later (Potter & Christy, 1962).

In the process, the concept of natural resources has been broadened somewhat. Thus, in recent decades, the notion of "amenity resources"—particularly as it reflects a special juxtaposition of climate, topography, coast and seashore, etc., especially attractive for the location of economic activities and family living—has been incorporated into the resources concept. Similarly, there have been increasing references to "open space resources", that is, open areas, particularly on the outskirts of cities, that offer breathing space and recreation possibilities for city residents.

The time has arrived, however, to rethink the basic concept of natural resources in a more general way so that it has the greatest possible relevance to our own day and to the foreseeable future.

At the core, the more traditional commodity resources *and* the newer environmental resources ultimately yield services to consumers; to use the jargon of economics, they enter the individual's utility function. However, the newer environmental resources are much more subject to externalities than are the commodity resources: the activities of all kinds of production and consumption units—whether family, business firm, or government—may generate either direct or indirect external effects on other units. This is the case when a firm emits wastes into the air or into streams, when one building cuts out the sunlight from other buildings, when planes roar over a residential section of the city, when a car adds to the congestion on a highway, or when a great new subdivision uses up a beautiful open area on the edge of town. In each case, costs or "illfare" are imposed on others. Analysis of the newer resources thus forces us to face up to a basic defect in classical economics: the assumption that the utility functions of individual human beings are independent of one another. Actually, resource economics has been concerned with this issue for some time, but now the questions of externalities and of collective goods must be brought front and center.

It has long been accepted that, in a socioeconomic sense, natural resources are those elements of the natural environment that have a use to man, and are therefore in demand, but whose supply falls short of the demand. Thus, as developments occur in science and technology, new resources (uranium, for instance) come continually into being; or existing resources greatly increase in value (for instance, with advances in construction, vertical transportation, and communication technology, airspace becomes more valuable), while others pass out of use. Where an element of the natural environment is in demand but supply is either plentiful for all or cannot readily be packaged for individual ownership and exchange, we have the case of a "free good" which is not considered a natural resource in the socioeconomic meaning of the term.[3] In almost all earlier economic texts, the classic case of a free good was fresh air. While in technical economic terms fresh air remains a free good, in a social accounting sense this is no longer the case in cities, where it entails large personal and group expenditures. If the meaning of natural resources is to be tied to the basic concept of features of the natural environment that are in relatively scarce supply, then it becomes necessary to invent a new category for those elements that, although they are in relatively scarce supply, still are not subject to individual ownership and exchange. This category would usefully serve to distinguish fresh air from, say, sunlight. The concept of free goods will clearly require rethinking.

Because natural resources have been associated with basic commodities important in national production for so long, there has been a lag in general appreciation of the extent to which the scarce elements of the natural environment today are of a noncommodity character. It takes quite a wrench in thinking to get away from the commodity view of natural resources and to be able to include in the resources category such elements as relatively pure air and water, three-dimensional space (including airway space, radio-spectrum space, city land, and underground space) and valued amenity features of the natural environment. Yet, in our crowded urban age, these are resources that count.

In trying to absorb the new resources elements into our conceptual scheme of things, and yet retain the major features of the more traditional interpretation of natural resources, there has been a tendency to associate these new elements almost exclusively with qualitative aspects of the environment and interpret this as essentially important for consumption rather than production. While the qualitative and consumption considerations certainly must loom large in any view of the newer resource elements, the quantitative and production aspects must also be seen as significant. A more complete view of the newer resource elements is provided most readily when we see them in terms of an extension of the basic natural resources concept—that is, when we accept an uninhibited interpretation of "needed elements of the natural environment that are in relatively short supply." This becomes particularly salient when we begin to grasp how different the whole production process is in the United States today compared to the past. Thus, less than 30 percent of the labor force is engaged in commodity production and the proportion continues to decline.[4] The service

---

[3] A feature of free goods has been that they do not become property. Insofar as they have value, they are expected to be capitalized as a component of land value. Land is thus viewed as a *collection* of fixed-to-a-place natural environmental features, including not only the geographic territory and soil, but also the associated water, climate, sunlight, air quality, and other amenity features.

[4] Even this figure is too high in a realistic sense. A substantial part of what the census puts in the commodity (or product) category actually involves service activities, ranging from R & D activities to paper work and promotional activities.

industries loom increasingly large. The recreation and education industries, for example, will soon pass farming in importance in both labor force and GNP terms. Project these trends another generation and the picture of the economy has very little resemblance to the one that was pertinent when the early conservation movement in the United States first gathered momentum.

All this is familiar and yet we have a hard time getting away from the more traditional picture of the "productive plant" or the "economic base" as represented largely by the farms, the mines, and the factories. These are certainly still very important, but the productive plant must now be seen increasingly as a series of *interrelated networks* of training, research, communication (which is at the heart of an automated plant), transportation, water and air use, and many other processes, together with their capital embodiments, established mainly in an urban setting. Productivity changes are increasingly influenced by the efficiency of the urban "plant" or urban environment.

In the past, when agriculture was at the center of the economic stage, both the quantity and quality of the land and water resources in an intimate interrelationship (as well as the know-how and vigor applied in the production processes) were important to the results obtained. Similarly, when industrialization took hold, the quantity and quality of mineral as well as forest and farm resources were of central importance. Today, even if in a different setting, quantitative as well as qualitative factors are significant (always in an inextricable mix): for example, the volume of water available for drinking, cooling, and waste disposal; the volume of air for waste disposal; the space available for the movement of planes or trucks; the land available for the construction of efficient industrial plants and for parking; the space available for radio-spectrum communications; and many other similar elements are a critical part of the production picture.

It is no trivial matter to establish the fact that the newer resource elements involve not only highly significant consumption and quality-of-living aspects but also equally significant production considerations. For example, if public annoyance with air and water pollution and traffic congestion should result in severe restrictions on industrial location, extremely heavy costs in industrial waste disposal, or severe limitation on the use of trucks, we may indeed pay a high price in rising costs of production. This is not to suggest, of course, that restrictions may not be appropriate under certain conditions; what is important is that the policy decisions should be made with a full appreciation of the production as well as the consumption factors. For in dealing with matters of the city, we are dealing with the very foundations of the nation's productive plant.

Once we begin to view features of urban land, air, and water, and space and amenity as significant natural resources, certain well-established principles, long associated with natural resources, come readily into play. These associations are not only significant intellectually (to the extent that meaningful classification is always important in the study of a subject), but also have important policy overtones. In the United States, the concept of natural resources carries certain strong connotations that influence the way in which we tend to approach an item that comes under the resources rubric. These connotations stem both from the impact made by the conservation movement, especially in the first third of this century, and from our experience with the use of our material (commodity) resources. They center on the well-established trinity of "conservation, development, and use of natural resources" and on at least some appreciation of the requirements and limitations posed by ecological considerations. Thus, in the United States, the term *natural resources* sets up an image encompassing several principles:

1. Resources are part of the national heritage; they should not be used unthinkingly and selfishly by any one group at the expense of others or by any one generation at the expense of future generations.
2. The value that the nation can receive from its resources depends on its willingness to *invest* in the *development* of such resources, whether it is a matter of enriching the soil, harnessing river basins or harnessing the atom, or experimenting with the best means for desalinization of water.
3. To get the most value out of the nation's resources, development wherever possible and appropriate should seek to achieve *multiple* uses. The multiple-purpose development of river basins comes most readily to mind, but the same principle applies to the use of farm land at the outskirts of cities for open space and recreation as well as for agricultural output.
4. While man has demonstrated a remarkable capacity for manipulation of nature for his own ends, there are basic ecologic principles he must understand and respect if he is to achieve his objectives over an extended period of time and without extremely high costs in real terms. Optimum returns can be obtained only through a knowledgeable and thoughtful mix of natural and man-made elements.

These principles can be described in other ways, but the core elements would be similar. The main point to be made here is that such principles have direct and important relevance to the newer noncommodity elements of the natural environment discussed here. Thus, by encompassing these newer elements into the natural resources rubric we achieve a unifying and simplifying end which, as suggested earlier, is extremely important in laying a foundation for coherent and consistent public policy and administration.

Thus, for example, under the first principle, the question can legitimately be raised as to whether certain resources—urban land, air, water, etc.—should be considered to be in the public domain[5] (or at least whether private holding and use should be extensively controlled) in order to protect the more general interest. Reference to established legal and traditional principles with regard to the "older" resources, while by no means binding, is instructive and helps to firm up the basis for public policy. Experience with law and policy touching on the more traditional resources, for example, can have important implications as we begin to make extensive use of air rights and underground or tunnel rights. Some legal scholars are beginning to make just this kind of extension; for example, with regard to air rights (Bernard, 1963).

---

[5]As Mason Gaffney has suggested for air.

In a similar light, the well-established principle of the desirability of *development* of natural resources to maximize social returns over time comes readily into play in thinking about the newer resources. Thus, for example, even in the face of a severe congestion problem in airways over and near cities, the existing approach is largely limited to the *regulation* of private commercial airlines, with limited investment in safety features and runways at the major airports. When airspace is viewed as a critically important natural resource, the desirability of addressing the problem through a developmental approach is immediately visible. The form and character of future city building should be examined in terms of achieving objectives with regard to the airways, as well as other objectives. For example, some airspace might well be set aside for the use of small airplanes only, to create what might be called air-commuting zones; this would clearly call for the development of a full ground-and-air approach to city building, in sharp contrast to the present two-dimensional approach.

The principle of multipurpose use of resources, which has evolved from, and has played such an important role in, river basin development, has great relevance for the urban-oriented resources. In fact, if sensibly applied, it is likely to achieve greater importance here than with regard to the more traditional resources. Communication and frequent interchanges are critical for most functions carried out in the city. The friction of space (transportation cost) not only produces the clustering of people and activities—that is, relatively high density—but in fact suggests that multiple-purpose use of space is at its essence a cost-saving device. Seen in this light, city building today tends to be highly inefficient. The present basically two-dimensional rather than three-dimensional city planning simultaneously promotes an outmoded single-purpose view of urban space (regulated by a simple set of zoning principles) and permits a wild jumble of incompatible uses, particularly on city streets.[6] Efficient and compatible multiple uses in a city require expert multiple-dimension planning. This is clearly a highly important area for additional thought and research. We urgently need principles that might guide decisions on when and how much multiple use is appropriate.

Finally, the importance of careful attention to ecological considerations in "conserving, developing, and using" urban-oriented resources should hardly need any special stress. It is evident that water and air can handle different amounts of pollution in different mixes under varying natural conditions; the capacity to make multiple use of these critically important resources is dependent in no small part on our knowledge of these natural conditions and the extent to which they can be modified. Builders who have constructed artificial lakes as space- and vista-providers often learn some quite interesting lessons about the ecology of still waters as algae emerge in abundance. The same is true of those who use or provide other amenity resources. A nice item along this line comes from Honolulu. It seems that Waikiki Beach may someday soon be scratched off the tourist's guide list because it is losing its sand. New shore-front

---

[6]As Lawrence Halprin (1963, p. 11) has put it: "It is too much to ask of a street that it serve, at the same time, for pedestrians and traffic and parking and shopping and children's play, and also provide amenity and quiet to the inhabitants along its way.

hotels have been built where there are no beaches, so the hotel owners have created their own. These synthetic beaches have upset the normal action of the ocean tides and currents off Waikiki's shoreline so much that the ocean is reclaiming the sand. Beaches far from these hotels are also being denuded. (Incidently, sand costs about $6 a cubic yard in the islands.)

City people may find it a little harder than their country cousins to grasp the importance of ecological principles, but it will be a little easier to get the lessons across if they can first grasp the notion that natural resources are a significant part of their environment, not things way out there in the countryside. And once these lessons are learned, it might even be easier to talk publicly about externalities, and about costs imposed on others, and why new rules of the game may be needed if we are to achieve desirable urban environments.

THE URBAN ENVIRONMENT AS A SUBSYSTEM

At an earlier point, I suggested that two concepts could play a useful simplifying and unifying role in creating a foundation for coherent and effective public policy with regard to the urban environment: in addition to the extension of the "natural resources" concept, there is need to see the urban environment as a contained highly interrelated system or subsystem. (Damage one part of it and other parts are immediately or soon affected; improve one part and other parts may be improved as a result.) In one sense, the system concept is an extension of the ecological considerations discussed above, but because of the importance of man-made features in the urban environment, the man-made as well as the natural elements must be seen as part of the relational system. Good and bad results are normally obtained as a result of the special *mix* of the two and therefore the two must be seen in all of their complex interrelationships.[7]

All urban units, whether city, metropolis, or megalopolis, are an integral and intimate part of the national scheme of things. None of them functions in isolated glory. It is not surprising, therefore, that all urban features, including the urban environment, comprise *open* systems. Roads, trains, and planes tie one city to others; messages go out and come in from everywhere; polluted water is carried from cities upstream to those downstream; polluted air is transported to distant areas; the size of the downtown of a given city will depend in no small part on how much of the nation's business is carried on there (thus, there is only one New York); urbanites vacation all over the country and the world; and so it goes. But the important consideration here is that the urban environment does comprise a meaningful and important system, signifying that, as with all systems, the internal elements—in this case, the main features that characterize the urban environment—have greater and more intimate relations among themselves than they do with units or features outside the identified system. Geographers, economists, human ecologists, and other students of

---

[7]This is true, of course, of the rural environment as well, but the sheer volume of manmade items in the urban setting is so great that the question of mix has a special relevance.

the city generally define the urban unit itself in terms of its nodal characteristics; that is, in terms of the quantity and intensity of the interactions. For example, they may define it in terms of the movement of persons and goods (while there is a great deal of movement *between* urban units, it does not compare to the daily movement back and forth *within* such units), in terms of the volume and frequency of messages sent, in terms of the extent of the local labor market, and the like. The physical areas covered by such intensity-of-flow items do not coincide exactly, but while the edges may be fuzzy, the urban community emerges as an identifiable nodal-type unit.

The nodal characteristics, while physically presenting a seemingly chaotic picture in our metropolitan and megalopolitan regions, have a clear and understandable logic. This has been an important part of the field of study of urban economics. The importance of centrality of location of economic activities stems from a number of factors, key among which is the significant—and generally increasing—specialization of function in manufacturing and service industries. Such specialization calls for the shipping of goods to and from a large number of producers, each adding value through specialized activity and sending them on. Thus, clustering is an important cost-saving device. Most of the production activities, in turn, call for the assistance of many specialized services, including professional services. The services themselves are linked not only with manufacturing activities but among themselves, with forward and backward and lateral linkages of every imaginable type. Those who ship goods need ports, railheads, highways, and airports that are linked with other major centers, and these facilities are, of course, necessarily localized to achieve the economies of scale to which they are subject.

The highly sophisticated manufacturing and service industries that are characteristic of our day require a wide and varied set of worker skills, and call for large labor pools. These are to be found only in population centers. Members of the skilled work force—including the managers—who are in demand choose to work in areas that they find pleasant for family living, and industry adjusts to this preference. Since many such persons prefer to live in communities which provide a large number of services, facilities, and amenities, cities draw activities for this reason as well. Here, centrality is a factor, since the costlier services and facilities (for instance, a symphony hall) must draw on a large population, but with urban growth many of the services and facilities can be provided in subcenters. This, however, only means that although centrality is somewhat more complex than in an earlier day, the economies-of-scale factor still comes strongly into play.

Taken together, all this adds up to the creation and maintenance of an elaborate *system* of people, capital, and movement with an inherent logic.

Nodality is a physical as well as economic phenomenon. This is true of the key elements in the *urban environment*. Thus, we can usefully speak of an airshed and a watershed encompassing an urban community, each with a focal zone; we can demarcate the open spaces and amenity areas reachable within, say, a Sunday's drive (an open-space-recreation zone if you wish) on the basis of a "gravity model"; we can separate the city into characteristic areas such as the central business district (CBD), inner city residential areas, suburbs (including high-income enclaves), and exurbia; we can demarcate the major transportation movements in nodal terms; and we can characterize work environments— downtown, in industrial estates, and scattered.

Systemic elements of the urban environment are generated not only by interrelations of natural and man-made features, but by *trade-offs* between these features (as well as within them). For example, more airconditioning of homes and workplaces can serve as a substitute for more air pollution control (that is, controlling the micro- rather than the macroenvironment). Polluting plants can be moved to the edge of or beyond the local air- or watershed instead of providing waste removal features within these plants. More open space might be provided in town, or people may be encouraged (by good roads, etc.) to drive out to the natural open spaces at the edge of town.[8]

Urbanites are not accustomed to thinking of their environment as a contained, highly interrelated system. Thus, they will complain loudly about air pollution conditions and yet vote for a mayor who promises to bring new manufacturing plants into town and to build superhighways right into the heart of the city. They will complain about the rapid loss of open space and yet vote for severe restrictions on the height of apartment and office buildings, for large-lot zoning, and for building highways through parks in order to reduce their cost. They will decry the loss of amenity resources nearby and yet permit private building right up to the beach edge and the pollution of nearby lakes. Of course, all this is not simply a matter of overlooking an important concept or a lack of understanding of systems analysis. Diverse interests are involved (different people are affected differently by these seemingly contradictory policies) and there are profits to be made, costs to be avoided, and elections to be won. But the point still needs to be made that the creation of a common ground of understanding of what is involved in working towards a desirable urban environment is essential for the building of a foundation for sensible, coherent public policy concerned more with a broad range of interests than with powerful but limited special interests.

---

[8]The trade-off notion is not always readily accepted. Thus, for example, a *Washington Evening Star* editorial (16 September, 1967) concerned with airplane noise, states: "The Los Angeles Department of Airports has come up with an unusual solution to the problem of noise from jet aircraft. . . Officials are planning to award contracts soon for sound-proofing a dozen homes around International Airport and measuring the before-and-after level of decibels. The project, which will cost some $200,000, seems designed to prepare the way for soundproofing of many dwellings with the help of local government subsidy. . . But one can't help wondering if this isn't exactly the kind of solution that the airlines would like best, since it involves no effort on their part. By the same reasoning, why not put a filter on every homeowner's faucets to cope with water pollution, or install universal air-conditioning to 'solve' the question of polluted atmosphere?"

Why not indeed? The editorial writer has overlooked the fact that most homes in the United States are individually heated while group heating is practiced in Sweden and elsewhere and that many other services have gone one way or the other over the years (including movie watching). The Los Angeles Department of Airports is indeed to be congratulated for carrying out a sensible experiment. I would hope that they are simultaneously looking into another alternative—that of location and relocation policy to cope with the noise problem—as well as into the question of the relative cost of building quieter planes.

ELEMENTS WITHIN THE ENVIRONMENTAL SYSTEM

If we are to develop an understanding of the urban-environment system, it will be necessary as a starting point to identify the key elements involved, that is, those elements whose relationships and interactions define and give special character to the system. This is a complex matter and can probably be done at various levels and in various frameworks. As a starting point and at a very general level, it is helpful, in order to sharpen the contrast between open and closed systems, to think of the key environmental elements involved in collective-living, high-density situations of an essentially *closed* character so as to identify similarities and differences with a more open situation of the type we are discussing.

At a very simple level, one thinks of the cave-dweller situation (which evidently comprised the human environment for a certain group of early man over a very long period of time, possibly a million years). Key elements in such cave environments evidently were the maintenance of relatively pure air (smoke pollution must have been a serious problem); acquiring and storing drinkable water; provisions for warmth and general bodily comfort; and division of space between family living quarters, work activities, recreation, and other clan activities. (Development of different types of enclosures for various groups and activities was related to technology; for example, the use of animal skins as cave dividers.) Environmental aesthetics were evidently not neglected, as suggested by the numerous cave paintings which have been found.

Essentially the same elements are identifiable when we think of other relatively closed environmental systems, such as that of the present day submarine, bathysphere, and space capsule.[9] At the other extreme of complexity from the old cave environment, diving into the wild blue yonder, are the environmental elements involved in a space satellite of the far distant future. In *Beyond tomorrow* (1965), D. M. Cole, a senior space scientist at General Electric's Space Technology Center, gives some attention to the environmental factors. His vision of "a new home among the stars" accommodates between 10,000 to one million people in a hollow asteroid, possibly 20 miles long, 10 miles in diameter. Such colonies, Cole suggests, could cruise space in their self-powered, closed cycle worlds by using new forms of macro-ecological relations and by developing flexible and extremely attractive interior environmental conditions. Here, too, air, water, weather conditioning, sunlight, space, and amenity features are pictured as key elements of the environment.

The closed-system view not only helps to highlight the basic elements that are essential for man's survival and comfort, but also suggests the many varieties of collective-living, high-density environments that are conceivable at different levels of technological development and different kinds of socioeconomic patterning. There is a strong tendency in our cities today to accept existing forms and relationships as given, merely because they are familiar. We simply do not

---

[9]A lively and informative treatment of the problems and possibilities in the realm of closed ecological systems is provided in "2000+," the February 1967 issue of *Architectural Design*, John MacHale, Guest Editor.

think about these matters unless some problem emerges which makes us uncomfortable, such as excessive air pollution or noise. Actually, with vast opportunities for achieving varied and attractive urban environments, the key elements of the environment and the ways in which they are interrelated, or can be made to interrelate, should be subjects of continuing study and private as well as public concern. The existing uses made of urban and nearby land; of three-dimensional space; of air and water; of structures for living, working, and collective activities; of climatic elements; and of amenity features of the environment must be recorded in meaningful ways, so that the interrelationships and interactions can be highlighted as a base for decisions that will influence the environment in desired directions.

While discussing elements of the environment, it is well to note also that for the greatest part such elements do not interact only at the scale of the urban unit as a whole—say, the metropolis—but are found in different intensities and in special mixes at smaller scales. Thus, air and water quality (or degrees of pollution) are different in different parts of the metropolis (air pollution, for example, will be more intense at congested transportation points or in parts of the metropolis dominated by manufacturing industry). Similarly, availability (nearness) of open space is different for every section of the urban unit; the condition of structures and their spacing will be different in each neighborhood; and the condition of the water, sewerage, and waste disposal facilities will differ from section to section. A careful recording of these differences and of the total impact of the special mixes to be found in each identifiable section of the urban unit is critical for sound policy making. The issue is generally not how some hypothetical average individual is faring, but the quality of the environment within which different real groups are living, working, and moving about. Information on distribution of qualitative levels should not be overlooked. This can be summed up by saying that the reality of the slum, as well as of the magnificent high-income enclaves, must be recognized in any meaningful approach to the problems of the urban environment.

Differentiation must not only be provided in geographic terms, but also in terms of the various groups making up the urban society. Different groups react differently to various aspects of the environment and also make different contributions to the environment or detract from it. This is seen most readily when the question of crowding in the urban environment is considered. Edward T. Hall (1966), a student of the subject, has pointed out:

> The degree to which peoples are sensorially involved with each other, and how they use time, determines not only at what point they are crowded but the methods for relieving crowding as well. Puerto Ricans and Negroes have a much higher involvement ratio than New Englanders and Americans of German or Scandinavian stock. Highly involved people apparently require higher densities than less involved people, and they may also require more protection or screening from outsiders. It is absolutely essential that we learn more about how to compute the maximum, minimum, and optimum density of the different cultural enclaves that make up our cities.

Hall suggests that the various ways in which different groups handle time is reflected in their need for space. "Monochronic" and "polychronic" styles of time use are characteristic of what he calls low-involvement and high-involvement groups and this in turn influences their relative degree of need to separate activities in space.

Beyond group characteristics, there are important individual differencesthat must also be taken into account.

THE URBAN ENVIRONMENT AND THE ENVIRONMENT OF URBANITES

It has been noted that the urban environmental system is an open one. It is open in various ways. Thus, instead of ending discernibly at one line, the built-up relatively dense sector of a city or metropolitan region fades gradually out into the countryside. City and countryside intermingle in a rather wide belt. Villages, towns, and farms provide a somewhat different setting for living and working than does the more built-up portion: open space is hardly in scarce supply, travel distances tend to be longer, water and sewerage facilities are often not tied in to the core systems. Yet the people living in such zones are largely urbanites (or farmers much concerned with the question of the appropriate time to sell their land) and these zones are mainly areas for future building. Roads and utility lines built here, open space set aside, and other activities (or lack of them) will influence the future urban environment in important ways.

The system is also open, as suggested earlier, in its direct transportation and communication linkages with other urban centers. This deserves particular attention because of the tendency for "string" construction along highways in many parts of the country to provide a very special—and in many cases aesthetically horrendous—urban environment. Often such string developments are found in the outer zone mentioned previously and are thus an integral part of the general exurban picture.

Finally, the system is open in the sense that urbanites living within the built-up, high-density areas—that is, within the core urban environment— spend greater or lesser periods of time away from that environment, largely for recreation purposes, and particularly for vacations. Some have vacation homes in recreation environments. In this regard, amenity resources achieve particular significance. The quality of these resources and their closeness to urban centers (which has a great deal to do with frequency of visits) thus is part of the "environment of urbanites" if not part of the urban environment itself. These resources, of course, also comprise part of the environment of rural populations, but for present purposes we are limiting attention to the urban population. The problems are clearly different for the rural population.

The value of recognizing these factors in any full-bodied treatment of environmental issues suggests that we have to be concerned not only with spatial elements—that is, the extent of the urban environment that is being described, analyzed, or controlled by public policy and action—but also with function, time, and intensity dimensions. We want to know how much time during the week, month, or year various groups in the population are "exposed" to the different kinds of environments and, if possible, the intensity of the exposure. These matters will be touched upon at a later point.

POLICY MEASURES AND A DECISION FRAMEWORK

It seems evident that the quality of the urban environment—as well as the environment for urbanites—will increasingly be a matter for public concern. The caliber of governmental policy and action with regard to environmental issues can be expected to be improved as our knowledge of the environment increases and as we develop better tools for decision making. It therefore seems appropriate to devote major attention to the question of reporting on the environment and on means for evaluating public action with regard to the environment.

Reporting on and evaluating the urban environment presents different problems from those presented by the more traditional commodity natural resources. While in the latter case there are usually some externalities to be considered and complex systemic interrelational elements to be dealt with, these features are so much greater in the case of the urban environment that it is a matter of kind more than of degree. The interrelationships among the elements of the environmental system and the externalities are so central in the scheme of things that we must come to grips with the question of how these can be highlighted meaningfully. This underlines the importance of a useful reporting and analytical framework. The problem of creating such a framework is hardly new. City planners have been struggling with the issue for over half a century. However, city planning has emphasized—almost to the exclusion of other considerations—past, present, and future *land uses*. Other urban natural resources (air and water, for example) have rarely received major attention; this is true also for systemic elements within the urban environment, such as the multiple relationships between land use and man-made structures.

We can probably go a substantial distance toward providing a useful reporting-and-evaluation framework through the use of what have come to be known as social indicators and social accounts. I have found particularly stimulating the proposal for an annual Social Report of the President, parallel to the Economic Report, but concerned with a different set of issues, including the quality-of-the-environment question. A system of reporting which would fulfill the requirements of such an annual report would have to characterize changes in environmental quality through the use of a few particularly pertinent measures, and to evaluate the results obtained through various public and private efforts to improve the environment. A national reporting scheme would necessarily have to be quite broad—and essentially limited—in scope. It should, logically, be supplemented by reporting on a local basis, that is, by state-of-the-region reports, which can provide a useful foundation for policy making and governmental action at the local and metropolitan scale. The problem of reporting at the national level would be much eased if the appropriate information was available for all the urban units within the nation.

What might such a system of reporting appropriately contain?[10]

First, it is necessary to decide just how much is to be included under the environmental rubric. It is evident, at one extreme, that it cannot be limited merely to physical (including natural) factors if the information is to provide a useful foundation for decision making. At the other extreme, it cannot usefully cover all matters that at one time or another are referred to as "environmental." The latter would bring in just about everything. The term environment is often used not only to cover the natural and man-made surroundings but also much of the social-political-economic ambience—that is, frequent references are made to "a democratic environment", "a competitive environment," etc. These types of issues can be covered more appropriately under other headings in either a Social Report of the President or a state-of-the-region report at the local level, say, with regard to a discussion of "equality of opportunity" or under "political participation."

Any delimiting of a field, even for reporting purposes, involves all sorts of cultural (including language) and political considerations, particularly the explicit and implicit public objectives or goals that are currently dominant. For present purposes—mainly to introduce some ideas for discussion in a preliminary way—it may be appropriate to start with an attempt to look at the more important elements that directly influence *conditions of living and working of the urban population* and particularly where they influence *the health, comfort, safety, and aesthetic satisfaction of individuals.* This would suggest limiting coverage to those aspects that are necessary to *differentiate localized situations* of some importance to the lives of the people; for example, those aspects that are essential to describe either slum conditions in our cities or the relative purity of the air within given metropolitan regions, but not those features that are common for people everywhere, the host of essentially *national* economic, social, cultural, and political factors in the quality of American life.

The differentiation of localized situations would have to proceed at various levels to distinguish between significantly different *settings.* Thus, as already suggested, it would be necessary to distinguish between metropolitan and nonmetropolitan (basically, small town) settings; between built-up and low-density zones, residential and nonresidential areas; and among the various characteristic types of communities, such as slum areas, middle-class areas, and the like.

ELEMENTS TO BE COVERED

It is proposed that the following items be included under the environmental rubric for metropolitan areas:[11]

---

[10]The materials presented here are based on a "Preliminary Report on Environment" which I prepared for the Panel on Social Indicators of the U.S. Department of Health, Education, and Welfare (May 1967) with the help of Joseph L. Fisher and Robert Gold. I want to acknowledge the many useful suggestions I have received on the earlier report from my colleagues, Irving Hoch, Lowdon Wingo, and Blair Bower, as well as from Fisher and Gold, which I have incorporated in the present statement.

[11]The metropolitan region is highlighted here because it calls for the most extensive coverage.

The Natural Environment

1. The airshed (to describe relative purity of air and air pollution)
2. The watershed (to cover water supply and water pollution)
3. The open-space-recreation "shed" (to cover conditions within an area that can be reached on a one-day recreation trip)
4. Quiet-and-noise zones (to describe relative degree and time-span of noise exposure)
5. Olfactory zones (to describe relative degree and time-span of exposure to unpleasant smells)
6. "Micro-climate" zones (including uncomfortable heat, wind blockage, etc.)[12]
7. Sunlight exposure (relative condition of buildings with regard to good, bad, or indifferent sunlight exposure).

The Spatial Environment

While basically part of the natural environment, it differs enough from the items under "The National Environment" to deserve special treatment. This category would attempt to characterize the use of underground space,[13] land, and overground space in terms of standards of efficient use (e.g., relative congestion and duration of what might be called low-quality conditions), changes in values of space, and degree of allocation of space in terms of relative values (thus, amount of subsidy would be highlighted).[14]

The Transportation–Utilities Environment

These have the characteristic of tying the metropolitan area into an integrated unit through a series of superimposed networks (or what might be called the skeletal features of the region). They tie directly into the natural environment through those utilities that provide water supply and provide for sewerage and solid waste disposal; also as they use underground, land, and overground resources. The latter is additionally significant in the case of electric and gas utilities, as well as telephone utilities. Aesthetic considerations with regard to such facilities have come increasingly to the fore.

The transportation network is particularly important for the urban environment. Accessibility, including relative accessibility to amenity resources, is a basic consideration in many aspects of the environment. The reporting should

---

[12]Because of traditional usage, "micro" is used here, although on a different scale from that employed in the case of home and work environments, where the term is also employed.

[13]It is reported (American Public Works Research Foundation, 1967, p. 7) that in about a hundred cities in the U.S.S.R., 35 percent or more of the investment in structures is in the portion that lies underground.

[14]Urban ground and near-ground spaces cover a remarkable (and fascinating) variety, including streets of various kinds; alleys; freeways; minor and major plazas; gardens; playgrounds; neighborhood, central, and regional parks; waterfronts; rooftops; open parking lots; etc. etc.

cover such items as availability of mass transit and other forms of transportation and the conditions surrounding movement in general, including considerations of trip time, congestion, safety, and stress.

The Community or Neighborhood Environment

This item would cover the main environmental elements within markedly differentiated communities or neighborhoods—for example, slum areas, other central city areas, and suburban and exurban areas. The term community or neighborhood here is intended simply to imply the existence of distinguishable common characteristics of physical elements, together with important interactions between people and physical environment within a contiguous geographic area by the fact of juxtaposition and "mix." At the same time, in order to provide adequate coverage of public service and facility conditions, it would be desirable not to restrict the areas too narrowly in geographic terms. The services environment is necessarily variable (since different services extend over different zones) so that in defining areas some fuzziness at the edges might well be appropriate.

The Microenvironments

The family or household shelter and the workplace are the settings for the individual's most intimate social relations as well as for his most direct and frequent contacts with the man-made physical environment.

The framework that is thus provided can be described as one of several environmental "envelopes" (although the term should not be taken too literally) through which the quality of the urban environment can be characterized: the large natural resources, and space-use envelope, the community–neighborhood envelope, and the home and work microenvelope, all tied together in various ways and literally tied together through the transportation–utilities set of networks. Each of these is characterized by different underlying conditions, the first through the special role of urban-oriented natural resources, the second by the interrelations of group behavior patterns and these with the man-made physical environment, and the third—the microenvironment—by the primacy and intimacy of social relationships as well as by the special needs and characteristics of a limited group (the household in one case, and employees of specific workplaces in the other). The importance of the microenvironment is attested to by the fact that some 68 percent of the total time of urban adults, on the average, is spent at home. The figure is 76 percent for the total urban population.[15] Of the remaining time, almost two-thirds is spent at work.

INDICATORS, ACCOUNTS, AND POLICY MEASURES

A broad framework for what I would call a system of "policy measures for the environment" is suggested here (see Table 1). First, let me make some

---

[15]Taken from a time budget study of forty-four U.S. cities. See Alexander Szalai (1966).

TABLE 1. FRAMEWORK FOR EVALUATING POLICY MEASURES FOR THE ENVIRONMENT

Elements in the environment	Indicators of present condition	Costs of environmental maintenance at present levels		Costs (or other adverse consequences) of environmental abuses and shortfalls		Costs of achieving standards at various levels		Benefits of achieving standards at various levels	
		Private	Public	Private	Public	Private	Public	Private	Public
	(1)	(2)		(3)		(4)		(5)	
A. The natural environment									
1. The airshed									
2. The watershed									
3. The open space–recreation "shed"									
4. Quiet-and-noise zones									
5. Olfactory zones									
6. Micro-climate zones									
7. Sunlight exposure									
B. The spatial environment									
1. Underground space									
2. Uncovered land									
3. Covered land									
4. Radiospectrum space									
5. Airways space									
C. Transportation–utilities environment									
1. Transportation:									
a) commuting time; b) alternative modes, including mass transit;									
c) congestion; d) safety; e) stress;									
f) aesthetics (e.g., billboards, landscaping)									

2. Water supply facilities
3. Sewerage facilities
4. Solid waste disposal
5. Electricity facilities
6. Gas facilities
7. Telephone facilities
8. Other communication facilities
D. Community–neighborhood environment
   1. Community characteristics:
      a) mix (e.g., degree of segregation);
      b) types and condition of structures and land uses;
      c) community stresses; 3) design environment (densities, street lighting, billboards, interest points, landscaping, zoning, etc.)
   2. Services environment (measures of quality and nearness):
      a) educational–cultural environment; b) personal safety and protection; c) health facilities and services; d) commercial facilities and services; e) recreation facilities and services; f) caretaker functions
E. Household shelter
   1. Housing condition
   2. Crowding
   3. Rats, roaches, and other pests
   4. Plumbing
   5. Household equipment
F. Workplaces
   1. Safety
   2. Amenities (e.g., eating facilities, sanitation)
   3. Work challenge indicators (assembly line, freedom of movement, etc.)

comments about the terms used. *Indicator* is normally used to describe the condition of a single element, factor, or the like, which is part of a complex interrelated system (employment, cost of living, production, etc., in the case of economic indicators). It is evident that in the case of the urban environment equally revealing indicators can be provided to describe existing conditions—say, with regard to air pollution, quality of housing, amount of open space available, etc.

Accounts, on the other hand, refer to comprehensive systems of data characterized by a balance between inputs and outputs or inflows and outflows (such as national income accounts, input–output accounts, or flow-of-funds accounts) or providing the value of the total stock of various items in a total system, as in the case of wealth accounts. We have a long way to go before we are able to work out comprehensive social accounts for the environment. However, as noted at a number of points, it is important to provide a broad picture of the urban environment because it is essential to be able to highlight interrelationships and externalities. What seems possible at the present time is the provision of rather comprehensive policy measures or decision measures that, while not fully comprehensive or characterized by balanced two-way flows, could nevertheless serve a unifying purpose in reporting on the environment specifically as an aid to governmental policy decisions. These must include both stock and flow items and, because of the focus on public policy, emphasize outlays and investment and the returns on these.

Table 1 outlines the main elements of the data framework proposed.

The first task involved would be to work out meaningful "indicators of present condition" (column 1) for each of the items listed. These would reflect present goals and standards (both legislative and informal) with the data attempting to indicate where we stand with regard to these goals and standards. The establishment of standards is no mean task. It would require a good bit of research as well as a sensitive reading of the standards that have the broadest and most strongly held acceptance. This clearly is an evolving task. In the first instance, the best standards at hand would be employed. At the same time, it would be useful to highlight the weaknesses of existing standards, particularly where too narrow an interpretation of objectives to be achieved could be misleading, and to explore the special characteristic of measures within the different categories.

As Joseph Fisher has pointed out (in his chapter in the "Preliminary Report on Environment" for the Panel on Social Indicators of the U.S. Department of Health, Education, and Welfare), the quality characteristics of the environment tend, to a considerable extent, to be subjective, with considerable variation in the views of different individuals. Further, air pollution and recreation opportunities, for example, affect different individuals quite differently, both physiologically and psychologically.

Another point deserves attention: the various aspects of the natural environment are interrelated in numerous and sometimes confusing ways. One way of abating industrial air pollution is by filtering and washing smoke to prevent contaminants from going into the atmosphere, and instead sluicing them out into the water courses, thereby adding to water pollution. The interrelations extend beyond the realm of natural resources. For example, one way of reducing pollution from automobiles would be to discourage or prohibit certain uses, but this would greatly affect transportation and might also drastically alter the microenvironment in which people live and work. Just as the various kinds of environmental pollution tend to be interconnected, so also the measures for abating and controlling them tend to be interconnected. And one should be cautious about interpreting a favorable movement over time in an indicator of air pollution lest it is accompanied by an equal or greater movement in the opposite direction in an indicator of water pollution.

Concern for arriving at some overall indicator of environmental quality in which the various interrelations and trade-offs can be included leads one toward the concept of *net social benefit*—that is, total (or incremental) social benefit less social cost. This concept of net social benefit can be applied to a particular kind of environmental disturbance or it can be thought of in connection with a large range of environmental effects.

The social indicators alone can provide only a limited part of the story. If we are looking ultimately to policy, it would be essential to get a picture also of the costs of our shortfalls, as well as the costs and anticipated benefits of actually fulfilling existing goals and standards, or higher-level goals and standards. But this calls for more than indicators; here we would have to put policy measures to work. The key categories that might be employed are suggested in Table 1.

Thus, the reporting system proposed would set out, as a second item, "costs of environmental maintenance at present levels" (column 2), broken down by private and public costs wherever possible. In almost every instance, substantial sums are already being spent in order to maintain existing environmental conditions—no matter how unsatisfactory. This is true of the present expenditures involved in keeping down air and water pollution; it is also true of the costs involved in trying to create a relatively safe street environment and transportation environment. The setting down of current cost figures would provide a rough measure of the relative amount of effort directed at any one of the items of interest in the environment. It would raise issues about the priorities attached to the various subjects and it would also raise questions such as whether we are getting our money's worth. There is a tendency in most discussions of the environment to think only in terms of the additional expenditures necessary to achieve somewhat higher levels. This can be misleading, certainly as regards the relative emphasis to be given to different activities. As in the other major items to be covered, breakdowns in terms of the various sections of a metropolitan region (slums, suburbs, etc.), would provide a useful picture of the relative attention being given to the various parts of the region.

Column 3 in the proposed reporting system calls for estimates of the costs— or other adverse consequences—of environmental abuses and shortfalls. In this, an attempt would be made, not only to obtain rough estimates of such items as the costs resulting from air pollution, but also of inadequate public services. Such costs would be recorded in dollar terms wherever possible, even if some heroic assumptions have to be made. In cases where dollar costs are simply not to be had, sharply focused descriptions or indicators of a noncost nature would be useful.[16]

---

[16]A sense of how much information can be conveyed by focused description is provided

Here, again, the specification of the standards to be achieved would be essential, particularly in measuring shortfalls. It is necessary to establish a wide variety of fairly narrow and specific standards—for example, for housing quality—as well as broader, more aggregative goals, such as a satisfactory home and community environment. Not only must standards be quite specific in the case of the environment, but they are also inevitably rather variable, that is, they often have to cover a wide range. Thus, it is possible to set up standards for various degrees of purity in the case of air and water and to measure the cost of achieving such standards as well as the cost of falling short of their achievement. The same is true in the case of housing standards, standards of congestion, and many other features that might be included under the environmental rubric. To round out the picture, then, it would be necessary to provide estimates of costs of achieving standards at various levels (column 4).

Thus, the whole system is built on a recognition of the fact that the quality of the environment is judged by the values of the society, that different levels of achievement are possible, that each of these has cost features attached—both in achieving the given levels and in falling short of achieving them—and that benefits are also to be derived from improvements in the environment. Unfortunately, these benefits are very much harder to define. In some cases they can be fairly firm, particularly when the benefit amounts to an avoidance of the cost of abuse or shortfall. But in other cases they are much more general. Over time, however, it might be increasingly possible to provide benefit estimates. Even short of such figures, it would be possible to describe in general terms the benefits of achieving specified standards and, thereby, to provide a better basis for public judgment.

At a later stage it might be possible to introduce additional types of indicators or other measures to round out the picture and provide a better basis for evaluating the present and alternative futures. One of these would be a time budget or measure of time expenditures, which would provide a picture of the time spent in major activities by various categories of individuals, and thus, in a general way, suggest the relative importance of different kinds of environments and the uses made of them. Such a measure, together with direct measures of intensity of use of services and facilities as well as of homes, workplaces, and transportation, would provide the basis for measurement of relative exposure and the development of risk ratios. This, for example, would tend to show the tremendous importance of the street in poor neighborhoods, the extent to which some public facilities are overutilized and others underutilized, and the relative exposure of people to various areas of the city (thus emphasizing, for example, the relatively great importance of small intown open spaces—such as squares and school playgrounds—as compared to vast open spaces far beyond the reach of most people). An intensity index could be a very powerful tool for decision making in some of the environmental items.

Differentiation in the policy measures not only needs to be made with regard to various classes of communities within a metropolis but also with

by the statements in the Supreme Court 1954 school decision on the losses attendant on a "separate-but-equal" education system.

regard to various age groups, income groups, and racial and ethnic groups. Wherever pertinent, the indexes or measures should be in terms of age, income, and race and ethnic categories as in the education-cultural environment, in health, and in recreation.

The indicators of present conditions should, wherever possible, provide information on three kinds of items: (1) the *average* situation in the various communities for the key items, as well as group distribution around the average; (2) improvement or deterioration over time, and (3) extreme situations that deserve special attention. In general, treatment of extreme situations is necessary so that significant *special* problems are not overlooked: without such items any reporting scheme would tend to be much too bland. If the scheme is to serve policy and action purposes realistically, a description of community stresses when the situation is explosive or of pollution conditions when health is directly threatened should not be lost in a mere deluge of data on averages.

FINAL NOTE

The information framework proposed here is essentially a decision-making model, highlighting the present state of affairs, what is deemed good and bad about it, the costs we suffer as a result of the shortcomings, and what is needed to bring the situation up to higher standards. The implementation of such a model would clearly require substantial effort but, when operational, it would provide an extremely valuable decision-making tool. It has the clear advantage of being close to policy and operations both in terms of its inputs and outputs; that is, on the one side, administrative or operating data could be used as the main sources of information while, on the other, it would provide a basis for policy decisions in a direct and meaningful framework. It is taken as an article of faith that governmental policy and action will be improved as knowledge about the urban environment increases and alternative possibilities can be reviewed in a broad and meaningful decision framework.

REFERENCES

American Public Works Association Foundation (APWRF). *Better Utilization of Urban Space*. Chicago, June 1967.

Bernard, M. M. *Airspace in Urban Development: Emergent Concepts*. Urban Land Institute, Technical Bulletin 46, (July 1963).

Cole, D. M. *Beyond Tomorrow*. Amherst, WI: Amherst Press, 1965.

Hall, E. T. *The Hidden Dimension*. New York: Doubleday, 1966.

Halprin, L. *Cities*. Reinhold, 1963.

Holden, M., Jr. *Pollution Control as a Bargaining Process: An Essay on Regulatory Decision-Making*. Cornell University Water Resources Center Publication no. 9 (October 1966).

Perloff, H. S., E. S. Dunn, Jr., E. E. Lampard, and R. F. Muth. *Regions, Resources, and Economic Growth*. Baltimore: The Johns Hopkins Press, 1960.

Perloff, H. S. and L. Wingo, Jr. "Natural Resources Endowment and Regional Economic Growth." In *Natural Resources and Economic Growth*, edited by Joseph J. Spengler, 191–212. Resources for the Future, 1961.

Potter, N. and F. T. Christy, Jr. *Trends in Natural Resources Commodities: Statistics of Prices, Output, Consumption, Foreign Trade, and Employment in the United States, 1870–1957.* Baltimore: The Johns Hopkins Press for the Future, 1962.

Szalai, A. "Multinational Comparative Social Research." *American Behavioral Scientist* 10, no. 4 (December 1966).

6

Urban Planning and the Quality of the Urban Environment

We are not likely to do much about the quality of the urban environment until we begin to sharpen the meaning of the concept and get a substantial area of agreement on what we are after. Second, urban planning is *potentially* a useful tool in achieving environmental improvement, but its major thrust to date has been to protect individual property values more than the total environment. Third, it is proposed that we use the concept of *regional assets* to highlight the focal points for urban planning concerns, particularly to achieve fitness among the major urban activities and encourage a healthy relationship between the natural and man-made features of the environment. More questions will be raised than will be answered, but it is hoped, this paper will at least sharpen some of the issues involved in environment quality in an urban setting.

THE QUESTION OF MEANING

The meaning attached to the term "quality of the urban environment" has been changing over time, and has tended to focus on one aspect of the total environment at a time. Today, environmental quality is taken to be mainly a question of pollution, and all other environmental considerations very much in the background. So popular is the pollution connotation, that as new issues come along they are fitted into the pollution rubric, we now talk about noise pollution and not just noise and quiet as environmental factors; and people concerned about too rapid a rate of population growth are beginning to talk about population pollution.

Going backward in time, before pollution became *the* popular environmental issue, we can remember that in the earlier 1960s the dominant environmental concern centered on what the urban highways and freeways were doing to our cities, cutting up established communities and taking up valuable urban land to accommodate moving and parked automobiles. Earlier yet, in the postwar 1940s

I wish to express my thanks to Chung-Tong Wu for valuable research assistance, in a review of pertinent literature, in the preparation of this chapter.

and 1950s, two environmental questions dominated the Sunday supplements and public activities. One was cleaning up the slums and blighted areas of the central cities (recognized governmentally in the Federal Housing Acts of 1949 and 1954, which launched the national urban renewal effort). The other was the supposed sterility and inadequacy of the suburban and exurban environments and destructive quality of urban scatteration. (Some may remember the book titles, if not the books, of the period: *The Crack in the Picture Window*, *Exurbia*, and *The Organization Man*.)

Poor housing and slums, the great environmental issues of the 1930s, were seen as poisoning all aspects of the urban environment as well as the lives of the slum dwellers. Going still further back in time, to the earlier part of the present century, when the City Beautiful movement was at its peak, the dominant environmental issues centered on the need for breathing space and urban beauty; that is, for city parks, playgrounds, attractive waterfronts, and magnificent public buildings that could give character and style to our prosaic, dull cities.

By now we have moved backward to the end of the nineteenth century, when the modern city planning movement was born. It was born precisely because some urbanites were concerned about the quality of the urban environment. This raises an intriguing question, or set of questions, about where city planning has been all this time and why it has not been more effective in looking after the urban environment.

OMISSION AND COMMISSION IN CITY PLANNING

Again, starting where we are today and noting the great upsurge of interest in the quality of the environment, we would expect urban planning to be a truly popular and highly favored activity. Urbanites who have only recently discovered environmental quality as a matter of great personal concern should, it would seem, be very much impressed when they discover that the quality of the urban environment has been the raison d'être of city planning for more than three-quarters of a century—not an insignificant period. Yet if there has been any gain in popularity or in support or in influence of city planning, it is hardly discernible.

It is interesting to contemplate why this should be so. I hope an understanding of this seemingly strange phenomenon might provide some insights into what might be done in the future to improve environmental quality more effectively than in the past.

One factor is already apparent; at no time has the concept of urban environment been comprehensively defined or broadly attended to. As already noted, some one or two environmental features have been receiving major popular—and, usually, political—attention for a period of time, with other equally important matters forgotten or very much in the background. This has created the up-and-down syndrome of environmental "fashion," without a build-up of sustained and effective follow-through in public policy and action. City planning has been following the changes in fashion rather than leading the way.

City planning has, until very recently, been only peripherally interested in the natural environment. And, since it is the degradation of the natural environment—of the air, water, and land—that has aroused so many people lately, it is not surprising that they are not turning to city planners as their saviors. Until literally forced to attend to these matters in the last few years, urban planners seemed to have been proceeding on the assumption that, except for some city and regional parks which had to be looked after (mainly against the inroads of the highway agencies), the natural environment was something "out there" in the countryside. Air and airspace, water and river basins were someone else's concern, and land was something on which urban activities took place. If, in some aspects, land was seen as "natural environment," it was supposedly the concern of the park people or some other operating agency.

I had had the advantage of working with a natural resources research foundation, Resources for the Future, Inc., for many years and therefore could early discern the gap that had developed. I gave a number of talks and wrote several papers referring to what I called "new resources in an urban age," making the point that human settlement takes place within a natural environmental "envelope," that we had to be much concerned with this envelope if we hoped to live well, and that this indicated the need for three-dimensional urban planning, carefully interweaving the man-made and natural elements in a new urban ecology. A similar point was being made on a global scale, under the concept of "spaceship earth," by Kenneth Boulding and others. The urban aspects, which are basically much more complicated, were receiving less attention, however.

As a direct result of the recently evolved interest in pollution, urban planning agencies have finally begun to concern themselves with the relationships of land uses to air and water pollution. Coming as late as it has, this interest has not yet produced any particularly useful planning concepts and tools for dealing with the degradation of the natural environment.

Another area of omission might be noted. City planning to date has been involved only peripherally with major region-forming activities: highway construction, airport construction, the extension of water and sewerage facilities, and the forces which direct them. These activities have been especially important in influencing where new urban settlement was to take place within the metropolitan region, whether closer to or farther from the city core, whether in a less or more compact form, and whether with less or greater protection against air, water, and land pollution. The major decisions with regard to highways, airports, water, and sewerage have been largely in the hands of national, state, regional, and local operating agencies, while urban planning agencies have had only marginal impact, if any. The fragmentation of local governments (with dozens of them in every major metropolitan region) to date has prevented any meaningful regional planning, so that major region-forming activities have largely gone their own way, subject to a host of economic and political pressures, usually not greatly concerned with environmental quality.

There are errors of commission in urban planning as well as errors of omission. Against the criterion of broad environmental-improvement objectives, city planning, in fact, can be said to have been in the wrong ball park.

Urban planning, as already noted, came into being specifically because of concern for the quality of the human environment. This was interpreted—rhetorically, at least—to require coverage of all aspects of man's physical environment. The watchword was comprehensiveness in planning. The "Master Plan" or "General Plan" would supposedly set out a framework for the whole municipality, within which individual public and private decisions with regard to land development and investments could be made. Various regulatory tools, especially building codes and zoning and subdivision controls, could be employed to ensure that the plan was carried out as designed.

From the very beginning, however, the quality of the urban environment was equated with planned *land uses*. Everything else was secondary. Thus, comprehensive planning in practice turned out to have a special meaning; namely, coverage of every bit of territory within the planned area—the municipality—with designated land uses: single-family residential, multi-family residential commercial, industrial, recreational, and so on, and the prevention of "nonconforming" mixes of land uses through zoning. A municipal zoning ordinance typically divides a municipality into mutually exclusive zones or districts. These areas can be categorized according to use, height, and area restrictions as well as to the allowable exceptions to these restrictions which may be granted by administrative authority. The insulation of the single-family detached dwelling has been zoning's primary objective. Generally, about half of the time devoted to all its tasks by the city planning agency is taken up by zoning activities (although, of course, there are substantial variations from agency to agency).

Richard F. Babcock, one of the nation's outstanding experts on zoning, has written:

> If, in the beginning [the early 1920s], zoning owed much to the fears of Fifth Avenue merchants in New York City that the garment industry would further encroach on their elegant side walks, zoning can thank the residents of the North Shores and Westchesters of this country for its remarkable survival. John Delafons, a recent English observer of American zoning noted, "It was as a means of strengthening the institution of private property in the face of rapid and unsettling changes in the urban scene that zoning won such remarkable acceptance in American communities."[1]

A conservative bench, as Babcock puts it, could be induced to permit municipalities, by an extention of the common-law nuisance doctrine, to build an all-encompassing land-use regulatory scheme under the aegis of the police power. Protection against nonconforming uses has generally been protection against heterogeneity, human as well as physical. In exurban, suburban, and wealthier "intown" areas, planning and zoning have been handy weapons to keep out so-called undesirables. Large-lot zoning and other legal weapons have been effective in many areas in preventing the intrusion of any low-cost housing and any low-income residents.

In recent decades, urban planning has also been much concerned with the elimination of slums and blight. In line with federal legislation, the designation of slum and blighted areas has been on the basis of the proportion of physically deteriorated structures within given areas, Not surprisingly, this has involved the

---

[1]Richard F. Babcock, *The Zoning Game: Municipal Practices and Policies* (Madison: University of Wisconsin Press, 1966), p. 3.

destruction of many homes of poor families, generally in minority communities, making way for homes of wealthier families and commercial development.

We might also note the quite ineffective urban planning approach to the regeneration of the declining central business districts (the CBDs) with total disarray as to the purposes and value of density controls—whether to direct traffic toward or away from the central business district, and whether or not the nice little intown malls help or hurt downtown businesses. The key issue of the logical future role of the central business district in the viability and attractiveness of the urban region as a whole has received little planning attention.

Beyond the immediate questions, there is the larger question of the basic factors behind urban decay and deterioration and what it would take to generate genuine renewal forces in our cities. Neither the narrower, practical issues of providing for the housing needs of the poorer families and reviving the CBDs, nor the broader issue of urban regeneration as a process, have been attended to in urban planning.

This covers only part of the total picture (and there are many positive elements as well as additional negative elements that could be alluded to in a more balanced presentation), yet the point that emerges is that, contrary to its supposed concern for *all* aspects of the human environment—present *and* future—urban planning in the United States has had a narrow and disjointed base of concern for existing property values and a class-conscious and essentially "delicate" view of the urban environment.

WHY PUBLIC INTERVENTION ANYWAY?

The judgments presented to this point were based on *implicit* assumptions. But the question, "Why public intervention in urban development anyway?," is too central to our discussion to be kept in the background. The fact is that there is no widely accepted answer as to why the collective guidance of urban development is called for. Each historical period, starting with the City Beautiful phase, seems to have provided its own rationale, with the most persistent argument centering on the notion of external diseconomies—the rationale for zoning controls. Robert Haig's formulation is a classic:

> It so happens that unless social control is exercised, unless zoning is fully and skillfully applied, it is entirely possible for an individual to make for himself a dollar of profit but at the same time cause a loss of many dollars to his neighbors and to the community as a whole, so that the social result is a net loss.[2]

From Haig's day on, the case for detailed public planning and developmental controls has rested largely on neighborhood effects.[3]

---

[2]Robert Haig, "Toward an Understanding of the Metropolis: The Assignment of Activities to Areas in Urban Regions" (Parts 1–2), *Quarterly Journal of Economics*, 40 (February and May, 1926), 179, 402, 433–434.

[3]Empirical evidence which places into question the importance of neighborhood effects is presented by Crecine, Davis, and Jackson in their article "Urban Property Market: Some Empirical Results and Their Implications for Municipal Zoning," *Journal of Law and Economics*, 10 (1967), 79–96. The evidence either way is pretty thin, however.

It seems to me that there are much stronger reasons for collective action with regard to urban development. Such action is needed in order to optimize for urbanites the full advantages of agglomeration, to provide a wide variety of choices in urban activities, and to prevent unnecessarily damaging collisions among competing uses of the urban environment, that is, the achievement of fitness among the major urban activities.

The urban environment is the setting within which all urban activities must take place. It is a setting made up of many natural environmental and man-made features, which, while normally sturdy and flexible enough, do have limitations on capacity and are subject to degradation and environmental static. This view recognizes externalities, but these are the externalities of a community wide nature, and not the highly limited and delicate third-party damages of neighborhood effects.

An urban area must accommodate a wide variety of activities simultaneously. It provides a place for living, for working, for fun, and for cultural activities. (If these four are defined broadly enough, they can encompass all urban activities, but a much longer list is equally suggestive of the main point.) In the nature of the case, the quality of each of these activities is in no small part determined by the location and character of the other activities, and the nature of the interrelations among them. Thus, on the urban scene, externalities not only describe special conditions (as when a factory belches smoke that descends on homes all around—the justification for the common-law nuisance doctrine and modern-day zoning) but describe a general state of affairs.

All the major types of urban activities are intimately intertwined: almost every urbanite takes part in all of them, and all urbanites are affected by them. The character and location of the economic activities within an urban region significantly affect the quality of living, since they influence the level and stability of family income, the amount of time that must be devoted in getting to and from work (how much time, for example, does father have left over to spend with his children after working *and* traveling?) and even whether some of the personal services, like shopping and hairdressing, can be carried out during lunch hour. Cultural and recreational activities not only enhance the quality of family living but can be factors in attracting industries and workers to a region. The quality of the "residential function" is directly influenced by the quality of the educational and other public services, and families and businesses within an urban region move about to improve their accessibility to all the many services they require. A planning framework is needed to provide the necessary information for individual, family, and business decisions, particularly in the face of the tremendous complexity of the modern urban region and the rapid rates of change. It is also needed to maximize accessibility and choices in a general sense, by supplementing and guiding the private market in order to generate supportive fitness among the major types of urban activities.

Beyond the close relationships among urban activities themselves, there is another set of significant relationships between the man-made and the natural elements. As already noted, urban activities take place within a natural environmental envelope. Each element in the natural environment can, and does, serve many urban purposes. This is particularly true of land. All urban activities ultimately rest on the land. There is no shortage of land in an absolute sense in a country like the United States. But given the importance of the communications function on the urban scene, land that is readily accessible to the focal centers of urban activity *is* in short supply and the subject of more or less intense competition among potential users. Beyond that, land containing particularly desired amenity features (for example, lake front or beach front), or is both accessible and open, is in particularly scarce supply. Thus, within the framework of the technological, economic, and taste limitations on height of buildings, accessible urban land has a circumscribed carrying capacity. Air, likewise, serves many purposes, including the removal of wastes, as space for building, as airspace for planes, and as space for the transmission of signals (e.g., the radiospectrum), among others. The same is true of water, which is used not only for municipal water supply and the removal of wastes, but also for recreation, irrigation, transportation, and power generation. Air and water also have circumscribed carrying capacities, based on a host of natural and man-made factors. Thus, as between the man-made and natural elements also, fitness is a key requirement.

CONTRIBUTIONS TO THE QUALITY OF THE URBAN ENVIRONMENT

Against the background that has now been painted, we can present the following proposition: an effort that seeks to enhance, or at least preserve, the quality of the urban environment should be expected to contribute importantly to the quality of the key urban activities and the fitness of interrelations among these activities, and to encourage a healthy relationship between the natural and the man-made features.

First, let us note what might be involved in contributing to the quality of the major urban activities; that is, to making a living, living in the urban community, having fun, and participating in the cultural life of the community (and beyond these, the more general objective of maximizing the individual's effective range of choice).

People are attracted to urban communities in order to make a living; and, we hope, a good living at interesting and steady work. Those who have become sophisticated about the economic factors need only have a member of the family or a friend unemployed for a period of time, or even more so, find themselves unemployed, to rediscover the importance of the city as an economic machine.[4] Concern for the economic health of the urban community forces at once a focus on the urban region, since it makes up the labor market, the major local consumer market, and the housing market. High priority attaches to accessibility. Accessibility can be brought about by locating points of origin and destination close together and by decreasing the friction of space, largely through improved transportation, as well as by increasing contact potentials through institutional and other means. Thus, a good urban environment is not one that has removed

---

[4]Hans Blumenfeld "Criteria for Judging the Quality of the Urban Environment," in *The Quality of Urban Life*, Henry J. Schmandt and Warner Bloomberg, Jr., eds. (Beverly Hills, Calif.: Sage Publication, 1969), p. 141.

places of work far from the inviolate residential quarters, safely away in industrial estates of which planners as well as developers seem to be so fond. Rather,
what is called for is a search for means of bringing jobs and homes together,
without unpleasant intrusions on basic residential qualities. At the same time,
mobility (broadly conceived) is important for both persons and goods.

Given the importance to people of making a living (acquiring income), the
economic vitality and growth potential of the central city as well as of the other
major commercial centers of the region are high-priority issues in urban development. Where important social ends are to be served by strengthening such
centers, availability of cheap space and good facilities for labor training—in a
general sense, the encouragement of "opportunity niches" or entry points into
urban activity—deserve more attention than the pretty little malls that are now
such an important feature of downtown planning.

Key industries—that is, the so-called basic or export industries plus other
large employers in the region—must obviously be major subjects of concern.
Their present and future locational and facility requirements must loom large in
urban plans. Matters which touch on urban-influenced cost increases, skill availability, and local market range deserve continuing attention.

Also vital for the present and future of an urban community is the regional
infrastructure. The ability of a community to attract a wide variety of industries
(thus enhancing stability) that can afford to pay relatively high wages and salaries is, given the character of modern industries, closely related to the quality of
living in the community, the quality and convenience of the educational and
research institutions, and the quality of the utility systems of the community.
Wilbur R. Thompson has made the case that, in general, the larger communities
have certain advantages with regard to levels and stability of income. His argument is particularly pertinent:

> The local social overhead—the infrastructure—that has been amassed is,
> more than export diversification, the source of local vitality and endurance.
> Stable growth over short periods of time, say up to a decade, is largely a
> matter of the number of different current exports on which employment and
> income are based. But all products wax and wane, and so the long-range
> viability of any area must rest ultimately on its capacity to invent and/or
> innovate or otherwise acquire new export bases.
>
> The economic base of the larger metropolitan area is, then, the creativity
> of its universities and research parks, the sophistication of its engineering
> firms and financial institutions, the persuasiveness of its public relations and
> advertising agencies, and all the other dimensions of infrastructure that facil-
> itate the quick and orderly transfer of old dying bases to new growing ones.
> A diversified set of current exports—"breadth"—softens the shock of ex-
> ogenous change, while a rich infrastructure—"depth"—facilitates the ad-
> justment to change by providing the socioeconomic institutions and physical
> facilities needed to initiate new enterprises, transfer capital from old to new
> forms, and retrain labor.[5]

---

[5]Wilbur R. Thompson, "Internal and External Factors in the Development of Urban Economies," in *Issues in Urban Economics,* Harvey S. Perloff and Lowdon Wingo, Jr., eds.
(Baltimore: Johns Hopkins Press, 1968), p. 53.

The points that Thompson makes with regard to economic change can be generalized beyond the large metropolis to smaller urban communities and beyond infrastructure to other aspects of the urban environment and quality of life. Studies in the field of urban and regional economics have highlighted the fact that, thanks to the great expansion of our service economy, there is an increasing convergence between what is widely thought of as aspects of good living and what turns out to be good business.

As already suggested, environmental quality depends not only on supportive relationships among the major urban functions but also on maintaining a healthy relationship between the natural and man-made features. Clearly, to seek environmental enhancement or preservation requires continuing concern for the natural environmental envelope of the urban region, specifically, for the condition of the airshed, the watershed, the quiet-and-noise zones, and the amenity resources or what might be called the open-space-and-recreation-shed of the urban region.[6]

An important key to this relationship is the concept of carrying capacity. It has been most highly developed with regard to the notion of waste disposal and our ability to predict how much waste both air and water would be able to remove, at given standards and under varying conditions.[7] Since waste removal by air, water, and land are alternatives to each other, it is evident that the capacity concept is most fruitfully handled in a systems framework.[8] We are also beginning to get some useful information on the capacity of lakes to absorb urban development around the shorelines and on the results of different levels of user pressure on recreational resources. The concept is suggestive also in learning to predict the outcome of different levels of user pressures on streets and on land in various parts of the urban region and in different uses.

All this is in an early stage of development, yet it does help to clarify the nature of the concerns that need to be associated with any effort looking toward the enhancement of the urban environment, including a consciousness of the constraints of our urban setting, natural and man-made or man-run.

REGIONAL ASSETS

Urban planning in the past, joined with zoning, has sought comprehensive coverage over a narrow base. What would be needed instead, if the urban

---

[6]For a discussion of these features of the urban region, see Chapter 5.

[7]For a discussion of factors involved in air carrying capacity (also discussed as dilution capacity, dispersion rate, or mixing height), see Albert F. Bush and H. B. Nottage, "Carbon Dioxide as an Indicator of Air Pollution," *Journal of the Sanitary Engineering Division*, Proceedings of the American Society of Civil Enineers (December 1967), 211–253; G. C. Holzworth, "Large Scale Weather Influences on Community Air Pollution Potential in the United States," *Journal of the Air Pollution Control Association*, 19:4 (April 1969), 248–254; J. C. Mosher, W. G. MacBeth, M. J. Leonard, T. P. Mullins, and M. F. Brunelle, "The Distribution of Contaminants in the Los Angeles Basin Resulting from Atmospheric Reactions and Transport," *Journal of the Air Pollution Control Association*, 20:1 (January 1970), 35–42.

[8]On this point, see Robert V. Ayres and Allen V. Kneese, "Pollution and Environmental Quality," in *The Quality of the Urban Environment, op. cit.*, pp. 35–71.

environment is to be protected and enhanced, is highly selective coverage on a broad base—a base that extends to all the major urban functions and the interrelations of the man-made and natural environmental elements. What is proposed here, for consideration and future discussion, is the desirability of redefining the basic focus of urban planning activities. Put the detailed individual neighborhood plans in the background (ultimately to be judged in terms of their contribution to the advancement of regional policy), deemphasize the municipality as an independent focus of urban planning, and concentrate on a few selected features across the metropolitan region, encompassing the labor market area and the major natural environmental "sheds." That is, *planning and zoning concerns should be focused centrally on those features of the urban region that sustain and support the major urban functions and the natural environmental setting.*

These can usefully be conceived of as the major *regional assets.* They comprise the more important natural environmental features, the more important elements of the regional infrastructure, and the key regional industries. But, while all of these have physical embodiment—in fact, on a map of the region, these physical embodiments might well be colored golden, or whatever other color might suggest top priority—major attention needs to be focused on the key sets of relationships involved.

Such relationships are of many sorts, of course. First and foremost are the relationships of the regional assets to the overriding goal of providing opportunities for the residents of the region to achieve satisfying patterns of living (in their own light). Other relationships of major concern are those that underlie what are now called life-support systems (such as the water supply), those that are characterized by unusually high or intense interactions, involve unusually vulnerable aspects of the social or physical fabric (such as race relations, or transportation during emergency periods), and those that have the greatest potential multiplier effect on social and other kinds of changes. A case in point, illustrating how these types of concerns might influence urban planning in the future, would be to emphasize policies aimed at strengthening the maintenance (or repair) capabilities of the region, since this would be of value in extending the usefulness and life of public *and* private facilities of every kind.

The focus on regional assets is essentially a way of centering attention on those features in which there is common interest or commonality. This is essential since, as John Friedmann has pointed out, "To accomplish anything, different interests must be concerted through intricate procedures of persuasion." This, as Friedmann has argued so persuasively, involves the "linkage of a scientific-technical intelligence to organized societal action."[9]

The issue of common interest or commonality is exceedingly complex in our pluralistic society, and as important as it is complex. The key point can be illustrated by reference to a quite different area, the gradual establishment of a sense of common interest (among businessmen, workers, and other major groups in the economy) in the maintenance of full employment and relative

---

[9]John Friedmann, "The Future of Comprehensive Urban Planning: A Critique," *Public Administration Review*, 31:3 (June 1971).

price stability through national government policy, although such a policy might affect any one of these groups negatively at one period in time. In the same way one might refer to the establishment of regional river-basin commissions as reflecting a convergence of group interests in the conservation and balanced development of waterways in some parts of the country. On the urban scene, efforts to achieve a convergence of group interests on the maintenance and enhancement of environmental quality have been minimal to date.

Thus, what is proposed is a deliberate focusing of attention on the very elements in the evolving urban situation that are keys to the future welfare of at least a large segment of the regional population if not the entire population— with the technical planning task consisting of assistance in the development of lines of policy and action that can enhance the quality of urban life and the persuasion of the disparate interest groups that such recommended lines of policy and action (hopefully evolved through broad community participation) are in the interest of most, if not all, of these. This would, in effect, give the urban planning function characteristics with regard to recommendations of policies and programs not too dissimilar to those of national economic policies shaped through the Council of Economic Advisors, the Treasury, and the Federal Reserve Board. But there are differences, too, since in the case of national economic planning, there are agreed-upon objectives, set down in federal legislation in fact, a condition missing in the case of urban planning. However, a good case can be made for the existence of *implicit* objectives in urban planning, namely, the very objectives that justify collective action on the urban scene.

And this takes us back to the regional assets, defined in circular fashion as those features of the total environment that are critical for the future health and well-being of the urban region. In this light, I would like to propose a new principle, the Perloff Principle: individuals and groups will press their own *immediate* interests in urban affairs (as in other affairs) except where social policy directs attention toward common wealth-fare (if I may be forgiven a play on words).

In broad categories, the regional assets can be taken to comprise four elements in their physical embodiment.

- The amenity resources (the beaches, lakes, forests, and so on, and the selected reserved open spaces) as well as the air- and watersheds.
- The utilities infrastructure, including major transportation, communications, power, water and sewerage facilities, the networks that tie the region together and support the other regional activities. The trunk lines are particularly important so that major concerns should, for example, be centered on points of maximum access in the region.
- The cultural infrastructure, including the major cultural facilities, the higher-education and research centers, and the primary and secondary education systems. Thus, for example, in this view, the universities would be seen as regional assets, since they help support and sustain major regional activities and enhance the viability of the region. The capacity of the universities to carry out their education, research, and ser-

vice functions would be of major concern. This would involve not only the campuses and direct university facilities but also the surrounding communities, to the extent to which they enhance or subtract from the total "output" of the university.
• The key industries of the region, the export industries and other major employers, as well as the major commercial clusters.

These categories can be said to make up what might be called the regional *skeletal* features, that is, those features that provide structure and form to the region, and tie its activities together, and whose characteristics have a great deal to do with the quality of the urban environment. These skeletal features make up an evolving set of key links comprising nonredundant relationships with large multiplier effects. Planning and zoning should attend to their needs closely.

This is not to suggest that the task of planning and related activities is forever to maintain these assets as assets or to work endlessly to increase their individual value. Rather, as in well-established business practice with regard to corporate assets, the task is to guide change in such a way that the assets *overall* are enhanced, with individual elements of the total system growing or declining (or in fact being eliminated). Regional infrastructure and other assets may, in fact, hold back needed change. Thus, often the problem is to promote change (and ease the friction.

Aside from the skeletal features, the region is made up of a great variety of local communities and of more or less ubiquitous services, facilities, and industries, or what might be termed the cellular features. Seen in the context of regional assets, only the totals in the various cellular categories should be seen as regionally significant, with planning attention most appropriately focused on setting standards (such as of amenity and service quality), avoiding bottlenecks, and generating multipliers in the processes involved. Thus, attention needs to be centered on such matters as the adequacy of housing for families at various income levels and for persons with various kinds of special needs, within a satisfying settlement pattern; standards for open space; standards for transportation service to be provided, and the like. Individual local communities deserve special detailed attention only when that is essential to the achievement of major and difficult social objectives, such as the encouragement of racial and income integration. Thus, it might not be too fanciful, within the context of the scheme suggested, to see top-priority designation attached to communities within the region that are on the way to achieving a substantial amount of income or racial integration. Such communities might well come into the asset category and, as with the other designated regional assets, they would be eligible to receive special public assistance—in this case to help them retain the integrated state with a minimum of friction. Given a society in which the "natural" pressures are in the direction of homogeneity in residential grouping, it is not homogeneity that needs special collective support (as through current practices in planning and zoning), but rather it is heterogeneity that needs such collective assistance: to encourage upward mobility of minority groups and to encourage more, and more meaningful, communications among various ethnic and income groups in a highly interdependent urban society.

Except for such special cases, it would be logical for the cellular units to be provided for through general policy (rather than through detailed planning and zoning provisions); for example, region-wide policy with regard to housing, public services, and *internal* transportation and communications, as well as community-oriented standards.

Within the conceptual framework suggested, urban planning would seek to enhance the quality of the urban environment by policy and action aimed at preserving and improving the regional assets, the high-priority (or golden) features, taken as a whole. It would seek to *prevent* (1) damaging mixes, (2) a density or intensity of use beyond capacity (as in the case of air pollution and natural recreation resources), (3) damaging and costly deterioration or decline, and (4) lower rather than higher returns on the use of the regional assets—but always from the overall regional standpoint (to the extent that this can be determined), rather than from the standpoint of property protection in highly limited zones. Thus, urban planning might seek to speed up changeover from low-return uses of land to higher-return uses of land near very-high-accessibility points; to slow down the intrusion of large-scale, high-cost housing in lower-income neighborhoods that are being integrated or are already integrated; and to guide the location of new subdivisions so as to minimize the additional waste load on the air- and watersheds of the region.

CHANGES IN OBJECTIVES, SCOPE, AND TOOLS

To carry out effectively the kind of urban planning suggested here would require some rather substantial changes in its objectives, in its territorial scope (that is, focusing on a broadly defined urban region rather than on the present jurisdictionally defined areas), and in its tools. On the score of objectives and territorial space, one might well ask why the powers-that-be, who are now so strongly behind the use of planning and zoning procedures for the defense of individual property rights within a narrow neighborhood-effects concept, should agree to a thorough overhauling of the urban planning process. Actually, I suspect that the federal government *could* induce the type of regional planning proposed here within a reasonably short period of time (say, ten to fifteen years) by using well-established carrot techniques—and the federal government has lots of carrots. What would induce a national administration to take this course is, at the moment, beyond me. I really have no answer except to reveal my built-in weakness for expecting rational, socially oriented solutions ultimately to win out no matter what the objective situation seems to be.

As for the tools, it is evident that, among other things, there would be need for measurement concepts and techniques that would permit fairly refined evaluation of changes in actual and required regional assets, in the same sense that national accounts are such valuable tools in national economic policy. Some of the existing concepts and techniques can, of course, be adapted to this need. In addition, I can see at least two fruitful new avenues. Both are downright primitive at the present time, but useful work is beginning to be done in both areas, so we may look forward to some progress over time. One is in the field of asset accounting and the other is in the realm of social indicators. Charles Leven and I made some suggestions for developing asset accounts in an article published in 1964.[10] Leven and his colleagues followed through in a book entitled *An Analytical Framework for Regional Development Policy*, which treats asset accounting in some detail.[11] The "social indicators" work[12] has attracted a fair number of scholars, and we are beginning to get some useful suggestions on the establishment of environmental and other standards and measurement of improvement or retrogression. An annual roundup and analysis of regional asset accounts and indicators could be brought together into a State-of-the-Region Report, which could become a flexible tool in a new kind of urban planning concerned mainly with broad policy.

Such measurement tools can be useful in urban planning as rough guides to policy even in our present limited state of knowledge about urban development. They would undoubtedly be much more useful when we develop a better theory and models of urban change. Work on regional accounts and indicators, however, will probably advance progress in the realm of theory, so that such work is to be encouraged on immediate practical grounds and because of its potential contribution to theory.

In conclusion, then, if my analysis is close to the mark of what is required to permit urban planning to contribute importantly to the enhancement of urban environmental quality, there is need for rather substantial changes in both the political-organizational and the intellectual realms. These changes, however, are at least conceptually within reach.

---

[10]Harvey S. Perloff and Charles L. Leven, "Toward an Integrated System of Regional Accounts," in *Elements of Regional Accounts,* Werner Z. Hirsch, ed. (Baltimore: Johns Hopkins Press, 1964), pp. 175–214.

[11]Charles L. Leven, John B. Legler, and Perry Shapiro, *An Analytical Framework for Regional Development* (Cambridge, Mass.: MIT Press, 1970).

[12]These might more appropriately be called urban indicators or just simply indicators.

7

National Urban Policy: Stage I

Building the Foundation

If we are now more appreciative of the severity of our urban problems than we were in the past, we are still far from agreement on the need for a basic national urban policy. One difficulty is that it is hard to distinguish between a miscellany of federal, state, and local policies and what might appropriately be called a basic national policy for a given area of concern. Historically, we have arrived at a relatively coherent set of policies on various matters of national interest by trial and error over a fairly long period of time. Unfortunately, under current conditions in our cities, we would pay a high price for a leisurely movement toward effective national urban policy. The process must be compressed if at all possible.

I want to present the following case: we will begin to cope effectively with the difficult problems of our cities only when we evolve *national* policy which can, on a broad front, guide urban development toward certain equity and quality-of-life objectives and enhance individual welfare. The urban problems are a product of our national socioeconomic system and way of doing things, and it is to bringing about changes in the total scheme of things to which we must initially address our efforts. Thus, the first stage should look to the creation of a foundation on which more specific policies—say, with regard to housing or new towns—might be firmly built.

EVOLVING A NATIONAL FRAMEWORK OF POLICY AND ACTION

It is in the nature of public action that attention first be directed at the outer manifestations of pressing public problems, for it is there that the political heat is generated. Thus, it could have been expected that in the New Deal days, under the pressures of widespread and long-lasting unemployment, there would be PWAs and WPAs, and other measures established by government directly, to provide jobs. A more effectively focused policy to get at the underlying causes of unemployment could only come later, after a certain amount of experience and a learning from the past, and after certain concepts and a system of information to guide policy and programs had been developed.

In the same light, it is not surprising that in the first reaction to the building up of political pressure around certain urban problems—inadequate housing, slums, traffic congestion, and the like—the government should seek directly to provide housing for low-income families, directly to remove slums and blighted areas, and to pour tons of concrete to try to overcome traffic congestion. But we now do have a good bit of experience in coping with urban problems, and it is time we emerged from the PWA–WPA stage into one that tries to get at more basic causes and tries to overcome the problems through a well-developed and sharply-focused strategy.

There is today a vast array of federal, state, and local policies and programs concerned with the problems of the urban communities—dozens in the housing field alone and more dozens in the realms of transportation, urban planning, water and sewerage, health, welfare, training, and so on. Many of these, in spite of relatively large expenditures, seem to get at only a small corner of the problem attacked, as in the case of urban transportation, urban renewal, and public housing. They also seem to generate a great number of new problems as they go about trying to solve the ones at which they are directed. This is not only true of the urban highway and renewal programs, but also of most urban-oriented policies and programs. This has been so well documented in recent studies of the various urban programs that I need not dwell on this aspect of the question at hand. What does deserve attention is why the apparent failure and what can be done about it.

The problem is not so much that the individual programs are poorly conceived—although that is true in some instances—but rather that a *foundation* has not been laid on which successful specialized programs can be carried out. One gets a sense of what is involved when he compares the smoothly administered, relatively successful public housing programs in the Scandinavian countries with the trouble-plagued programs in the United States. One realizes that the significant differences do not relate to methods of construction and financing but rather to the fact that the programs in the United States are too overburdened with a heavy load of human pathology and social problems to be able to fulfill the housing objectives. In the same light, it should be easy to see that a large number of physical-development programs can be piled one on top of the other with only limited, marginal improvements unless greatly improved urban planning and governmental admnistration can be brought into being.

What we have now is a huge jumble of programs without a clear conception of what we are really trying to accomplish and without much logic as to which level of government is equipped to do what. Thus, we find the federal government deeply involved in the specifics of neighborhood programs, to the point where localities become mere agents of the federal bureaucracy. And we find local governments trying to achieve ends, as in welfare programs and in large-scale physical-development programs, that can only be achieved at the national level or at the level of the metropolitan region.

HISTORICAL PERSPECTIVE

In looking toward the development of national urban policy concerned with fundamentals, it is instructive to review some history with regard to evolution of national policy on matters of central concern.

Consciously directed change is not new in the United States. There is a tradition for it. (Unfortunately, there is also a tradition of serious policy lags.) Guided development, as we normally use the term, implies change in directions which promise a convergence on highly valued objectives.

The national government has taken a major role in guiding development, setting the broad framework for private as well as state and local decisions and activities. While this history is too well known to require much elaboration, one feature does deserve special attention. Behind the continuous struggle for power and privilege and behind the ins and outs of conservative versus progressive politics, there has been a sensible appreciation of the importance of developing and consciously channeling the basic national resources—including not only the natural resources and capital resources but the human resources and the institutional resources as well. While the official ideology was *minimum government*, the minimum generally included a strong governmental concern for rapid development and a broadening of the welfare base.

NATIONAL DEVELOPMENT AND NATIONAL POLICY: THE AGRICULTURAL AND INDUSTRIAL PHASES

The United States has gone through several major developmental phases, each with a different impact on our basic resources and each calling forth a rather large and complex set of national policies and programs that ultimately added up to a discernible national policy for that phase. A key feature in each case, as noted, was the focus on the building up of the basic capacity of the human and institutional resources. While in a short paper it will be necessary to generalize outrageously, and to omit consideration of many significant variations and details, it is nevertheless instructive to review the types of approaches that we have used in coming to grips with the problems posed by each of the major national developmental phases.

The *agricultural development phase* was, of course, the dominant one in the earlier history of the country and, in fact, can be said to extend all the way to World War II. The natural resources that counted were land and water; and in both regards, the nation was blessed. National policy extended to distribution of public lands to farmers in a relatively orderly fashion, and the method of distribution had a great deal to do not only with the efficiency of production but with the social structure that evolved. Thus, the family-size farm was instrumental in integrating vast numbers of people, including the great flood of immigrants from Europe and elsewhere, into the mainstream of national society. In the twentieth century, increasingly the national government turned its attention to policies that helped to encourage conservation and sensible development and use of natural resources.

Human resources, too, were a major focus of public policy and expenditures, involving the federal and state governments as well as the localities. Of tremendous importance was the institution of universal free education and the establishment of land-grant colleges and extension services. It is well to remember that this was a revolutionary approach, breaking with centuries of tradition, projecting the idea that farming was not an art to be learned from one's father and grandfather but rather was to be based on the expansion of scientific knowledge and brought to the individual farmer by an elaborate system of experiment stations and extension services. Thus, at a remarkably early stage, the nation undertook to help its farmers achieve *a high level of competence* in all aspects of production, merchandizing, and farm life.

It is well to note also that throughout the agricultural era, the government was concerned with the capital needed for sound farming operations. Not only was the most important element for capital—the land—provided to individual farmers as section after section of the country was settled. But at a relatively early stage, the government concerned itself with the provision of irrigation facilities as well as farm-to-market roads and the extension of credit to meet the input and sellings needs of the farmers. While it is quite easy to be critical of the imperfections of certain aspects of the policy as implemented, it is evident that government policy and assistance were of the greatest importance in the creation of an effective agriculture.

On the institutional front, representation at the federal and state governmental levels was such that the farm interests could be guarded and promoted (although, of course, the larger farmers could generally get the best of the bargain). Direct federal expenditures and indirect federal aid to state and local governments covered the more costly investment items and gave a boost to local budgets. The rural county served the relatively simple needs of the countryside—as then perceived—at the local level, with the property tax financing the modest services that met these needs.

The *industrial development phase* overlapped the agricultural phase, covering the period from about the middle of the nineteenth century to about the middle of the twentieth. From an early stage, national efforts were directed at the discovery and exploitation of the basic industrial resources, with an increasing interest, especially after World War I, in the sound conservation, development, and use of resources needed in the industrialization processes. Concern for the caliber of human resources was reflected in the establishment of local school districts in all the industrial centers to provide a fairly high level of literacy, although some regions, particularly the Southeast and Southwest, lagged badly in this regard. In addition, state universities, with federal help, established many technical schools geared to providing the needed skills in mining and manufacturing. Many of the great technical universities of today are the products of this public policy. The government responded to capital needs through the establishment of national and state banking systems and helped provide the elaborate system of infrastructure necessary to an industrial society by massive subsidies for railroads and by direct investment in river and harbor construction, dams, and highways. Needed institutional development was reflected in the evolution of a legal structure which encouraged industrial production and which sought to prevent the more extreme business abuses by antimonopoly laws and a host of specific business regulations. Important also for the industrial era was the establishment of labor unions and their increasing strength and scope. The nation was quite slow in appreciating the role that government might play in the development of healthy labor–management relations, but this too came with time.

The 1930s and 1940s, with the trauma of depression and war, in a very real sense, marked the culmination of both the agricultural and the industrialization phases. Public policy was directed at shoring up and filling gaps in the institutional base for the late-industrial era. First, there was need to right the balance between the encouragement of private entrepreneurship and imposing social responsibilities on business. This involved increased public regulation of banking, insurance, the stock market, and other business activities as well as public support of organized labor, as in the Wagner act. Second, it meant the acceptance of public responsibility for maintaining a floor under farm incomes to prevent a squeeze on the farmer between the prices of farm inputs and farm outputs. Third, there was need to cope with the problem of the business cycle whose severity tended to increase with the growing importance of durable-good production. The acceptance of national responsibility for full employment and price stability, on top of the other reform measures, meant the maturing of national economic policy to parallel the maturing of the industrial economy.

There is one feature of public policy during the agricultural and industrial phases that deserves particular attention because of the negative impact it was to have on the future. This was the relative indifference to equity questions as contrasted with the deep interest in efficiency issues. Governmental policy was essentially national in scope and concerned with economic growth rather than with the problems of falling behind and of depressed areas. The race was to the swift. The main thrust was promotional and developmental. A vast nation was to be opened up and developed, and those who raced ahead were encouraged. Only the most extreme abuses were prohibited. If a section of the nation or a group fell behind or was disadvantaged for one reason or another, only limited and temporary help would be provided. Thus it was that certain regions of the country could be abandoned as stagnant pools of poverty and ignorance. Not until the deep depression of the 1930s shook the nation to its foundations, did a concern for the poor and disadvantaged and for equity in general really begin to surface. But by that time, social, cultural, and economic patterns had caught the more disadvantaged in an iron vise. Thus, for example, the Southern hold on the congressional committee structure, added to the post-reconstruction patterning of relations between whites and blacks, revealed itself as a formidable block to rapid and meaningful improvement in the lot of the Southern Negroes. Only slightly less formidable were the barriers to improvements in the other backwashes of the rapid American thrust to national development, in Appalachia, in the cutover regions of the Upper Midwest, in the Four-Corners area and other sections of the Southwest, and in isolated pockets in other regions of the country as well.

Before the New Deal effort towards greater equity could be well started, World War II intervened and speeded the nation into a new phase of development.

THE POST-INDUSTRIAL PHASE

Shortly after World War II, by the midpoint of the present century, the nation was entering a new socioeconomic phase, one that has been referred to as the post-industrial or the services era. Employment in materials production—that is, in agriculture, mining and manufacturing—had stopped growing in relative terms and in the case of forming and mining in absolute terms as well. Materials production had become highly capital intensive, with automization increasingly important and with higher and higher human skills being called for. Employment growth was concentrated in the service activities—trade, professional services, business services, banking, communications, government, and the like. These rapid growth activities were all urban oriented so that national development ordained rapid urban expansion. This was urban growth piled on top of the extremely fast urban growth of the industrial period.

Urban evolution of the industrial period had had two major characteristics. The city had evolved as an "Americanizing," skill-upgrading mechanism, quickly turning new immigrants into workers for the factories, the railroads, and the shops, and rapidly absorbing them into the American mainstream. And the city had grown in a relatively compact manner, tied first to the horse carriage and then the trolley, as well as to the railroad. The evolution of the new period was, however, to take some different forms.

One aspect of post-World War II development was to have a particularly important impact on the cities. This related to employment patterns. World War II, with its tremendous demands for military goods added to the civilian requirements, meant great pressure on industrial capacity and extremely high employment needs. With many of the men in the armed services who normally would have been in industrial employment, and with wages at an all-time high, rural workers, many of them Negroes from the South—who in normal times might have hesitated to leave the countryside for the competitive urban environment—were drawn into the cities. For example, between 1940 and 1950, the rate of migration out of agriculture ran as high as 90 percent in some Southeastern states and of course geographic migration was closely tied to this movement. For example, during the 1940–50 decade, some 465,000 persons left farming in Alabama, amounting to a movement out of agriculture of 93.4 percent. (This loss was more than made up by an exceedingly high rural-population replacement rate.) The war, thereby, opened up migration channels that normally would have stayed closed or would have been filling up at a very much slower pace. As it was, the movement became a virtual flood and developed a momentum quite typical of migrational patterns. Thus it was that people who had been trapped in some of the most economically and culturally deprived areas of the nation began to trek to American cities.

They clustered in the older areas of the central cities, the only areas where they could find housing they could afford, and which were open to them, while the whites who had lived there earlier fled to the suburbs. Soon these areas of in-migration become giant ghettos of minority groups, in many ways effectively cut off from the remainder of the urban society.

Hardly had these new migration channels been opened up and the flow become well established than the war ended. Men—with greater skills—returned from the war and took up old and new jobs while industry very rapidly converted to modern, and often, automated plants. Once the patterns had been established, however, the migration continued—particularly of the younger people—intensified by the mechanization of cotton production and governmental restrictions on agricultural output. Jobs or no jobs, the "revolution of rising expectations," associated with the move to the cities, had touched even the most backward of the backwaters and was not to be denied. In many cases, the later moves were from town to city and from one city to another. The search for opportunity and a better life was having its repercussions in every corner of the land. But unlike the situation that had faced the European immigrant in an earlier day, the poor white and Negro migrants of the post-World War II period had few unskilled jobs readily at hand and little preparation for the more skilled jobs that were available.

It is well to note, then, that the current developmental phase of our national life—the services phase—started with the highly distorting impact of a major world war. Actually, the full consequences were to be delayed until after the impact of the Korean War had played itself out, but the die had been cast. Millions had been drawn to greater opportunity in the cities only to find themselves unprepared to grasp such opportunity—particularly in the face of long-established racial prejudice—and forced to reside in limited areas of the city, generally far from the sections of the burgeoning metropolitan regions where the greatest growth in jobs was taking place.

Other aspects of the new era have also caught the nation unprepared. Almost all the developments have been in association with a greatly increased use of communications (in its broadest sense) in all of our socioeconomic activities: the tremendous proliferation of service activities that are essentially oriented to face-to-face contact, the increasing importance of R&D and other noncommodity aspects of production which also call for more elaborate communications, and the tendency for more and more activities to be national and often international in scope, so that rapid communications have become a critical element in overall efficiency. The city, in effect, has become something of a production "shell" or plant in itself. The efficiency of the patterns of location of various activities in relationship to each other, and movement among them, has become as important as the efficiency of the beltline in mechanized factories. The nation has not been in the habit of viewing the city as an efficient or inefficient productive environment; attention has been focused on the *individual* production units. Consequently, our institutions are not geared to the task of consciously creating efficient productive contexts for socioeconomic activities. In fact, we have permitted ourself to drift into a situation where land uses in the city tend to be, in no small part, the unplanned consequences of racial segregation and political confrontation rather than the result of rational guidance on the basis of efficiency, equity, and quality-of-life objectives.

In other respects, too, we entered the new era unprepared. The basic structure of state and local governments had been set down during the earlier agricultural phase. Certain inadequacies were becoming apparent during the latter part of the nineteenth century and the first part of the twentieth as the industrialization phase gathered momentum. The shortcomings of our state and local governments have been described so frequently in recent years that they need not be detailed here. The main point to note is that the agricultural and indus- trial development phases, the states and localities were called upon to deliver only limited public services. As a general matter, the power elite in agriculture, mining, and industry was satisfied to keep the state and local governments weakly organized. Where certain services were deemed particularly important, as in education, special districts were established for the delivery of the services instead of strengthening the basic governmental units. Thus, we entered the post-industrial or services era with governmental units completely unequipped for positive developmental roles in the exploding metropolis which characterizes the new period. As a matter of fact, it is very much in keeping with the ideas of the previous period that local government should be at its weakest in the outly- ing areas of the metropolis where the new construction is going on. This fits the spirit of the former phases nicely. But the local governmental system as now organized has little relevance to the needs of today.

Not unexpectedly, state and local finance has also been geared to the gov- ernmental system of the previous phases and not to the requirements of the current phase. The property tax, which could meet the needs of local units established to deliver a certain minimum of public services, could not provide an adequate base for the much more elaborate requirements of the post-industrial era. The tremendous proliferation of categorical federal aids to states and lo- calities reflects the inadequacies of local finance to provide for new needs—in welfare assistance, in education and health, and in the construction of airports, hospitals, institutions of higher learning, and public housing units.

One more item is needed to fill out this story of cultural lag and unprepared- ness. This is with regard to the handling of urban land. During the agricultural and industrial phases, land became one of the most important of the develop- ment leverages. The granting of public lands to individual farmers, to corporate units, and to states had been an outstanding device for settling the land, build- ing the railroads, encouraging education, and achieving many another develop- ment purpose. This, on top of an inherited common-law view of private proper- ty, had given the nation a special regard for the private use of land. Naturally enough, the prevailing view had been extended to the use of land in the building of cities. While always accepted as having certain special characteristics, the ownership and transfer of land at the edge of cities had nevertheless long been regarded as the logical way to promote urban development. The land spec- ulators and the land developers of the modern-day city are as much a part of the national development picture as their counterparts have been in the coun- tryside—but in a totally different developmental setting.

Coming closer to today, with a growth of concern for order in urban devel- opment and for the quality of the urban environment, a whole series of controls were superimposed on the basic structure of private property. Thus, zoning, subdivision controls, and building controls were introduced to achieve greater order and improved quality—only to be found entirely lacking in the context of traditional approaches to ownership and transfer of land. For local governments are at their weakest in precisely the zones where the controls are most needed.

Organized in small enclaves, suburbanites tend to use such controls to keep "undesirables" out and to keep governmental costs down to a minimum. The needs of the metropolis as a whole rarely are a part of anyone's reckoning in the suburban communities.

All this adds up to a picture of a nation unprepared in both concepts and institutions to cope with the requirements of a quite new socioeconomic era. If we were to extrapolate current developments in a straight line, we could expect that in the decades to come, all our major cities would have three things in common. They would have a black core, they would be financially bankrupt, and they would be politically unmanageable.

THE PROBLEM AHEAD

The major problem that we face on the urban scene is not the lack of clear-cut goals with regard to the kinds of cities we want, as is often suggested. It is doubtful that we can collectively decide whether we want many giant cities or very many small ones, whether or not we want to encourage high density in central cities, whether or not our future lies in developing new towns, and the like. Rather, it is a problem of greatly increasing basic competence in certain key areas of our national life, in the same sense that key policy in the agricultural and industrial eras was concerned with the basic factor endowment of human resources, natural resources, material resources, and institutional resources.

If, today, national urban society is to get at fundamentals, it must initially try to fulfill three basic requirements: (1) to rapidly increase the competence of individuals, particularly those in the "bottom third," (2) to rapidly increase the capacity of states and localities (as well as of the national government), to carry out needed developmental activities, (3) to rapidly increase our capacity in R&D (research and development) geared to guiding public policies and programs with urban impacts.

It should be stressed that meeting these requirements is not a panacea for solving all urban problems. Rather they are the basic ingredients for the nation to begin to cope with the uniquely urban problems, such as the problems of agglomeration and high densities, and the problems of reconciling long-lasting urban physical capital with rapidly changing tastes, social needs, and technological possibilities.

Increasing Human Capacity

The first requirement calls for a priority focus on human beings. The nation needs to provide a basic structure for the development of people capable of dealing with the high-skill requirements of the post-industrial era. We have to make up for decades of neglect by bringing the formerly bypassed and disadvantaged to a relatively decent level of personal competence. In a society that is overwhelmingly urban and largely affluent, poverty and prejudice can no longer be swept into isolated rural corners and in equally isolated urban ghettos. The contrasts are sharp and open and of explosive potential. The key need is to help individuals develop competence in every sphere of urban life; the capacity to cope must extend to the political and social sphere as well as the economic (family self-support). We cannot possibly build a satisfactory urban life when a substantial proportion of the total population is unable to amass and use political power or to achieve social and economic standing.

It is time that the nation said quite simply and openly: humans are by far the most important resources in our post-industrial age. Every individual not only deserves to achieve the dignity that comes with being adequately prepared for a productive life but, just as important, the nation urgently needs productive individuals with skills beyond those required during earlier periods.

The key requirement for the future is a *national floor* under the basic human services, that is, for education, health, and welfare. Alvin H. Hansen and I proposed such a national minimum for human services in a book published in the early 1940s—*State and Local Finance in the National Economy*—looking ahead to the new era that was then dawning. This proposal still answers a critical requirement. Hopefully, we have reached the stage where the proposal can receive serious consideration. While we cannot say with any certainty just how much education and health care is "enough" for any one individual to achieve his "full" potential, we do know something of the disadvantages that are suffered by persons in, and from, those urban and rural districts whose education and health services are at a low level. The education and health care that a person receives should not be dependent on the locality where he happens to be born and grow up. People need the capability to cope with the modern era no matter where they are reared since they are likely to spend their working years in totally different communities. A national floor does not mean an equal expenditure per person but rather that expenditure needed to achieve a reasonable level of human competence and well-being. Thus, the national expenditure could be expected to be higher in areas with a disproportionate number of disadvantaged persons. At the other end of the spectrum, states and localities could add as much as they desired to achieve higher levels of services where local residents were willing to tax themselves for this purpose.

By the same token, as many thoughtful persons (and study commissions) have suggested, there is much to be gained by the provision of some form of minimum income for poor families in the United States—as long as this is not employed as an excuse for cutting back on needed specialized payments and services. A guaranteed income would help to bring many presently poor families into the national mainstream. Extreme poverty—particularly in an urban setting—is an attack on human dignity that generally deprives an individual of the capacity to cope with the world around him. Thus, a minimum income financed by the federal government could be expected to substantially reduce the extent and depth of the manifest difficulties our urban communities face: the continuing strain on the body politic caused by the dead weight of a population that is unable to care for itself, is rejected by the majority group, and is often ruthlessly exploited. Again, it should be stressed that this is not a proposal to *solve* human resources problems but is a needed ingredient in programs to meet the wide range of human needs. A move by the federal government to provide an income floor at a level where all American families are taken out of debilitating poverty will be the surest, and probably the fastest, route to the improvement of the urban environment, by reducing now severe urban problems to manageable proportions. Thus, for example, it seems logical to assume that a substantial part of the substandard housing problem would be solved by the national provision of a minimum income that brought every American family above, say, the sum suggested as the budget floor by the Bureau of Labor Statistics in its family income-and-expenditure studies. The removal of debilitating poverty is essential, not only to greater personal capacity, but also to better relations among various social groups and to a more equitable distribution of political power among the different groups.

Until a reasonably adequate level of basic public services and of family income are provided across the whole nation, cities will find themselves in an anomalous position; the more they do to ameliorate their difficult human problems, the more these problems can intensify, since poor and disadvantaged persons will pour in to take advantage of the superior services and assistance they provide. The overall net gains from the improvement of basic human services will become much more apparent than they are today once there is a solid floor of services and income for the whole nation.

Increasing the Capacity of States and Localities

The second major requirement is to increase the capacity of states and localities to cope with urban-development needs.

Beyond federal government support of human services, the whole system of federal, state, and local finance must be adjusted to the era in which we live and must be employed as an instrumentality for thoroughly modernizing state and local governments. While finance is hardly the stuff around which much excitement can be generated, it turns out to be almost as much a key to the achievement of urban objectives as it is a key to the achievement of full-employment and economic-stability objectives.

Much higher levels of local public services are needed to meet the pressing problems of urban life; yet localities cannot possibly raise the money needed to finance such public services. They cannot tax beyond a certain point for fear of losing industries and higher-income families, a fear which has reality in an open and mobile society. The provision of a national floor under the basic human services would be the first and most critical step in overcoming the current dilemma. However, looking ahead over a relatively long period of time, there is also need for general-purpose federal grants to states and localities or tax-sharing arrangements to enable them to plan orderly development within the cities and on their outskirts. Cities will not undertake planned development of this kind unless they can look forward to an assured flow of funds for that purpose. Nor can they be expected to do a decent job of planned development unless their political and administrative structures and processes are thoroughly modernized.

Federal finance can be used as a powerful lever for improving states and local governments, that is, to equip them to deal more effectively with the extremely difficult problems of the present day. A sensible approach (as proposed by Representative Henry Reuss of Wisconsin) would provide for federal tax-sharing with the states contingent on the modernization of state and local governments. The objective would be to encourage the creation of more equitable and viable local governments and more representative and better equipped state governments. Just what "modernization" in today's context implies is itself a good question; it is surely a mild word for the substantial changes that are needed. If it were limited to the use of more up-to-date management methods, its payoff would probably be slight. The critical problems are clearly in the realm of politics and human relations. Minority groups and the poor must somehow acquire political and economic leverage, a real voice in decisions that directly or indirectly affect them.

Such an approach to financial assistance would put the national government in the business of up dating state and local governments. General purpose federal grants or tax sharing, if used specifically as a lever for modernization, would aim at bringing about a high level of state and local governmental competence in the same sense that a federal floor under human services and a guaranteed minimum family income would aim at creating a minimum level of individual competence throughout the country.

Yet another use of the federal financial lever is to promote urban development that has an inherent regional logic. While we cannot yet claim to understand fully the forces behind the present patterns of urban development over the national landscape, neither can we weigh properly all the costs and benefits of alternative forms of development. The element that has emerged most clearly is the clustering of activities around the metropolitan cores so that the commuting range has taken on a substantial significance in suburban and new-town construction as well as in the thrust of both private and public redevelopment. The very strenuous efforts that have to be made to establish independent, free-standing new towns, as contrasted with the rapid continuing expansion of suburbs and the building of new *satellite* communities, underlines the power of the metropolitan commuting element.

There is clearly need for an advanced kind of region-wide developmental planning that aims at tying together suburban and new-town construction with the layout of transportation, water, sewerage, and other utilities that have communications and developmental impact, so as to go as far as possible in achieving efficiency, equity, and quality-of-life objectives. Few states and localities can be expected to move quickly in joining forces for the achievement of this kind of planned development unless the federal government uses a very powerful financial carrot-and-stick strategy toward that end.

The establishment of a national floor of policy and expenditure supports would permit the state and local subsystems of our highly integrated national system to begin to function properly. This is not to suggest that they would necessarily function as models of efficiency and foresight. After all, the federal government, with much greater organizational capability, is hardly such a model. I would, however, expect them to rather quickly develop the capacity to bring key decisions into the political arena and to work out programs that bring together disparate interests around certain general, longer-range improvements.

What is proposed is in keeping with the traditional American practice of providing a national framework within which individual, local, and state activities can be carried out effectively. Actually, rather than undermining local self-government and scope for individual choices in patterns of living as is sometimes assumed, federal support would strengthen the former and greatly add to the latter. Today, local self-government has become essentially an empty slogan. Once a national floor of financial support is provided and funds for planned urban development are made available, local people would be in a far better position to control their environments.

R&D with an Urban Focus

There is yet a third requirement, that is, to rapidly increase our capacity in urban research and development (R&D) so as to have better guidelines for public urban policies and programs. We have seen the contribution that research has made to the various national science, health, and space programs, and also its contribution to national economic policy. It is at least as important for the evolution of urban policy—both the foundational kinds of policies discussed here, and the more detailed and specific policies that need to follow. We do not at the present time have nearly enough knowledge to have any assurance about the detailed content of such policy. Thus, for example, the poverty program and the many experimental educational programs have served to highlight the enormous difficulty and complexity of raising the achievement levels of culturally deprived youths; the various housing programs have underlined the difficulty of getting better housing to low-income families; and, along the same lines, the limited impact of the federal 701 regional planning grants have made it evident that there is much about regional development that still has to be learned.

Unfortunately, a mere extension of present research capabilities and approaches will no more do the job that is needed than would the mere extension of present federal categorical aids. As with the first two requirements, the need now is for a major restructuring and an entirely different conception of the appropriate quantitative levels.

The question of appropriate scale and quality looms large with regard to basic data. The need for more and better data is stressed so often that everyone gets "turned off" by the mere mention of data. Somehow this problem has to be overcome and an appropriate volume of resources—multiples of what are now employed—channelled to the task. Two organizational changes deserve priority attention. One is the establishment of a mid-decade census (given the speed of urban change in the United States), with extensions into a broad range of longitudinal studies by the Census Bureau. The other is the establishment of expertly manned data centers within every major metropolitan region of the nation, serving data-generation, clearing-house, and analytical purposes. A key feature of such centers must be the availability of resources to permit them to service the data needs of scholars and research centers within their region at minimal costs to the reseachers.

The consideration that gave rise to the establishment of the Urban Institute in Washington, D.C. applies also to the need for setting up strong research centers—under university and other auspices—within the various metropolitan regions; namely, the ability to achieve economies of scale and the capacity to tackle interdisciplinary problems. It should not be necessary to make a case for regional centers, as against total reliance on a single institute, given the many significant differences among the various parts of the country. One has only to compare the Los Angeles region with the San Francisco metropolis, within a single state, to make the point. The problem here, however, it should be noted, is not merely one of adequate financial resources for research but also the willingness of scholars to work with others on questions that will necessarily take many years to resolve. Academic institutions are today not well organized for interdisciplinary, long-maturing research. If we are greatly to extend our research capability in the urban realm, some far-reaching changes in research organization will have to be achieved.

The "D" in R&D also deserves attention. It is all too easy to be critical of the federal government's fumbling with its so-called urban "demonstration projects" as well as other forms of experimental development efforts. Certainly, in most cases the scale has been much too small and the available resources much too limited to make for a genuine learning experience. Also, the critical evaluation component has been missing entirely or much too perfunctory to be helpful. The fact is that we urgently need fresh thinking about experimentation in the urban realm, and we need greatly to strengthen our evaluation capabilities.

It is disconcerting to note that the very R&D component expected to help provide firm, tested content to the general policy framework outlined above itself needs substantial improvement in human and organizational capacity. But this is not a surprising situation given the overall national lag with regard to the needs of the post-industrial urban world of today. It is not helpful to underestimate the scale of the problems we face in this realm as in others, any more than it is to be too impressed with the difficulties involved. We clearly have the resources needed to develop an appropriately scaled R&D capability in the relatively near future. Our job is to bring this about as quickly as we can.

To sum up, this paper stresses two key points in looking to a better urban future for the United States. First, it urges a sharply focused national-policy thrust aimed directly at greatly increasing the overall competence of individuals, particularly those formerly disadvantaged, as well as the overall competence of states and localities—in both cases through the use of a highly traditional policy lever, namely, federal finance. And second, noting the complexity of the problems involved, it urges the importance of developing an R&D capability that can assist in the design of effective specific urban policies and programs.

REFERENCES

Beckman, Norman. "Our Federal System and Urban Development: The Adaptation of Form to Function." *Journal of the American Institute of Planners, 29 (August 1963): 152–67.*

Canty, Donald, Ed. *The New City: The National Committee on Urban Growth Policy.* New York: Praeger, 1969.

Connery, Robert and Richard Leach. *Federal Government and Metropolitan Areas.* Cambridge: Harvard Univ. Press, 1960.

Fitch, Lyle C. "Eight Goals for an Urbanizing America." *Daedalus, 97: no. 4 (Fall 1968): 1141–64.*

Hansen, Alvin H. and Harvey S. Perloff. State and Local Finance in the National Economy. New York: W. W. Norton, 1944, Chapter 8 ("Federal Underwriting of Minimum Service Standards").

Hoover, Edgar M. (with Raymond Vernon) *Anatomy of a Metropolis.* Cambridge: Harvard Univ. Press, 1959.

―――, (study director), *Economic Study of the Pittsburgh Region 1― Region in Transition. 2―Portrait of a Region. 3―Region with a Future.* Pittsburgh: Pittsburgh Regional Planning Association, 1964.

―――, "The Evolving Form and Organization of the Metropolis." In *Issues in Urban Economics* edited by Harvey S. Perloff and Lowden Wingo, 237–284. Baltimore: Johns Hopkins Press, 1968.

Meyerson, Martin. "Urban Policy: Reforming Reform." *Daedalus,* 97 no. 4. (Fall 1968): 1410–30.

Okun, Bernard and Richard W. Richardson. "Regional Income Inequality and Internal Population Migration." In *Regional Development and Planning: A Reader,* edited by John Friedmann and William Alonso, 303–18. Cambridge: M.I.T. Press, 1964.

Perloff, Harvey, S. "Modernizing Urban Development," Daedalus, 96, no. 3 (Summer 1967): 789–800.

Perloff, Harvey S. and Richard P. Nathan, Eds. *Revenue Sharing and the City.* Baltimore: John Hopkins Press, 1968.

Siegel, Irving H. *The Kerner Commission Report and Economic Policy.* Kalamazoo: W. E. Upjohn Inst. for Employment Research, 1969.

U.S. Advisory Commission on Intergovernmental Relations Reports: *Government in Metropolitan Areas,* 1961. *Governmental Structure, Organization and Planning in Metropolitan Areas: Suggested Action by Local, State and National Government,* July 1961. *Metropolitan America: Challenge to Federalism,* August 1966. *To Improve the Effectiveness of the American Federal System Through Increased Cooperation Among National, State and Local Levels of Government,* 1968. *Urban and Rural America: Policies for Future Growth,* April 1968.

U.S. Chamber of Commerce. Task Force on Economic Growth and Opportunity. *Rural Poverty and Regional Progress in an Urban Society.* Washington, D.C.: Chamber of Commerce of the U.S., 1969.

U.S. Congress. Committee on Government Operations. Subcommittee on Executive Reorganization. *Federal Role in Urban Affairs:* Hearings, December 30, 1966, Appendix to Pt. I. Washington, D.C.: Government Printing Office, 1966.

U.S. Congress. Committee on Government Operations. Subcommittee on Government Research. *Full Opportunity and Social Accounting Act,* 3 pts. Hearings—June 26; July 19–20, 26, 28, 1967. Washington, D.C.: Government Printing Office, 1968. *Human Resources Development,* 2 pts. Hearings–April 8, 10, 18, 23–24, 1968. Washington, D.C.: Government Printing Office, 1968.

U.S. Department of Health, Education and Welfare. *Toward a Social Report.* Washington, D.C.: Government Printing Office, 1969.

U.S. National Commission on Urban Problems. *Building The American City.* Washington, D.C.: Government Printing Office, 1968.

U.S. President's Commission on National Goals. *Goals For Americans.* New York: Columbia Univ., The American Assembly, 1960.

U.S. White house. *"To Fulfill These Rights,"* Conference—June 1–2, 1966, Washington, D.C.: Government Printing Office, 1966.

U.S. Congress. Joint Economic Committee. *Employment and Manpower Problems in the Cities: Implications of the Report of the National Advisory Commission on Civil Disorders,* Hearings—May 28–29; June 4–6, 1968. Washington, D.C.: Government Printing Office, 1968.

U.S. Congress, Subcommittee on Economy in the Government. *The Planning-Programming-Budgeting System: Progress and Potentials,* Hearings—September 14, 19–21, 1967. Washington, D.C.: Government Printing Office, 1967.

U.S. Congress, Subcommittee on Urban Affairs. *Urban America: Goals and Problems,* Hearings—September 27–28; October 2–4, 1967. Washington, D.C.: Government Printing Office, 1967.

U.S. Department of Housing and Home Finance Agency. *Metropolis in Transition: Local Government Adaptation to Changing Urban Needs* (By Roscoe C. Martin.) Washington, D.C.: Government Printing Office, September 1963.

U.S. National Advisory Commission on Civil Disorders. *Employment and Manpower Problems in Cities.* Washington, D.C.: Government Printing Office, 1968.

Alternatives for Future Urban Land Policy

Given the land use situation in the United States, what are the policy alternatives facing the nation? Substantial parts of our population are disadvantaged by the land use policy that has emerged over the past several decades, primarily from the independent action of hundreds of local planning and zoning bodies. The various minority groups that have been effectively excluded from living in new housing in suburbs are naturally unhappy over their situation and strive to do something about it. But other sectors of the total electorate are also unhappy about the situation, and they, too, seek to do something about it. Land use measures are not solely responsible for the discrimination that exists or for the generally disadvantaged position of racial and ethnic minorities and the poor. Reform of land use planning and zoning alone will not cure the unsatisfactory conditions.

Various measures have been taken, or might be taken, that will lead to substantial modification in land use planning and zoning practices. The actual events are far more significant as indicators of change than they are for their accomplishment. Perhaps they presage a hurricane, perhaps they will subside. In this paper we explore some of the possibilities for change, make some tentative appraisals, and suggest some possible lines of desirable action. If change is coming, from what direction is it coming, at what speed, and at whose impetus?

Traditional land use controls have been under attack from several directions. Heyman points out that municipal land use regulation is under attack by the environmentalists, the lawyers, market forces, the proponents of open housing, state governments, and the federal government[1] Fessler has traced the recent rise of legal services to the poor and shown how these services have enabled poor people to challenge governmental actions inimical to their interests[2] Dissatisfaction with the results of local land use controls has caused

---

This chapter was written in collaboration with Marion Clawson.

[1]Ira Michael Heyman, "Legal Assaults on Municipal Land Use Regulation," in Marion Clawson (ed.), *Modernizing Urban Land Policy* (Baltimore, Md.: Johns Hopkins Press, 1973), pp. 153–174.

[2]Daniel Wm. Fessler, "Casting the Courts in a Land Use Reform Effort: A Starring Role or a Supporting Part," in Marion Clawson (ed.), *Modernizing Urban Land Policy* (Baltimore, Md.: Johns Hopkins Press, 1973), pp. 175–203.

many states to adopt statewide or regional approaches. In Alaska, Colorado, Connecticut, Delaware, Georgia, Hawaii, Maine, Maryland, Massachusetts, North Carolina, Rhode Island, Vermont, and Wisconsin, either a new state organization or an existing agency is required to implement some degree of *statewide* land use planning or zoning, or both, or to carry out some sort of planning and land use regulation aimed at particular classes of land, such as wetlands or tidal areas.[3] In addition, in some states, as in California with its San Francisco Bay Conservation and Development Commission, or California and Nevada with the Tahoe Regional Planning Agency, or New Jersey with the Hackensack Meadowlands Development Commission, or New York with the Adirondack Park Agency, a regional agency has been created to deal with some special problems of land use planning and control. These various measures are primarily directed at resource-use problems—the preservation of some unique resource or area. Their primary focus is ecological (or physical). This is not to imply that they are lacking in social consequences, but social objectives are not the primary aim. Their significance for our present purposes does not lie in their aims or in their mechanisms, or even in their results (which to date have been small), but rather in the fact that they do represent a distinct break with past sole reliance on *local* land use planning. Some establish state controls that replace local controls; others provide a combination of state and local controls, with statewide concerns clearly dominant.

In a few instances state legislation has been directed primarily at the social issues of land use control—particularly, at the exclusionary aspects of local land use zoning. Massachusetts enacted a Zoning Appeals Law, which enables developers of low-income housing to apply to a local zoning appeals board for a comprehensive permit instead of applying to various agencies for the many permits required under local regulations. If the application is denied, the developer can appeal to a Housing Appeals Committee created at the state level, which has the power under the law to reverse the decision of the local zoning board. In New York, the Urban Development Corporation has the legal power to override local zoning ordinances and building codes that would otherwise prevent the Corporation from building housing for low-income groups.

The statewide and regional approaches to land use planning and control are, in general, too recent to have been fully tested for either their competence and efficacy or their legal powers. They are significant, however, as portents of a growing dissatisfaction with the operation of land use planning and zoning at the strictly local level.

Bills before the Congress in 1972 provide for a much larger federal role in land use planning. Senate bill 632, which passed the Senate in September 1972, included a statement of national policy, expressing a national interest in land use planning; provided a system of grants to states to enable them to conduct land use planning for certain critical environmental and development areas and to give some degree of supervision to units of local government in their land use

---

[3]Fred Bosselman and David Callies, *The Quiet Revolution in Land Use Control* (Prepared for the Council on Environmental Quality. Washington, D.C.: USGPO, 1972.)

planning; and provided for the establishment of a small new unit in the Department of the Interior to handle the federal grants. The bill as reported out of the Senate Committee had included severe penalties for states that did not carry on land use planning; by Senate action these were reduced to a simple withholding of the planning grants. This bill had been supported, with minor suggested changes, by the executive branch. A similar but different bill had been considered by the House Committee but was not acted upon by the House. Although many important differences remain to be ironed out, ultimate passage of national legislation on land use planning seems likely. Most of the discussion about national legislation has focused on environmental problems, but social problems can surely not be ignored if any machinery for land use planning is devised. Who is to benefit, who is to lose, who is to be excluded, and from where?

Every analyst who deals with the future faces several choices. Will he try to project or forecast the changes that he thinks are most probable, or paint a picture of what he personally thinks is most desirable, or take some intermediate and often poorly defined approach? We recognize the problem, and, in what follows, we try to be explicit about our choices. We sometimes use one approach, sometimes another. On the one hand, we do not accept trends or forces as inevitable and unchangeable; one purpose of an analysis such as this is to provide the basis for alternatives. On the other hand, we do not believe that pure wishful thinking is likely to be productive; there must be some consideration of reality.

As we contemplate the future of cities and of land use, we make one basic assumption that underlies the rest of what we have to say here. In our opinion, a nation that has undertaken changes in education, in voting, and in civil rights such as have occurred in this country in the past twenty years or so cannot long continue to turn its back upon discrimination in housing. True, and to the surprise of those of us who lived through the New Deal, the lead has been taken by the courts, and more particularly by the Supreme Court. But it is a mistake to underestimate the degree of legislative, executive branch, and general electorate support for the changes that the Court has imposed. There have been grumbling and threats of revolt, and here and there outright defiance of a court decision; but the dominant fact has been the degree to which people generally have gone along with, if not positively supported, the Court in its reforms. Despite some talk in recent months about the new Supreme Court being likely to be a strict constructionist one, the present Court has pushed educational desegregation further than its predecessors did. The Court, like the public, will change its views over the next decade or two; but there is perhaps as much reason to expect the Court to go forward on the removal of racial and other barriers as to expect it to retreat.

In the remainder of this paper, we consider the possible directions of change in land use controls, with only modest consideration either of how such changes might come about or of the chances that they will. We are convinced that some change is inevitable and that a reduction of discrimination in housing is highly probable, but we are not sure how these changes will be realized or exactly when. The task of developmental statesmanship is to explore and to invent alternative policies; choice is possible, and urban land use can be what we collectively choose to make it.

PROCEDURAL REFORMS

One possible avenue for change in land use zoning and other land use controls is procedural reform—procedures in planning, in zoning, in public works, and in other measures that largely determine the public input into urban and suburban land use. Anyone even modestly familiar with these procedures knows how often they violate the accepted principles of good government and even legal requirements of due process. Babcock has amply documented this for zoning.[4] Fessler has also described some of the deficiencies of zoning.[5] Planning and zoning actions are often taken in closed sessions, or without due notice to affected parties, or in contradiction to rules established by the organizations concerned; members of zoning commissions and other bodies act on cases in which they have an interest, direct or indirect, or enter into reciprocal trade with other members, each to advance the other's cases without direct action by the involved party, outright bribery is proven in some cases and suspected in many others. Zoning and other actions are taken without any standards, or are inconsistent with other actions by the same public bodies. All in all, there is scarcely a field of local government activity where procedural sloppiness and outright favoritism are more prevalent than in zoning and related actions. As Babcock has shown in his book, the local courts have been scarcely more consistent; many have shunned zoning cases and have let virtually anything slip by in order to avoid serious work and thought on zoning. Fessler has described the reluctance of appeals courts to disturb administrative local zoning actions.

All this would seem to cry out for reform, and there may indeed be persons or groups who will work for reform on these grounds. Some political conservatives, for instance, may favor racially oriented local zoning but still be outraged at the slovenliness of local governmental processes. Legal attacks on land use zoning for its procedural inadequacies face great difficulties, as Fessler has shown. The basic problem is standing to sue; this is often denied to nonresidents of the county or other area concerned on the grounds that they lack the requisite personal interest or stake in the outcome. Yet the local gentry who do have standing to sue may have reached an informal agreement among themselves that no one will upset the cozy arrangements by which they benefit (or think they do). Outsiders from racial and income groups not represented in the county but de facto excluded by local zoning may find it extremely difficult to get their cases before the judicial machinery. Nevertheless, difficult as challenges to procedural deficiencies may be, one should not wholly foreclose them from judi-

---

[4]Richard F. Babcock, *The Zoning Game—Municipal Practices and Policies* (Madison: University of Wisconsin Press, 1966).
[5]Fessler, "Casting the Courts in a Land Use Reform Effort," pp. 175–203.

cially imposed reform, or judicial stimulus to legislative reform, or self-inspired legislative reform.

Let us first explore some of the directions procedural reform might take, and then consider what, if anything, a new method might accomplish if adopted.

Since cities and counties exercise control over private land use by means of powers granted to them by the states, the states might arouse themselves to exercise some degree of control over the use of those delegated powers. One avenue would be to enact legislation that would spell out the legal and administrative procedures for planning, zoning, and other controls over private land use. One element here might be a statement in the law of the kinds of considerations that should be faced, and discussed, in development plans for an area. For instance, the law might require that the plan state its goals, that it explore and present evidence on its benefits and costs to affected groups, and that it include some governmental procedure adequate to implement its objectives. One might here draw an analogy with the environmental impact statements required under the National Environmental Policy Act of 1969 and subsequent amendatory measures. The local government to which legal power to control private land use had been delegated might be required to analyze the economic and social impact of its regulations. State legislation might also spell out such procedures as due notice of action, public hearing requirements, provisions for appeal, and others. While these might not alter current practice in some of the better-managed local zoning and planning bodies, they might raise the standard of practice in many others. If any such legislation were adopted by any state, the grounds for appeal from planning, zoning, and related actions would be laid.

This type of state action would be vastly more effective if interest groups or various kinds, whether resident within the local area or not, had clearly established standing to sue. This might be specified in the same or in other legislation. However, the effectiveness of the concerned citizen organization should not be exaggerated; few organizations are equipped to fight all the battles for racial minorities, and still fewer are equipped or willing to fight battles for economically depressed groups. Nevertheless, states could go a long way in bringing a procedural orderliness to local government actions in the zoning and related fields.

A state law governing local zoning might include a special measure requiring that specific zoning actions conform to, or at least not violate, an area's general plans and policy frameworks, and that these, in turn, be established only by proper procedures of hearing and appeals. This would provide some guide for specific zoning actions. Zoning board members could no longer state that cases were heard "on their merits" without defining a "merit" and subjecting their definition to citizen review in open hearing.

Conformity to general plans and policy frameworks would help to reduce the arbitrariness and favoritism of local zoning actions. This would be particularly effective if local plans and policy frameworks set out local plan objectives and principles of developmental action in specific terms and if the local plans showed the relationship of the local unit to the metropolis in economic, social, and political terms as well as in physical and service terms. Tying zoning to general plans would not guarantee wisdom or fairness. General plans are also subject to prejudiced and parochial thinking. But at least the zoning rationale and purposes would have to be formed in the open.

State legislation might go further and provide that appeals from local governmental planning and zoning action be heard by a body outside the area concerned. This might be a state body like the Massachusetts Housing Appeals Committee or a metropolitan wide body such as a subsidiary of a metropolitan Council of Government. Or it might be a special court—after all, special courts have been established to decide other special types of problems. If an appeals system of this kind is to be effective, it should be open not only to the parties directly involved, and perhaps the professional staffs of the planning and zoning organizations, but to any interested citizen group as well. Here, the right of citizen groups to bring class action suits would be extremely important if not critical. A principle might easily be established that any citizen within the larger area served by the appeals board could have the right to appeal.

A system of appeals from local planning and zoning actions to an agency of a higher unit of government that serves a larger area would have some similarities to the procedures under the British Town and Country Planning Act of 1947, as amended (including the amendments still pending, but likely to be adopted).[6] In Great Britain, under this act, local units of government prepare land use plans for their area of jurisdiction. If a tract of land is designated on the map for residential or other development, this in itself is "planning permission," and its owner is thereby granted the legal freedom to develop it in accordance with the plan. If the map shows that a tract is to remain in some undeveloped use, then planning permission has been refused. There is no separate step of land use zoning such as we have in the United States. The plans have to be approved by the appropriate Minister in London (originally, the Minister of Town and Country Planning, later the Minister of Housing and Local Government, and now the Minister of the Department of the Environment). Refusal of planning permission has almost always meant a substantial loss in land value compared with the value of the same land with planning permission; any citizen feeling aggrieved by such loss of value could appeal to the Minister who could, if he chose, hold a public inquiry into the matter. If the local government sought loans or grants for public housing—and about half of all housing since World War II in Britain has been publicly built—the approval of the Ministry for the loan or grant was required. Thus, in effect, the Ministry had three opportunitites to review the local plans. The Ministry could, and in fact almost always did, modify the plans before granting approval. This process was very time consuming; the delays in planning review were very great. In 1968 an act provided that thereafter local authorities would prepare "structure" plans, or statements of general policy, showing trends and broad patterns of future development; these are approved by the Ministry, as before. The detailed proposals to implement the structure plans come in local plans, which are not normally approved by the Minister, although he has the legal right to intervene. This process in Great

[6]This and other references to the British experience come from Marion Clawson and Peter Hall, *Planning and Urban Growth: An Anglo-American Comparison* (Johns Hopkins University Press for Resources for the Future, 1974).

Britain has reduced the arbitrariness and parochialism of local planning, and—though such conclusions must be largely subjective—it seems greatly to have reduced fraud, bribery, and personal profiteering from the individual's actions as a public official. The *overall* social consequences may not be much better than the results in the United States, but for different reasons.

If appeals from local planning and zoning action could be taken to a body with jurisdiction over a wider area—at least a metropolitan area—the metropolitanwide effect of local actions might receive consideration. Thus, the type of large-lot zoning that may seem defensible when practiced on a small scale by one suburban municipality would be seen to produce significant and undesired effects when practiced by all suburbs in the metropolis. The appeals process *might* be able to force consideration of regional interests and results in this way.

When one begins to contemplate the possibility of appeals from zoning and other land use controls being made to regional or statewide bodies, the recent California and Richmond, Virginia, school cases assume paramount importance. These decisions may or may not be upheld on appeal to higher courts and, even if upheld, must be fleshed out with additional decisions. In the Richmond case, the court rejected the defense of school integration within counties when this led to segregation between counties. In effect, the court was sweeping county boundary lines, at least for some purposes. Many boundaries of local government arose from historical accident. If carried to its logical end, the court's attitude would reject the defense of suburban cities or counties that they were not responsible for a segregated housing situation in the larger metropolitan community. Again, one should not assume that the potentials of these school cases will be realized—whether one regards this as good or as bad. The decisions to date are significant as straws in the wind rather than as actual firm results. But it surely is not inconceivable that the highly localized land use zoning we have known for about half a century might be changed materially in the future.

There are those who take a dim view of the efficacy of procedural reform. In their view, legislation prescribing proper procedures may force local governments to do properly and neatly what they had previously done sloppily and with frequent favoritism, but the end results will be the same as far as the poor and the racial minorities are concerned. This view assumes that procedure can be made subservient to ends and that, given the ends, legally defensible procedure can be found that will attain the ends. Some might go further, and argue that there would be insufficient interest and power to require local governments to live up to the improved procedures established by law. One can surely sympathize with the "procedural pessimists," for good procedure alone does not guarantee wisdom, fairness, or positive results.

We take a rather different view of the advantages of procedural reform while admitting the arguments of the pessimists. We think that procedures do matter, that the end product of governmental action is directly affected if not governed by the processes of government, and that the reform of procedures will affect the outcomes of the processes concerned. If some or all of the foregoing procedural reforms for zoning and other land use controls were adopted, a different pattern of land uses would result. One key feature of a reformed procedure would be the use of public hearings or other open review of actions by local governmental bodies; anyone familiar with public hearings knows that they are no panacea—often attended only by the directly interested and by the crackpots, often eliciting nothing but junk testimony, often ignored when the decisions are made. But the mere possibility that a public hearing will be held, or can be insisted upon by opponents, surely acts as a strong restraint against favoritism and illegality.

If zoning had to be based upon general plans and policy frameworks, and if both had to conform to certain legal standards and be arrived at by a governmental process subject to citizen scrutiny, then at least one could say that the results represented the considered decision of the people of the area or of the unit of government making the decision. This would reduce the ill-considered actions and those in the personal interest of one of the actors; it would by no means guarantee a socially enlightened action. But, when combined with review at a higher and geographically wider level, it would be less locally oriented and more considerate of the metropolitan or regional interest. We think these differences would be real gains.

SUBSTANTIVE REFORM

The dividing line between procedural and substantive reform is obviously not a clear and sharp one, yet there is some difference between efforts to make old established approaches work better and efforts to institute new and different approaches. The preceding section was concerned, in the main, with measures to improve the working of the zoning and other land use controls that have existed for the past half century or so—to make these controls work more effectively, more democratically, less parochially. Now we consider some new measures to replace or supplement the old ones.

First, we must consider and dismiss as unworkable any suggestion to abolish land use zoning. The experience of Houston, Texas, where private covenants have largely governed land use, is sometimes cited as evidence that public zoning is unnecessary and costly. Comparatively few persons, we judge, would accept this view. We do not. Private covenants may raise more problems than they answer; in particular, their social accountability is weak. On a more practical level, private covenants do not exist on hundreds of square miles of residential areas in the United States, and the negotiation of such covenants among the many landowners in such residential areas would be impossibly difficult. Were zoning to be abolished for these areas, their residents would feel that they were not adequately protected from intrusion by nonconforming and discordant uses. Thus, should land use zoning be totally overthrown by some court decision, we think that legislatures would immediately act to restore it in some legally acceptable form at least for the areas where zoning has existed for many years. We think that a total rejection of land use zoning is both undesirable and politically unacceptable. Reform, not abolition, seems called for.

Proposals for drastic reform of land use zoning fall in a very different category than proposals for its abolition. In "Requiem for Zoning" and "The Future of American Planning," John Reps sharply criticized land use zoning as it has worked in practice, but he proposed major changes to cure or reduce its demonstrated deficiencies.[7] Our own proposals, in the paragraphs that follow, bear considerable resemblance to his. Without attempting to review or appraise his proposals, we proceed to develop ours, merely warning the reader that ours are not wholly new.

One major substantive change would be the provision that every land use plan or land use zoning ordinance require every residential development to include some provision for low-income and/or racial-minority populations. This requirement upon land use planning and zoning might conceivably be imposed by a court decision or by legislative action arising either spontaneously or in response to court pressure. In fact, an ordinance requiring residential builders to include housing for low-income families was adopted by the county government of Fairfax County, Virginia, in 1970, but was not upheld in a court test. If mandatory mixing of a majority and minority groups were proposed, two major questions would immediately arise. Should it apply to economic classes as well as to races? For what unit of area should it be applicable? These questions merit consideration at this point.

Racial discrimination in housing surely still exists, and is likely to be struck down whenever it is too overt or whenever it can be proven—not an easy task. But dealing with income discrimination is vastly more difficult. How much good would it do poor people of any race or ethnic group to have discriminatory land use controls abolished if they cannot afford to buy or rent housing of standard or better quality? Elimination of bias in zoning would remove one obstacle to their ownership or occupancy of better housing, but their limited ability to afford something better would remain a barrier, unless removed by other measures. Thus, requirements in land use plans and in zoning ordinances that provision be made for racial minorities and for the poor would not, in itself, produce much housing for these groups. Other measures would be needed, as Weaver has pointed out.

Perhaps more important is the question: At what geographic scale should a mixing of income classes and/or races be required in land use plans and zoning ordinances? Should it be required at the subdivision, suburban satellite town, or metropolitan scale? If the requirement is imposed at the subdivision scale, the developer would have to provide some housing at specified price levels for poor and/or racial groups, with no discrimination in sales to the latter. The required amount would probably not exceed a relatively small percentage of his total housing construction. Presumably, the developer's profit prospects are such that he would not provide this housing unless he had to—if he would, there would obviously be no problem. If the developer must suffer some reduced income by providing housing for low-income and/or racial occupants, then he must make up this loss by higher prices or larger profits from the other houses

[7]John W. Reps, "Requiem for Zoning," *Planning 1964: Selected Papers from the 1964 ASPO Planning Conference;* and "The Future of American Planning: Requiem or Renascence?," *Planning 1967: Selected Papers from the ASPO National Planning Conference* (American Society of Planning Officials, Chicago, 1964 and 1967).

he builds; their purchasers are, in effect, bearing the social cost of providing housing for the low-income and racial groups involved. Is this the proper incidence of such costs? Is this the proper scale of mixing? Will small numbers of persons from low-income and racial groups find their best social opportunities in otherwise high-income subdivisions? Such questions clearly challenge the idea of mixing at the subdivision level.

Mixing at the suburban–city or suburban–county level would avoid some, but not all, of these difficulties. If a unit of suburban government were forced to make provision for both low-income and racial groups in its land use plans, it would have somewhat more flexibility than a single subdivision developer. Since the low-income workers would often be the service employees for the higher-income residents, provision of land on which housing could be erected for them could be justified on grounds of simple equity and of the efficiency of people living reasonably near their jobs. It has been stated that less than 10 percent of the garbage collection staff of Montgomery County, Maryland, actually live within the county. Here are regularly employed public employees receiving low but not substandard wages, who are forced to commute long distances because there are no practical housing opportunitites nearby. Such extreme separation of home and work place may be attacked on both efficiency and equity grounds. In the case of suburban counties, a strong case could be made that their land use plans and zoning should provide land for housing for all major groups of workers in the county. Provision of housing within their means would involve its own problems; appropriately zoned land is essential but may not be sufficient. At the level of the suburban city, especially the small one, a requirement to provide land for low-income housing might be more difficult to meet and perhaps less defensible. In each case, an attempt to provide for all would raise the question of whether there is any place in the future for the exclusive high-income residential area. If there is, how large can it be without creating social consequences unacceptable to a large proportion of the electorate?

The case for requiring land use planning and zoning to take account of the needs of racial minorities and low-income groups is strongest at the metropolitan level. If genuine planning exists or can be created at the metropolitan scale and if land use zoning is either formulated or subject to review at the metropolitan scale, provision could be made for housing all income classes within reach of job opportunities, public services, and recreational and cultural facilities. This would undoubtedly produce some separation of housing by income levels, and probably by race also—in each case, perhaps more de facto than proclaimed. But such metropolitan planning and zoning does not exist today; possibly a series of court decisions would provide the impetus to legislation which would provide for it.

There are various ways in which lower-income and minority groups can be helped to achieve better living and working conditions. One is for large-scale public purchase of undeveloped suburban land to be made available for subdivision, sale, or lease to private developers. The idea would be for some public body to purchase undeveloped suburban land or land for the construction of balanced satellite communities, well in advance of the need to develop it, and to attain a desired pattern of suburban or new town growth by making this land available for private development.[8] As Reps has pointed out a number of specific proposals to this end have been made in recent years[9] Public ownership of land for urban development is an old and well-established American practice that has fallen into some disuse in recent decades but which might well be revived.

One issue in implementing such a proposal is: What proportion of the potential development land should the public agency buy—all of it, most of it, or just some? The argument can be advanced that sound suburban development requires control over land use on all land, hence the public agency should buy all the developable land. Certainly it can be argued that a few intermingled tracts of private land might go a long way to thwart the general plans for an area. On the other hand, purchase of *all* development land would surely raise many difficult political as well as economic problems. The negotiations and problems involved in buying land from every holdout might become intolerably complex and time-consuming; public agencies as monopolies may become as barnacle-encrusted as private monopolies; and a public agency that was forced to meet all demands and requirements for buildable land might face unnecessary problems in dealing with developers. Considerations of this kind have led to the suggestion that the public body avoid a monopoly position but buy enough land to be the major factor in the suburban land market—something on the order of 60 percent of development land, for instance.[10] In the case of land purchase for the development of satellite communities or new towns, a stronger case can be made for 100 percent public ownership.[11]

Closely related to the question of how much land to buy is the question of how far in advance of the time of expected development to buy. Land likely to be developed soon is also likely to be the object of some developer's plans and not easily acquired. Its price is likely to be high. Land not likely to be developed for some years can be bought more readily. Owners may even welcome a good buyer. For this type of land, the price is likely to include some allowance for risk or uncertainty as to timing and ultimate form of development. Since a public body might be in a position to make its own forecasts come true, a price that is attractive to a seller might also be a good bargain for the purchaser. But purchase far in advance of development calls for a relatively large capital investment and postpones the political or social payoff of the program for several years.

Public purchase of development land for later resale or lease to private developers implies substantial fiscal problems for the unit of government buying the land. A public agency cannot expect to buy much land at the market price

[8]Bernard Weissbourd, "Satellite Communities: Proposal for a New Housing Program," *The Center Magazine* (Center for the Study of Democratic Institutions, Santa Barbara, California), January and March 1972.

[9]John W. Reps, "Public Land, Urban Development Policy, and the American Planning Tradition," in Marion Clawson (ed.), *Modernizing Urban Land Policy* (Baltimore, Md.: Johns Hopkins Press, 1973), pp. 15–48.

[10]Marion Clawson, *Suburban Land Conversion in the United States: An Economic and Governmental Process* (Baltimore, Md.: Johns Hopkins University Press for Resources for the Future, 1971), pp. 358–59.

[11]Weissbourd, "Satellite Communities," pp. 11–13.

that prevailed before it began its purchases; its act of land purchase pushes up the land price. Calculations based upon desired acreage of land and upon appraised land prices prevailing before the land purchase program starts will prove far too low. The public agency cannot operate as if the market were determined by others and that it only accepted the market prices, when in fact the scale of its operations would largely determine that market. If any public agency seeks to buy a substantial acreage of land on the assumption that the preprogram going prices will continue throughout the program, it is in for serious disillusionment—as federal, state, and local park executives learned long ago.

When the public agency that has bought land for development purposes begins to sell that land, or lease it on long-term leases, its disposal actions then push the market price for land downward. In the long run, a program of public land purchase and disposal may lower land prices on a net basis; that is, prices may average less for the long run than they would have if there had not been a public land purchase program. But the effect in the short run may be different.

One argument that has been used against public land purchase for development purposes is that public purchase takes land off the tax rolls, hence imposes a financial burden upon the local unit of government that loses the real estate tax that the private landowner would pay. But this argument ignores the fact that the public land purchase pushes up the price of the land not bought, as well as of that actually purchased. If the tax assessment procedures are efficient and alert, land will be reassessed promptly as land values rise; and tax revenues from the remaining private land will rise also. A fairly extensive program of public purchase of land need not lower tax receipts from private land at all. In many instances, the unit of government that buys the land will be able to obtain some receipts from various forms of temporary land use, pending permanent development for some purpose.

In any discussion of public agency purchase of land for development, one immediate question is the power of eminent domain. Must the agency have the legal power to take land from its owners by payment of a fair compensation but without the owner's consent? Political obstacles often preclude the large-scale use of this legal power when it is available to an agency. But it can be argued that a public agency that is to acquire land for suburban development must have the power of eminent domain, both to acquire critical tracts and to permit serious bargaining with private landowners. To some extent, real estate tax programs and extending (or withholding) public facilities can be made to substitute for eminent domain as a means of bringing private landowners to the bargaining table.

Another major question is: What public agency should buy the land, make plans for its development, dispose of it by lease or sale to private developers, and generally use the land program as the mechanism for the realization of plans for the development of the area? A surburban satellite city or a suburban county, unless relatively large in area and population, is likely to lack the governmental revenues or credit, the administrative expertise, and the political stability to undertake a program of large-scale acquisition of lands. In general, regular governmental agencies, at any governmental level, are likely to be poorly organized to carry out such programs. Special land agencies or development authorities may be more appropriate. Mixed public and private corporations may have many advantages, including the possibility that present landowners may wish to acquire an equity participation in the corporation in return for their land, because this land venture may improve their tax position. Such corporations might operate with fewer bureaucratic hindrances also. State and national corporations, as well as regional units, have been variously proposed as best able to carry out a land development program. For each of these proposals there are pros and cons that should be thoroughly analyzed.

If a major program of suburban land acquisition were undertaken by an established unit of local, regional, or state government or by a newly created instrument politically responsible to one of these levels of government, what are the prospects that the acquisition and disposal of lands would be managed with more skill and higher standards of performance than they are now? Are not the same individuals and groups likely to run the new agency and to continue to serve their personal interests? Obviously, neither a new program nor a new agency will serve as a magic wand, but they have something to offer. A program of land acquisition, planning, and disposal would provide new tools for suburban development—positive tools that would supplant the negative tools of zoning and enable dedicated and able people to do a vastly better job than has been done in the past. With a new agency and a new program that could, and probably would be forced to, operate in the public limelight, the kind of preferential treatment that often destroys the effectiveness of land use zoning would be immensely more difficult.

As one contemplates the history of urban land use change and urban growth over the past quarter century or so and the kinds of suburbs that have resulted from the processes involved, one is forced to conclude that nothing less than major public involvement in the suburban land market will make any real difference in the kinds of urban growth that will take place. Better planning, more carefully operated land use controls, reorganization of local government, and many other proposed reforms are helpful but not sufficient, and must be supplemented by a program of public land purchase to achieve a real change in urban growth and land use.[12] If we are dissatisifed with the kinds of suburbs that have been produced in these years and want to change them, we must be prepared to adopt adequate measures.

Another major substantive change in urban land use policy would be the restructuring of private speculation in suburban land. The sprawling nature of suburban growth is a direct outgrowth of private speculation in land, and the exclusionary character is an indirect result of the same speculation. The speculation itself grows directly out of three kinds of programs that reward and encourage speculation in land: (1) zoning, which restricts the supply of land to a greater or lesser degree; (2) a system of charges for public services that penalizes neither withholding land from development nor jumping to distant tracts for development; and (3) various forms of preferential tax treatment for land speculation. These three programs deserve more detailed treatment.

---

[12]Clawson, *Suburban Land Conversion*, pp. 355–63.

Zoning and other land use controls, when effective, are a restriction upon the supply of buildable land; one is tempted to say an artificial restriction, in the sense that they are manmade, not inherent in the physical land availability. But, it is also well to note that all markets for all commodities are artificial to a degree; they operate within a framework of laws and institutions made or governed by public action. Even where zoning is so weak that it can usually be overthrown by a determined assault it exerts a substantial effect upon land prices. It takes both money and time to appeal a zoning decision. If the demand for buildable suburban land is modestly inelastic (as we judge it is, in the absence of any rigorous analysis of the question), the price of suburban land moves upward more than proportionately to the decrease in supply resulting from zoning. A 10 percent reduction in the effective supply of land would push land prices per acre up more than 10 percent—perhaps a great deal more. If one intervenes to affect the supply of buildable land, he must either accept the price consequences or intervene adequately to offset or prevent them.

Two characteristics of the typical system of local government charges for public services also favor speculation in suburban land. First, usually no charge is made for availability of services not yet taken advantage of; and, second, charges do not reflect differences in location and the costs arising from them. When a sewer line is extended beyond a piece of idle suburban land, usually no charge is made for the availability of such service, until a new house on the lot is connected to the sewer. The owner of this land has all the advantages of sewer availability, with no costs on his part, until he chooses to use the service. The same relationship is true for roads, schools, water supply, and other services typically provided by the local government. When building does occur and such services are utilized, the charges do not reflect location and the costs associated therewith. That is, the sewer charges for houses in a subdivision a mile beyond the nearest housing are not likely to be any higher than they would be in the lots adjacent to the presently developed area. These two aspects of charges for local governmental services serve to encourage the discontiguous subdivision type of sprawl. Under a different system of charges, sprawl could be discouraged.

Favorable tax treatment for suburban land speculation arises in several ways. Numerous studies have shown that unimproved suburban land is typically treated with great tenderness by the assessors, even though most states have laws requiring that the idle land, like other real property, pay local real estate taxes based upon the full market value of the land. In cases where it is hard to distinguish the real market price from inflated claims, the assessor's caution may be defended, at least in part. Frequently, however, there is a lag in reassessments, and land with a rapidly rising price pays taxes based upon values of some years earlier. In many cases, outright favoritism is suspected but cannot well be proven. Often the landowners and the assessors have mutual interests. In some states favorable tax treatment has recently been extended to "farmland" in suburban areas, and tax farming has become profitable.

Land speculation gets favorable treatment in federal taxes also. Real estate taxes are deductible from income in calculation of federal income tax; so is interest paid on money borrowed to finance land speculating. Also, with some exceptions, gains from land sales may qualify for treatment as capital gains and be taxed at a distinctly lower rate than ordinary income.

Each of these preferential tax treatments for suburban land speculation could be removed by government action. Local real estate taxes could in fact as in theory be based upon the full market value of land; federal income tax laws could be changed so that real estate taxes and interest could not be claimed as a deduction if the land were relatively unimproved; and capital gains on unimproved land could be treated as ordinary income.

Adapting measures that make private speculation in suburban land a less profitable practice would result in much lower prices for building lots, as well as in much more closely settled suburban areas, which would make for certain economies in provision of public services. Under these conditions the building of lower-priced houses becomes possible. When building lots are expensive, a developer tends to build more expensive houses so that the land price is not an unreasonably high proportion of the total price of house and lot. The provision of lower-priced new suburban houses would open the suburbs to people of somewhat lower incomes. It would not solve the problems of the poorest people, but it might ease them somewhat, as the housing vacated by the near poor would become available to a lower-priced group. The filter-down process might thus be made to work faster and more to the advantage of the lowest-income persons.

A discussion of possible substantive changes in urban and suburban land use planning and control would not be complete without a brief reference to the situation in the older sections of inner cities and the possibilities for facilitating private action in urban renewal. Public urban renewal programs have not been as effective in supplying housing to those who need it as it was hoped they would be. The time between the purchase and clearing of a site and its rebuilding for any purpose has too often been unduly long—land has sometimes lain idle for years. In a large proportion of the cases, the price at which the public agency could sell the land was substantially less than what it had paid for the land and for site clearance; large public subsidies have been necessary, and these have gone to the owners of the decadent properties—hardly a group in financial need of public subsidy. When cleared sites were redeveloped, the resulting residences were usually far too costly for occupancy by the former residents of the area, and these people were pushed into other decaying residential areas. The whole process has been clouded by racial overtones; in many instances the displaced population was black, while the new residents were white. "Urban renewal has been black removal." And, finally, the scale of public urban renewal has been too small to cope with the large backlog of decayed urban centers and with the constant accumulation of slum areas as old housing becomes virtually uninhabitable. For all these reasons, some new approaches that would enlist private business as well as public efforts in urban renewal seem called for.

Various devices might be adopted to make private urban renewal more feasible economically.[13] The developer might be given the power of eminent domain, under carefully prescribed conditions so that land assembly would not continue to be as difficult and as time consuming as it is now. Taxation of real estate might be shifted more toward the land and less toward the improve-

[13]Marion Clawson, "Urban Renewal in 2000," *Journal of American Institute of Planners* (May 1968).

ments, thus removing one major obstacle to rebuilding. Provision might be made for accumulating a demolition fund for each building by an override on the mortgage payment or by special taxes; this would be effective for buildings that still have a fairly long life ahead of them. Owners of seriously deteriorated housing might be given subsidies for demolition purposes as a means of speeding up rebuilding. While these and other measures might facilitate rebuilding of slum residential areas, they would have to be supplemented by other public programs such as rent subsidies or income maintenance if they are to help produce new housing for low-income people.

IN CONCLUSION

Land use controls, particularly zoning, have operated—and are still operating—to exclude low-income and racial minorities from many urban areas, particularly from many suburbs. Current land use controls are under heavy new attack from several quarters: from the environmentalists, from professional associations of lawyers, from large business firms that operate in the residential-building business, from various proponents of open housing, from state governments, and from the federal government. The motives and the objectives of these groups differ somewhat, but they are united in their opposition to existing land use controls. The road to substantial revision of the land use planning, zoning, and control process is a rocky one; assaults on existing practice may be made on various grounds, yet may not be uniformly successful. Powerful economic and political groups have much to gain from present arrangements and will resist change. The several challenges to existing practice made thus far are more significant as straws in the wind that suggest how social attitudes are changing and may be effective than they are in actual results. The conclusion of several of the authors, and one with which we agree, is that change is coming, but its timing, its exact form, its origins, and its final results are unclear at this time.

We believe that social change is within the control of our whole society, that choices are possible, and that the course of events is not immutable. In this essay, we have outlined some of the possibilities for modifying land use controls for the next generation. Our analysis is neither all-inclusive nor greatly detailed. Others can doubtless think of different approaches or restructure our ideas in major ways. In any case, new approaches would have to be spelled out in detail before they could be applied, and experience in their use would almost surely reveal the need for refinement.

For urban and suburban land use, as for so many other facets of modern life, the future promises to be interesting, even exciting. It may not always be simple or easy, but surely ways can be found to modify urban land policy so that it will better meet future needs.

III

REGIONAL PLANNING AND ANALYSIS

INTRODUCTION

Regional planning traditions reach into United States history as far back as the canal-building projects of the 1820s. The beginnings of the modern era date from planned multipurpose river basin development, as exemplified by the Tennessee Valley Authority, which aimed at developing by-passed regions, and includes the more recent legislative and administrative history of the Area Redevelopment Act of 1961, the Appalachian Regional Commission, and the Public Works and Economic Development Act that set up commissions to channel aid to economically distressed areas.

Perloff's introduction to regional planning came via multipurpose river basin development, and particularly the TVA. As each subsequent landmark was legislated, he maintained a watchful and critical eye on the course of development.

Perloff's work on regional planning falls into two categories. The first is aimed at broadening and deepening understanding of past and current economic growth and the forces explaining it. The second consists of policy analysis of economic growth at state and regional level. This part includes essays of both types. The work can also be distinguished between essays dealing with the United States and those oriented to developing nations in the rest of the world. The first two items fall into the latter category.

As Perloff notes in his autobiography, one of his first assignments during his consultancy with the Government of Puerto Rico was to reorder the Commonwealth's expenditures accounts by function rather than by reporting agency. Revised in this way, the accounts better described the expenditures' purposes and provided a more realistic basis for assessing progress toward developmental goals. The accounts are analyzed in "Public Services and Social Priorities," a chapter excerpted from his seminal monograph on *Puerto Rico's Economic Future*. Published in 1950, the book has stood the test of time not only for its current relevance to Puerto Rico but for what it says and the way it speaks to those who today struggle with the formidable challenges of developing the Third World. The major dilemma then, as now, was how to cope with population growth that swallowed up real economic progress.

The sources of Puerto Rico's underdevelopment are identified as a natural resource base far too narrow to support a large and rapidly growing population; agricultural stagnation; a backward manufacturing sector hampered by poorly trained labor, a scarcity of venture capital, and restrictions on sales in the continental United States markets; dependency on the United States for developmental capital that fluctuates with the business cycle; and import dependency. The consequences of underdevelopment, on the other hand, are high levels of unemployment and underemployment, low wages, and slow (or no) growth in output, employment, and income; high inflation rates and large balance of payments deficits; and, finally, negligible savings with virtually no net additions to the capital stock.

The statistical analysis shows the gap between capital improvements required and the capital supply available for their financing. Various alternatives are explored for increasing and spending revenues. On the revenue expansion side, Perloff recommends stricter enforcement of income tax collections, reassessment of real property, taxing idle land and estates, removing the regressivity from consumption taxes, and strengthening the rum industry as a major producer for export. In regard to expenditures, priorities should be shifted from relief (the "poorhouse" approach) to expansion of the productive base particularly in light of the fact that welfare payments were increasing by many multiples of expenditures for education. Moreover, 87 percent of external assistance received between 1930 and 1946 was spent for emergency, "ameliorative" services, with only a small share of total federal aids and expenditures left to bolster the underlying structure. These figures show

> the pressing need for long-range development programs of sufficient scope to bring about a decided and lasting improvement in the production–population balance and indicates at the same time that it would be extremely difficult for the island to initiate sufficiently rapid progress out of its own resources.

In the early sixties, a bold program to integrate Latin America along lines similar to the European Economic Community took form in the efforts of the Alliance for Progress to consolidate socioeconomic development processes by emphasizing national planning, urging social reform (particularly in land and tax realms), and facilitating United States and international financial assistance. For four years, Perloff served as United States representative on the Alliance's Committee of Nine. Popularly called "The Nine Wise Men," the prestigious group was charged with reviewing applications for financial assistance from Latin American member nations. "National Planning and Multinational Planning Under the Alliance for Progress," one of a series of papers drawn from this experience, sets out the problems of planning at national and multinational levels as well as the directions hoped-for multinational economic integration would take. In it, Perloff and Raúl Saez promote "framework planning," a methodology consisting of analyses and projections of socioeconomic trends at the regional scale; of regional markets within and outside Latin America; of capital flows, terms of trade, balance of payments, and requirements for external financial aid; and of development potentials specified in terms of the regional complementarity of industries, trade, and infrastructure. Aside from its description of the proposed methodology, the essay is interesting primarily as an historical document, reflecting the hopes for Latin American progress under the Kennedy and Johnson administrations.

"Lagging Sectors and Regions of the American Economy" assesses the influence of demographic, occupational and regional factors on the spatial distribution of United States income. A full employment policy that ignores regional differences promotes underemployment and social polarization. The longterm path to equalizing regional incomes is found in policies that encourage locating new industry and the workforce at their most advantageous sites and, for the lagging regions, investing in education, providing government assistance to stimulate migration, developing underutilized natural resources, and creating regional study and planning agencies. Thus, on the choice between promoting place versus people prosperity, Perloff comes down squarely in favor of assistance to people and encouraging their mobility to areas offering good jobs.

In "Natural Resource Endowment and Regional Economic Growth," Perloff and his coauthor, Lowdon Wingo, relate the economic growth of United States regions with compositional change in their resource endowments. Three resource-oriented stages—an agricultural phase (1776–1840), a minerals dominant period (1840–1950), and the services era and "amenity resources" period (since 1950)—capture the swings of United States development. Changes in national demand, production technology, and economic organization, it is demonstrated, continuously redefine a region's resource endowment. Spatial economic growth depends on an area's comparative advantage in exporting resource products and its access to national markets. The Mountain States' minerals endowments, the Northwest's timber, the Southwest's natural gas reserves, and Florida's amenities, furnish examples. Cumulative growth, however, occurs only in those regions where production in high demand nationally is characterized by locationally associated forward and backward linkages and by large intraregional multipliers. Low-grade agricultural production and most minerals production do poorly on this count, but cumulative growth characterizes the Great Lakes region, for example, with its excellent accesses to prime national markets.

An index of regional specialization, calculated by using a three-sector classification of economic activity in eight multistate regions, identifies a spatial pattern of industrial nucleation dichotomized between heartland and hinterland. The industrial heartland (consisting of New England plus the Middle Atlantic and Great Lakes regions) specializes in fabrication, is situated at the focal point of national markets, and serves as the "industrial seedbed of the economy." Radiating from the heartland, regions comprising the resource-exploiting hinterland are dominated by processing industries that, by producing for intermediate demand, serve the heartland.

With the blossoming of urban and regional research, the need grew for more detailed and better organized data to more accurately measure progress, identify problems, and inform policy. Perloff realized this necessity early in his career. As he insists in his revealing autobiography, the assembly of data to describe the development of a nation, region, city, or program is a first and necessary condition for rigorous analysis. Perloff notes his early fascination with the empirical information ordered into flow-of-funds accounts that uncovered causes of the 1937 recession, and the data that helped compensate for the impending deficits in the social security system, and the necessity for reordering accounts by function to determine whether social programs were realistically funded. Indeed, good information was fundamental for successfully transforming knowledge into action. As one response to the challenge, Perloff proposes developing and estimating regional accounts and preparing from them periodic state of the region (or city) reports, both with antecedents at the national level. "Relative Regional Economic Growth: An Approach to Regional Accounts," one of several essays contributing to this direction in research, proposes a system of subnational accounting for regions and metropolitan areas, and defines its contents and potential uses. The article presents considerable detail on the manner of organizing the accounts for maximum effectiveness and identifies the criteria that the data should meet.

"Key Features of Regional Planning," by defining what planning is about, comes as close as any of the essays in the Perloff corpus to developing planning theory. Planning process, says Perloff, has two principal foci. The political aspect, as it is here termed, consists of setting goals, choosing among alternatives, and evaluating results; the technical aspect involves information analysis, regional designation, planning and programming, and, finally, operations.

Perloff's contributions to regional planning were substantial. But in the federal system of the United States, the regional approach to economic development found little resonance. The United States was primarily a national market. Even though a certain redistribution of resources towards disadvantaged regions was, from time to time, attempted, there was no accumulation of planning experience. Regional planning agencies, the TVA excepted, had typically very few powers to realize their ambitions, and the American system of "checks and balances" made coordinative planning on a regional scale virtually impossible.

The matter was quite different in developing countries, where some form of national planning is generally attempted. Where there is national planning (the governmental powers at local and regional levels being relatively weak), a spatial framework for investment planning is an absolute necessity. (In most Third World countries, public capital expenditures account for 60 percent or more of all investments.) Hence the very favorable reaction to Perloff's writings on Puerto Rico.

It must surely be counted as one of the supreme ironies of planning that major contributions to theory—in this instance to the theory of regional planning—would come from a country that did not practice it. Does theory need practice? One would think so, but the extant literature suggests otherwise.

9

Puerto Rico's Economic Future

Public Services and Social Priorities

The concentration on the development of productive resources and industries through collective action is a relatively recent phenomenon in Puerto Rico and is a reflection of the growing awareness in the island of the nature of the basic social and economic problems, coupled with the growth of democratic institutions and social and political responsibility.

PURPOSES OF PUBLIC EXPENDITURES

An indication of the changes that have taken place in the scope and direction of public action within recent decades is furnished by a breakdown of insular government expenditures. Between 1972 and 1976, there was substantial expansion of annual outlays devoted to resource development and economic improvement programs: from $4.7 billion annually to $35 billion.[1] Much of the latter has taken the form of contributions from the general fund to the public enterprises established specifically for developmental purposes. These enterprises have been called "Puerto Rico's Bootstraps," as a reflection of their central role in the island's efforts at self-improvement.[2]

Nor have public services been neglected. In fact, during the same twenty years, there was a fivefold increase in expenditures for administration and public services, which is substantial even if account is taken of the price increases during that period. Total governmental outlays for all purposes were $105 million in fiscal year 1945–46 as compared with only $19 million in 1927–28, or an increase of some 560 percent.

---

[1]Editors' Note: These and many of the subsequent statistics are drawn from tables excised from this version but appearing in the original document, Harvey S. Perloff, *Puerto Rico's Economic Future* (Chicago: University of Chicago Press, 1950), pp. 378–394.
[2]See Grace and Rexford G. Tugwell, "Puerto Rico's Bootstraps," *Harper's Magazine*, February 1947, pp. 160–169.

OUTLAYS MEASURED IN TERMS OF NEEDS

In spite of the very large expansion in public services within the past few years, they are still far short of what is needed even on a minimum basis. The Puerto Rico Planning, Urbanizing, and Zoning Board, in the financial program submitted in March 1947, presented an estimate of "how far the allocation already made, and those included in [the Financial Program], go toward the realization of the reasonable goals that have been set up for several public services.[3]

> For Health and Welfare, it is believed that, with the Insular Funds allocated and the Federal funds anticipated, well over half of the desirable program should be achieved. . . .
>
> In the field of Education, the present Program would provide for about half of the Island's minimum needs.
>
> Provision for the various types of Protective and Penal buildings and institutions probably exceeds 50 percent of the needs. . . .
>
> All in all, it would not be far wide of the mark to say that the appropriations already made and those now contemplated may be expected to provide about *half of what is needed to achieve minimum standards of public service for Puerto Rico*, with notable exceptions in the case of highways, where a longer term of years will be required, and of housing, where the alternative solutions and their financing are still far from clear.[4]

When actual and anticipated appropriations are weighed in the scale of minimum *capital* needs, including those essential to the development of the basic economic resources, the gap is at least equally great. The Puerto Rico Planning Board estimates that $675 million is required to fund necessary capital improvement programs. Of this, only $189 million had been authorized as of December 31, 1948, and an estimated $102 million would be available for the proposed six-year program, 1949–50 to 1954–55. This gap arises, of course, from the fact that financial resources available for public purposes are quite limited. Thus, even assuming that the proposed capital-improvement program can be carried out, there will be a gap of some $378 million in terms of the minimum existing capital needs calculated on a conservative basis.

There is a serious question as to just how much can be accomplished through a halfway provision of essential services and improvement programs. John Stuart Mill once suggested: "When the object is to raise the permanent condition of a people, small means do not merely produce small effects, they produce no effects at all." Possibly a halfway financing of crucial services should not be considered in the category of "small means," but certainly there is the very serious danger that when needs constantly overrun limited accomplishments, many of the accomplishments will be largely nullified. This is especially the case when the combined and cumulative effects of the improvement programs are not sufficient to dampen the rate of population growth, that is, when

---

[3]Puerto Rico Planning, Urbanizing, and Zoning Board, *Fourth Six-Year Financial Program,* submitted March, 1947, pp. xiii, xv.
[4]*Ibid.*, pp. xiv–xv.

the expansion of the productive base is not so great as the expansion of population.

GOVERNMENTAL RECEIPTS—PAST AND FUTURE

There is the additional danger that governmental revenues will not be adequate to finance basic services and improvement programs on even a 50 percent basis. The increased provision of public services and the undertaking of developmental programs in recent years have been possible, in very large measure, because of the fortuitous circumstances which resulted in large insular government receipts from the rum tax. A full appreciation of the extent to which this quite accidental development was the basis of the expansion of recent years is essential to any evaluation of the economic future of Puerto Rico.

Rum tax receipts enabled the insular government to enjoy substantial current budgetary surpluses, and these surpluses provided the basis for the extensive program of improvement both in the field of economic development and in the expansion of essential public services.

The increase in insular revenues from sources other than the rum tax was due in very large part to the increase in the island's net income. Receipts from the insular income tax, for example, rose from $2.2 million in 1939–40 to $24.8 million in 1945–46 and to $31 million in 1947–48. The increase in net income, in turn, was based to a very great extent on the expansion of federal activities in Puerto Rico. Income derived from such activities constituted a large proportion of the total insular income, rising from 9 percent of the total in 1939–40 to a peak of 25 percent in 1943–44 and declining to 19 percent in 1945–46.

The diminishing rate of federal outlays (together with the indication that there may be a further sharp drop in federal expenditures as veterans' benefit payments decline) and the diminishing returns from the rum tax suggest the possibility that the Puerto Rican government may have serious difficulty in maintaining public services and capital outlays on even the inadequate current basis of 50 percent of minimum need. A sharp retrenchment in the provision of essential services and in the effectuation of the developmental programs could be expected to have undesirable effects on the welfare of the island.

Under the circumstances in which Puerto Rico finds itself, the resources which can be made available to finance a collective attack on the basic social and economic problems of the island, and the effectiveness with which these resources are employed, becomes a matter of the first importance. As a general principle, these can be said to depend essentially on (1) the tax effort involved, or, in essence, the proportion of the insular income devoted to collective purposes, (2) the degree to which a system of social priorities (that is, a strict adherence to the principle of "doing first things first") is applied in the expenditure of public moneys and in the weight given to the various public programs, and (3) the amount of external assistance which is forthcoming.

TAX EFFORT

There is no objective measure for testing the adequacy of an area's tax effort. Much depends on the nature of the economy and the relative scope for public and private activities as they have developed over time. But in very large measure it is also a question of the decisions made by the people (acting through their representatives in the government) as to how much they are willing to give up of their individual incomes to devote to public purposes.

In this connection, it must be recognized, however, that individual and family needs are felt more directly than are social needs and that a tax payment always involves a recognizable sacrifice, while collective accomplishments tend to be diffused in their effect and are not readily identifiable. Yet, it seems clear that many of the pressing social and economic problems of Puerto Rico require concerted long-range collective action if lasting solutions are to be found. This is especially the case since the important function of new capital formation (which, on the mainland, is assumed in largest part by private enterprise) requires a large degree of public financing in Puerto Rico. Very little economic improvement can be hoped for in the island unless new industries are developed and existing industries expanded and unless agriculture is diversified and improved farming methods are introduced. It is, therefore, a matter of the greatest importance that a widespread and increasing appreciation of the fiscal, as well as economic, problems of the island be developed among the people of Puerto Rico so that the foundation may be laid for a continuing collective effort (including a tax effort) commensurate in scope with the problems involved.

There is no escaping the fact that real and lasting gains can be made only if the people of Puerto Rico are willing to make present sacrifices for the sake of future improvements. For the majority of people at the lower-income levels any sacrifice of current income seems completely out of the question, since their incomes are inadequate even for the purchase of the basic necessities. As a consequence, the tax burden must inevitably fall on the relatively small percentage of the population whose incomes are above the levels necessary to maintain an acceptable standard of living.[5]

Given the fact that, even under the most favorable circumstances, only relatively limited internal resources can be devoted to public purposes, it is extremely important that the greatest pains be taken to develop a revenue system which is effective and economically sound.

The most immediate needs would seem to be for:

1. The strict enforcement of the income-tax law. All indications point to the fact that at the present time the rate of income-tax avoidance and evasion is extremely high. It may well be that an additional 20 or 25 percent of income-tax revenues at current income levels can be collected through strict enforcement and the plugging of existing loopholes.

2. The complete reassessment of real property in the island. Such property is, at the present time, inadequately and unequally assessed, and there is a very strong likelihood that this involves a sizable loss of revenue to the government. Provision should be made for the taxation of capital gains involved in property

---

[5]At the same time, it must be recognized that all sectors of the population can contribute to the collective effort, through hard work and the learning of new skills wherever possible, as well as in the recognition of the social responsibility involved in marriage and childbearing.

sale, beyond the value added through capital improvements. There is every reason why socially created values should be taxed and devoted to public purposes rather than result in private speculative gains. While very high taxes on income and profits can cause a flight of capital, it must be recognized that taxes on land do not involve this risk, since land is an asset which cannot be removed. At the same time, it is important that taxes do not discourage capital improvements on land.

3. The taxing of idle land.

4. The directing of efforts to strengthen the rum industry and to foster the sale of its products in the mainland market. The Planning Board pointed out in its Fourth Six-Year Financial Program:

> The greater part of the proposed social and economic program depends upon a prosperous and stable rum industry in Puerto Rico. For this reason, all the proposals suggested by the liquor industry as measures that may lead toward the improvement of the competitive position of the industry in the American market and the world rum market should be carefully studied by the lawmakers. Prompt and effective action should be taken on those measures that are finally judged to be of benefit in stimulating this important part of our economy (p. iii).

5. A revision of the inheritance- and gift-tax law (together with an efficient administration of the law) to make the transfer of property at death a substantial source of revenue to the government.

6. A revision of excise taxes and excise tax rates, with a clear-cut distinction between necessities and goods used in production, on the one side, and luxury items, on the other. This would call for a high tax on expensive wines and jewelry and no tax at all on basic necessities, a high tax on expensive cigars but a low one on cheap cigars, a high tax on expensive automobiles but a low tax on trucks. Most of the present excises stand in need of consolidation and simplification.

7. The elimination of all trust funds in insular accounts, except those which involve an insurance, pension, debt-payment, or business-reserve feature. It should be recognized that the establishment and maintenance of a large number of trust funds for a variety of special purposes is chiefly a reflection of political immaturity and irresponsibility. Neither of these is characteristic of present-day Puerto Rico. The maintenance of a great variety of trust funds makes it extremely difficult, if not impossible, for the people and their representatives in the government to know the purposes for which public funds are being spent. A logical system of social priorities can be established and effectuated only if the total picture can be seen and all expenditures periodically reviewed. This cannot be done when a sizable share of the public moneys is set aside in the hidden corners of trust funds.

SOCIAL PRIORITIES

When we consider the many pressing social and economic needs of the island as against the extremely limited resources availble to meet these needs, it is of the utmost importance that attention be focused on the question of priorities, that is, the weight to be given the various public programs.

Where poverty, disease, crowding, and malnutrition are as widespread as they are in Puerto Rico, there is a strong humanitarian urge to attempt to ameliorate the suffering through the use of the available public resources. But, unfortunately, the direct relief of distress rarely makes any contribution to the solution of the underlying problems which are the cause of the distress in the first instance. And the more resources which are devoted to this purpose, the fewer are available for the attack on the basic problems.

Certainly it is far better to employ public funds in the expansion of the productive base and in the provision of new job opportunities than to use the funds for relief handouts. Similarly, it makes better sense to attack the problem of malnutrition through a basic reform in landholding and land use, together with improvements in farm methods and in marketing, than to attempt to distribute small quantities of relief food.

Undoubtedly, the entire insular budget could be employed in meeting the most immediate welfare, nutrition, and housing needs alone. But this would be to accept the "poorhouse" approach to the island's problems. The people of Puerto Rico have, in fact, rejected this approach and have embarked on a series of long-range economic improvement programs to which they have devoted a sizable proportion of the available public funds.

Whether these programs have received the relative share of the public effort which they deserve may, however, be questioned. Between 1941 and 1947, when public revenues were at peak levels, some $74.5 million was allotted as contributions to the public enterprises *directly* concerned with resource development and economic improvement programs, or an annual average of $10.6 million. This compares with total expenditures of $75.4 million in 1944–45 and $104.9 million in 1945–46 and with public welfare expenditures alone of over $6 million in the former year and over $7 million in the latter.

An examination of public service expenditures within the past years similarly raises the question of the logic of the social priorities reflected in these expenditures. If the public service outlays of 1945–46 are compared with those of 1927–28, the increases involved are strikingly disproportionate. Thus, for example, while total expenditures increased by 560 percent, welfare expenditures increased by 2,500 percent, those in housing by 2,300 percent, on nutrition by 2,820 percent, and on health by 617 percent; but the increase in educational expenditures was only 342 percent. While it may well be that certain of the services were relatively neglected in 1927–28 and that this former neglect is the main cause of the disproportionate increases, nevertheless, such a comparison suggests the need for a careful evaluation of the present emphasis given to the various services, and especially the ameliorative services.

Comparisons of expenditures for various purposes during the fiscal year 1945–46 are also worth noting. Thus, for example, the amount spent for food distribution for relief purposes was roughly equal to the total spent for soil conservation, improving land use, and the protection of watersheds. The amount spent on public assistance payments was as large as that spent for high-school and university education and was double the total spent on vocational education. The sum spent on hospitals and health institutions was three times as great as that spent on disease prevention and health regulation and 150 percent as large as the expenditures for sanitation and water supply. Many similar comparisons could be made to reveal the relative emphasis on ameliorative services.

The Planning Board, in the report referred to above, has noted (p. xiii) that "the government of Puerto Rico, like most governments, is under constant pressure to increase its current operating expenditures" and that various factors, including "the temptation to vote special appropriations, whether or not they are part of a well-considered program, so long as there are surpluses in view," have tended "to create an increase in the Insular Government's current expenditure outlays which might prove disastrous." There are indications that the current operating budget is expanding to the point "where it alone will soon exceed anticipated income, leaving nothing whatever for additional capital improvements either for needed new facilities or further economic development." The Planning Board has pointed out, further, that "if any continuing program is to be pursued, ways must be found to restrain current expenditures, to increase income, or both, so that there may remain some working margin available for essential improvement projects."

The discouraging prospects have seriously affected the board's plans for the long-range developmental projects so that in the six-year financial program "the new funds for capital improvements and contributions to public enterprises diminish rapidly as the Fourth Financial Program proceeds, with little more than small amounts in the final year 1952–53."

It should be pointed out, however, that in view of the primary importance of the developmental programs, it does not seem appropriate to consider their financing as subject to "some working margin" remaining after all other outlays have been provided for. There seems to have developed an unfortunate tendency in Puerto Rico to associate the economic improvement programs with the war-created budgetary surpluses and to regard their support as subject to the continuance of high-level budgetary receipts. But it might well be asked whether such programs should not receive a substantial share of the available public revenues even if the total receipts fall far below their wartime peak, in other words, whether a logical system of social priorities would not dictate the continued support of extensive agricultural and industrial development and population-control programs, even at the expense of the ameliorative services.

EXTERNAL ASSISTANCE

Experience has shown that developmental measures can be expected to bring about substantial economic progress *only if they are carried out in a concentrated and effective manner*. This means that they must be adequately financed and expertly administered. It is this element which underlines the importance of external assistance, for while a great deal could undoubtedly be accomplished internally through intensive tax efforts and the evolution of an effective system of social priorities, a balancing of the relatively limited resources which can be made available as against the enormity of the task involved cannot help casting doubt on the probability of initiating sufficiently rapid economic progress out of the island's own resources.

The question of external assistance does not introduce an entirely new element into the picture. As has been the case with all the other areas within the political and economic sphere of the United States, Puerto Rico has received federal assistance in various forms throughout the period that it has been under American sovereignty.

In the seventeen years between 1930 and 1946 direct federal grants and expenditures in the island (excluding all military, veterans', and other defense and war outlays)[6] have added up to a total in the vicinity of $403 million or an average for the period of about $23 million a year. Of this federal contribution, about 83 percent was in the category of relief, other "emergency" outlays, and subsidies, and only 17 percent was of a *regular* service or developmental character. In other words, the federal contributions to Puerto Rico have been essentially in the nature of amelioration rather than directed at basic improvements in the Puerto Rican resources and in the island's economy.

The question of federal grants-in-aid and expenditures in Puerto Rico involves many complex political problems, examination of which must be considered as beyond the scope of this study. At the same time, it seems pertinent to consider the implications of the facts which have been highlighted thus far, namely:

• That the federal government has made contributions to Puerto Rico, in the form of grants and expenditures, throughout the period that the island has been under United States sovereignty and that these contributions have averaged some $24 million a year during (roughly) the last two decades.

• That these contributions have, with very few exceptions, arisen from general provisions (covering Puerto Rico) within federal statutes enacted for specific national purposes and geared to specific mainland conditions. The result has been that the overwhelming majority of the contributions has been of an "emergency" ameliorative character and that only a small share of the federal aids and expenditures has directly served to improve the underlying socioeconomic structure of the island.

• That, although the federal contributions have been of great assistance to the Puerto Rican people and have raised the insular income beyond what it would have been without such contributions, there seems little doubt that outlays of the same magnitude could have accomplished a great deal more if they had been geared specifically to Puerto Rican conditions and problems and if they

---

[6]Military expenditures cannot be considered in the category of federal "contributions" to Puerto Rico. As the U.S. Tariff Commission pointed out in its report of May, 1943 ("Puerto Rico's Economy with Special Reference to United States–Puerto Rican Trade"): "If Puerto Rico had not been under the United States flag the United States might have maintained additional military facilities elsewhere and possibly at greater cost than those in Puerto Rico. The direct military costs are not included in the table, but it is not clear that some of the expenditures included, such as those for harbor improvement, . . . and some other purposes, should not be regarded, partly at least, as for the maintenance of United States defenses."

had been spent according to a long-range plan and according to a logical system of social priorities.

• That an analysis of Puerto Rico's economy and basic problems indicates a pressing need for long-range developmental programs of sufficient scope to bring about a decided and lasting improvement in the production–population balance and indicates, at the same time, that it would be extremely difficult for the island to initiate sufficiently rapid progress out of its own resources. Puerto Rico is not unique in this respect. Studies throughout the world have stressed the fact that external assistance is almost invariably necessary to permit an overpopulated, economically underdeveloped area to break out of a vicious circle of poverty and rapid population growth, since such assistance is needed to make possible a change in the tempo of economic improvements.

As long as United States–Puerto Rican relations are such as to involve federal grants and expenditures in the island and as long as the island's most pressing need is for the broadening and strengthening of the productive (income-earning) base of its economy, serious thought might be given to the possibility of redirecting federal assistance so that it may make the *maximum* contribution to the island's welfare.[7]

In contrast to many other areas of the world which have been subject to frequent political upheavals and whose economic programs have largely been a compound of wishful thinking and restrictive measures, the Puerto Rican people have displayed a noteworthy political maturity as characterized by their ability to evolve an essentially sound and balanced development program in the face of inordinately difficult conditions. There is every reason to believe that, with a certain amount of external assistance which would permit an increased tempo of development at the crucial points, coupled with a persistent and expert administration of the programs which have been initiated, Puerto Rico can make real and lasting improvements in its social and economic structure.

---

[7]A study by the national government of federal grants and expenditures in Puerto Rico in terms of the island's specific needs seems called for. At the same time, it seems clear that the question of a reorientation of federal assistance can be examined effectively only in the light of an *over-all,* long-range program of economic improvement for the island prepared by the insular government, involving an estimate of costs and suggesting a system of priorities. Questions of priorities and costs are already receiving detailed attention, especially in the financial programs of the Insular Planning Board, so that an over-all long-range improvement program of this type would require only an extension in terms of measuring costs as against internal resources and defining the areas in which external assistance is most urgently needed.

10

National Planning and Multinational Planning under the Alliance for Progress

The possibilities of achieving high level self-sustained economic growth by the less developed countries of the world has taken on a new dimension in the past generation with the emergence of three powerful forces. First, widespread desire by the people of these countries to rapidly raise their standards of living and a belief that this is a feasible goal. Second, the provision of substantial financial and technical assistance by the more developed nations. Third, the forging of regional institutions to advance economic growth.

These elements have come powerfully to the forefront in the Western Hemisphere and have been given form and substance through the cooperative system called the Alliance for Progress—La Alianza para el Progreso. While the Alliance is quite young, having been proposed in March, 1961, and organized in August of that year, it provides certain general features which should be of interest to persons concerned with the problems of development.

Although the Alliance as a formal arrangement is recent, the ideas and forces behind it have been developing over many years. Thus, over the past few decades the countries of Latin America have increasingly devoted themselves to the goal of economic development. The joining of forces for the achievement of common goals through the inter-American regional system is an idea of long standing—which was given a new form in the Alliance. The emphasis on internal structural reforms to ensure that all the people of a nation benefit equitably from economic improvement—a key feature of the Alliance—is a natural outgrowth of the far-reaching ideas of reform stemming from the various popular movements in Latin America.

Formal planning as a valuable tool for designing and implementing an effective, consistent development effort has increasingly come to be accepted as a result of successful experience with planning in the Western Hemisphere, as well as in other parts of the world. Western Hemisphere scholars, many of them associated with the United Nations Economic Commission for Latin America, as

---

This chapter was written in collaboration with Raúl Saez.

well as other scholars and practitioners, had over a long period of time devoted themselves to strengthening planning and programming techniques. The know-how and technical skills thus developed could be drawn on by the Alliance program.

Far-seeing individuals from universities, government and business, over the years saw the need and developed ideas for commodity stabilization and for regional economic integration, and movements to foster both of these ideas preceded the establishment of the Alliance program.

In addition, the experience with the Marshall Plan in Europe, with a full awareness of the great differences involved, provided a valuable background for the design of an assistance program in Latin America. Among the pertinent aspects of the European experience was the use of country programs as a basis for external financial assistance, the review of country programs by an international body, and the general multilateral approach to assistance programs. The idea of what came to be known as "confrontation" within the framework of the Organization for European Economic Cooperation not only helped strengthen the forces of regional cooperation, but provided a truly suggestive plan of action that could be drawn upon.

So the key elements for a far-reaching cooperative hemispheric effort had been maturing over the years. It was evident, finally, that for implementing such an effort an adequate base of financial support for Latin American development programs would be required and that all potential sources of external financing would have to be tapped.

Certain present features of the Alliance for Progress program, and even more, its potentialities in the future are, we believe, highly suggestive, and of direct significance for development efforts in every part of the world.

THE STRATEGY OF THE ALLIANCE

The Alliance for Progress seeks to accelerate the economic and social development of the participating countries in Latin America. The Charter of Punta del Este,[1] looking toward the achievement, within a reasonable time, of self-sustaining development, has set a goal of per capita income increases in each nation of not less than 2.5 percent annually. With population increasing on the average at an annual rate of some 2.6 percent, the minimum per capita goal requires an average rate of increase in national income of at least 5.1 percent per year. Relatively few Latin American countries have maintained such a level of growth over the past decade.[2] At the time of the Charter, it was estimated that the achievement of these growth rates would require over the decade about $100 billion in capital funds, of which at least $20 billion would have to come from sources outside Latin America. These figures are on the low side and now it

---

[1]Named after the small resort outside Montevideo (Uruguay) where the Alliance was organized.
[2]During the period 1950–1961 the annual average increase in the gross national income for Latin America was 4.3 percent.

seems likely that larger sums will have to be made available to achieve the goals set.

Country planning has been given a large role in the Alliance program. Each nation is to formulate plans to provide (a) a firm direction to its development effort by establishing goals, priorities, and a general development strategy, (b) guidelines for carrying out needed structural and social changes, (c) a general framework within which to develop specific sector programs and projects (as well as the priority programs and projects), and (d) a rational basis for estimating required internal and external financing (assuming a maximum effort to mobilize internal resources). Planning has been emphasized because of the contribution it can make to a more effective and disciplined channeling of resources into developmental purposes. Given the ambitious growth goals on the one side and the severely limited internal resources on the other, there is need to ensure that an adequate volume of both public and private savings are generated and are invested in an optimum fashion in the development of the natural, human, capital, and organizational resources. The programming of needed investments of specified categories encourages appropriate production scale and production linkage, while the projection of the flow of funds provides a strong weapon in the achievement of monetary stability. Country plans can also help highlight conflicts with plans of other nations and thus provide a basic framework for working out continentwide policies geared to common objectives.

A highly significant feature of the Alliance is the emphasis placed on basic social reforms, particularly land and tax reforms. All the signatory nations of the Charter of Punta del Este have agreed to carry out "programs of comprehensive agrarian reform leading to the effective transformation, where required, of unjust structures and systems of land tenure and use . . ." Similarly, all the nations have agreed to promote tax reform where necessary both to provide for the effective mobilization of internal resources and to bring about a more equitable distribution of income. Since such, among other reforms, are deemed essential to lay a foundation for sustained economic and social advance within the countries of Latin America, their implementation is considered a key requirement for the extension of long-term plan-related financial assistance under the Alliance. The dual function of structural reforms—the increase in productivity and the mobilization of resources on the one side and the satisfaction of equity requirements on the other—is critical to rapid development under current conditions in democratic countries. The optimum use of natural resources (and particularly the land) and the tapping of the great potential energies of the human resources (which requires widespread involvement in development by the people of a nation) are at the very foundations of economic advance. People who have relatively little cannot be expected to work hard and accept the discipline of a development effort, unless they feel that they are receiving and will continue to receive a fair share of the total returns.

The reforms are matters of extreme complexity, compounded by the great variations in national situations and institutions. There are important groups within each of the Latin American countries who are strongly opposed to social reforms and such groups can be expected to resist the implementation of such reforms with all means available to them. At the same time, the formal acceptance of the concept of reforms by all the participating countries, plus the pressures involved in the tying of reforms to long-term financial assistance, provide a foundation for meaningful progress along these lines.

A central feature of the Alliance is the provision of long-term United States and international financial assistance based on country plans comprising all the above-mentioned elements. The idea of foreign assistance being provided to finance a development plan rather than isolated projects was first utilized in the case of India's Third Five-Year Plan. This approach is currently in the process of being adapted to the specific factors involved in the Latin American situation.

EVALUATION OF COUNTRY PLANS AND THE "COMMITTEE OF NINE"

The evaluation of national development programs has been given a pivotal role in the execution of the development strategy under the Alliance. The evaluation mechanism has been established for three interrelated purposes. First, it provides the nations submitting plans with expert judgment on the adequacy of the policies and methods proposed for achieving the national development goals and targets which the country has set. Second, this serves as a means of advising the signatories of the Charter of Punta del Este on matters related to their obligations under the Charter. The evaluation covers the extent of consistency with the Charter. Third, and as a direct counterpart of the other two, it serves as a technique for helping to bring national plans up to a qualitative level where the possibilities of obtaining an adequate amount of public and private external financial assistance is maximized.

Any Latin American government, if it so wishes, may present its plan for evaluation of an ad-hoc committee composed of three or less members from a panel of nine experts[3] together with an equal number of experts not on the panel.[4] The ad-hoc committee studies the development program, exchanges opinions with the government and, with the consent of the government, reports its conclusions to other governments and institutions that may be willing to extend external financial and technical assistance.

The ad-hoc committee, in examining a national plan, is concerned with a number of key elements. Thus, it will test the realism and consistency of the goals and targets set, in terms of the rate at which programs can be implemented, the distribution between economic and social projects, the provision of adequate overhead facilities to make the production targets feasible, and the

---

[3]The Inter-American Economic and Social Council of the Organization of American States has selected a panel of experts, the so-called "Committee of Nine", organized in such a way as to enjoy "complete autonomy in the performance of their duties." Seven of the nine members are Latin Americans.

[4]Thus far, there has emerged a certain pattern in the composition of the ad-hoc committee. The membership has been predominantly Latin American; in each case there have been four members from Latin America, one from the United States, and one from Europe or elsewhere outside the Western Hemisphere.

like. It will evaluate the plan, as well as the means of implementation, in terms of the specific criteria set forth in the Charter of Punta del Este. This includes a review of the social investments and structural reforms. The committee will analyze in great detail the provisions made in the plan concerning the achievement of an equilibrium in the balance of payments, as well as the provisions made for the mobilization of internal resources. On the basis of such an analysis, the requirements for external financing can be evaluated. In addition, the committee studies carefully the major policy proposals—with regard to such matters as prices, wages, imports, subsidies, and the like—to decide whether these are consistent with the development objectives set forth in the country's development plan.

The ad-hoc committee, of course, has at its disposal the reports of national, foreign, and international agencies on various aspects of the economy under study and may commission special reports in areas where it feels they are required.

The ad hoc committee is, among other things, a technique of confrontation which gives the country under study the opportunity to discuss recommendations informally and make changes in its plan before it is presented for financing. The significant element here is the support provided by an independent international group, without any special-interest motive, to a government to adopt and carry out sound economic and social policies. Aside from the general prestige of the committee, the backing of the U.S. Government and international financial agencies gives substantial weight to the "confrontation" of the committee.

The committee's findings are presented in a report addressed to the nation which has submitted the plan for evaluation and, with its approval, to financial institutions and governments that may be prepared to extend external financial and technial assistance in connection with the execution of the nation's development program.

While the experience with this mechanism is quite limited—as of September, 1962, it had been applied to only three country development plans—it seems to be fulfilling its central purposes. In each of these cases, the recommendations of the ad-hoc committee have provided a stimulus for the introduction of important policy changes and new measures by the governments and have provided terms of reference for international financial arrangements.

This is not to suggest that an ideal mechanism has been invented. There are many problems yet to be overcome before there can be assurance that this is a truly viable mechanism, working as an integral part of a well-functioning scheme. Thus, for example, since the scheme depends on the ability of the Latin American countries to chart and carry out important economic and social changes, the fact that the Alliance concepts are not yet generally understood by the public means that the planning cannot yet be deeply rooted. In addition, given the importance of a high quality of national planning and execution of plans, there are problems stemming from the inexperience of the planning agencies, the lack of adequate planning personnel, the inadequacy of statistics and economic information, and the inadequacies of institutional arrangements for plan execution. Also, it is evident that there are serious problems of scale since the key objectives of regional integration and commodity stabilization cannot be achieved until a large share of all the Latin American countries have come into the scheme and taken the necessary steps to promote regionwide progress. Finally, there is the problem of adequate international financing of national investment programs, which is something of a chicken-and-egg proposition, since assurance of such financing is needed in many cases to generate truly significant self-help efforts, while such efforts are themselves the best assurance of adequate international financing.

However, with improvements that can be anticipated over time on the basis of experience, and a strong start in a few of the countries that are ready to move ahead, the scheme described above may well turn out to be one of the most important of the levers in Latin America's economic and social development.

MULTINATIONAL PLANNING

The evaluation of national programs on the basis of formally established criteria is in effect a beginning of multinational planning. Programs and policies within national plans are, as indicated above, tested by the evaluating committees for consistency with what other Latin American countries are doing, or propose to do, and potential conflicts are brought to the forefront. Thus, for example, a country seeking to diversify its exports might be proposing greatly to increase the production of a crop, which in its own country in the past has been minor, but which is the chief earner of foreign exchange in another Latin American country and already tending toward world oversupply—for example, coffee or sugar. In such a case, the ad-hoc committee could be expected to highlight this fact and discuss with the government the possibility of introducing alternative crops or livestock. Potentialities of greatly increasing trade, particularly among nearby neighbors—where transportation bottlenecks can be overcome—will be carefully reviewed. And, of course, the potential role of the nation's economy in the evolving regional common market would be a matter of special interest. Clearly, the value of such a review increases progressively as more countries prepare their plans and submit them for evaluation.

The force of such evaluation stems from the fact that it is rooted in the core principles of the Alliance for Progress. The search for effective means to promote the stabilization of income derived from exports both by stabilizing the income from present exports and by encouraging diversification to reduce dependence on a limited number of primary export products is, as mentioned earlier, a central feature of the hemispheric strategy for development. Diversification is an aim of development planning in each of the Latin American countries in which the present commodity exports provide a limited and unstable base for economic expansion. In addition, the problem of commodity stabilization, being world-wide in scope, requires multilateral solutions through international agreements and arrangement. The member nations associated with the Alliance have established study groups, such as the coffee study group, focusing specifically on the particular commodity problems of Latin America. In the case of coffee, extensive preparations preceded the working out of an International Coffee Agreement, signed in August, 1962, which provided for export quotas and production controls. Special attention is also being devoted to the possibility of creating a compensatory financial mechanism designed to reduce fluctuations in annual export earnings from commodity transactions on an international or on a hemispheric basis.

The same principle is true of the effort to strengthen regionwide economic integration. The broadening of markets in Latin America is deemed essential to accelerate the process of economic development in the hemisphere; it is seen as an important means for obtaining greater productivity through specialized and complementary industrial production.

In general, then, the conception of the Alliance for Progress as a simultaneous, cooperative, and multilateral development effort provides an initial base for multinational planning.

It will undoubtedly take a number of years to implement completely the elaborate framework outlined by the Charter of Punta del Este. However, already over three-quarters of the countries of Latin America are in the process of preparing national development programs. The Central American Common Market—covering five countries—is almost an accomplished fact, while the Latin American Free Trade Area—covering nine countries—is going through the slow, tedious process of working out product-by-product trade arrangements. In addition, a significant start has been made toward the solution of the coffee problem, while stabilization arrangements for other basic products are being discussed.

This progress, as much as the great problems yet to be overcome, highlights the need for an additional tool which can strengthen the present efforts and mechanisms. A regional approach to development calls for relatively extensive direct regionwide planning. The key objectives of the Alliance for Progress and the mechanisms which have been set up to implement them would be strengthened significantly through more extensive regionwide planning—what might be called "framework" planning—viewing *all* of Latin America in relation to the changing "rest of the world" situation.

What is meant by framework planning here is (a) the preparation of analyses of economic and social trends on a regionwide basis and projection of key series to reveal the interregional implications of the evolving situation. Such projections would be broken down by economic sub-regions as well as by sectors. This would call for a central institution to provide detailed information far beyond anything now available; (b) analyses and projections of regional markets within and outside Latin America for major products and services, as well as production, exports, and imports within each commodity category, prepared within the context of analyses of world market developments;[5] (c) analyses of capital flows, terms of trade, balance of payments, and requirements of external financial assistance; and (d) the detailing of the developmental potentialities of the region, seen as a single cooperating unit, in terms of complementary indus-

---

[5]It is assumed that such data would be used with extreme care in practice. Forecasts for commodity markets are often wrong. Furthermore, there are at times reasons for a low-cost producer to expand in spite of a relatively unfavorable world market outlook.

tries, increased trade, and development of regionwide infrastructure facilities, such as transportation and communication.

This type of multinational planning would furnish extremely useful specific terms of reference for the preparation of country plans and of expansion plans by private firms. It would, at the same time, provide a key element in the strengthening of Latin American economic integration. The major objective of such integration is the speeding of *new* economic development, particularly in manufactures, rather than merely the freeing of current trade. The basic need is to encourage internal (within-region) investment in productive enterprises as well as to attract investment from outside. As Europe is now demonstrating, broad planning can help reduce certain kinds of risks and encourage productive expansion.

The question of economic integration among lesser developed countries is, of course, quite different from what it is in the case of an economically more advanced region, such as Europe. In the latter, intercountry trade accounts for a large part of their total trade; by contrast, inter-Latin-American trade is only a minor share—amounting on the average to some 10 percent of the total external trade of the countries concerned. While there are sizeable variations from country to country, it is evident that Latin American countries have separately geared their economy to complementarity with the outside world, predominantly the United States and Europe. It is noteworthy that there is a practical absence of any exports of manufactures from one Latin American country to another, suggesting the lack of competition and excessive protection under which these industries have evolved. Even more important, however, is the fact that the process of industrialization has still a long way to go in the region. Thus, for Latin America, integration is not so much a question of competition among already existing industries—with all the extensive adjustments that are involved—as an opportunity to promote and plan the development of new industries collectively, avoid unnecessary duplication or uneconomic location and ensure from the beginning the most appropriate scale of production for the industries to be started. This does not mean, of course, that the appropriate route to development is the establishment of vast multiproduct cartels, for these can be just as stultifying on an international as on a national basis. The key question is one of markets and scale, but within a context of lively competition for sales in a rapidly growing regional market, reinforced by international competition.

Multinational planning is also required to arrive at some basic decisions as to the degree of autonomy and types of external trade that the region should seek in a world which is increasingly becoming regionalized. Such a decision requires cooperation among regions. It would not be wise to develop product surpluses which were not exportable to other regional markets; nor to encourage dependence on external sources of capital goods and raw materials without seeing to it that the corresponding means of finance were available. It is to be hoped that Latin American regional economic development can take place in a world economy increasingly geared to extensive and relatively free international and interregional trade.

The evolving multilateralism and planning of the Alliance for Progress suggests that a foundation for regionwide planning is being laid stage by stage. In the not-too-distant future, a point may well be reached where the merging of national and multinational planning will be a key element in, as well as a symbol of, a high level of economic and social development throughout the whole of Latin America.

11

Lagging Sectors and Regions of the American Economy

The problem of low incomes has a number of facets: (1) the economically disadvantaged groups in our society; (2) the low-income industries; (3) the low-income regions; and (4) the national costs arising from the underemployment of part of the labor force. Each of these adds something to the total picture and each involves some special policy issues. Also, while these various elements—group, industry, region, and nation—are interrelated, they are significant in themselves. The most severe difficulties arise when all these are compounded, as in the case of isolated agricultural regions with limited resources, worked-out land, small farms, and a majority of Negro farmers.

Certain groups in our society tend to receive much lower incomes than the bulk of the population, no matter what they do or where they live. This is especially true of the Negroes, older persons, physically and mentally handicapped persons, and younger persons with limited education and skill. For example, nonwhite persons receive lower incomes than whites, whether they are urban, rural nonfarm, or farm residents, and no matter what part of the country they live in. The income figures for 1949 provided in the 1950 census show that the median income of rural farm nonwhites in the Southeast was $486 compared with $933 for rural farm whites. While the differentials were not as great in nonfarm sections and in other regions, they were substantial. In the case of urban and rural nonfarm persons in the relatively wealthy Middle Atlantic region, for example, the median income of nonwhites was $1,344 compared to $2,330 for whites, or 42 percent less.[1] This represents very low incomes indeed for Negroes at the lower end of the spectrum. A substantial differential between whites and nonwhites remains when age, sex, education, and occupation are taken into account. The various studies that have examined this problem most closely conclude that the white–Negro income differential is largely explained by racial discrimination. At the end of 1959, the Labor Department data on unemployment indicated that of the number who had been jobless for more

---

[1] The data referred to in this paper are largely drawn from Harvey S. Perloff, Edgar S. Dunn, Jr., Eric E. Lampard, and Richard F. Muth, *Regions, Resources and Economic Growth* (Baltimore, Md.: Johns Hopkins Press, 1960.)

than twenty-six weeks, one out of four was nonwhite, at a time when nonwhites were one out of ten in the labor force as a whole.

A somewhat similar situation obtains with regard to the other economically disadvantaged groups, but this need not be spelled out here. The main point is that the low-income problem of the disadvantaged groups would remain even if the industry and regional aspects of low income were somehow overcome. Thus, even the highest income northern cities have a substantial problem in the inadequate employment opportunities and very low income of Negroes, older persons, and other groups. The low-income problem migrates with the Negro when he leaves Macon County, Georgia, for Washington, D.C., or Chicago.

The problem of the low-income industry is of a different nature and is associated with the structural characteristics of certain economic activities. There is a broad spectrum of average incomes paid out to individuals employed in the various industries of the country. Incomes range from the very low levels of persons in some branches of farming, such as cotton and tobacco, in manufacturing groups, such as apparel and leather manufacture, and in service groups, such as personal service, amusements, and retail trade; going by stages on up to the very high incomes paid out in industries, such as petroleum products manufacture, automobiles, pipeline transportation, banking and finance.

Wages and salaries tend to be significantly associated with capital per worker, although other factors also come into play. Thus, the average level of income paid by an industry is associated with the relative amount of skilled labor employed within the industry (or the occupational structure more generally), the relative ages of the persons employed, the relative proportions of males and females, and the like. These factors are interrelated, of course; for example, the less-skilled jobs tend to be filled by younger persons, females, and nonwhites. The location of the industry also influences the level of income payments, and this bring us to the question of lagging regions.

The extent to which low incomes are regionally associated is suggested by the data on state per capita personal income. In 1957, for example, with only one exception, all the states with a per capita income above the national average were in the manufacturing belt and the Far West—the most industrialized-urbanized regions of the nation. At the same time, the lowest per capita incomes were—excepting only North Dakota—all in the Southeast. In this region, only the peripheral states, such as Virginia and Florida, had a per capita income as high as $1,500 at a time when the national average was above $2,000; Mississippi's per capita income was under $1,000.

The level of income within an area is clearly associated with its industrial structure; that is, whether low-income industries predominate or not. Thus average per capita income within the states tends to vary inversely with the relative importance of agriculture within the state and also with the relative importance of processing industries (those for which the products of agriculture and mining are important), since both of these sectors are on the low-income paying side. Incomes are positively associated with the relative importance of employment in the fabricating industries and in the business services.

More refined industrial-regional breakdowns show additional significant relationships. Among farmers the only important regional variation in income levels is that between the southern farmer and the farmers of the rest of the nation. Thus, as has long been recognized, while agriculture in general faces some serious problems, it is the southern farmer who presents the most extreme low-income problem.

It is highly significant that both the favorable and the unfavorable elements tend to cluster in spatial or regional terms. As Frank Hanna has shown, in states in which average earnings are above the national average, the average earnings in almost all occupations, as well as in almost all industries, tend to be above the national average for that occupation or industry. Moreover, in states where the average wage and salary earnings of workers are above the national average, workers tend to be concentrated in the higher paying occupations and industries. This is not surprising. Interstate differentials in income of workers in the same industry are related to differences in the marginal productivity of labor and the latter is related to differences in the proportion with which labor is combined with other factors, especially capital. Labor-intensive industries tend to locate where wages are relatively low and all industries, to the extent that their production function permits flexibility with regard to the combination of labor and capital, will tend to use less capital-intensive methods in the lower income areas. Thus the low-income effect can be seen to be self-reinforcing.

But why does not capital flow into the low-wage areas (to take advantage of the lower labor cost) in volume sufficient to equalize wage levels? Some industries are, of course, attracted to such areas; the apparel and textile industries, among others, have moved to the Southeast and to communities in the mining regions. There seems to be a limit, however, to the flow of capital that can be attracted by the lower wage levels of certain regions. Every industry has its own special locational preferences based on its particular input and market requirements. A detailed study of industrial location which we have carried out at Resources for the Future shows clearly that for the great majority of industries the location of material input sources and even more the location of markets tends to exert the dominant locational pull. Also important are such factors as the need for specialized services, requirements of communication and speed of transportation services, and the attractiveness of the living environment. In the language of the industrial location economists, relatively few industries are labor oriented. One has only to think of the steel industry or of machine tools or women's high-fashion dresses or the whole host of specialized services that cluster in the great urban centers like New York, Chicago, and Los Angeles to get a mental image of what is involved. As a matter of fact, there is a good bit of evidence to show that market considerations are playing an increasingly important role in our economy. If this is as significant as it seems to be, then the great national-market and regional-market centers might well be the receiving areas for the bulk of American industry, while the more isolated areas might well have difficulty in holding on to the limited industry they already have.

The classical solution for raising wages in the low-wage industries—that is, workers leaving the industry to get better-paying jobs elsewhere (reinforced by organized bargaining)—is still the basic solution within those industries and areas characterized by a high degree of factor mobility. The problem arises when either an industry or an area is characterized by inadequate mobility over a long period of time. In the instances which present the most difficult problem, inadequate industry and regional mobility reinforce each other, as is the case of a large section of farming in the Southeast. Here an understanding of the difference between immobility and inadequate mobility becomes important. There has been a tremendous amount of movement out of agriculture in the poorer areas of the country, but it simply has not been enough to overcome the low-income problem. That such movement helps with relation to income is suggested by several facts; for example, between 1939 and 1954, the states that had absolute decreases in population—such as Oklahoma, Arkansas, and Mississippi—had some of the greatest relative increases in per capita income in the nation for the period. Our analysis suggests, in fact, that over recent decades perhaps the most important single factor pulling the per capita income of the Southeast upward was the decline in agricultural employment. But the movement out of agriculture has not been enough to raise income levels in these areas close to the national average.

One can conjecture that the amount of out-migration required to bring wages and income within a given area close to national averages would depend on many factors, and that important among them would be: (1) the rate of natural increase and of in-migration, if any; (2) the ratio of labor force to population and the number of new entrants into the labor force; (3) the existing amount of unemployment and underemployment; and (4) the rate at which new job opportunities are being created. All of this can add up to the requirement for a tremendous amount of out-migration from disadvantaged areas.

Reference to recent migration is instructive. Thus between 1940 and 1950, the rate of movement out of agriculture ran as high as 90 percent in some southeastern states. For example, some 465,000 persons left agriculture in Alabama. This amounted to a movement out of farming during the decade of 93.4 percent. However, during the decade Alabama had a rural farm replacement rate of 203 percent. (By comparison, New York State had a replacement rate of 115 and California of 122 percent.) Altogether, then, farm employment in Alabama was reduced by a total of only some 127,000 persons—a farm employment decrease of 25 percent.

Translated into geographic terms, a predominantly agricultural region may continue to be subject to underemployment and limited improvements in income levels, in the face of substantial out-migration, as long as birth rates continue relatively high. Moreover, out-migration from farm areas, even if involving reductions in total numbers, cannot be expected by itself necessarily to increase levels of living within such areas. The out-migration would normally have to be accompanied by a number of changes—such as the creation of larger farms, a higher ratio of capital inputs, and a more efficient use of labor—which add up to a higher productivity per farm worker. Without this, the rate of improvement in income levels can be painfully slow.

The experience of nonfarm depressed areas, such as certain of the coal mining areas of Pennsylvania, Kentucky, West Virginia, and Illinois and the textile mill communities in New England, has been similar to that of the southern farm regions with regard to the persistence of low incomes in the face of quite substantial out-migration. Here, too, while large numbers of workers have left such areas in the face of limited employment opportunities, many others have stayed on over the years in spite of unemployment or employment at very low wages in industries, such as apparel, or in assembly operations, and the replacement rates, in some instances, have continued to be very high.

This brief account hardly touches the surface of the problem, but it is suggestive to see it in broad outline. And here I would like to refer to the fourth facet of the problem I mentioned at the beginning: the cost to the nation of having a significant share of its labor force underemployed. (Secular underemployment is, of course, the other side of the coin of low incomes.) In simple terms, we are not producing as a nation what we are capable of producing.

The national rate of economic growth has lately become a lively issue in the face of the Soviet economic advances, but of course the issue of optimum national production has relevance aside from the cold war situation. The United States has not yet seriously come to grips with the question of nationwide secular full employment, including the removal of pockets of unemployment and underemployment.

Actually, at the present time there are some serious efforts to improve employment opportunities and income levels. For example, there are over 14,000 agencies concerned with area development in one way or another; also there are a number of federal and state programs concerned with depressed regions and certain of the disadvantaged groups. While some very effective things have been done, and are being done, taken as a whole, the results thus far have not been very impressive. Possibly the difficulty is one of inadequate scale and impact. The few figures on population replacement given earlier suggest how in rural areas a limited effort can be literally drowned in the counterinfluence of high birth rates. We are in a situation with regard to the problem of low incomes and secular underemployment similar to the one that characterized countercycle efforts in the early thirties—too little, disorganized, and often misdirected. As we become more successful in maintaining general prosperity nationwide, the employment and income problem increasingly reduces to the lagging sectors.

It is evident that the problem of sectors of low incomes and secular underemployment will not readily yield to solution. The forces at work are extremely complex, including physical, social, cultural, political, and psychological factors as well as economic ones. Also, there are all sorts of booby traps involved. Activities that prevent or delay needed adjustments on the part of individuals, industries, or regions can of course do more harm than good. The mislocation of industries by way of subsidies would fall into this category, as would efforts that delay the migration of workers from areas with few employment opportunities. Industries, to remain competitive, must generally be well located with regard to all their inputs as well as with regard to markets, and it is obvious that not all areas with problems of surplus labor are capable of economically absorbing new industries. One can go further. An essential ingredient of a sound program of full employment would be the encouragement of location of new industry and of work force in the most advantageous locations, weighing not only input and output factors over the foreseeable future, but also the social and cultural opportunities likely to be offered to people at every stage of their life, but particularly when they are young. A good many of the presently depressed areas are by no stretch of the imagination favorable environments for the growth of our future citizens. In general, it is clear that the problem of low incomes is directly tied to factor immobilities, to add to the immobilities, in the name of doing something about low incomes, would hardly make good sense.

It is very difficult indeed for the people of a local community to be able to launch a full-fledged program which can equate labor force and relative employment opportunities, when this involves sizable out-migration. However, there are clearly very many important steps that a local community could—and should—take within the framework of a well-developed national program. But the latter is not yet in being; so that today local efforts are, with very few exceptions, limited and basically ineffectual. What this suggests is that there is need for the adoption by the national government of a policy of fostering secular full employment in the lagging sectors as well as in over-all national terms. This could readily come under the rubric of the Full Employment Act of 1946, but there is much to be said for a more conscious and dramatic broadening of the federal full employment program to include a strong and continuous effort to remove pockets of underemployment and getting at the more important personal, industrial, and regional factors. In addition to the broadening of the federal effort, it would take a more concerted effort on the part of all the other levels of government, working with private individuals and groups, to make substantial progress with such a persistent and difficult problem.

The details of a program of nationwide secular full employment would have to be worked out, of course, year by year through study and planning, in the same way that our stabilization program is worked out through the continuous work of the Council of Economic Advisers, the Treasury, the Federal Reserve Board, and the other agencies and groups. However, in the absence of this type of study and planning, one can draw on our limited knowledge and experience to point to some measures that would seem to be needed and appropriate.

I would put at the top of the list an intensive effort to improve education in the depressed areas, to prepare young persons for a lifetime of skilled, productive work. Compared to other potential governmental measures that have been proposed, public investment in education promises the greatest relative returns. This might include federal and state funds specifically provided for the low-income areas—with both total expenditure per pupil and the nonlocal share increasing in inverse ratio to the average level of income in the area. Such an effort might well focus on the establishment of quite large consolidated schools, bringing in students over a wide area, staffed by well-paid teachers, and providing far better than average general and vocational education. A highly developed system of vocational guidance would be attached to such consolidated schools. I would take this to be the best and most effective measure to help wipe out underemployment. Educated, skilled persons can be counted on to seek out good employment and income opportunities and, equally important, situations favorable to continued development of the individual. It would be highly desirable if such a special educational effort extended to the low-income sections of our cities.

Such an educational effort might well be coupled with the provision of federal and state loan and grant funds in depressed agricultural areas to encourage the enlargement and improvement of farms and to provide special aids for those selling their farms and moving to areas of greater income-earning opportunities.

In some regions, the foundation for higher income economic activities can be broadened and strengthened through the intensive development of underutilized natural resources, such as forestry, water, and recreation (or amenity) resources, where such development promises to attract new industries and service activities.

High-caliber regional study-and-planning agencies are needed within the various metropolitan communities and rural economic regions to probe continuously the problems and the consequences of economic and other changes under way and projected and to point the direction for sensible programs to cope with such problems and consequences. Attention needs to be focused, not only on areawide problems and programs, but also on the groups with small economic problems, such as the nonwhites and the aged.

Every low-income section of the country has its own special set of problems and quite different potentialities for economic growth and improvement. Some have natural resources that have yet to be fully tapped; some have locational advantages for attracting industries; others, however, have to face up to their very limited potentialities for economic expansion and to the urgent need for a high rate of out-migration. In many instances, significantly higher income levels can be achieved only by combining a really effective economic development program with a substantial amount of out-migration. The experience of Puerto Rico is suggestive in this regard. It has taken a brilliantly conceived and executed economic development program—coupled with a rate of out-migration over the past decade high enough to keep the island's population at almost a stationary level—to permit Puerto Rico to realize a substantial and continuous increase in its level of per capita income. And Puerto Rico has not hesitated to help the migrants. Such a twofold effort is called for in a number of regions in the United States and, to be sensibly focused, requires careful planning.

Such study-and-planning efforts could be most effective if they were backed, as suggested earlier, by federal study, plans, and programs which set up a framework for the state, regional, and local efforts. Low incomes deeply involve all levels of our economy and society. The national scope of the problem requires recognition by the federal government if policy at any level is to be effective in ameliorating it.

12

Natural Resource Endowment and Regional Economic Growth

We are concerned in this chapter with the relationship between the natural resources within the various parts, or regions, of a country and what might be called the geography of national economic expansion.

The development of the economy of the United States provides a case study of resources in space interacting with the other elements of economic growth that is especially illuminating: (1) it covers an extended spectrum of growth from early agricultural beginnings to status as an advanced, industry-and-service-oriented economy, thus affording an opportunity to examine the role of resources in different stages of national economic growth. (2) It covers a wide variety of regional resources and growth situations, providing a rich set of variations on the interactions of the national economy with its geographic components. And (3) it can be examined with the help of a wealth of historical information and statistical data. Specifically, Resources for the Future has concluded a three-year study of the regional characteristics of the growth of the United States economy. The results of this effort have been made available in a book entitled *Regions, Resources, and Economic Growth*.[1] This chapter draws heav-

---

This chapter was written in collaboration with Lowdon Wingo, Jr.

[1]Harvey S. Perloff, Edgar S. Dunn, Jr., Eric E. Lampard, and Richard F. Muth: *Regions, Resources, and Economic Growth* (Baltimore: The Johns Hopkins Press, 1960). We owe a great deal to Messrs. Dunn, Lampard, and Muth; we wish to absolve them, however, of responsibility for any errors or inadequacies in this paper.

The discussion of growth here will be limited to changes in what we refer to as the *volume* of economic activities (e.g., increases in population, employment, value added, and the like), acknowledging that this is but one facet of economic growth. Growth as defined by changes in *welfare* (changes in per capita income, for example) is discussed in Part V of *Regions, Resources, and Economic Growth;* changes in state per capita are analyzed in some detail by Simon Kuznets in "Industrial Distribution of Income and Labor Force by States, 1919–21 to 1955," Part III of "Quantitative Aspects of the Economic Growth of Nations," *Economic Development and Cultural Change*, Vol. vi, July 1958.

We assume that the broad features of regional economic expansion in the United States are familiar to our readers, and so we have presented no figures to describe them here. Those interested in such detail are referred to Chapters 2 and 3 of *Regions, Resources, and Economic Growth.*

ily on the research that went into this book and on the conclusions that emerge from it. Given this storehouse of materials, we have been tempted into speculation on the broad relationship involved in the resources–growth problem.

RESOURCES AND GROWTH IN A BROAD HISTORICAL FRAMEWORK

One of the insights emerging from an examination of the history of American economic development is the difficulty of defining "resource endowment" in any long-run, substantive sense. In the short run, endowment is simply the inventory of those natural materials that are required in some degree by the national economy responding to internal consumption demands and to its possition in international trade. As the requirements of the economy change, the composition of the inventory shifts, and in this sense resource endowment is a changing concept closely associated with the dynamics of economic growth. In short, the answer to what constitutes resource endowment is rooted in the determinants of final demand—consumer preferences and income distribution, as well as foreign trade—on the one hand, and in the current organization and technology of production on the other. As these variables change, so will the content of resource endowment. And, clearly then, as the composition of resource endowment changes, there will tend to be substantial changes in the relative advantage among regions supplying material inputs (and services) for the national economy.

The impact of these shifts can be sketched in with broad strokes by identifying stage by stage what have been the natural resources that count in the national economy. This requires us to tell again a familiar story, but with a special focus.

THE EARLY AGRICULTURAL PERIOD

From its colonial origins the American economy developed as a producer of resource inputs into the rapidly expanding European economy. To serve such a function the endowment which counted in early America was arable land with its environmental complements of climate and water, and this, with access to the growing European market for agricultural staples, set up the conditions for regional growth in early America. It was quite logical, hence, that the regional economies developed a certain archetype: a good deepwater port as the nucleus of an agricultural hinterland well adapted for the production of a staple commodity in demand on the world market.

The growth potential of these nucleated regions depended heavily on the extent and richness of the hinterland accessible to port. Since good agricultural land was almost a free resource while labor and capital were dear, the expansion of production was effected by bringing more land into production and so extending the limits of the hinterland. Much of early American history is dominated by the great rivalries for control of hinterland that emerged between New York and Boston, Philadelphia and Baltimore, Charleston and Savannah. This expansion of the hinterlands took place through social overhead investment in transportation facilities beginning with the Massachusetts road system in the seventeenth century,[2] later producing the Erie Canal, and finally motivating the half century of railroad construction stretching from the Baltimore and Ohio's first crude line reaching out to the rich wheatlands in Maryland and Pennsylvania to the driving of the golden spike at Promontory Point, Utah.[3] The force of the outward push for land is suggested by the fact that population west of the Alleghenies, which was estimated by the 1790 Census at 109,000, by 1840 had become almost six and a half million, with more than 87 percent of the labor force involved in agriculture.

Even though the data on this period are not very satisfactory, we can draw these general conclusions: (1) the *regional* endowment that made for growth was good land advantageously situated with respect to the market centers; (2) the distribution of economic activity in the period before 1840 was essentially a function of the expanding, nucleated, agricultural regions reaching into the economic vacuum of an unsettled continent to bring ever greater areas of land under cultivation; and (3) this resource-dominated expansion of the economy set the stage for the next important development by establishing a geography of markets, transport, and labor force to condition the nature of succeeding growth.

The Minerals-Dominant Economy

Somewhere around 1840–1850 the next important resource stage began—as a result of the emerging minerals-dominant economy. The rapid growth of the railroads and the expansion of processing industries resulted in a new input requirements: a new set of resources became important and a new set of locational forces came into play. The first part of this period was dominated by the growing demand for iron and steel and by the rapid elaboration of their production technology.[4] At this point it was the geographical juxtaposition of coal, iron ore, and the market which afforded the great impetus for growth. The importance of minerals, unlike agricultural land, was not alone in their direct contribution to regional growth so much as it was in the nature of their linkages with succeeding stages of production. It was not so much the mining of coal and iron that was important for growth, as the making of iron and steel products, which could not be separated from the sources of its mineral inputs. The early concentration of steel making in western Pennsylvania was a result of these rela-

---

[2]The importance of hinterland in the growth of the early centers is vividly described by Carl Bridenbaugh, *Cities in the Wilderness* (New York: Ronald Press, 1938).

[3]A detailed treatment can be found in Paul H. Cootner, "Transportation Innovation and Economic Development: The Case of the U.S. Steam Railroads." Unpublished Ph.D. thesis, MIT, 1953.

[4]In 1880, some 70 percent of steel output went into the rails. Cootner, *op. cit.*, Chapter v, pp. 13–14.

tionships, for this area was not only well endowed with deposits of iron ore and coal but was central to a concentrated market stretching from Boston and New York westward. As the center of gravity of the market shifted west and as Mesabi ores replaced depleted local ores, the iron and steel industry also shifted westward along the southern shores of the Great Lakes.

With the increase in the demand for nonferrous metals, the depletion of accessible ore deposits in the East and the penetration of the West by the railroad net, a new role in regional growth was played by mineral resources endowment. In the Mountain region stretching from the Canadian border to the Southwest states, the mining of metal ores was the lead factor in economic development: in 1870 when mineral extractions involved the employment of 1½ percent of the labor force nationally, in the Mountain states it accounted for no less than 26.54 percent, after which it declined until in 1950 the proportion was 3.44 percent, still twice as much as the national average. Except for primary processing of ores, however, this resource base did not induce the location of any substantial amount of linked activity in the Mountain states. With most of the weight loss taking place during concentration and smelting, the distribution of the market governed the location of succeeding stages of metals fabrication, and the major markets were concentrated in the Northeast.

The extent to which changes in both demand and supply conditions influenced regional resources activities is suggested by the data in Table 1, showing figures for interregional production shifts for pig iron, copper, and lead. Several points are worth noting: (1) the period of great growth in the output of these mineral products (1870–1910) corresponds with the most extensive interregional shifts in their production; (2) truly huge shifts in lead and copper production took place from the Great Lakes region to the Mountain states (and to a lesser extent to the Southwest and Far West) during this period; and (3) there has been a steady shift in pig iron production throughout the entire period 1870–1950 from the Middle Atlantic states to the Great Lakes and, to a lesser extent, the Southeast. These data underline the highly selective regional effects resulting from the growth of a mineral-based economy.

Some notion of the extent of changes in national requirements of material resources is provided by a measure of the changes in the composition of the value of purchases in constant dollars within the broad mineral categories over the period 1870–1950. (This measure is the same as that employed in Table 1; namely, the end of period total which would have to be redistributed among classes to create the beginning of period percentage distribution.) Thus, within the mineral fuels the total shift over the period was equivalent to 57 percent away from bituminous and anthracite coals and toward petroleum and natural gas fuels, that is, towards materials which would hardly have been considered as resources ten years before this period. Among the metals during the same period the total shift was almost 34 percent, away from iron, lead, and tin and in the direction of the light metals and ferroalloys—one-fourth of this shift has been in the direction of metals for which the economy of 1870 had little or no use, such as aluminum, manganese, nickel, and molybdenum. Finally, among the nonmetals (and here the availablity of data limits us to the period 1910 to 1950) the internal composition in this shorter period shifted by 31 percent, away

TABLE 1. PERCENTAGE CHANGE IN REGIONAL DISTRIBUTION OF U.S. PRODUCTION
OF PIG IRON, COPPER AND LEAD, 1870–1910 AND 1910–1950

	Pig iron		Copper		Lead	
	Percentage Shift[a]		Percentage Shift[a]		Percentage Shift[a]	
Region[b]	1870–1910	1910–1950	1870–1910[c]	1910–1950[d]	1870–1910[c]	1910–1950
New England	− 1.62	− .06	− 6.90	0	− .41	0
Middle Atlantic	−15.98	−15.65	− 1.44	− .08	− 1.02	+ .34
Great Lakes	+11.13	+ 7.37	−62.36	−17.72	−58.89	− .45
Southeast	+ 4.90	+ 5.80	− 6.39	− 1.57	− 3.89	+ .75
Plains	0	0	0	+ .33	+ 7.09	− 7.89
Southwest	0	0	+27.73	+23.77	+ 1.63	+10.30
Mountain	0	0	+39.49	− 2.28	+54.61	−10.17
Far West	+ 1.57	+ 2.54	+ 9.86	− 4.03	+ .88	+ 7.12
Total Shift	17.60	15.71	77.08	24.10	64.21	18.51
Percentage growth of output	1,538%	115%	2,727%	67.8%	1,983%	11.7%

[a]The end-of-period percentage of total national production *less* the beginning-of-period percentage. Thus, with respect to pig iron in the period 1870–1910, New England percentage share of national production was 1.62% less in 1910 than it was in 1870. The figure for Total Shift (sum of the absolute value of the shifts × ½), then, represents the percentage of total national production which would have to be redistributed in order to recreate the beginning-of-period percentage distribution by regions.

[b]The states composing the regions are as follows: *New England*—Maine, New Hampshire, Vermont, Massachusetts, Rhode Island, Connecticut. *Middle Atlantic*—New York, New Jersey, Pennsylvania, Delaware, Maryland, District of Columbia. *Great Lakes*—Ohio, Indiana, Illinois, Michigan, Wisconsin. *Southeast*—Virginia, West Virginia, Kentucky, Tennessee, North Carolina, South Carolina, Georgia, Florida, Alabama, Mississippi, Arkansas, Louisiana. *Plains*—Minnesota, Iowa, Missouri, North Dakota, South Dakota, Nebraska, Kansas. *Southwest*—Oklahoma, Texas, Arizona, New Mexico. *Mountain*—Montana, Idaho, Wyoming, Utah, Colorado. *Far West*—Washington, Oregon, California, Nevada.

[c]The 1870–1910 shift figures for lead and copper should be viewed with caution. The 1870 figures upon which the shifts are based represent the regional composition of the *current dollar value* of domestic mine production (the only data which were available), while all later figures used express domestic mine production in *short tons*. Since we are dealing with regional composition, the resulting shift figures would be seriously compromised if there were substantial price differentials at the mine head among the major producing regions in 1870. For the purposes of the discussion following, it is assumed that such price differentials would exert at worst a modest influence on the 1870–1910 shift figures.

[d]Excludes unallocated production in Pennsylvania, Tennessee, and Vermont of 1.59%.

Sources for Table 1: Shift figures computed from Perloff, Dunn, Lampard, and Muth, *Regions, Resources, and Economic Growth* (Baltimore: The Johns Hopkins Press, 1960), Table 75, p. 205; Table 76, p. 208; Table 77, p. 210. Growth of output computed from the long-term series in an RFF study by Neal Potter and Francis T. Christy, Jr., "U.S. Natural Resource Statistics, 1870 to 1955" (Preliminary Draft, with revisions to 11/1/59), Lead, Table MT-14; Copper, Table MT-12; Pig Iron, Table MT-28.

from stone and toward other construction materials, as well as toward basic chemical materials. Something more than one-fourth of the shift was to materials which would not have been considered as resources in 1870.[5]

An especially important instance of the regional effects of changes in national requirements is provided by the case of petroleum and natural gas in the Southwest in recent decades. Here the effect resulted not only from a powerful, direct mining leverage (as was noted in the case of the Mountain region), but also from the availability of a cheap, convenient fuel which altered substantially the region's relative advantages for certain classes of industry. The happy coincidence of these mineral fuels with rich deposits of salt and sulfur provided a resource base for a rapidly expanding chemical industry. Thus, petroleum and gas extraction and refining, responding to a huge and growing national demand, served to change the economic conditions of production throughout the entire Southwest.

Summarizing the broad sweeps of the period of very rapid growth from about the middle of the nineteenth century, we note that during the first half of this period (to the end of the nineteenth century) there were two great overlapping resource effects conditioning the subnational distribution of economic activity: (1) geographically the more widespread effect was that of agriculture continuing to spread out over the arable lands—as in the early period of economic development, but pulling with it an increasing component of processing and servicing activities; and (2) the developmentally dominant effects emerged from the growth of the minerals economy, shifting rapidly among regions, triggering, intensifying, or transforming the nature of regional growth patterns.

The second part of this modern period—that is, the first half of the twentieth century—has been largely characterized by an elaboration and deepening of the subnational economy building upon the geographic pattern of activities brought about by the great interregional resource shifts of the ninteenth century. Resource activities defined in relative importance in the national economy throughout the period, but their real importance lay in the role they had played historically in defining the economic basis for the succeeding stages of regional growth—in the movements of population and industry among the regions. In a very real sense the classical resource effects were playing themselves out, as the service sector moved into a dominant position and as technological and other changes (such as price changes which made recapture of waste products economical) brought about a long-range reduction in the proportion of raw materials to total output,[6] thus weakening the linkages of economic activities to their

---

[5]Calculated from data in a forthcoming RFF study by Neal Potter and Francis T. Christy, Jr., "U.S. Natural Resource Statistics, 1870 to 1955" (Preliminary Draft, with revisions to 11/1/59), Tables McT-22, 23, 24, 33, and 35.

[6]The Potter–Christy data indicate that between 1870 and 1955, when real GNP expanded 16 times, the output of the resources industries expanded only 5½ times. In terms of output (in 1954 prices), the extractive industries dropped over this period from ⅓ of GNP to 12 percent. The greatest declines were in the products of forestry, fishing, and agriculture. Output in mining rose as a percentage of GNP until the 1920s and since has shown a moderate decline relative to GNP. Kindleberger finds a similar trend in the declining relative use of raw materials in Europe. Charles P. Kindleberger, *The Terms of*

resource inputs. The power of the "market magnet" loomed as the dominant locational force operating in the economy.

The Services Era and Amenity Resources

By midcentury, moreover, an additional resource effect was beginning to influence the distribution of economic activity among the regions. To understand the importance of this effect requires us to move away from a definition of resource endowment which sees resources exclusively as tangible materials upon which technology works in the production of goods, and toward one which sees natural resources as including other features of the natural environment which have consequences for economic decisions. Natural resources, then, need not *enter* directly into the processes of production, but only *influence* directly the location of markets as well as of production. This broader definition embraces a group of physical environmental conditions which we will refer to as the "amenity resources"—that special juxtaposition of climate, land, coastline, and water offering conditions of living which exert a strong pull on migrants from less happily situated parts of the nation.

This amenity-resource effect derives from the interplay of a number of developments within the national economy and society. First, there is the growing importance of the non-job-oriented, as well as the job-seeking, migrant. Some 8 percent of the United States population is over 65 years of age, and the proportion of this age group in the total is growing. Approximately two-thirds of these persons are not working and many enjoy some form of paid retirement. Since most consumption items can be acquired with only minor interregional differences, many of these persons will seek out the more intangible resource services, such as climate and coast, that do have substantial interregional variations.

Another important development is the growth in the number and significance of industries whose ties to resource inputs and national market centers are relatively weak. These are the so-called "foot-loose" industries which are distinguished from other industries in the fact that they have an unusually broad spectrum of locational alternatives available. Such an industry may be labor-oriented in terms of requiring unskilled or semi-skilled labor, such as the apparel industries, or in terms of a highly technical labor requirement, such as the research and development industries. It may be climate-oriented, as in the case of the aircraft industries. Or it may be an industry whose unit transportation costs are negligible in terms of the value of the product, such as instrument and optical goods producers. All of these have in common an array of locational possibilities which permits them to settle in amenity-rich areas without doing violence to the economics of their activities. The growth of the transportation equipment industry (mainly aircraft) in California is an excellent example. During the period 1939–54 California realized some 35 percent of the national shift in

Trade: A European Case Study (Cambridge and New York: Technology Press and Wiley, 1956), Chap. 8, pp. 176–212.

employment in the industry, and this accounted for a very large share of California's total increase in manufacturing employment.

Finally, there is the effect of a rising per capita income throughout the nation. Given the high elasticity of demand for travel and recreation, rising incomes have meant an increasing export market for regional amenity resources in the form of tourist services to vacationers.

Even before mid-century the great shift in population was in the direction of states that had advantages in these amenity resources: Florida, the Southwest, and the Pacific Coast states. During the 1940–50 Census period, this great arc of states stretching from Florida on the southeastern rim to Washington on the northwestern rim[7] (which contained 16 percent of the national population in 1940) absorbed some 40 percent of the total increment of national population growth.[8] The movement in the direction of the amenity resources is strong, and even though we are not certain how much of the movement to specific regions can be attributed directly to this resource influence and how much to other factors, given a highly mobile population with rising incomes and retirement payments, it seems fairly certain that the direct influence of the amenity resource will increase rather than diminish.

And so, in the broad perspective of history, the changing content of resource endowment has had a succession of effects in the interregional distribution of economic activity. As new resources moved to the forefront of the national economy, new advantages for economic growth were created for those regions well endowed. This much seems certain: in terms of the distribution of national economic activity over the landscape, resource endowment has mattered a great deal.

RESOURCES AND THE MECHANICS OF REGIONAL GROWTH

Regional growth typically has been promoted by the ability of a region to produce goods or services demanded by the national economy and to export them at a competitive advantage with respect to other regions. We have already referred to three such cases touching upon resources—the leverage of minerals in the growth of the Mountain states, of petroleum and natural gas in the growth of the Southwest, and of amenity resources in the growth of Florida. The role of timber in the development of the Pacific Northwest and the role of agricultural commodities in the development of the Plains states are equally instructive. This ability to export induces a flow of income into the region which, through the

---

[7]Florida, Texas, New Mexico, Arizona, California, Oregon, Washington.

[8]In the case of Florida, between 1940 and 1950 the native white population of the state increased by 54 percent, adding an increment of 707,300 to the 1940 population of 1,304,000. Of this increment the increase in Florida-born residents accounted for 210,000, while the increase of residents born in other states accounted for 497,300, some 251,600 of which were born in states north of the Ohio River. New York alone accounted for 30 percent of these. Everett S. Lee, Ann R. Miller, Carol P. Brainard, and Richard A. Easterlin, *Population Redistribution and Economic Growth, United States, 1870–1950* (Philadelphia: The American Philosophical Society, 1957), Table P-3, p. 257.

familiar multiplier effect, tends to expand the internal markets of the region for both national and region-serving goods and services. The extent of the multiplier effect is related to certain internal features that characterize the economic and social structure of the region. Regions tend to differ substantially in the degree of development that becomes associated with the growth of the export industries and in what happens to the income that flows in from the export sales.

Some of these internal features are related to the nature of the export industries and particularly to the localized industrial linkages, and services attaching to the export sector are also important here. Thus, for example, it has been noted by historians that the shipment of *heavy* export products from a region has influenced the development of substantial transportation facilities and services within the region. The quantity and type of labor required by the export industries and relative levels of wages paid has, of course, an obvious relationship to the internal development of a region. Another important feature is the income distribution that tends to be associated with a given type of regional export product. Douglass North has pointed to the differential effect on regional development in the nineteenth century of the plantation system in the Southeast for the production of cotton and tobacco—with its highly unequal distribution of income, as compared to the independent-farmer production system of the Midwest—with its broad income base and its growing markets for local goods and services.

Internal regional development takes the form both of internal structural changes (such as an increase in the proportion of the labor force employed in manufacturing and service industries) and an expansion of the local market for all sorts of goods and services. As the regional market expands and region-serving activities proliferate, conditions may develop for self-reinforcing and self-sustaining regional growth, and new internal factors may become important in determining the rates of regional growth, such as external economies associated with social overhead capital and the agglomeration of industries, and internal economies of scale. At any rate, the occurrence of rapid self-sustaining growth involves a shift in the relative importance of growth factors—away from the dominance of the export sector and in the direction of the internal organization of production—which makes it possible for the region to play a more elaborate role in the national economy. This highly simplified exposition of the regional growth process needs to be hedged with many reservations, but it brings to the fore the context within which the effects of resource endowment play out their role.

The export and internal determinants of regional economic expansion can be brought together in the concept of *cumulative advantage.* But any advantage which a region may have vis-à-vis other regions is, of course, always relative. This is so whether the focus is in terms of input and market advantages in the production of a single product or the products of a single industry, or whether the focus is in terms of cumulative advantages for over-all economic growth.

The conditions making for relative advantage can be of many sorts. Given our focus on the role of natural resource in growth, it is suggestive to view relative advantage as resource-based and non-resource-based. As already noted, resource-based advantages have afforded the conventional route to regional economic growth in the United States. In terms of their consequences for regional economic expansion, resources can be described as "good" or "bad" depending on their capacity to provide a vigorous economic linkage with the national economy and to extend the internal markets of the region. A good resource for a region can be identified, first, by its ability to support an extensive stream of nationally wanted production. Here attention is focused on the characteristics of the national demand curve for the resource and the relationship of the region's supply conditions to those of the other regions: these must afford a substantial promise that production of the resource in the region will expand. In short, the demand for the resource must be derived from final and intermediate demand sectors of the national economy exhibiting a high income elasticity of demand. Secondly, production of the resource must be characterized by extensive locationally associated forward and backward linkages. And, finally, the resource must be characterized by a high regional multiplier—that is, a substantial proportion of the returns from the export sector must find its way into active demand for regionally produced goods and services.

Thus, a region's resource endowment is good to the extent that it is composed of resource products which rate high by these criteria. A poor resource endowment is one whose potential for inducing growth is, accordingly, not very high. In general, the importance of resource endowment in regional growth derives from its ability to alter the region's overall cumulative advantage position. This will vary among regions and among resource components, and especially will it vary over time as shifts in the composition of rapid and slow growth sectors of the national economy change the bill of inputs.

Most agricultural products rate low on this growth scale. The agricultural sector in recent decades has expanded at about the rate of population growth[9] and its products have had an income elasticity of much less than one.[10]

Thus, taken in aggregate, agriculture will rarely make much of a contribution to the cumulative growth advantages of a region, except in the case of a region whose relative advantage for the production of agricultural products is improving relative to the rest of the nation, as in the Plains states for the period 1870–1910.[11] However, to focus our inquiry at the 1-digit level is to conceal by

---

[9]The index of per capita agricultural production has changed as follows:

1870 . . . 86.33
1910 . . . 100.00
1950 . . . 100.05

Source: Agricultural production data from Potter and Christy, *op. cit.*, Series AT–28; Population data from *Historical Statistics of the United States*, 1789–1945, Series B–2, and 1950 Census of Population.

[10]Income elasticity of demand for food has been estimated at 0.2 to 0.3; Harlow W. Halvorson, "Long Range Domestic Demand Prospects for Food and Fiber," *Journal of Farm Economics*, vol. 36 (December 1953), p. 760.

[11]The index of the share of the Plains states in the value of the national agricultural product is:

1870 . . . 41.48
1910 . . . 100.00
1950 . . . 91.07

Source: Perloff, Dunn, Lampard, Muth, *op. cit.*, T. 38 p. 138, and T. 100 p. 249: "Regional

aggregation the considerable variation among agricultural products at the 3- and 4-digit level. Some agricultural products in some specific instances can make significant contributions to regional economic growth. Thus, where cotton and cattle would rate low across the board as growth-generating items, the ability of California to engage in capital-intensive cotton production, and of Florida to exploit new breeds of cattle on the basis of excellent feed conditions, make these comparatively good resource products for these states. In other cases, there are agricultural specialties whose patterns of consumption have suggested a relatively high income elasticity of demand—such as fruits, nuts, and horticultural specialties—so that they tend to contribute to the economic growth of those areas which are suited to their production.

The minerals sector has expanded much more rapidly than agriculture as a whole and regional endowment in mineral resources has always been looked upon as a positive asset for regional growth. As in the case of agriculture, there are great variations among the various mineral categories as to their contribution to regional growth. In addition, there are two characteristics of minerals that deserve special attention: first, minerals are nonrenewable resources, so that the depletion phenomenon becomes important in assessing the relative advantage conveyed by them; second, there is a high degree of substitutability among mineral products, so that the advantage of an endowment involving bituminous coal, for example, may become ephemeral as petroleum products become utilized as a substitute fuel. The impact of substitution cannot always be easily identified; it would be difficult to say, for example, how much production of steel, copper, lead, and zinc have been displaced by the growing production of aluminum. In general, the big mineral-using manufacturing industries, and particularly, the metals-using industries, have been among the most rapidly growing sectors of the economy. Also, at the level of final demand, the products of these industries have a high income elasticity of demand. Equally important, they are the terminal products of an intricately-linked production sequence.

The role of petroleum and natural gas deserves a special comment. Throughout the first half of the twentieth century their production has continued to increase at a tremendous rate: over the period 1910 to 1950 the increase in output was almost elevenfold, and during this same period almost half of the total interregional shift in mining activities was accounted for by the oil-rich states of Texas, Oklahoma, and Louisiana. During the more recent period of 1939 to 1954, while employment in mining as a whole declined by 8.84 percent, employment in this sector increased by 92.4 percent. In terms of national levels of consumption, petroleum and natural gas have clearly been good resources. In terms of their multiplier effects and their linkages these resources do not rate so high. Production and refining of petroleum products is one of the most capital intensive activities in the economy, so that a considerable proportion of the returns to these activities is in the form of returns to capital, which is largely imported. At the same time, while petroleum extraction and the manufacture of petroleum products are tightly linked together, the more general backward and

---

Distribution of Value of Resources Extracted, by Major Resource Industry, 1870, 1890, 1910, 1930 and 1950."

forward linkages are relatively limited—for example, almost 80 percent of petroleum products were destined for final demand in 1947, while absorbing only 13.1 percent of the total inputs from other manufacturing activities. The answer to the question of how good an endowment is petroleum and natural gas is also affected by the nature of the regional supplies. These mineral fuels are strongly conditioned by the discovery–depletion cycle, so that areas narrowly specialized in the production of these mineral fuels may well find these products to have substantial disadvantages for growth if the depletion of reserves takes place at a greater rate than the augmentation of reserves by new discovery.

The fairly limited, direct, localized linkage with other economic activities is not only a characteristic of petroleum and natural gas, but of other minerals as well. For regional economic growth, the linkage between resources and other economic activities is not only a matter of *product linkage* and value added (since the value may be added elsewhere geographically), but is even more a question of *locational linkage*—the extent to which other activities cluster in the same general area as the resources. There is some evidence to suggest that these types of geographic linkages are fairly limited, and that they are becoming even more so. In this category are data showing the rank correlation of employment in manufacturing with population and resources employment, by states, some of which are presented in Table 2, using data for 1954.

The proliferation of stages in the manufacturing processes has permitted the increasing separation of resource processing stages from later stages. Since the processing stages are generally the primary weight-losing points in the production process, remaining stages become increasingly freed from their resource bases to seek more strategic market locations. This is reflected in the different

TABLE 2.   RANK CORRELATIONS OF SELECTED RESOURCE-USING MANUFACTURING GROUPS WITH RESOURCE EMPLOYMENT AND POPULATION, BY STATES, 1954

Correlated sectors	Coefficient
(1) Employment in 1st stage resource-using manufacturers with resource employment	.677
(2) Employment in 2nd stage resource-using manufacturers with resource employment	.583
(3) Population with resource employment	.666
(4) Employment in 1st stage resource-using manufacturers with population	.915
(5) Employment in 2nd stage resource-using manufacturers with poulation	.935

Note. These groups were based upon input-output relationships. The industries classified as 1st stage resource users were those sectors in the 200-industry BLS table that received more than 10 percent of their inputs (by value) from the resource sectors. The 2nd stage resource users received little directly from the resource sectors but received more than 10 percent of their inputs from the 1st stage resource users. These two groups combined accounted for slightly less than half of the total manufacturing employment. The 10 percent dividing line was an arbitrary choice, but was based on what seemed to be in both cases a logical division in terms of the nature of the basic productive process involved.
Source: Perloff, Dunn, Lampard, Muth, *op cit.*, Table 148, p. 394.

correlations for the 1st stage and 2nd stage resource-using manufacturing groups with relation to resources employment and to population.

Employment even in the 1st stage, resource-using manufacturing industries has a high degree of geographic association with population, but a relatively limited association with resource employment (roughly equal to that between resource employment and population). The 2nd stage resource users show a higher degree of association with population and a lesser degree with resource employment. The major part of manufacturing (those not included in the two classes shown) is even further removed from resource association. For all stages of manufacturing, taken in broad categories, closeness to markets (intermediate and final) tends to be the dominant locational factor.

This underlines the point made earlier: while export of resource products provides the basis for regional economic development, extensive and continued growth can be expected to take place only in those regions which achieve sizeable regional (internal) markets. Here the notion of *cumulative* advantage is useful. Rapid advances are possible as a region reaches threshold size for the internal production of a wide variety of goods and services. This type of regional development is greatly enhanced where the building up of social overhead proceeds rapidly—especially in the development of an extensive internal transportation network—and where particular attention is paid to the human resources and to the conditions for living. The latter, as noted earlier, is in no small part helped by the natural conditions of the area. Where resource and non-resource advantages come together are to be found the best conditions for a high level of economic development.

RESOURCES IN THE RELATIONSHIP OF THE REGIONAL AND NATIONAL ECONOMIES: HEARTLAND AND HINTERLAND

In the development of the United States economy the role of cumulative advantage is most clearly seen in the growth of the Middle Atlantic region and, later, of the Great Lakes region. Here are regions which have enjoyed unequaled access to national market. Each was endowed with unusually good agricultural resources from the beginning, and the emergence of the minerals-dominant economy found each with excellent access to vast deposits of iron ore and coal. With these resource and market advantages, they developed into the most significant feature of regional economic growth on the American scene—the emergence of an industrial heartland coincident with the center of the national market.[12]

The emergence of the industrial heartland set the basic conditions for regional growth throughout the nation—it was the lever for the successive development of the newer peripheral regions: as its input requirements expanded, it reached out into the outlying areas for its resources, stimulating their growth

---

[12]New England, which is also part of the Manufacturing Belt, can be considered a lesser-endowed, junior partner in the industrial heartland.

differentially in accordance with its resource demands and the endowment of the regions. The rapid growth of the United States economy was accompanied (and to some extent achieved) by this process of industrial nucleation.

A major consequence of the process of expansion and regional differentiation has been the *specialization* of regional roles in the national economy, and the nature of this specialization has influenced the content and direction of regional growth. In following this process of growth, we see the working out of the general principles touched upon in the previous two sections.

Using a three-sector classification of economic activity and eight multistate regions (as in Table 1) for the period 1870–1950, we can use a simple index of specialization[13] to describe the dynamics of regional specialization in the national economy during this period. This is plotted for two of the three major industrial sectors—resource activities and manufacturing—in Figure 1 (100 = national average). The data serve to highlight the nucleation process. In the three regions which have coalesced into the industrial heartland—New England, Middle Atlantic, and Great Lakes—strong manufacturing specialization has characterized the entire period; however, during this eighty-year period there has been a relative decline in manufacturing specialization (i.e., as compared to the nation as a whole) in the eastern end (New England and Middle Atlantic) and a continuing increase in the western (Great Lakes) end as (1) the center of gravity of the national market shifted toward the west, and (2) the superior resource endowment of the western end helped tip the scales in its favor.[14] The great outlying regions (with the exception of the Far West) have maintained or increased their relative specialization in resource activities over the whole period, while in the heartland resource activities in relative terms have continuously declined, suggesting the progressive reaching out of the heartland into the hinterland areas for its resource inputs.[15] These data highlight the significance of the heartland–hinterland construct in the development of the national economy, and its persistence and stability in the face of dramatic structural changes during this period. The nature of this process has a number of important implications for regional growth.

---

[13]$I = 100 \times \dfrac{\text{percent of region's labor force in given sector}}{\text{percent of nation's labor force in given sector}}$

[14]It is worth noting that the industrial heartland itself is not a static geographic area, but an area whose size and extent (and even role) shift with significant changes in the national economy.

[15]As in so many other indexes, the Far West (especially California) emerges as a unique case which, at least since the end of the 19th century, has followed neither heartland nor hinterland patterns, but which can be described in terms of a subnucleation in the national economy, or, if one prefers, as a second nucleation. The development of California thus suggests some interesting questions—for example, about the possibilities of second-growth (or new-conditions) nucleations, as well as the possibilities of a gradual spreading out of nucleation-type or high-level development in advanced stages of national economic growth. Even under the latter circumstance, the heartland–hinterland concept retains valuable explanatory power in analyzing regional development over time.

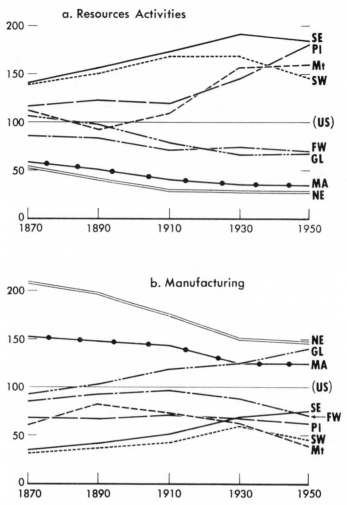

FIGURE 1.   Indexes of specialization in resources activities and manufacturing, multistate regions, 1870, 1890, 1910, 1930, and 1950 (U.S. = 100).

In the hinterland regions the working out of comparative advantage can result in a narrow and intensive specialization in a single resource subsector, in effect tying the future of the region to the vicissitudes of national demand for the products of that subsector. This will set at least ultimate limits to the region's growth rates: shifts in national demand patterns, the emergence of substitutes, depletion, technological advances, or the relative shifting of regional advantage may at any time choke off growth and leave behind enclaves of unemployed resources and economic stagnation. At its extreme, the western experience of "boom-town to ghost-town" is a dramatic illustration, but almost as severe has been the history of the tobacco and cotton producing areas in the South. These consequences are not confined to single-product specialization. Broader, sector-wide regional specializations may produce similar problems where the degree of specialization is great and where the products in the aggregate have a low income-elasticity of demand. Typical of this kind of problem is the experience of the Plains states which has been increasing specialization in agriculture since 1910, at the same time that their relative contribution to total national value of agricultural products has been declining.[16]

On the other hand, a broad and diverse resource specialization involving products in growing demand may provide a continuing impetus to regional expansion, especially where there is some complementarity among the resource activities. The Southwest illustrates the advantage of such a condition. Here a flourishing chemical industry has emerged based on rich endowments of petroleum, natural gas, sulfur, and salt—this is doubly fortunate, considering the high rate of growth of chemicals industries in the national economy.[17]

In short, the economic expansion of the hinterlands is closely associated with their resource endowments and the manner in which their endowments contribute to the evolution of favorable patterns of specialization or substantial levels of cumulative advantage.

When we look at the manufacturing sector, some important regional facets also emerge. Thus, the economic expansion of the hinterlands is accompanied by a certain amount of induced manufacturing growth. This falls into two general classes: (1) Industries devoted to the processing of regional resource products loom large. If we classify all manufacturing into first-stage resource users, or processing industries, and later stage, or fabricating industries, and plot by State Economic Areas which class of industry is dominant, we find that the processing industries dominate throughout the resource hinterlands, while the fabricating industries dominate in the industrial heartland. Thus, the process of industrialization not only defines the resource role of the hinterlands, but also sorts out the kinds of manufacturing activities between the heartland and the hinterland. (2) Less distinct is the role of region-serving industries in the regional growth process. These are generally market-oriented industries, producing products for regional final demand: as regions grow, their expanding markets offer increasing opportunities for economies of scale, so that one dimension of regional growth is a kind of "filling-in" generated by emerging regional market

---

[16]See n. 12.

[17]Annual growth rates of the following chemical end-products groups are suggestive:

	Period	Average Annual Growth
1. Synthetic fibers (not including rayon and acetate)	1940–1954	36.1%
2. Synthetic organic plasticizers	1936–1954	16.8%
3. Synthetic plastics and resins	1940–1954	16.6%
4. Fixed nitrogen in fertilizers	1939–1955	13.4%

Source: Harold J. Barnett and Frederick T. Moore, "Long Range Growth of Chemical Industries," *Chemical and Engineering News*, April 7, 1958, p. 81.

possibilities. This kind of growth frequently takes place at the expense of imports from other regions, so that one characteristic of regional growth may be a decline in the relative advantage of other regions from which imports have flowed in the past.

A general idea of this total effect is provided by a measure of the differential shift in manufacturing employment, as shown in Figure 2. This measures the extent to which the growth of employment in the major (2-digit) manufacturing industries within each of the states of continental United States has exceeded or fallen below expected growth, that is, the average national growth for each of the industry categories during a given period (here, over the period from 1939 to 1954). These within-industry shifts are netted out for each state, and each state total is shown as a percentage either of all the above-average growth states taken together (i.e., a percentage of the upward shift) or of all the below-average growth states taken together (a percentage of the downward shift), depending on which category the state falls into. Thus, for example, Texas had 11.4 percent of the total gain—or greater than expected increases—of all the states that experienced above-average growth in employment for all the 2-digit manufacturing industries taken together.

At the same time, however, the rapid-growth (often the new) manufacturing industries have continued to find their most favorable location to be in the industrial heartland. This is shown by the proportionality shift in manufacturing employment—a measure of the relative change in manufacturing employment

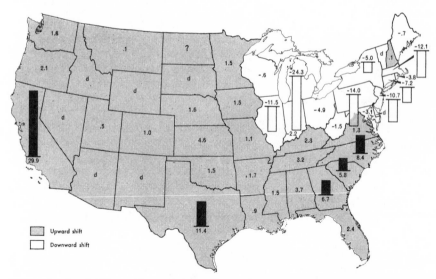

FIGURE 2. Total differential net shift in all manufacturing employment, 1939–54. (Disclosure problems made it difficult to measure this dimension accurately for those states marked "d"; the direction of shift was ascertainable, however, in all states but North Dakota. The % figures are rough indications of dimension only.)

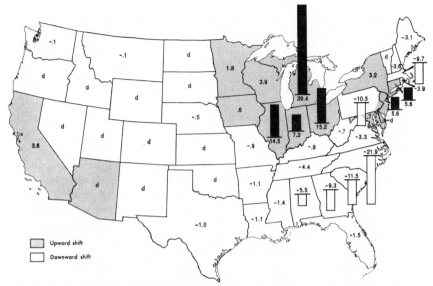

FIGURE 3.   Total proportionality net shift in all manufacturing employment, 1939–54. (Disclosure problems made it difficult to measure this dimension accurately for those states marked "d"; the direction of shift was ascertainable, however. The % figures should be taken as rough indications of dimension only.)

among the states due to their industrial *composition.*[18] (See Figure 3). The significant role in regional economic growth of industrial composition is highlighted by noting the very wide range of industrial employment growth rates during the same period, 1939–54. The regions which have contained or attracted the machinery, metals, and chemical industries have, of course, gained volume-wise through the unusually rapid growth of these industries. It would seem that these industries find that the massive markets, economies of agglomeration, and the extensive social overhead investment of the Manufacturing Belt provide them with the economic environment most conducive to their growth and prosperity.

As highlighted by a comparison of Figures 2 and 3, the industrial heartland tends to grow in a different way than do the hinterland areas. The industrial heartland serves not only as the focal point of the national market taken as a whole, but also as the industrial seedbed of the economy. The newer products

---

[18]Even if manufacturing employment in each industry had grown at the national average for the industry within each state, some states would have had a greater than average increase in total manufacturing employment because of a favorable industrial composition; that is, a high proportion of rapid growth industries. That is what is measured in the "proportionality" or composition effect, shown in Figure 3. For a more detailed description of these measures, see Perloff, Dunn, Lampard, and Muth, *op. cit.*, Chapter 5.

tend to be started here, nourished along, and as they find wide acceptance and volume grows, often the manufacturers find that they can supply the outlying markets more economically by producing on a decentralized basis. There are cases, of course, where the reverse is true and experimentation begins away from the center, but these have been relatively limited in number. In broad terms, the hinterland areas have grown mainly by the filling-in process referred to above, a threshold-by-threshold upward movement as resource exports expand and as the regional markets grow in size.

Focusing, then, on the specialized role of the regions in the national economy we get a picture in broad strokes of the spatial dimensions of the national economy. Central to it is the great heartland nucleation of industry and the national market, the focus of the large-scale, nation-serving industry, the seedbed of new industries responding to the dynamic structure of national final demand, and the center of high levels of per capita income.[19] Radiating out across the national landscape are the resource-dominant, regional hinterlands specializing in the production of resource and intermediate inputs for which the heartland reaches out to satisfy the input requirements of its great manufacturing plant. Here in the hinterlands, resource endowment is a critical determinant of the particular cumulative advantage of the region, and hence of its growth potential. This heartland–hinterland relationship seems to be the basic morphology of the subnational economy; through it we can better understand the role of resource endowment in regional growth.

SUMMARY

In summary, the United States experience suggests the following set of propositions. Resource endowment is continuously redefined by changes in

---

[19]While a discussion of the welfare aspects of regional growth is beyond the scope of this paper, it is worth noting at least briefly that among the more dramatic features of the evolving heartland–hinterland relationship has been its consequences for levels of per capita income. If we divide the nation into two parts—the heartland (including the Far West as a subnucleation) and the resource hinterland—and take the per capita personal income in the former as an index of 100, the comparable index for all the hinterland regions taken together is 58 for 1920 and 69 in 1950. Thus, although the per capita income differences have tended to narrow with the process of hinterland development, the advantage in welfare terms for the industrial heartland is still tremendous. As several studies have shown, the structural origin of the income differences is associated with the agricultural-nonagricultural dichotomy, so it is not surprising that we find such significant income dominance by the nuclear regions. This is, of course, not a hard and fast relationship. That a high degree of manufacturing specialization in industries with a relatively low income-elasticity of demand not only can dampen regional growth rates but depress a region's relative welfare levels has been indicated by the New England experience. At the same time, it is possible for resource regions to enjoy comparatively high per capita incomes, as the Mountain states have proven by turning up periodically with per capita incomes exceeding the national average. The important conclusion, however, is that so long as income differentials are associated with industrial structure, and structure is regionally determined by this ongoing process of nucleation, there are likely to continue to be interregional differences in welfare levels.

national final and intermediate demand, production technology, and economic organization. The relative economic growth of a region is directly related to its relative advantages in the production of goods and services for the national market; these may result from resource endowment on the one hand, or from a favorable degree of access to the national markets on the other—more generally, from a combination of the two. These advantages are normally conditioned by other elements, such as the quality of the labor supply and relative labor costs. The working out of cumulative advantage is exhibited in the specialized role that a region plays in the national economy, and this specialized role can best be described in terms of the heartland–hinterland relationships.

13

Relative Regional Economic Growth

An Approach to Regional Accounts[1]

Many kinds of decisions made by both private and public units depend on analyses of past growth and estimates of future growth of subnational areas. A significant proportion of all the capital investment and service expenditure decisions made by state and local governments, as well as capital investment and production decisions of private industry, is concerned with estimates of regional changes in population, in the volume of economic activities, and in the levels of living—that is, in the key elements of relative regional growth. Because of the importance of such estimates, it seems logical that they have a central place in any system of formally organized regional economic accounts.

A REGIONAL-GROWTH FRAMEWORK AND A TWO-LEVEL SYSTEM OF ACCOUNTS

A focus on relative regional growth and on the factors behind it, in fact, provides a useful way of viewing the requirements for regional accounts as well as the potentialities for constructing such accounts. The regional-growth–industrial-location framework of analysis provides a relatively comprehensive and consistent context for understanding and evaluating subnational economic and physical development. This framework has the additional advantage of tying regional accounts to the mainstream of theoretical and applied work in economics. By its very nature, such a framework tends to focus attention directly on

---

[1]A central purpose of this paper is to try to provide an overview highlighting the relationship between research in the field of regional economic growth and industrial location and work in the field of regional accounts. Both fields are in a period of rapid development so that one cannot hope to do more than suggest potentially fruitful lines of approach. Essentially, the paper deals with the "external" forces as they influence the growth and development of individual regions and the focus generally is "from the outside in."

The author wants to express his appreciation to Jesse Burkhead, William Vickrey, Werner Z. Hirsch, and Lowdon Wingo, Jr. for their thorough and thoughtful review of the manuscript.

meaningful economic relationships, rather than turn in on itself to provide a neat set of bookkeeping arrangements for their own sake. As will be shown in some detail later, industrial location and localization—using these terms to refer to the location of all economic activities, including production and consumption activities—furnish valuable reference points for all types of analyses. This extends to questions concerned with the geographic form of, and physical relationships in, the metropolitan region (one of the most important and difficult elements in the planning and development of local communities).[2]

The regional-growth–industrial-location framework suggests that a system of regional accounts would have to be built up at two levels: (1) at the national level covering all the regions (i.e., those specifically designated for accounts purposes), and (2) within the individual regions, so that adequate detail can be achieved and due consideration given to the special circumstances and special problems of each community. The information provided at each of these levels would be useful to the other, and would tend to strengthen the other. Over time, individual consumers of regional accounts may be expected to learn how to use each of these types to advantage.

A complete coverage at the national level is needed for federal government decision making as well as for decisions made by private enterprises whose activities extend over more than one community or state. It is equally necessary for the analysis of problems and for decisions made within any particular region. The development of any region can adequately be understood only within the context of national economic and social development; the relationship between the parts and the whole is always a critical element in regional analysis. In addition, comparative data of the type provided by nationwide coverage are a powerful tool in regional analysis. The need for nationally prepared, across-the-board estimates is especially evident with regard to growth projections (and, as already indicated, projections are crucial in subnational decision making). Growth projections developed for a single local unit often tend to be exaggerated; it is only too easy to claim a larger share of the anticipated national total increase than is reasonable. Projections for the whole nation provide a corrective for this. And, of course, they provide a tremendous saving through the "economies of scale."

A system of regional accounts built up at two levels would be particularly useful in application if both employed the same geographic building blocks. Since various kinds of public and private decisions necessarily cover a variety of types of subnational units (from the small county to the multi-state region in various combinations), the main possibility for general usefulness lies in providing information for sensible and flexible data "building blocks." If we focus attention on the possibilities for the decade of the 1960s, a strong case, I believe,

---

[2]This is not to suggest that the economic and physical features are the only ones of importance on the subnational scene. Social, political, and other considerations are, of course, centrally involved in many types of decisions made in states and localities. The key point is that the economic and physical features tend to be the *direct* foci of the great bulk of public and private decisions involving information on aggregates; thus, they provide a useful *starting point* for a regional accounts effort, no matter how encompassing the latter turns out to be over time.

can be made for using the states and the Census-defined Standard Metropolitan Statistical Areas as the basic data units for regional accounts. Given data for these units, some breakdowns will be possible for the sub-SMSA units and for the nonmetropolitan areas of the state, by way of allocation techniques. Even units as large as the SMSA's will provide plenty of headaches—for example, with regard to the disclosure problem in manufacturing industries—but these are highly significant units for decision making and deserve particular attention in the construction of regional accounts.

What types of data and what kinds of accounts does the logic of the regional economic growth model suggest? While it might be interesting to follow through this logic without any regard to feasibility, it seems preferable to discipline the approach by weighing the possibilities of obtaining the necessary data within some middle-range period, say, a decade. Within such a period we can look forward to data and accounts progress in a number of directions.

Extremely important in this regard is the work under way within the Office of Business Economics of the U.S. Department of Commerce to prepare interindustry sales and purchases (input–output) data for 1958, integrated conceptually and statistically with the national income and product accounts. When completed, the basic estimates "will be maintained on as current a basis as the available data permit." What is particularly significant as regards future possibilities for regional accounts is the fact that the sales–purchases information will involve a deconsolidation of the national income and product account *along industry lines*. As explained by the OBE, income and product accounts for the various industries will be established. The product (credit) side will show, in addition to sales to final users and inventory change, the sales of goods to each intermediate industry. The debit side will show, in addition to gross product originating in each industry, the purchases of intermediate goods by each industry. When set up in matrix form, the final demand columns will reflect the expenditures for gross national product; the value added rows will show gross product originating on an industry basis. This information will provide an extremely valuable framework for regional estimates and projections, as well as for regionally constructed input–output tables.

Another important development is the fact that we can expect to have personal income data on a regional basis for the major metropolitan areas as well as for the states.

Most of all, looking ahead, we might hope that to an increasing extent key national income and product and sales–purchases aggregates—or, more specifically, the major "control totals"—will be developed centrally for states and metropolitan areas and that there will be provided at the national level those state and metropolitan tabulations of data which can be obtained by normal data processing methods in the course of developing the national aggregates (such as regional tabulations of the data from the Economic Censuses and from the Internal Revenue Service).[3]

---

[3]Richard Ruggles and Nancy Ruggles, "Some Relationships Between National Accounts and Regional Accounts," *Proceedings,* American Statistical Association, 1959, pp. 278–81.

We can take it for granted that over time there will be continuing play back and forth between improved concepts and tools for regional economic analysis and the strengthening and improvement of regional accounts. What is involved at this state is necessarily an early effort to develop the logic of a systematic approach to the design of regional accounts, starting from where we are in our understanding of regional economic growth. This suggests, first, determining the needed measures of economic growth (or change) and then a look at what would seem to be the key analytical variables.

MEASURES OF CHANGE

How is regional growth (or change) to be measured? It can be assumed that at least four types of socio-economic change are significant for decisions made within or about metropolitan communities and states.

1. Changes in the volume of economic activities and in population
2. Changes in welfare
3. Changes in productivity
4. Changes in economic stability

Several tests seem logical in choosing indexes of change. One is inherent interest in the index itself, as in the case, say, with total population or per capita income. A second is its usefulness as an analytical variable. And a third is the possibility (or ease) of obtaining the data.

Employing such criteria, a case can be made for measuring changes in *volume* by way of the following items: population, labor force, number employed, total personal income, and total value added by various industrial sectors. The key *welfare* index is normally taken to be per capita income. However, a more meaningful picture could be provided if in addition there are data on distribution of income by family income classes, on wage levels, on number of unemployed, and on net fiscal residuum (as suggested by Hirsch). *Stability* might be represented by changes from a trend line—monthly, quarterly, or annually—in employment and unemployment and in value added. Changes in the productive *efficiency* of the regional economy can be measured in terms of changes in the value of output of goods and services (value added) per worker. All these elements have been discussed at great length in the literature[4] and it is

---

[4]Among other sources, see *Regional Income*, vol. 21 of Studies in Income and Wealth, National Bureau of Economic Research (Princeton: Princeton University Press, 1957). Suggestive materials on the measurement of economic stability are provided by George H. Borts, "Regional Cycles of Manufacturing Employment in the United States," *Journal of the American Statistical Association*, 55 (March 1960), 151–211. On the relationship between these indices of change and the designation of social objectives or goals, see Werner Z. Hirsch, "A General Structure for Regional Economic Analysis," in Werner Hochwald (ed.), *Design of Regional Accounts* (Baltimore: Johns Hopkins Press, 1961), 1–32.

useful here only to refer to them as background for the discussion which follows.

In terms of regional accounts, such a listing of measures of change, tested against currently available data, suggests several new requirements: (1) the need for value added estimates for states and metropolitan regions for all major economic activities on a periodic basis; (2) the need to place employment security data on employment and wages on a consistent basis (particularly with regard to industry and occupational classification) and regularly publish the data for all states and metropolitan regions; and (3) the early need for detailed periodic information on family income through Internal Revenue Service data and other sources.

ANALYTICAL VARIABLES: A REGIONAL GROWTH MODEL

If we had all of these indexes for all the states and metropolitan regions of the nation over a number of years, we would certainly have a great deal of valuable information concerning socioeconomic change. However, it is evident that more would be needed for analytical and projection purposes. More than anything else, we are concerned with having—in an effectively organized way—the raw materials for analysis of the problems that concern the public and private decision makers, and, of course, the general public.

We can refer to current knowledge of the factors behind regional economic growth to identify key analytical variables, and therefore data requirements. Regional economic growth is clearly a highly complex phenomenon. However, certain central features can be identified.[5]

A useful procedure is to visualize the requirements for making regional growth projections (assuming a comprehensive, eclectic approach), since this *directly* relates regional growth theory to the accounts question. Taking the projected national demand for various products and services as a starting point and translating this into total production by industry classes (gross value, value added, and employment), the problem is to allocate supply among the various regions of the nation. In turn, it would be necessary to allocate purchases on a regional basis—that is, to identify on a geographic basis the markets for the various goods and services. The interrelations of the two would have to be worked out, of course, by successive approximations. Relative regional growth (in volume) would be the reflection of the relative proportion of the total increases in supply and demand accounts for by each of the regions (but with different figures expected for increases in value added and in employment, because of the regional variation in labor productivity).

Production and consumption data (with income data serving as a bridge

---

[5]The analysis here draws on materials presented in Harvey S. Perloff, Edgar S. Dunn, Jr., Eric E. Lampard, and Richard F. Muth, *Regions, Resources, and Economic Growth* (Baltimore: Johns Hopkins Press, 1960). This book, in turn, draws on the work of many analysts, including Alfred Weber, J. H. von Thünen, August Lösch, E. M. Hoover, Jr., Walter Isard, W. H. Dean, H. A. Innis, D. E. North, Colin Clark, Bertil Ohlin, and others.

between the two) have to be played back and forth because each so directly influences the other, and these are, in fact, the logical organizing foci for most of the data. The subcategories are, then, the aggregates which highlight the more meaningful relationships. One of these arises from the significant differences between the export industries and the derived or residentiary industries. This distinction can be symbolized by comparing the role of the steel industry as against the role of retail trade in the growth of the Pittsburgh metropolitan region, or comparing the place of the aircraft industry as against that of personal services in the development of California. In other words, the major export industries (which include the federal government activities) are seen to have a special lead role in regional growth and to be autonomous from the standpoint of any particular region. The employment and income generated by the export industries provide the main base on which the so-called derived or residentiary industries will be built. This relationship is not uniform everywhere or over time.

The extent to which the derived industries will be built up will depend on various factors—such as the types of forward and backward linkages provided by the export industries, the service requirements of these industries (e.g., the nature of the freight shipments and the volume of business services used), the wage and salary levels set by the export industries, and the like. These are analytically important and have to be considered specifically in making the regional projections. But while the growth of the derived industries is by no means automatic, it tends to take place within a fairly circumscribed range. It is this feature, rather than any inherent sense of relative economic importance, that makes the export-derived industry distinction analytically useful.[6]

On the consupmption side, the important distinction is between final consumption and intermediate consumption. The former is closely associated with the derived industries, but not entirely; most of the export industries that produce final goods and services will sell at least part of their total product locally. In fact, the size of this local sale could be an important factor in the location decisions of certain of the industries. In the case of the goods-producing export industries, however, the important element is the purchase of intermediate goods—since the relative costs of acquiring (and selling) such goods is weighed in location and production decisions.

In making the regional projections, then, the starting point is a determination of the probable location and production of the export industries (specifically, those serving markets that extend beyond one state or one SMSA). This is not so much a matter of industries literally moving from one part of the country to another, within the projected period, as it is a question of where the new capacity will be built and the increases in production will take place. The answer has to be determined on the basis of *relative regional advantage* with regard to the

---

[6]It should be noted that these categories are treated here as useful organizing classes in an industry-by-industry approach to national-regional projections and not as an automatic "basic-nonbasic" technique for regional projection. For the limitations of the latter, see Ralph W. Pfouts (ed.), *The Techniques of Urban Economic Analysis* (West Trenton, N.J.: Chandler-Davis, 1960).

quite specific requirements of each of the major industries. These relative advantages can be analyzed in terms of the classic factors of accessibility to natural resources, quality and quantity of labor (including elasticity of supply of labor), and size of markets (together with other factors related to economies of scale), as well as the somewhat newer factor of the relative desirability of the working and living environment. These, taken together, will determine which region or regions would seem to offer the best overall economic (profit-earning and/or capital-preserving) position for each of the major industries. Where one consideration is dominant, as is often the case, the industry can be characterized as resource-oriented, labor-oriented, market-oriented, or amenity-oriented.

All this suggests that both the requirements of the major industries and the relative regional advantages with regard to these requirements have to be examined separately and in some detail. This calls for a variety of data, and these can be usefully organized in three major categories: data centering on (1) manpower or labor characteristics; (2) input-output and income-outgo; and (3) stock (assets or wealth). The first are data concerned with the human resources facet; the second, the intermediate-flows facet; and the third, the nonhuman capital facet. The key factors involved in analyzing *relative regional advantage* can be subsumed under these categories.

On the production side, the manpower information should throw light not only on numbers but on characteristics (such as sex, race, etc.) and on occupational and skill groupings as well as on levels of labor payments. The flows data, covering the interindustry purchases and sales, can provide insights on relative transportation costs and linkage advantages or disadvantages, as well as on growth of markets, investments and returns on investment. The stock category ideally should provide information on resources and amenities, as well as on output capacity and value of assets. The difficulty of obtaining information within this last category is obvious, but its importance should be equally obvious.

On the consumption side, the flows are of course of particular interest. The income and expenditures of households, as well as the purchases of firms, are needed to provide a measure of the changing levels of final markets and of the intermediate markets. The totals are important because of the increasing market orientation of industry generally and because of the significance in regional growth of the achievement of higher regional market threshold levels. The latter refers to increases in market size adequate to attract a whole new set of industries—say, meat packing or automobile assembly—that find they can now achieve adequate economies of scale by production within a given region to satisfy regional final or intermediate demand.

Since we are going through the exercise of visualizing the requirements for making regional growth projections as a way of highlighting the requirements for regional accounts, it is useful to note how the analytically significant data might be organized for making the regional projections. The problem is one of breaking down national projected population and economic tools (employment, output, income, purchases, etc.) into regional components—that is, totals for the states and metropolitan regions. To do this, it is necessary to look both backward and forward, the historical series providing the first approximations from which departures can be made by way of analysis of changing conditions

and their impact on the key relationships.[7] The initial question is one of relating the regional totals to the national totals—the parts to the whole—in a meaningful way. This can be done by translating the regional time series into "share" and "shift" terms so that it becomes easier to relate the parts to each other as well as to the whole—that is, who has gained at whose expense? These data could also be used in analyzing hierarchical relationships where they exist, such as any ties between the growth of the metropolis and the growth of the state or multistate region.[8]

The data showing year by year what proportion or *share* of the national totals are to be found within each of the regions, not only provide valuable across-the-board information, but also provide a useful type of discipline. They indicate clearly that, given certain assumptions about national growth, unusually rapid gains in certain parts of the country must be offset by stagnation or decline in other parts of the country; and then one immediately has to answer the question of where these declines as well as gains are to take place. In the same way, the *shift* data for the major measurement items—for example, for total population, employment, income, and value added—serve to relate each region's growth to the national averages. Here one can see clearly whether regional changes, even if generally upward, have been greater or less than the national average change. Thus, if a metropolitan region or state has been growing in employment and income faster than the nation as a whole, an upward shift is recorded—that is, a shift greater than that expected on the basis of the national average—and the question of what is behind this immediately comes to the forefront.[9]

---

[7]Burkhead highlighted the dangers inherent in any automatic projection of relationships from historical data, particularly given the problems associated with the instability of production coefficients and trading coefficients and the likelihood of the coefficients being more unstable in the future than in the past (stemming from the impact of the federal highway program, the appearance in certain regions of blocks to development such as water shortages, etc.). See Jesse Burkhead, "Comment," in Werner Hochwald (ed.) *Design of Regional Accounts* (Baltimore: Johns Hopkins Press, 1961), 66–68.

[8]As a matter of fact, metropolitan areas within the various large multistate regions show similar over-all growth patterns in many cases. See Perloff, Dunn, Lampard, Muth, *op. cit.*, p. 44. See also O. D. Duncan, *et al.*, *Metropolis and Region* (Baltimore: Johns Hopkins Press, 1960).

[9]An illustration here might also be useful. The table below shows for 1939–54 the state changes in population relative to the change in population for the nation as a whole for the states that have experienced the greatest departures from the average. All the upward shifts add up to 100%, as do all the downward shifts taken together. Thus, California had some 44% of the total above-average shifts during the period 1939–54. For some types of information year-by-year shifts needed to be calculated.

PRINCIPAL POPULATION SHIFTS AMONG THE STATES, 1939–1954

Percentage net upward shift		Percentage net downward shift	
(1) California	43.9	(1) Pennsylvania	14.1
(2) Florida	11.9	(2) New York	8.7
(3) Michigan	7.7	(3) Oklahoma	7.3
(4) Texas	6.7	(4) Arkansas	6.3

(continued)

A good starting point to arrive at an understanding of the changes that have taken place as among regions are the shift data in terms of the industry components. Thus we would want to have figures for the shifts in employment and in value added for each of the major export and derived industries for each of the regions. To get at what is behind the shifts in relative standing among the regions, a distinction needs to be made between the composition effect—that is, the consequences of a region having a favorable or unfavorable mix of the rapid-growth versus the slow-growth industries, as against the differential (or local factor) effect—that is, shifts among regions *within* given industries due to changes in relative regional advantages for these industries. The importance of this distinction stems from the fact that regions can grow either because they have industries that throughout the whole nation are enjoying a rapid growth or because they are getting a larger and larger proportion of a given industry—whether it is growing or not.[10]

The composition—or rapid-growth industry—effect arises from certain significant national factors, such as changes in taste, relative income elasticities for products, price elasticities, productivity, etc. In making regional projections, a large part of the total effort must necessarily center on analysis of just these factors as they relate to the relative growth or decline of *specific* industries on a *nationwide* basis.

The differential effect will require a look at the special local factors as they play themselves out with regard to the requirements of each of the major industries. The point here is that industries, whether growing or declining nationally, will not grow in such a way that each region retains its exact share of the total, but rather that some regions are likely to get a larger and larger share of the total capacity and production over time. Thus each region has to be looked at with regard to its changing relative advantages as to its input and market position for each of the major industries.

It is here that the various manpower, flows, and stock data, as described above, come into play. An especially important focal point is relative marginal productivity of capital among regions and the reasons behind the differentials. It can be assumed that as new capacity within an industry is required due to anticipated increases in demand, such capacity will be built in those regions where the returns on investment can be expected to be largest.[11] Thus, past data

Percentage net upward shift		Percentage net downward shift	
(5) Maryland	4.6	(5) Mississippi	5.7
(6) Washington	4.4	(6) Missouri	5.7
(7) Ohio	3.8	(7) Massachusetts	5.6
(8) Arizona	3.5	(8) Kentucky	5.1
(9) Oregon	3.3	(9) Iowa	4.6
(10) North Carolina	2.3	(10) Alabama	4.1

Source: Perloff, Dunn, Lampard, Muth, *Regions, Resources, and Economic Growth*, Appendix Table H.

[10]For a detailed explanation see Perloff, Dunn, Lampard, Muth, *op. cit.*, Chap. 5. Also Edgar S. Dunn, Jr., "A Statistical and Analytical Technique for Regional Analysis," *Papers and Proceedings of the Regional Science Association*, 6 (1960), 97–112.
[11]Stein and Schupack have used relative marginal product of capital to predict regional

on marginal productivity of capital is highly pertinent. However, since relative advantages with regard to inputs and markets are constantly subject to change, the regional analyst has to go through more or less the same kind of analysis that the businessman does in making his decisions with regard to new construction of capacity. That is, the past is a valuable indicator but not the total picture. The new situation as it is evolving must be taken into consideration.

Once estimates have been made for the export industries,[12] and the independent population additions, the base has been provided for making volume estimates for the derived industries. Here studies of changes over time in the relationship between the export and derived industries and the relative sizes of derived industries among different regions would be highly suggestive. However, in looking at the future, additional analysis would be called for, to account for forces such as the following: (1) the effect on the construction industry of requirements for new overhead, that is, social capital as well as for anticipated building of plant and equipment; (2) the generation of unusually active renewal programs within given metropolitan regions; (3) anticipated changes in regional income distribution; (4) the effect on services of an unusual rapid increase in income, if such is anticipated; and (5) the effect of identified organizational trends in various industries, such as the decentralization of banking services. A useful distinction can be made between minimum-size derived industry totals (i.e., the per capita volume below which no region falls—or the amount that can be assumed will be added with every increase in population) and the above-minimum volume which is the result of the special conditions of the individual region, as revealed by factors such as those outlined above.[13] Generally, shifts in

---

employment. See Jerome L. Stein and Mark B. Schupack, *Forecast of New England Machinery Industry in 1970*, Research Report of the Federal Reserve Bank of Boston, 1970 Projection No. 11, December 1959. Ideally, we would want to have figures on the value of capital assets, on capacity, on replacement and new investment, and on return on investment. An outstanding study employing these measures in projecting employment growth is T. Y. Shen, *New England Manufacturing Industries in 1970*, Research Report of the Federal Reserve Bank of Boston, 1970 Projection No. 1 (no date). The surveys that have been carried out by the Federal Reserve Bank of Boston suggest that rough estimates, at least, are feasible (although just how accurate present estimates are is an open question). In general, it is clear that we need a good many studies on capital, both national and local, to provide a firmer basis for estimates. This is a weak link at the present time and attention needs to be devoted as to how we might obtain the needed data on capital and on investment returns.

[12] One of the special categories that deserves particular attention is the localized forward- and backward-linked industries; that is, the industries that cluster in space so that they make up localized industrial complexes. These are industries that tend to obtain their best over-all position by clustering together within a relatively limited space rather than trading over a wide area. For these industries we would need detailed data on sales and purchases within the various regions. The petroleum–petrochemical complex and the various metals complexes are cases in point. For a thorough examination of the locational aspects of one such complex, see Walter Isard, E. W. Schooler, and T. Vietorisz, *Industrial Complex Analysis and Regional Development* (Cambridge and New York: Technology Press and Wiley, 1959).

[13] On this point, see Gunnar Alexandersson, *The Industrial Structure of American Cities* (Lincoln: University of Nebraska Press, 1956); Irving Morrissett, "The Economic Structure of American Cities," *Papers and Proceedings of the Regional Science Association*, 4 (1958) 239–56; and Edward L. Ullman and Michael F. Dacey, "The Minimum Requirements

industry and in population are closely related, but because of the increasing volume of the non-job-oriented population movement, an independent estimate of the latter is called for. We know that the amenity resources—that special constellation of climate, shore, water, etc., which attracts people in large numbers—are playing an increasing role. Some of the current studies on the older groups in the population contain suggestive data. The trends are very powerful here, particularly with regard to the movements to California, the Southwest, and Florida, so that the highly significant shares of this movement can at least be identified.

Projections normally have to go through a series of successive approximations, and this is true for the regional projections discussed here, particularly for the market-oriented industries and the derived industries generally. For these industries, successive market threshold effects have to be estimated to avoid too much piling up of multiplier effects on one side, and to avoid an underestimation of the role of changing scale economies. Here the discipline of employing the share and shift techniques is particularly valuable.

The application of trend lines to the future from the historical series might be done by way of regression analysis, with a good dose of judgment. The objective would be to come up with future values—possibly set out with ranges—for all of the measurement indexes; that is, for regional population, labor force, employment, income, and value added. From the standpoint of the users of the regional projections, however, the associated analytical materials would be at least as useful as the projected measurement indexes. This is true whether the focus of interest is on increases in the volume of activities or on changes in income levels, in productivity levels, or in economic stability levels.

PROJECTIONS FOR INDIVIDUAL REGIONS

Anyone preparing growth estimates for an individual region—whether a multistate region, a state, or a metropolitan region—would obviously seek to relate them to the across-the-board projections (assuming that these were available). Otherwise the task for the individual region is formidable. Given the across-the-board projections, however, the estimates for an individual region can focus on a few special considerations in detail and also test alternative projections as possibly influenced by way of public policy and programs. Here impact analysis, as outlined by Hirsch, would come into play.[14]

In addition to providing greater depth, the individual-region studies (and,

Approach to the Urban Economic Base," *Papers and Proceedings of the Regional Science Association*, 6 (1960) 175–94.

[14]Werner Z. Hirsch, "Regional Accounts: Objective and Framework," *Proceedings*, American Statistical Association, 1959, pp. 282–90. See also his valuable series, *Three Studies in the Measurement of the Impact of Metropolitan Growth* (Washington: Resources for the Future, Inc., 1959), mimeo. An important step forward in impact analysis is marked by the National Planning Association study, *Local Impact of Foreign Trade* (Washington: 1960).

particularly, metropolitan region studies) are needed to emphasize another element that does not appear in the across-the-board studies—that is, the localization patterns, or where economic activities (production and consumption) take place *within* the metropolitan region, and the relative rates of growth of the variou sections of the region.[15]

The localization patterns and localization requirements provide a significant link between the national and large-regional location factors and the specific public planning and investment decisions that are normally made within a metropolitan region. Thus, on the *intra*regional scene, the general requirements for a given type of labor supply are translated into the ability to obtain the necessary labor within reasonable commuting distance. The general considerations concerning the costs of collecting materials and shipping products are related to the ability to get industrial sites near rail lines or near main highways, as well as to relative traffic and terminal conditions within the metropolitan region. Special requirements, such as the availability of adequate water, also come into play at the localization level, and of course the amenity considerations have their localization features as well as the more general regionwide feature of climate. Clearly, relative regional growth and location considerations extend to the intraregional situation.

On the other side, assumptions about additions to population and above growth of economic activities in a given region carry with them a whole series of concomitants at the localization level. These are, for example, requirements for a certain amount of land and for certain specialized sites[16] (based on the kinds of industries anticipated and the characteristics of the persons who will be manning these industries), and changing requirements for transportation and for a whole host of social overhead items like education and health facilities. Here we find our knowledge particularly limited. We need a great deal more information than we have about the relationship between the growth of various types of industries and land requirements, transportation requirements, water requirements, and social overhead requirements in order to translate the generalized regional projections into specific localization requirements. This type of information is needed to understand what has been happening with regard to both land use and service requirements within the metropolitan regions, as well as what changes can be anticipated on the basis of overall growth.

THE LOCALIZATION VARIABLES

The usefulness of the regional growth-location-localization framework for evolving regional accounts can be highlighted further by noting the extent to

---

[15]The terms "location" and "localization" are not used in any uniform sense in the literature, and only rarely is "localization" separately treated, but it is clearly useful to have separate terms which permit differentiating between the *intra*regional considerations and the broad *inter*regional considerations.

[16]Estimates of land and building use by various types of industry are provided in the *Economic Report 1959*, prepared by the City Planning Commission of Sioux City, Iowa, under the direction of Charles L. Leven.

which, on the intraregional level, the same types of analytical variables are needed as on the larger region location level. This grows out of the fact that on the intraregional level, as well as the other, both the producing units and the consuming units normally seek to optimize their over-all position (or values).

On the production side—including manufacturing, commerce, government, and other service activities—there are the autonomous and derived units. The latter are those tied to specific population or market aggregates (such as nonspecialized retail stores, schools and many other types of public services, and various kinds of private trade and service establishments), and tend to be added in organic cell-like fashion. These are the counterparts of the derived industries—as against the export industries—in regional location analysis and, like the latter, tend to vary within relatively limited ranges with given additions in population.

The autonomous units normally seek specialized localization features and, in fact, can be characterized in terms of their "orientation" (depending on how large the item looms in the total costs and/or returns of the firm—as well as how much variation is offered by the different localization opportunities). As a tentative listing of such orientations, the following might be suggested:

1. *Transportation-oriented:* requiring special facilities such as ports or rail lines, or sensitive to high transport costs (e.g., cannot afford to fight heavy in-town traffic).
2. *Large-market-oriented:* drawing on the entire region, usually in the central business district, but also in "regional" shopping centers.
3. *Communications-oriented:* requiring a great deal of face-to-face communications and/or nearby specialized service operations.
4. *External-economies-oriented:* overhead service costs loom large and therefore such firms seek locations where these services are or can be provided at minimum cost, as in industrial estates or central business districts.
5. *Labor-oriented:* emphasis on ability to acquire a given quantity or type of labor at a reasonable cost (such as high-skill industries drawn to suburbs or industries requiring many workers drawn to locations along main highways).
6. *Large-site-oriented:* such as coal yards and lumber yards as well as manufacturing enterprises whose technology calls for one-story operations; also hospitals and certain other public facilities.
7. *Water-oriented:* requiring location along a river or at a point where large quantities of water can be acquired at low cost.

The projected localization of anticipated new autonomous units can be worked out by relating the industry requirements (or orientations) to: (1) the environmental features of the region, (2) the estimated holding capacity of the different subareas of the region,[17] (3) accessibility (transportation cost), and (4) the costs of land in each of the subareas.

---

[17]Defined in terms of the established zoning and density standards. However, as William Vickrey has suggested, for certain purposes, holding capacity and development standards need to be viewed as parametrically variable.

Governmental facilities and activities fall within both the autonomous and the derived categories. For first approximation projection purposes—that is, assuming a continuation of existing governmental policy—the governmental units can be treated in basically the same manner as their private counterparts. It could be expected that such trend estimates would be one of the types of information employed in the development of new governmental policy.

The localization of the derived units is essentially tied to the relative size and character of the consuming publics in the various subsections of the region. The most important of the derived items are the construction of new housing and the provision of housing services, followed closely by the provision of public services and the construction of public facilities, and followed in turn by the more or less ubiquitous private trade and service establishments.

Several techniques have been developed for estimating the future distribution of households in the metropolitan region. These commonly approach the problem by distributing a given number of new units (new households, dwelling units, or population) among the subareas of the metropolitan region by some explicit rule. Lowdon Wingo, in a current study,[18] classifies the various methods as follows: ad hoc allocations, gravity (or potential) models, and economic models.

Ad hoc methods are characteristic of current city planning practice and typically begin with the determination of holding capacities for the subareas based on such factors as the available land, prevailing population densities, and standards of development.[19] For the prediction of future traffic requirements, the Chicago Area Transportation Study developed a technique which involves the distribution of the estimated population among a large number of small areas according to their distance from the central business districts and a "per-cent-of-holding-capacity" function evolved from existing relationships.[20]

The potential or gravity model has been applied to urban spatial organization in various ways. Walter Hansen has developed a potential model which will allocate an increment of households among subareas, given for each subarea its employment, a measure of its accessibility to all other areas, and the amount of developable land it contains.[21]

Economic models assume that the spatial pattern of the urban economy results from the optimum-seeking activities of firms and individuals, each bidding for his best combination of two variables: the amount of land and its location. Both linear programming and continuous equilibrium forms have been explored. Herbert and Stevens have developed a linear programming model to allocate households among a number of subareas in a metropolitan region which

[18]Lowdon Wingo, Jr., *Transportation and Urban Land* (Washington: Resources for the Future, Inc., 1961).

[19]Cf., F. Stuart Chapin, Jr., *Urban Land Use Planning* (New York: Harper & Bros., 1957), pp. 339–54.

[20]John R. Hamburg and Roger L. Creighton, "Predicting Chicago's Land Use Pattern," *Journal of the American Institute of Planners*, 25 (May 1959), 67

[21]Walter G. Hansen, "How Accessibility Shapes Land Use," *Journal of the American Institute of Planners*, 25 (May 1959) 79–91.

would take the journey to work and the household demand for space as the significant relationships to be observed. Allocation would be carried out to maximize some function of location rents, space per household, and accessibility to employment, subject to certain restraints such as the supply of space.[22]

Wingo has developed an equilibrium model for the allocation of households based on two key functions of households—the provision of labor services at specific production sites and the purchase of the services of urban land for shelter space. The model concentrates on how the labor services are organized in space, given the characteristics of the transportation system, the spatial arrangement of production, the nature of the labor force, and individual household demands for space. It brings together the supply and demand elements to generate a spatial distribution of location rents and household densities. Thus, the model is a close approach to a localization counterpart of an interregional industrial location model of the type described earlier, dealing with the interrelationship of production and consumption elements in space.[23]

For many types of decisions made in or about metropolitan regions involving a focus on subareas, information about numbers alone, whether of population or households, or industries, is not enough. All sorts of detailed stock and flow data for specific areas or spatial configurations within the metropolis are needed. This is particularly true with regard to data on human resources and data on public services, expenditures, and revenues. Examples are decisions touching on plans for building schools and other public facilities, on the provision of voluntary health and welfare services, and on estimates of property tax returns. At the present time in metropolitan communities where this type of subarea data is collected, it is done on a haphazard and not-too-well-organized basis, but in looking ahead to improved regional accounts it is evident that such data and their organization must receive high priority.

A great deal of work needs to be done to clarify just what data should be collected on a regular basis for all subareas, particularly given the high cost of providing a wide range of information for a large number of units covering multiple political jurisdictions.

Three important tasks emerge here. One is the development of a sensible basis for demarcating subareas within the metropolis for accounts purposes. Another is the design of a useful data classification system which can serve the major accounts purposes. And the third is the invention of a scheme for the recording and use of the subareas data so that significant spatial relationships— such as distances from the central business district (or the core of the city) or income-potential and population-potential measures—can be recorded and analyzed. The total system should be suited to modern machine techniques of data manipulation.

In general, what would seem to be needed is a dynamic picture of the localization of facilities, persons, and activities within the metropolis. The provision of such data would, clearly, be an enormous undertaking, but given the

_____

[22]John D. Herbert and Benjamin H. Stevens, "A Model for the Distribution of Residential Activity in Urban Areas," *Journal of Regional Science*, 2 (Fall 1960), 21–37.
[23]Wingo, *op. cit.*

nature of the decisions which call for this type of information—such as the multi-billion-dollar transportation proposals—the costs involved are likely to be justified. It might well be that within the decade data centers will be establshed in the major metropolitan communities and these could provide the information needs of the various types of decision groups on a cost basis.

IMPLICATIONS FOR THE DEVELOPMENT OF REGIONAL ACCOUNTS

The above examination of the information needed to understand and project large-regional and intraregional development would seem to point to a number of conclusions with regard to regional accounts.

There are a number of important advantages in seeking to provide information in an accounting framework, stemming from the inherent requirement that an effort be made to achieve:

- Comprehensiveness—accounting for the totality of the items involved (such as all of personal income received)
- Internal consistency—normally based on the double-entry nature of recorded transactions, but permitting other checks as well
- Comparability—resulting, among other reasons, from uniformly and consistently defined categories; and
- Periodicity—providing the data at given known intervals, so that potential users can count on their availability

These highly significant advantages suggest the extension of the accounting framework to cover as much of the basic data needed for decision making as possible.

Regional analysis calls for data of such a wide variety that a number of accounts would have to be developed, including stock (wealth) as well as flow accounts, to satisfy this need. No one type of account is likely to suffice, no matter how comprehensive. The same kinds of considerations which gave rise to the development of five major types of national economic accounts are at play on the subnational scene. The problems that have to be solved at the subnational level are complex and subject to rapidly changing forces; decision-makers have to be armed with various types of information and there are decided gains if the essential data can be organized into accounts.

Special purposes and unique data problems require a regional accounts system to be conceived in its own particular context, even though there are some parallels that can usefully be drawn between national and regional accounts. Some of the differences between national and regional accounting that seem likely to emerge are:

- Regional accounts need to be developed through a two-level approach, with the federal statistical agencies providing certain of the basic data for all of the regions and with the individual regions building on these and providing extensions and greater detail where needed for their own special purposes.

- Unlike the national income and product and certain of the other national accounts, the key regional accounts may, for some period of time, be based on data provided periodically but not annually.
- Because of this nonannual feature and because of the costliness of providing certain of the data needed for regional analysis, it seems likely that regional accounts, to achieve needed comprehensiveness, will have to depend on sample studies to a much greater extent than has been the case with national accounts.

There is a natural tendency to think of accounts in terms of the long experience with national accounts, so it is useful to focus on such differences to bring into relief the special problems posed by regional analysis and regional policy-making.

The most hopeful possibility is to build a system of regional accounts centering on a geographic breakdown of the national interindustry sales and purchases estimates. First and foremost, the purchases–sales estimates will be integrated—both conceptually and statistically—with the national income and product accounts, so that much of the key data will be available on an industry basis. And, as the analysis in this paper suggests, the industry breakdowns are the critical ones for regional analysis and projection. Moreover, since the interindustry estimates will be built on the data provided by the economic censuses, a high proportion of the information is subject to regional identification.

Difficult conceptual and statistical problems are involved in such a geographic breakdown, to be sure, but they do not seem beyond solution. Whether Congress will be willing to provide the necessary funds is another matter, but one can be hopeful even on this score—particularly considering the history of interindustry work in federal agencies and the other statistical progress that has been made to date.

Even without nationally provided estimates, integrated regional interindustry input-output-income-product estimates might be prepared periodically within individual states and metropolitan communities that are interested in having such accounts as an aid to decision making. Local data collection by governmental and private agencies could be organized through a coordinated effort geared to an accounts framework, and gaps in information could be filled through industry and household questionnaires. The large problem here (aside from the question of cost) is that of comparability, an essential in regional analysis. Thus, if there is to be no central provision of regional data (aside from those already being provided), a very serious effort would have to be made to get as much comparability in regional data collection as can be achieved without sacrificing special local data needs.

The provision of needed information within an accounts framework at the *local* level would of course be greatly simplified by a geographic breakdown of the national interindustry sales and purchases estimates: not only would interregional comparability be greatly enhanced, but the local efforts could be devoted to achieving greater refinement and detail.

A geographic breakdown of national interindustry estimates ideally would provide data for the states and the major SMSA's on (a) value added by each of the industry groups, (b) payments to labor and capital by each of these groups, (c) interindustry purchases and sales, including both intermediate and final users, (d) payments of taxes to the various governments and receipt of revenue by the various governments, and (e) final demand purchases of households and governments and as related to capital formation and exports.

The geographic breakdown of the national purchases and sales data will not provide information on an important item in regional analysis—the areas from which the purchases are made and to which the sales are made. This information, if it is to be made available, would have to come by way of industry questionnaires. It is the type of data that might be provided within particolar regions, employing the national accounts data as a framework and as a basis for comparison.

Even taking the optimistic view that all the practical problems could be overcome and these core accounts established, quite a bit of information needed for regional analysis and projection would still be lacking. Some of this information could conceivably be provided through an extension of the interindustry accounts, while some would call for data outside the direct core accounts framework. Among the former are the manpower data which are needed for analysis of relative regional advantage, for localization analysis, and for impact analysis. We would want to have breakdowns for various characteristics of the labor force (sex, age groupings, race), for skills (i.e., skilled, semiskilled, and unskilled), and for major occupational groupings. The manpower item in the interindustry accounts could be expanded by a supplementary table providing this information, estimating the average wage for each of the major categories rather than simply for all of labor within each industry group. The availability and price of different types of labor are of prime importance in judging the relative attractiveness of different regions for industry.

To the greatest extent possible, the manpower items should be related to the household item in the final demand column, again through a supplementary table. Thus, for example, such interrelated information should suggest the number of nonwhite workers and households that might be expected from a given increase in industrial production within a metropolitan area. Also an anticipated increase in manpower could be related to rather specific types of household purchases, as well as to the increase in regional purchasing power generally. The main point is that bringing such information directly into the basic accounts framework offers the various advantages spelled out previously and serves to strengthen the capacity for regional analysis and projection.

Some of the needed information does not readily lend itself to the basic accounts framework. This is especially true of the stock, or wealth, data where the double-entry feature is not particularly meaningful; that is, where either the asset value figure is of no great moment or there is no liability figure in a balance sheet sense—say with regard to public facilities financed by taxes. The major need is for data on stocks which are expressed largely in physical terms, as in the case of housing, land use, and productive capacity.

At the same time, there are important gains to be had by relating stock data to flow data wherever the relationship is analytically important and the value figures can somehow be produced. This is true, for example, in arriving at and analyzing gross and net investment figures which call for information on the depreciation and retirement of plant and equipment. These, in turn, call for estimates of depreciable assets. There is a great deal about regional economic growth and intraregional localization that can only be understood by relating current economic processes and flows to data on assets and liabilities and the physical units behind them. This can be exemplified by data on capacity, including both private productive capacity and public facilities. Estimates of regional growth must take into consideration excess productive capacity which can be employed to meet increases in demand: estimates of construction require production-capacity rations as well as information on changing use of housing stock; estimates of needed public facilities call for information on capacity as well as on use of existing facilities. Where there are such analytically significant ties with the interindustry core accounts, there may be some value in placing such data into what might be called an "accounts-associated" category. The value would arise from the pressures to achieve account qualities of comprehensiveness, analytically meaningful categories, and periodicity. However, this point need not be stressed; the focus must be on a sense of priorities with regard to needed data, whether they are in accounts form, accounts-associated form, or just available. The main point is that certain stock data are important to regional analysis and projection.

The development of a regularized flow of information on stocks or wealth will obviously call for substantial research and experimentation far beyond anything done to date. We have the pioneering work of Raymond W. Goldsmith and others to build on, although it is only too evident that the problems of developing estimates at the regional level are particularly severe. On the other side, however, the need for stock data is more direct at the regional level—since so many of the decisions center on construction, redevelopment, and control of land use—so that great interest and practical use can be expected to follow on the heels of any progress made in this area.

Because so many decisions at the subnational level center on what we have called localization, stock or wealth data should be organized in terms of intraregional subareas wherever possible. It is not enough to have figures for the inventory of housing within a given metropolitan area as a whole; it is important to know where the housing is located. The same is true for private productive facilities and government facilities, as well as for the major communication-flow channels such as highways, railways, and waterways. In general, the development of an accounts framework for data needed in decisions focusing on intrametropolitan localization patterns deserves high priority in future research on regional accounts.

14

Key Features of Regional Planning

Regional planning has developed along pragmatic lines with relatively little attention to formal theory. It may be premature to expect a fully developed theory in a young and highly disparate field, but it does seem possible to generalize about the common features of regional planning as it has evolved in various countries around the world. Such generalization is not only suggestive of areas for further study but offers the possibility of illuminating a path through the confusing reality with which we must deal. The emphasis here is on problems of broad-scale regional planning, including both urban and rural activities, in developing situations.

Regional planning is concerned with the ordering of activities and facilities in space at a scale greater than a single community and less than a nation, or, in the case of a common market situation where a number of nations are economically integrated, less than that of the integrated totality.[1] In regional planning we must deal with a varied assortment of regions which are subsystems of a larger whole and change with the whole over time in both internal structure and external relations.[2] Such planning focuses on clarifying objectives and on designing means to influence behavior (particularly locational decisions) so as to increase the probabilities of development in desired directions in selected homogeneous or nodal areas of a nation (or a multinational complex). Since we are dealing with *both* regions and planning, it is evident that space, time, and process are core concepts.

It is useful to distinguish between two aspects of the planning process: viewed in essentially political terms, it involves the setting of objectives, the making of choices from alternative means (or system designs) for achieving the objectives under existing constraints, and evaluation of results obtained (in substantive and political payoff coin); from the technical planning standpoint, that is, through the eyes of the technical regional planner, the key process elements can be said to involve information and analysis, regional designation, a planning and programming phase, and operations. The technical planner may relate him-

---

[1]The latter is mentioned specifically because the paper treats a hypothetical common market situation to illustrate the regional planning features discussed.

[2]The change may be extremely halting or may involve emptying out in the case of depressed regions, but even in such cases the impact of national (or systemwide) change tends to be critical.

self to the political process in special ways. He may point to inconsistencies in multiple objectives where these appear and are particularly damaging, or suggest more operationally meaningful goals.[3] In the offering of alternatives he may be merely suggesting policies so unattractive as to make the preferred technical solution a natural choice politically. Evaluation, if it exists at all, is likely to be resisted by the technical planner or used to demonstrate why more resources for the regional planning effort are required.

It is helpful to be aware of the two parallel sets of processes. Not only must there be recognition of the continuity of the planning process in both terms, including feedbacks, but also awareness of the very important *lateral* relationships between the two sets.

JOINT DEFINING OF REGIONS AND OF PLANNING OBJECTIVES

The fact that regions can be, and are, defined in various ways—which troubles so many people, some to the extent that they entirely reject the value of regional analysis and planning—can, upon reflection, be seen to stem from the very purpose for using the concept "region." Jurisdictional boundaries tend to have built-in rigidities for reasons that are both traditional and practical (particularly for administrative convenience). The hierarchial character of governmental units often puts the subnational units in a defensive position with regard to jurisdictional rights and privileges (even when they do not have the claims to sovereignty that American states do). Because of this, their existence as subsystems of a larger system gets lost to view and can easily interfere with the efficient execution of national policy, and particularly national development policy. Moreover, jurisdictions have varying degrees of power for "closing in" on themselves, or closing others out, through special duties, taxes, and regulations (such as health regulations). They have public service responsibilities, tax authority, and in most parts of the world they are bound by constitutional and other kinds of provisions to provide uniform treatment of persons and firms in services and taxes. All of these features are stiff barriers to the solution of special problems within an areal context.

Thus, the designation of regions for planning purposes[4] has as its raison d'être the highlighting of the open-ended, subsystemic elements important to the objectives for which the planning is undertaken.[5] Such objectives, or the priorities given to them, can be expected to change over time, and this might

---

[3]An example would be the proposed objective of bringing new industries to a depressed region in a poor country rather than attempting "to equalize income"—which may be the language of the political objective.

[4]This is contrasted with purely intellectual and analytical purposes, which may involve quite different considerations.

[5]An extremely useful theoretical analysis of the region as a subsystem within a larger system and what this implies for the study and treatment of regions is provided by Edgar S. Dunn, Jr., *Economic and Social Development: A Process of Social Learning* (Baltimore, MD.: The Johns Hopkins Press, 1971).

well cause a change in the demarcation of the planning and/or operational region.

Designating a region for planning purposes also permits differentiation of the area from national and state (or continental) norms, either to achieve an equity objective, by providing an equalizer for a disadvantaged group, or to exploit unusual opportunities with unusual political and administrative tools. If the region is enclosed permanently by having *jurisdictional* rights conferred on it, it is then in a position to close itself off to some degree at least, and, under some conditions, it may have to follow national norms. And, of course, it may both close itself off and follow national norms.[6] If the central purpose of region designation is not differentiation, then what is involved is administrative reorganization, which, while it might be enormously valuable, should be distinguished from region designation.

It is not surprising that a nation or supranational unit should find many objectives for which spatial and related differentiation are valuable. Their value is increased by the fact that planning objectives vary from region to region, and the priority and interpretation given to them can be expected to change over time. Planners must, in fact, deal with essentially conditional objectives and emerging localized perspectives.[7]

NATIONAL PLANS IN REGIONAL TERMS

A whole national territory can, of course, be divided into planning regions, as has been done in a number of countries, for example, Chile and Poland. Normally, the purpose is to strengthen and sharpen national planning—in particular, to test out in spatial terms the various governmental sector programs proposed. Such planning should be distinguished from regional planning that has a differentiated *operating* component and intent for each region. The former is essentially simulated planning, concerned with studying the convergence of national sector programs in distinct areas, programs for agriculture, industry, education, transportation, and the like.

The facilities and services provided through sector programs must inevita-

---

[6]In this case, it becomes appropriate to speak of provincial (or state) planning rather than regional planning. This contrasts with regional planning even where the same regional designation is maintained over a long period of time, as long as the open-ended and differentiation characteristics are also maintained, as demonstrated by the TVA case.

[7]Edgar Dunn usefully points out: "it should be clear that the development planner (as distinct from the activity manager concerned with marginal efficiency transformations) has to work with conditional objectives. He must see them as conditioned by the present state of his system and subject to modification under the influence of future states not fully discernible. He should not define his planning objectives in terms of a fixed terminal state of the system. It may be a great convenience in planning to deal with fixed state targets, but it is more than a semantic nicety to insist that they be conceived as open-ended and nonterminal. . . . An important consideration in each choice is the contribution that the current stage can make to the development options at the next stage. The temptation and the tendency to view development as a one-step process sorely needs to be resisted."

bly be distributed selectively, and perhaps prejudicially among the regions. If each agency, operating with relative independence of others, sets its own targets, priorities, and standards, as is usually the case, it is unlikely that all the individual programs and projects will fit together sensibly in time and space. Thus, the agriculture agency might be making a major effort to raise the output of a particular farm product in a given area in order to increase export earnings, but the plans of the transportation agency for farm-to-market roads may be out of phase, as may also be plans for the extension of farm credits. Much information vital to an effective national plan can be gained by testing national sector plans for locational coherence and by studying their convergence within regions of the country that have been established for that purpose. The decision focus in such a case should remain the national plan and its sector components. Specifically focused, differentiated objectives and programs for each region would not necessarily be part of the picture when the main purpose is the testing of national plans. (This distinction is not normally made in the literature).

In simulated planning, as in operational regional planning, a special effort must be made to maintain the open-ended, differentiated characteristics. Otherwise, the regional designations, if kept over a long period of time without change, could increasingly become a Procrustean bed, unnecessarily stretching out or chopping off activities. Regional designations tend to take on a life of their own very quickly. Even so, simulated planning can be of great value in helping to prevent the closing in of operational regions on themselves by serving as a framework for overall perspective.

To optimize its evaluation (or "shadow") role, given the basic requirements of open-endedness and differentiation, simulated planning must permit *overlays* of some regions upon others, particularly the system of metropolitan regions overlaid on the homogeneous areas. (For example, Recife in northeast Brazil needs to be analyzed as part of the Brazilian national system of cities as well as in its role within the depressed northeast region.) Of greatest importance in both simulated planning and operational planning are periodic reviews of regional designations. These are necessary in order to keep up with or anticipate the socioeconomic changes under way.

THE LARGER CONTEXT OF REGIONAL PLANNING

So likely are human activities to close in on themselves that, as we have noted, special efforts continuously have to be made to prevent the destruction of the basic advantages of regional planning, that is, its open-ended and subsystemic features. The *core* features of regional planning of whatever variety is its relation to national planning (or national policy in market economies where there is no national planning). The central purpose is national welfare,[8] even where an interregional equity objective is politically paramount. Obviously, it would be hard to justify a development program for a depressed region which

---

[8]We hope we will in the not-too-distant future be able to say *world* welfare.

served to weaken the national economy and to bring the other regions down toward the level of the depressed area. Nor can a nation accept the proposition that there should be no migration out of a depressed region but that jobs must be provided for everyone who happens to be living in the given region, if this course would significantly reduce the productivity of the whole nation. But there is much more to it than that. No region can solve its own problems or fully exploit its potentialities by itself. Because the region is a subsystem, the most important part of planning for it is that which guides the flows between the nation and the region of investment capital, goods and services, people, entrepreneurship, and other elements.

There are strong reasons, deeply embedded in the socioeconomic structure of the nation, why a depressed region is lagging in income growth, a frontier region is relatively unexploited, or a metropolitan region is growing at the rate and in the form that it is. In order to alter the course of events, quite extensive changes have to be triggered, thresholds passed, and new environmental conditions established. Thus, regional planning becomes highly dependent on an understanding of location factors.[9] Most of the basic concepts having a direct relevance to regional planning are brought together in the theory of "cumulative advantage." That theory views the rate and form of growth of cities and regions as determined largely by the *relative* advantages of each, that is, those advantages of the natural environment and man-made works which attact major industries and high-skill labor.[10] As the requirements for economic activities change, so do the relative advantages among any given regions. Determining relative advantages is itself a critical element in understanding the kinds of measures that would be necessary to influence location decisions. However, in such an analysis, various noneconomic, as well as economic, factors have to be considered, among them attitudes and motivation, education, and political and administrative considerations.

THE SYSTEM OF CITIES

The close relationship between regional planning and national planning or policy is, as already noted, a crucial and continuous link between national objectives and regional needs. Another specific link is the system of cities, which in a variety of ways encourages and makes possible an increasing degree of specialization, a critical ingredient of economic progress. The importance of division of labor and of specialization for socioeconomic development has long been

---

[9]Of great value here are the work of Lösch and the revisions and extensions of Weberian location theory by Hoover, Isard, and others. Also applicable are certain of the concepts stemming from economic base and interregional multiplier theory, exemplified in the work of Haig, Hoyt, Andrews, Tiebout, and others. A valuable bibliography on location theory is provided in Friedmann and Alonso, eds., *Regional Development and Planning*. Part I (Cambridge, Mass.: The M.I.T. Press, 1964), pp. 704–706.
[10]Harvey S. Perloff, "Relative Regional Economic Growth." Chapter 13 of this volume.

established. But there are certain important spatial concomitants that deserve attention.

A greater specialization of function implies that each specialized activity (whether farming, forestry, mining, manufacturing, or services) must extend its linkages to outside activities in order to obtain needed inputs and find markets for its products. Thus, growing specialization creates networks of activity subsystems that have strong functional ties growing out of complementarities. Such ties, essential to economic progress, tend to grow stronger and more complex as development proceeds. These interrelationships may extend great distances; across the whole world, in fact. However, because costs are always attached to the transport of materials and goods, economic access (which depends on the quality of the transportation and terminal system) plays a large role in determining the linkages and interrelationships between the activity subsystems.

The cities play a key role in this process: they (1) represent the focal points of the transportation and communications networks, (2) encourage labor specialization and areal specialization in productive activities, (3) encourage efficiency in the provision of the service components of the economic system, and (4) make possible economies of scale and of agglomeration. In every case, these characteristics actually or potentially are helpful to the nonurban areas of the country which depend upon the products and services of the urban areas to increase the value of their own outputs and family incomes. The advantages of linkages, of course, flow both ways; increases in incomes in the farming and mining areas mean more purchases of urban-produced goods and services, which become inputs in the farming and mining operations as well as consumer goods.

We have long understood that the entire process encourages the growth of a hierarchy of urban centers. Those at the peak represent the most complex of the process. The smaller communities at the base are simpler agglomerations which carry out limited processing and service functions, and are generally in more direct relationship with the countryside; that is, they tend to be farm and mining centers.[11]

Thus, the so-called homogeneous regions and the nodal regions are closely linked; in fact, the quality of this linkage is crucial in the socioeconomic advance of both. As development advances these linkages increase in closeness. John Friedmann has suggested, in fact, that in a highly industrialized nation these links are so close and urban life so dominates all activities that the only useful designation of regions is in terms of the metropolitan regions and their spheres of influence.

This formulation is provocative and useful, particularly since it attempts to put regional planning into a dynamic framework. Recent developments, however, suggest this stage has not yet been reached even in the most industrialized countries; in fact, most of the industrialized countries (including the United States) are only now coming to grips with the depressed areas problem. In the

---

[11]Again, Friedmann and Alonso contains valuable bibliographies, this time on the role of cities in economic development and on the system of cities. Note especially the articles by Brian J. L. Berry.

United States, in addition to the program for the Appalachian region, several other multistate regions have recently been designated for special treatment as depressed areas. On the continent of Europe, in the EEC area, the depressed area rehabilitation objective is gaining momentum and programs for depressed regions are being prepared. Both in the United States and in Europe, a good bit of attention in such programs is devoted to building up urban "growth poles."

Aside from the depressed area problem, regional designations in advanced countries may follow lines other than those suggested by the metropolitan region in various situations. Thus, certain emerging problems in the economically advanced countries, such as air and water pollution, suggest the possibility of a different type of regional effort, of which the regional program to clean up the Ruhr Valley is an example. Likewise, large-scale land development efforts for intensive recreation purposes, as in mountain areas or along a seacoast, would call for regional planning and development along lines not direcetly related to metropolitan regions.

A more general formulation of the issue raised by Friedmann is that the system of cities becomes increasingly significant as a focal point of spatial planning as a country develops, that is, as the ties among the urban communities and with their hinterlands are strengthened. This means that, increasingly, regional planning must be multidimensional planning in a special sense. It must guide public and private efforts not only in terms of the homogeneous regions chosen for differentiated treatment within themselves but also in terms of the ties between the urban communities of such regions with urban communities outside the regions. At the same time, it must strengthen the complex of specializations, complementarities, and linkages to achieve optimum efficiency and self-adjusting capacity within the region.

The developmental effectiveness of the linkages among the units within the national system of cities and between the urban communities and their hinterlands is not merely a matter of good transportation and communication facilities, although these are important. It is also a matter of how sturdy is the economic base of each of the urban units, how efficient its form, and how attractive the urban environment for daily living and working. These problems are, of course, of direct interest to city planners. Thus, the interests of the regional planner and the city planner converge at the metropolitan region; the regional planner is more concerned with "urbanism writ large"—the metropolis as a functional unit within the system of cities—while the city planner is more concerned with the intrametropolitan issues—generally, the efficiency and quality of life within the urban community. Both the regional planner and the city planner are concerned with national urban policy, for such policy provides an essential part of the framework within which specific regional and city plans need to be drawn up.

DEALING WITH THE VARIOUS PHASES OF THE PLANNING PROCESS

Each phase of the total regional planning process has its own requirements so far as scope, content, and methods are concerned. This is an aspect of regional planning that has not received the attention it should have, either in the literature or in practice. Its neglect in practice has caused the unnecessary rigidity that has characterized regional planning. Regional planning is concerned with the ordering of activities and facilities in space and time, but this does not imply that regional planning is necessarily concerned with the same space and the same time in all of its phases. Thus, the notion of changing regions applies to different planning phases as well as to different objectives and problem areas.

The information–analysis phase of regional planning can, and normally should, cover the total area of the nation (or of the multination region). This is particularly important in order to understand the evolving role of each activity, industrial sector, and area within the larger national scheme. Activity, sector, and region are simply various categories in which to record the totality, each being a convenient way of describing the subsystems involved. The interrelationships of all these among themselves are important, as are the relations of each to the total.

Total national coverage also makes sense at the planning–programming phase in simulating a national plan in spatial terms, although in this case, the regions may be differently established on the criterion of programming effectiveness. Such national coverage can serve as a useful check on sector programs devised by relatively independent departments or ministries. However, sound operational planning must work from the bottom up as well as from the top down. Planning from the bottom up is achieved in *sector planning* by reliance for program and project preparation on the bureaus or action agencies within the individual ministries. In *regional planning*, planning from the bottom up can readily pose severe problems. This can be highlighted by the experience of the U.S.S.R., where doctrine dictated that planning proposals must come up from each economic region. The results, it was found, were local proposals for resources allocation so far beyond national capacity and so subject to local political considerations that the problem of reconciling them with national "control" totals becomes very difficult indeed. While the trend has been toward greater decentralization of planning decisions in general, the role of regional planning within the national plan from the bottom up has been substantially diminished.

It is well to remember that, in most political systems, basic local interests are looked after through local representation in a national legislature. Each legislator, even when essentially national (or Burkean) in outlook, can be expected to seek local advantage; for many issues, after all, national interest can only be defined as the totality of local interests. Thus, with local interests generally provided for, regional planning and programming—beyond simulation purposes—can be limited to those areas where an unusually strong case for differentiation in governmental treatment exists. While this may seem fundamentally simple, actually, of course, we do not know too much yet, in spite of what seems like centuries of effort, about how to provide for local differentiation while giving top priority to national goals.

In operational terms, the key problem is to evolve an approach which permits an effective and fair reconciliation of diverse interests. This calls for political and administrative inventiveness. The operational objectives that have to be reconciled are (1) providing for meaningful participation by the people of the region so as to bring the local interests forward; (2) achieving flexible and hard-hitting administration, which at times may mean the establishment of a regional authority (as in the Tennessee Valley, Guayana, Southern Italy, and the Aswan Region); and (3) closely relating the regional planning to national policy and programs so as to protect national interests.

Other operating considerations must, of course, enter into the choice of regions and the design of regional programs. As mentioned earlier, administrative as well as political capacity are certainly of primary importance. The small supply of administrative and planning personnel in developing countries, for example, can be expected to influence the number of regional development programs undertaken at any one time. Even if this particular limitation is resolved, other operational limitations can be expected. The capacity of the various departments or ministries to carry out their sectoral programs when there are many separate regional programs under way is one such limitation. The main point is that decisions as to the number, form, and function of regional planning efforts must weigh operational considerations quite heavily in the balance. Regional planning, after all, is not an end or good in itself. It should be undertaken only if it contributes clear-cut benefits that are greater than the costs involved.

A HYPOTHETICAL EXAMPLE

To obtain an overview of the features of regional planning described above, it is helpful to imagine the regional planning process at work in a given situation. Since we are concerned with normative as well as positive elements (the "ought to be" as well as the "as it is"), this can best be done under hypothetical conditions. Thus, I propose to look at the problems of planning involved in making a success of a Latin American regional economic integration effort, projected some time into the future. Taking a situation to which we are not accustomed can help us to escape our traditional ways of looking at regional planning and to sharpen our awareness of the interrelationship of the basic elements.

We shall hypothesize that a Latin American common market treaty has been signed, that intraregional tariffs have been eliminated, and that there is a common external tariff (hopefully, a limited one so that Latin America is looking outward as much as inward). International movement of goods, investment, and people is free. Monetary and fiscal policies have been harmonized. A movement to achieve political integration is under way. Meanwhile, a Common Market Commission has been granted joint executive-legislative authority (of a parliamentary variety) covering certain broad, but specified, areas. The Commission members would be the top planners, but they would have a technical regional planning unit to assist them. It is assumed that continentwide planning has been accepted as essential in an underdeveloped continent to turn the integration effort into a substantive success.

A host of large problems emerges at the outset. If trade among the countries is to be substantially increased, international transportation facilities will have to be greatly extended and improved, since existing facilities are largely geared to a trade pattern that involves the shipment of a limited number of basic commodities overseas rather than to significant intra-Latin American exchanges. Natural resources, potentially ready for much more extensive exploitation under the new conditions, have to be identified, and strategies for their development worked out. Provisions for special help to the poorest countries and parts of the region have to be made (for the same reasons that special arrangements were made for southern Italy in the European common market effort). The most promising growth poles have to be identified and further developed. Expansion of manufacturing industries producing goods for sale in a regional market has to be planned for (probably working closely with a regional promotional organization equipped to provide special inducement to such industries).[12]

The Information–Analysis Phase

The members of our hypothetical planning agency will need a great deal of information. An early and continuing task will be the analysis of the major developmental problems and potentialities.

The planners will need information on every part of Latin America. Some information would be available within the various national planning organizations even though it initially was generated for internal planning purposes. However, the greatest part of the information needed would be transnational. While national boundaries could not, by any means, be overlooked, the main focus would be on the problems and potentialities that involve more than one nation and on the structural changes that would tie socioeconomic activities more closely together. The planners will want to have data for the more significant sections (mainly urban regions) of all of Latin America. They will want to trace the major flows among the existing centers and make estimates of future flows on the basis of the new trading conditions. Input–output matrices will probably be developed, on a from-to basis. In the same light, they will examine the existing trade patterns with nations overseas, also, on a from-to basis, and project anticipated trade patterns, recording the physical movements as well as the movements in terms of value.

A tremendous amount of information will be needed for these analyses and projections, particularly on human resources, natural resources, public and private capital resources, and institutional endowment. All of this would have to be recorded and analyzed not only in locational terms but also in dynamic (over

---

[12]The requirements for successful regional integration in Latin America outlined here are based on the literature in the field, which includes Victor L. Urquidi, *Free Trade and Economic Integration in Latin America* (Berkeley, Calif.: University of California Press, 1962); Miguel S. Wionczek, *Latin American Free Trade Association* (New York: Conciliation, Carnegie Endowment for International Peace, 1965); Robert T. Brown, *Transport and the Economic Integration of South America* (Washington, D.C.: Brookings Institution, 1966); national Planning Harvey S. Perloff and Raúl Saez, "National Planning and Multinational Planning under the Alliance for Progress," Chapter 10 of this volume; and Harvey S. Perloff and Rômulo Almeida, "Regional Economic Integration in the Development of Latin America," *Economía Latinoamérica*, II (November 1963).

time) terms; for example, figures of population density in the countryside and cities will have to be analyzed in accordance with expected changes in their patterns of distribution.

To achieve analytical significance relevant to the planning tasks, the information will have to be organized to highlight major features of the Latin American socioeconomic-physical landscape. Regional accounts would probably be employed for this purpose. These would have to include both stock items (natural resources, labor force, capital resources, and the like) as well as flow items (such as product, income, trade, communications, and migration). Such accounts would have to be built up from the smallest jurisdictions for which data are collected in order to provide the maximum flexibility in spatial combinations for the analyses that will have to be made.[13]

In general, the planning analysis could be expected to focus on the requirements for achieving optimal developmental and locational leverage under Latin American conditions. Such a focus, our hypothetical planners would know from the experience of others, would involve simultaneously bringing about an increase in specialization of functions and areas and an increase in activity linkages, through improvements in access from one area to another and other means. They will want to analyze the conditions under which economic activities could increasingly achieve economies of scale and of agglomeration, as, for example, conditions associated with a growing hierarchy of urban centers. They would thus be particularly concerned with actual and potential growth poles and with the linkages among them.[14]

Initial interest would probably center on the heartland regions or development axes (elongated corridors along principal transportation routes linking two or more metropolitan regions) because of their great potential developmental leverage. These are the urbanized regions that have outstanding resource and locational advantages; that is, they contain, or have easy access to, various resource inputs needed for both heavy and light industry; can obtain the necessary food supplies at reasonable prices; have been able to attract a wide variety of human skills, including management skills, and have nodal characteristics with regard to transportation.[15] Latin America, like the United States and Ger-

---

[13]Detailed analyses of the problems of developing appropriate regional accounts for planning purposes are provided in the three volumes sponsored by the Committee on Regional Accounts, Resources for the Future, Inc.: Werner Hochwald, ed., *Design of Regional Accounts* (1961); Werner Hirsch, ed., *Elements of Regional Accounts* (1964); and *Regional Accounts for Policy Decisions* (Baltimore, Md.: The Johns Hopkins Press, 1966).

[14]The idea of the urban community as a developmental lever has been elaborated by François Perroux, *L'économie du XXᵉ siécle* (Paris: Presses Universitaires de France, 1961). See also J-R Boudeville, *Problems of Regional Economic Planning* (Edinburgh: University Press, 1966), for a useful discussion of the "growth pole" concept as well as other concepts and methods appropriate to regional planning.

[15]For an analysis of this concept, see Harvey S. Perloff *et al.*, *Regions, Resources, and Economic Growth* (Baltimore, Md.: The Johns Hopkins Press, 1960); and Harvey S. Perloff and Lowdon Wingo, Jr., "Natural Resource and Endowment and Regional Economic Growth," Chapter 12 of this volume. Also see the highly suggestive treatment of the subject by Edward L. Ullman, "Regional Development and the Geography of Concentration," *Papers and Proceedings of the Regional Science Association*, 4 (1958), pp. 179–198.

many, has a manufacturing belt, in this case extending from Rio de Janeiro in an almost continuous belt of cities to Buenos Aires. (The fact that this particular economic heartland could extend across national boundaries, in a situation where relatively little had been done to enhance interconnections, suggests the economic power of activity-clustering for specialization and complementary linkages.) The hypothetical planners will want not only to analyze in depth the nature of the existing linkages within the heartland and how these might be enhanced through developmental measures, but they will also want to analyze the nature of the relationship of the heartland to the food-producing areas near by (the food-growing hinterland) and the raw materials and specialized products of the other economic zones. The latter, in turn, can expect to experience economic progress as their sales to the heartland, as well as to more distant countries, expand, and as their own manufacturing and service industries grow.

Our planners will also be interested in the incipient heartland-type areas evolving along the coast of Venezuela and across to the major cities of Colombia, as well as the anticipated megalopolization of the Mexico City region. Such a multiple development of heartland-type areas could be expected in a region as vast as Latin America. These areas, together with the other major metropolitan regions and their clustering communities, would be the backbone of an increasingly interlocked continent for increasingly elaborate interchanges.[16]

In addition to urbanized regions, the hypothetical planning agency will be interested in regions of other types. In studying the various potentialities for increasing food supply and producing raw materials for which there are anticipated markets, the planners will probably designate a number of particularly promising producing areas as development regions. The international agency would make the designation either because the areas cross national boundaries or, for intranational regions, because the country itself is not equipped to exploit the full potentialities of the region without substantial external assistance.

The agency will undoubtedly also want to study closely the various international river basins, such as the La Plata basin which is shared by Brazil, Argentina, Uruguay, Paraguay, and Bolivia; the Tumbes basin, shared by Ecuador and Peru; and the Lake Titicaca basin, involving Bolivia, Chile, and Peru, which have been discussed as offering rich opportunities for multiple-purpose development, including irrigation, power, and transportation. Elaborate study would probably be devoted to the Amazon basin in particular in an attempt to appraise the future potential of this highly complex region and to determine whether the barrier it imposes to internal transportation within the northern part of South America can be overcome.

Other frontier zones, including those whose development is already under way, as in Guayana, will be studied closely to determine whether a pattern of development already in progress should be changed, given the anticipated increased intraregional trade, or whether a pattern of development might now be undertaken for the first time. Entire countries (such as Bolivia) or parts of countries (such as the Brazilian northeast) would be studied as possibilities for special

---

[16]Brown outlines an intriguing program for the accomplishment of this objective.

treatment as depressed regions. Considering depressed regions in national units will help to provide a strong political base for successful economic integration of all of Latin America.

The Planning–Programming Phase

The information-gathering and analytical work ideally would cover every part of Latin America and extend to trading partners overseas. Such coverage would be needed to understand the economic, social, and physical interconnections of the whole continent, as well as the problems and potentialities that deserve special attention.

When it reaches the planning–programming phase, our hypothetical agency will necessarily be much more limited in the geographic coverage of its activities. Some of the sector programs (for housing, education, health, welfare, and so forth) will be treated largely within a national context. Only in the case of transnational programs will our planners be directly involved. Particularly important for them will be: (1) the design of programs for improving accessibility through transportation and communications of every type; (2) the working out of efficient and economical patterns of urbanization, and particularly the search for means to turn the urban regions into powerful levers for linkage and development; and (3) the selection of regions, such as those offering unusual potentialities for food production, for special attention and help in planning the major aspects of their development.

With only limited resources available, severe strains can be expected to develop as choices are made among areas for special treatment, between major objectives of *efficiency* (maximizing the net returns for all of Latin America), *equity* (the poorer countries would certainly make a strong case for special treatment), and regionwide *cohesion* (closer ties among the various countries in order to bind them together socially and politically). Such choices are likely to be an integral part of the continuing political dialogue. The technical planners will be interested in more operational formulations and will be concerned with probable impacts from alternative lines of action. They can, for example, estimate how much would be given up in gross regional product by public investment in depressed areas compared with investment in alternative growth areas; or, contrariwise, how much would be gained by slowing down the flood of migrants to capital cities and other major cities if development programs were initiated in selected depressed areas.

A major problem will be to achieve a truly continental point of view in evolving the general planning goals and making the specific investment decisions. It can be expected that all decisions will be shaped by conflict and the pressures of diverse interests. Every country will undoubtedly press for special consideration: In the case of the smaller ones, such as Bolivia and Paraguay, the pressure might be for special treatment for the country as a whole; in the case of the larger ones, such as Brazil, for various deserving (that is, special problem or special opportunity) subnational regions. Unless the advantages of special treatment are obvious, the planning agency will find itself trying to avoid designating regions for such treatment in operating terms, for its members will learn quickly that the mere designation of a special region will intensify pressures for additional public investment funds.

The Planning-Operational Phase

The payoff of plans comes in their implementation; our hypothetical planning agency will, therefore, have to weigh operational considerations throughout the whole planning process. If the members of the planning agency have paid careful attention to past experience with national planning in Latin America as well as to the frequent and large gaps between ambitious plans and the exceedingly limited capacity for carrying them out they are likely to prepare "plans for planning."[17] The availability of adequately trained personnel for the detailed planning, for project preparation, and for the administration of proposed regional programs will certainly be a key factor in the decision as to whether or not to encourage the initiation of proposed programs. Also, the probability of having the necessary budgetary funds available on a continuing basis, including funds to meet unexpected problems that arise in the course of execution (an inevitable feature of all regional programs), will play a significant role in the initial decisions.

Once a given regional program has been initiated through the combined efforts of the supranational and national authorities and the people of the region, one of the greatest challenges to the planners will be to maintain the necessary degree of freedom for change and adjustment during the execution phase. This will be true whether the regional program is being carried out on a centralized or a decentralized basis.

Changes in supply and demand will influence not only the growth of major industries, and, consequently, the growth of the regions in which they are located, but also the rate of expansion of the linked industries and services. Job availability and related migration movements will be influenced by changes in demand and supply and, thus, such changes will have an impact on both the major urban centers and the countryside. Major changes of other kinds can also be expected to have extensive repercussions.

All this suggests not only that plans will have to be adjusted often, but also that the entire regional program must be set up on an inherently flexible basis. A good example is the amount of in-migration that should be planned for. Experience in Guayana, Brasilia, and elsewhere has demonstrated that it is extremely difficult to accurately predict the amount of in-migration, since the effects of the drawing power of a new urban growth pole and the "rejection" power of the hinterland cannot be measured precisely. This suggests that flexible programs looking toward job creation, the provision of self-help and extremely low-cost housing, and some assistance to a large number of unemployed (an inevitable concomitant of a new hopeful area) will be more valuable than highly detailed

---

[17]The importance of execution in the planning process and of weighing operational consideration in laying out plans has been stressed by Albert Waterston in several publications. See especially his *Development Planning: Lessons of Experience* (Baltimore, Md.: The Johns Hopkins Press, 1966).

plans for land use and for construction of specific major buildings. The quality of the planning will depend not so much on the accuracy of the projections as on the ingenuity employed in creating self-guiding and self-adjusting mechanisms wherever possible.

Thus, our hypothetical planning agency can be expected to play out a unique role as far as content is concerned but to follow processes that would be familiar to regional planners, who may be working under equally unique circumstances in other parts of the world. These processes and features make up the common elements in regional planning of every type.

IV

FISCAL POLICY AND PLANNING

INTRODUCTION

As "Budgetary Symbolism and Fiscal Planning," the first of these chapters, was being written, the nation was emerging from one crisis, the Great Depression, and stood at the brink of another, World War II. The second article, "Fiscal Policy at State and Local Levels," was conceived during the dark days of that war. Besides their common context, both deal with the duties of government as the ultimate guardian of the public welfare, a veiw of public responsibility then undergoing radical change.

"Budgetary Symbolism," Perloff's first published paper and a spin-off from his doctoral dissertation, provides a penetrating analysis and critique of long-standing and archaic budgetary practices against the backdrop of a rapidly evolving society and economy. It starts by tracing the evolution of budgetary equilibrium, the doctrine that insists on regularly balancing government expenditures against current revenues; next demonstrates how rules that limit government programming to annual budgets are outmoded, given changes in "political and economic structures and in social concepts and ideals"; and concludes by admonishing government to "take a more active part in society's attempt to achieve security and the more abundant life."

The tradition of balanced budgets is "on the one hand the balance wheel of social organization and on the other hand one of its greatest elements of rigidity." It required courage to argue, as Perloff did, against the prevailing wisdom and in favor of deficits if these were what it took to stabilize economic activity. This meant a large and active public sector with control over substantial resources. As well, it presumably meant usurping the rights of the individual and meddling in what had previously been sacrosanct affairs. Even more awesome than size of government was its rapid growth during the depression. In spite of the largely successful efforts of the Roosevelt administration in pursuing a program of "reckless spending" to pull the economy out of the depression, prevailing opinion strongly supported fiscal conservatism. According to surveys cited in the article, most people opposed government intervention. Perloff's courageous and radical proposals thus flew in the face of widely held views.

Perloff saw the federal budget as the principal public instrument for translating knowledge into action. A budget larded with symbolism and beholden to past traditions—that is, if its ideology were one of control and economy—was neither flexible nor efficient. Insistence on a budget balanced annually rather than over the course of the entire business cycle prevents its use as a flexible device for correcting the business cycle. The arguments, incidentally, are as fresh today as they were then, as the political push for a constitutional amendment requiring a balanced budget gains power, and the public becomes increasingly sensitive to the size and growth of public spending (except in areas of national defense).

Perloff's concerns for national planning via the federal budget moved to the state and local levels in the second of the two articles reprinted here. The significance of subnational governments as taxing and spending units is often overlooked, yet their sheer size as fiscal entities alone warrants reckoning the consequences of their actions. Perloff notes that, in 1941, two years before the article was published, "state and local tax revenues amounted to more than 11 percent of the national income while . . . the expenditures of state and local governments amounted to almost 12 percent of national income payments." The comparable figures today are 18 and 20 percent. Moreover, relative to federal expenditures, and largely as a result of the devolution of formerly national programs to lower governmental levels in the wake of the New Federalism, state and local expenditures currently (in 1981) run nearly 80 percent those at the national level.

"Fiscal Policy at State and Local Levels," a contribution to a book dealing with the economic problems anticipated during post-war reconstruction, demonstrates how state and local government, without the national mandate of carrying out countercyclical policy, frequently spent in such a way as to frustrate federal fiscal policy. For example, during the depressed 30s, state and local governments were forced to curtail their expenditures as revenues fell in response to declining levels of economic activity. With federal policy pursuing countercyclical policy, state-local expenditure policy, which tended to be procyclical, stood at odds with national stabilization efforts.

The article illuminates the problems faced by subnational governments in financing their economies and, in tightly reasoned arguments, shows how they can only operate procyclically in light of constraints such as required annually balanced budgets. Moreover, various aspects of the system promote inequities or aggravate existing inequities. An ambitious, broadly based program of reform to increase fiscal responsibility, including a better distribution of resources, is proposed. Because of prevailing inequities in the system, the federal government should play a stronger role in financing certain state and local services and programs, such as public education. The fiscal capacity of the nation's poorer areas would be reinforced, economic growth fostered, and regional disparities reduced by a long-term resource development program if the federal government shouldered the responsibilities for supporting certain sectors of national concern, such as basic services for the poverty population. By assuming the cost of carrying out public functions of national concern, the federal government would insure the adequacy of local and state revenues to cover their remaining responsibilities. The proposed reform package includes federal responsibility for the unemployment program, standardized business taxes, removal of the wasteful interstate competition for business firms through favorable tax treatment, and a shift from taxing consumption (such as sales) to income.

Far-sighted recommendations of this sort, as we have seen, run throughout Perloff's later writings. They are as timely today as in the 1940s when they were first made.

15

Budgetary Symbolism and Fiscal Planning

POPULAR BUDGETARY CONCEPTIONS

It would be asking the impossible to expect the general public to grasp the intricacies and economic refinements of governmental fiscal activity. And because the budget stands as the only summary statement of all national financial policy, it is taken as a broad criterion for passing judgment upon the activities of government in the general field of fiscal relationships. As is to be expected, budgetary judgments are based upon oversimplified, symbolic ideals. This often leads to a popular distortion of fiscal realities. Special interests can be relied upon to use such distortion to their own particular ends. At certain times this merely amounts to a siphoning of public funds in one direction rather than in another. At other times, however, fiscal perversions may prevent necessary adjustment to social changes, with serious consequences for the national welfare.

Certain students of American government finance have been content with pointing out the irrationalities of fiscal activities. The formulation of fiscal policy, they conclude, represents a compromise between powerful economic forces in the community. The whole thing is nothing more or less than the play of pressure groups seeking to benefit at the expense of others. Although political reality demands a full understanding of this process, however, we cannot leave the matter at this stage if we are at all concerned with its implications for the general welfare (or whatever we wish to term that elusive something which is supposed to be guaranteed by the democratic process).

It must be clear that the use of public funds is the centrifugal force of collective action. Alexander Hamilton eloquently epitomized this basic fact in the *Federalist:* "Money is, with propriety, considered as the vital principle of the body politic: as that which sustains the life and motion, and enables it to perform its most essential functions." But if the motion of the body politic is to be steady and progressive, and in time with the movement of social change, then fiscal policy and the financial machinery of government must necessarily keep pace with the demands made upon them.

Unfortunately, we find certain forces of inertia converging with particular intensity to hamper adjustments to new fiscal situations and new communal needs. For one thing, certain groups in the community see in the financial machinery of government an essential balance wheel of the existing social order. They resist any changes in that mechanism on the ground that it will unbalance the social structure.[1] For another, certain symbols and traditions in the fiscal realm have become what amount to popular creeds demanding unquestioning faith. Since the budget is the focal point of government financial activity (from the standpoint of publicity and popular comprehension), it has been particularly subject to this phenomenon. The whole question of public budgeting is shrouded in a mist of traditionalism and symbolism to such an extent that it is rarely discussed at the level of governmental techniques and mechanisms.

The budget is the crucible into which the manifold issues of collective action, economic intervention, tax justice, economy, pressure groups, and so on, are dumped pell-mell and molded into a common shape—monetary figures. Thus, the whole activity called "governmental spending" can be treated as an abstract concept and closely associated with the words "recklessness" and "extravagance." The resulting color of the admixture—i.e., whether it is red or black—can be used as a final criterion for judging the "soundness" of an administration. An increase in taxes can be talked of as a drain on the private economy—even though such taxes may be used to finance subsidies to certain sections of the economy and to bring about a distribution of economic goods that actually promotes productivity. Generally, the basis of judgment is an emotional reaction to certain abstract concepts. Recent Gallup and *Fortune* polls, for example, reflected a large majority opinion against *spending* in general by the government.[2] But when it came down to specific items, there were majorities of 81 percent against reducing expenditures for armament, 82 percent were in favor of an adequate old-age pension, and 86 percent favored a continuation of farm benefits. Similarly, a majority were for work relief in preference to the dole, notwithstanding the fact that work relief is far more expensive. The only place where any sort of general agreement for reduction could be reached was in the ordinary operating expenses of the government. But here again we have a nonspecific item which can be discussed vaguely in terms of "administrative economy," "bureaucracy," etc.

Not only is the budget the dumping-ground for a variety of broad issues, but it is popularly conceived as being first and foremost an instrument of control and economy, rather than a tool of government fiscal planning. Thus, a depar-

---

[1] Typical of this reaction is the criticism of the Roosevelt administration by the American Liberty League, because, among other things, "the New Deal has prostituted the taxing power under the constitution to accomplish social and economic ends remote from the raising of revenue." From a statement made public July 19, 1936, as reported by the *New York Times*.

[2] The American Institute of Public Opinion poll was taken in April, 1938, that of *Fortune*, in March, 1939. Similarly, a study of the press reaction to the President's suggestion, in the spring of 1938, for a new program of spending revealed that for every editorial and dispatch in favor of the program, there were six against it. Burt M. McConnell, "The Press Looks at Pump-priming," *Current History*, vol. 48 (June 1938), pp. 30 ff.

ture from "sound economy" is viewed as a misuse of the budget and a danger to democratic control. D. T. Smith, for example, writes: "There is a real and very great danger that a democracy may spend itself to death, as it were, once it departs from a balanced budget."[3]

In totalitarian countries there is, of course, no such problem. Government budgeting is nothing more or less than fiscal planning aimed directly at the achievement of the objectives of the ruling clique. In the United States, on the other hand, the budget is an intermixture of many ingredients: a statement of expenditures, revenues, and debts, a document presented by the executive to Congress, a series of legislative measures, a political program, an instrument essential to democratic governments, a tool to enforce economy—as well as a planned financial program. All these ingredients are by no means given equal weight. The role of the budget in the social structure is conceived chiefly in terms of popular control and governmental economy. Such a conception derives directly from the traditional and symbolic elements which have attended the evolution of our modern philosophy of public budgeting.

The basic pattern of this development is not far different from that which has molded others of our beliefs and concepts. In the search for techniques and institutions to fulfill the social needs, "fundamental principles" are evolved. They constitute in part an ideal to be aimed at, and in part a justification of the existing structures and beliefs. As the institutions mature and the beliefs become traditional, the principles begin to be conceived as universal truths and in time they become creeds demanding unquestioning faith.

BUDGETARY TRADITIONS

Important to the development of our philosophy of governmental budgeting is the fact that the budget evolved as an instrument and symbol of the democratic, laissez-faire ideal.

The seeds of modern budgeting lie in the struggle over the power of the purse. Born in a period when this power was jealously guarded against the demands of royal prerogative, public budgeting reached its maturity in a later period, when "sovereign" peoples sought to safeguard the fruits of a hard-won victory. To the new classes seeking power it was clear that "he who controls the finances of the state controls the nation's policy." From popular consent to taxation, to parliamentary approval of expenditures through appropriations, to the periodic discussion by the legislature of expenditures and revenues set up in the form of a financial plan—these are the logical stages in the evolution of government by representatives of the people.[4]

It is natural that the budget, as the focal point of financial, and therefore of

---

[3]*Deficits and Depressions* (New York, 1936), p. 179.
[4]For an account of this development, see Gaston Jèze, *Théorie Générale du Budget* (Paris, 1922), pp. 10 ff. Also F. W. Maitland, *The Constitutional History of England* (Cambridge, England, 1920), and Charles A. Beard, Introduction to René Stourm. *The Budget* (American translation, New York, 1917).

governmental activity, should have developed as a powerful instrument of popular control. Thinking about the budget was constantly in terms of the democratic ideal. To perfect the budget, to improve budgetary procedures, was to perfect and improve democracy. H. C. Adams well expressed the typical attitude when he wrote:

> The comprehensive nature of budgets . . . is not suggested by regarding them either as a report or as a project of law: they must be conceived as a part of the political machinery essential to the realization of the ideal of popular government before their dignity and importance can be adequately appreciated.[5]

From England, the United States inherited a whole set of financial techniques and traditions aimed at preventing arbitrary executive power.[6] But when the people resorted to the legislature as the palladium of democracy, new problems of control arose. For, with time, the spending of public moneys became not so much a question of social necessity as of party politics. Congress became "the happy hunting ground" and "pork barrel" appropriations were voted with machine-like precision.[7]

In the campaign for the reform of governmental abuses and inefficiency, the budget became a keystone about which were centered the demands for economy and efficiency, for freedom from graft and corruption. It was a blazing symbol— the rallying ground for reform.[8] When the movement gathered momentum, the budget became a campaign issue and party managers "set their sails to catch the favoring wind in the hope that it would waft their chosen candidates into office."

The campaign for budget reform was successful, climaxed by the passage of the federal budget law, under the title of the "National Budget and Accounting Act," in June of 1921. The emphasis throughout had been on control and economy, and the budgetary techniques which were developed were aimed in that direction. Thus, regular meetings of "the responsible representatives of the business organization of the Government" became an integral part of the budget process. These meetings were directed at financial economies, as were the One- and Two-Per Cent Clubs, the Bureaus of Efficiency and the Coordinating Boards. The fetish for economy extended to the Budget Bureau itself. Its staff

---

[5]Henry Carter Adams, *The Science of Finance* (New York, 1898), p. 105.
[6]For a discussion of colonial struggles for the right to control the purse, see Charles J. Bullock, "The Finances of the United States from 1775 to 1789 with Especial Reference to the Budget," *Bulletin of the University of Wisconsin*, 1 (June, 1895), pp. 117–273.
[7]The 1916 *Annual Report of the Secretary of the Treasury* is illuminating on this point. Representative of the legislative attitude toward expenditures is the classic remark of Senator Tillman of South Carolina: "The whole scheme of river improvement is a humbug and a steal; but if you are going to steal, let us divide it out, and not go on complaining." *Congressional Record*, March 4, 1901, p. 3906.
[8]Frederick A. Cleveland, writing in 1915, rejoiced in the fact that "the 'budget idea' has finally come to be thought of as a constitutional principle—one which has been used effectively for the purpose of developing representative government and keeping it in harmony with the highest ideals of democracy." "Evolution of the Budget Idea in the United States. *Annals, American Academy of Political and Social Science*, 62 (November, 1915), p. 15.

and expenses were extremely limited—but so were its scope and achievement. It more than had its hands full in examining the requests of the spending agencies, relying almost completely upon previous expenditure records. A careful and detailed examination of the various government activities and the relative justifications for spending public moneys was out of the question. Thus was the association of the budget with strict governmental economy carried to its illogical conclusion.

But other factors also played a role in the development of our philosophy of public budgeting. For together with the growth of democratic government had come a new ruling class and a new economic pattern of life. "Sound" governmental financial policy was interpreted as calling for a limitation of public activities and expenditures to a minimum, and for a minimum disturbance of the pricing system. It was felt, quite generally, that social needs would best be fulfilled if private enterprise was left free to pursue its own ends; that government interference was, on the whole, harmful; that the abstraction of funds from the private economy by the government was undesirable.

It was from this background that certain budgetary principles were evolved as guides for statesmen and as bases for judging the soundness of government fiscal activities—"soundness" being conceived as adherence to the prevailing laissez-faire, democratic ideal.

Thus, the principle of *Budgetary Equilibrium* (which insists on a balance between all government expenditures and current revenues) was evolved, in the final analysis, as a demand that the state keep within its immediate means—for therein lies the assurance that the government will not indulge in reckless spending, that it will not expand its activities too quickly, and that it will not divert more funds from the private economy than it can obtain by the difficult and painful process of taxation. Since government borrowing enables a rapid expansion of public enterprise, it was alien to the ideals of a business civilization.[9]

From the principle that "revenues of a determined and short period were the best guarantee of the frequent convening of Parliaments" evolved the budgetary canon of *Annuality*. It was generally agreed that: "A year seems to be the maximum of time over which legislatures can afford to give the power (control of the purse) out of their hands. . . ."[10] But beyond guaranteeing the frequent convening of legislatures, the rule of annuality was to aid in maintaining "sound" financial practices by insisting that revenues and expenditure should *balance year by year*. This Hilton Young called "the golden rule of economoy."[11] The "economy" which this rule demands is clearly that of preventing capital funds from passing out of the private economy into the public field. It leaves no scope for government borrowing (beyond short-term borrowing in anticipation of taxes), and thereby imposes a very real limit on the expansion of governmental activities.

---

[9]For a typical interpretation of budget balancing, see Fritz Neumark, *Der Reichshaushaltplan—Ein Beitrag zur Lehre vom öffentlichen Haushalt* (Jena, 1929).

[10]René Stourm, *op. cit.*, p. 319.

[11]*The System of National Finance* (London, 1915), p. 11.

Again, the rule of *Unity* came to be considered an essential of "good" budgeting. It was a demand that all fiscal material be presented in a single budget, that there be no segregation within the budget system. "Budgetary unity," insisted Jèze, "is, for Parliament, the best means of *control* and comparison. . . ."[12] Infraction of unity—through the use of so-called extraordinary or emergency budgets—was conceived as implying a desire on the part of the government to conceal an increase in expenditures by dividing their totals and to justify unnecessarily large expenditures by characterizing them as of a unique vintage. "This, in reality," wrote Stourm, "is always the purpose underlying the separation of the extraordinary budgets: they are made to delude the country." This departure from "sound" finance was taboo, however, mainly because it generally involved government borrowing and thereby enabled the state to spend beyond the limits of its current revenue.

Similarly, each of the other canons of public budgeting had a raison d'être in terms of the prevailing social ethic. Back of the principles of comprehensiveness, publicity, prior authorization, specification, etc., stands a long history of bitter struggles against oppressive executive authority and against irresponsible representatives; a history marked by the rise to power of a class which assigned to the state a limited and purely protective role, and which imposed upon the state the methods and ideals of the civilization it evolved.

So universal was the ratification of these rules of public budgeting, and so honorable their history, that society in time forgot their raison d'être and accepted them as a final good. They became social symbols and, as such, have persisted until the present day. The result has been the perpetuation of a philosophy of governmental budgeting which arose as a rationalization of a social order, as a distillation of experience in a particular era.

POLITICAL AND ECONOMIC CHANGES

Certain it is that many changes have come about since the principles were first formulated, both in political and economic structures and in social concepts and ideals.

For one thing, the state has been called upon by the demands of a large section of the community, and by the sheer necessity of overwhelming social needs, to take a more active part in the social process. It has been called upon to bring about a more equitable distribution of wealth, to regularize employment and care for the unemployed, to control industries charged with a plain public interest, to prevent the private economy from breaking down under the weight of too severe crises—in short, to take a more active part in society's attempt to achieve security and the more abundant life.

Moreover, the conditions of the economy have vastly altered (at least from what laissez-faire, competitive theory would have it). We are now faced with an economy in which competition is not "free," allocation of resources is not sub-

[12]Gaston Jèze, *Théorie Générale du Budget* (Paris, 1922), p. 198.

ject to the pricing system alone, equilibrium is not the necessary rule, and factors of production are not fully utilized. Under such circumstances the role of the public economy in relation to the private economy is certain to undergo vast changes. The fate of the economy is left less in the hands of "natural law," and more emphasis is placed on human organization.

With these developments, the fiscal machinery of government has had to be utilized for purposes far beyond the financing of the so-called traditional government services. For quite some time, the fiscal machine has been employed to accomplish far-reaching social ends, such as the prohibition or discouragement of certain activities regarded as undesirable, the more equitable distribution of income, the expansion of collective consumption, and the raising of the national standard of living. But although severe and ever-recurring depressions have long since saddled governments with many social problems, the promotion of stability and security was, until quite recently, considered beyond the scope of state activity. Complete reliance was placed on what was thought to be the automatic, self-regulatory mechanism of capitalism.

During the last generation, however, a tremendous change has taken place. Stability and security have become inescapable governmental problems. The "invisible hand" has been entirely discarded in favor of direct control in nations under a dictatorial regime. But even in the democracies the management of the business cycle has become a public function in the face of the social hazards of instability and unemployment.

"NEW WINE IN OLD BOTTLES"

Governing groups can be expected to attempt a solution of at least the more immediate problems in periods of social stress, since popular discontent will clearly threaten their political existence. This is a factor which transcends even the force of diverse pressures and ideologies.

Thus, in the face of an unprecedented crisis, government spending on a large scale was undertaken by both the Hoover and Roosevelt administrations. "Shock funds" had to be thrown promptly into the breaches in the social and business structures. Demands for overcoming individual and institutional distress took precedence over demands for a balanced budget.

This phenomenon occurred everywhere. Studies by League of Nations experts[13] and Hugh Dalton and his associate[14] revealed that almost every national unit of any importance incurred at least one deficit during the last depression, and some experienced a continuous series of unbalanced budgets. Quite generally it was discovered that accepted fiscal notions were far removed from concrete realities. But only in one or two isolated cases was a concerted effort made to construct "a new scheme of legal and institutional regulations for the fiscal

---

[13]League of Nations, Economic Intelligence Service, *Public Finance*, 1928–35 (Geneva, 1936).

[14]Hugh Dalton and others, *Unbalanced Budgets—A Study of the Financial Crisis in Fifteen Countries* (London, 1934).

household."[15] Rather, governments tended to follow a policy of improvisation and to turn to "the window dressing ingenuities of public accounting."

Such was the course taken by the federal government. Through a dual bookkeeping arrangement—based on the principle of a balanced "regular" budget, which is made to balance by setting up a separate "emergency" category— the administration kowtowed to the principle and avoided the fact. Furthermore, to escape the straitjacket of traditional federal finance, the government felt it necessary to create numerous independent agencies with power to obtain their own funds, and to indulge in all sorts of financial contortions (as exemplified by the purchase of Home Owners Loan Corporation stock by the Treasury with funds provided by the R.F.C., which in turn had obtained its capital by sale of its notes to the Treasury). It was impossible, under such circumstances, for anyone, including Congress, to get a clear picture of what was going on.

The fiscal record of recent years has revealed only too clearly the manner in which budgetary traditionalism and symbolic concepts stood in the way of permitting the budgetary mechanism to be employed as an instrument in the planning and execution of the economic and social policies of the government. During a period in which revolutionary developments have been taking place in government finance as well as in the relationship of the state to the private economy, the administration has felt itself called upon to justify its actions in terms of principles which quite clearly have very limited application. Furthermore because of the traditional view of our federal budget as an instrument of control and economy, the budgetary mechanism has not served the needs of fiscal planning nor of revealing, in the more fundamental aspects, the results of current fiscal policy.

When the Roosevelt administration came into office in 1933, a serious attempt was made to balance the budget along traditional lines.[16] Yet, at the same time, the administration became convinced that the crisis conditions called for huge emergency expenditures. For some time there was an attempt to maintain that there was economic merit both in curtailing ordinary and in expanding extraordinary expenditures. Politically minded and fully aware of the popular conceptions concerning large government spending and budget balancing, Mr. Roosevelt constantly and publicly stressed the "emergency" character of the new expenditures and continued to make gestures towards a balanced budget.

Since governmental action must have a philosophical justification simplified into an acceptable symbol, the administration held out to the public the similarity of depression and war finance. It was a war against depression. Just as victory in battle was contingent on a huge public debt, so was recovery. The

[15]See Gunnar Myrdal, "Fiscal Policy in the Business Cycle," *American Economic Review*, 29 (March, 1939, Supplement) pp. 183–193. Reprinted with permission of the *Review*. Also "That Wonderful Swedish Budget," *Fortune*, 18 (September, 1938), pp. 65 ff.

[16]There was a general conviction that the government's credit would suffer if the budget was not promptly balanced and that economic recovery depended on an immediate balance. The legislation enacted at the request of the President was entitled "an Act to Maintain the Credit of the United States Government." The rate of pay of government employees was cut 15 percent, venterans' benefits were reduced, and taxes were increased.

emergency expenditures engendered by an economic crisis should not be viewed in the same light as the regular outlays of the government. Under such circumstances, we should not seek a balance between current income and all expenditure; a balance between current income and ordinary expenditure is all that is necessary to assure sound government finance.

The introduction of what was generally termed an "extraordinary budget" aroused a storm of protest and was severely criticized in many quarters. (*"We have two budgets but only one Treasury."*) The administration was accused of trying to deceive the public, of indulging in unsound fiscal practices and in extravagance on a monumental scale. Others came to the defense of the government and urged that the segregation of emergency from other expenditures was justified under the circumstances.[17] The debate over the extraordinary budget was clearly superficial and symbolistic; the issue, obviously, was not the form of the budget document, but the advisability, at the time, of a government spending program based largely on borrowing. Those who felt that business stability and the government's credit were seriously threatened by the huge deficits did not have their fears allayed by the balancing of a budget which "does not include any additional expenditures for extraordinary purposes."[18] On the other hand, those who shared with President Roosevelt the view that the emergency situation called for large government expenditures and that "the immeasurable benefits justify the cost," agreed that the incurring of deficits in the financing of such emergency outlays was completely justified.

CHANGES IN FISCAL POLICY

This emergency period marked, on the part of the administration, a new conception of the role of fiscal policy. In the face of unemployment and business stagnation, it was felt, the government could not afford to sit back and wait for a "normal" recovery. It must take positive financial action to alleviate suffering and bring about a rapid business recovery.[19]

For some time government deficits were looked upon as a necessary evil— the price to be paid for carrying out the essential relief and recovery measures. It was felt that a return to a balanced budget must be made as soon as it was

---

[17]See, for example, J. Wilner Sundelson, "The Emergency Budget of the Federal Government," *American Economic Review*, 24 (March, 1934), pp. 53–68.

[18]In his budget message presented January 3, 1934, President Roosevelt had declared that with the exception of debt retirement, the budget estimates for the fiscal year 1935 show a small surplus, but that this budget "does not include any additional expenditure for extraordinary purposes."

[19]The relief and recovery measures taken at that time included: (1) provisions for relief of the unemployed and destitute; (2) extension of financial aid to, and underwriting the credit of, distressed economic institutions and groups; and (3) stimulation of employment and purchasing power by means of the National Recovery Administration, extensive appropriations for public works, and the restoration of agricultural purchasing power through benefit payments and other devices provided by the Agricultural Adjustment Administration.

humanly possible. The administration came, in time, however, to view deficits in an entirely different light. It had discovered that there was at hand a better justification of huge government expenditures than that of sheer emergency necessity. Certain eminent economists were urging that vast governmental disbursements were the primary requisite for recovery. Interest in the so-called pump-priming theory reached its peak at the time of Keynes' visit to America in the spring of 1934. It was at about this time, it has been suggested, that the administration shifted to the view that large government deficits, far from being an evil, were a virtue in time of depression. During the emergency period, expenditures and deficits had been mounting; the government had been just swimming along, going with the current. Now it was beginning to defend and rationalize the process.

The pump-priming view held that the so-called natural forces could not be relied upon, in the existing situation, to counteract the powerful deflationary forces at work, nor to bring about recovery. Furthermore, even if a "natural" recovery should come in the course of time, the social cost involved in the continued nonutilization of the community's human and physical resources was too high a price to pay. Government expenditures would supply the missing spark; they would prime the industrial pump. And, moreover, a given amount of public spending would have an effect upon the national income far in excess of the actual volume of expenditures made. Since the purpose of the government spending is to compensate for the deficiencies of private spending, the funds must come, not from taxation, but from borrowing. Taxation might merely divert money which would have been spent anyway; the spending of borrowed money is a net gain, since during a depression there is a large amount of idle funds at hand. Consequently, a deficit becomes, not an evil, but a primary requisite for recovery. But such deficit spending in depression must be offset by surplus financing during subsequent prosperity. This means that annual budget balancing must be abandoned in favor of a policy of balancing expenditures and revenues over the period of the business cycle.

By the end of 1934 the administration had accepted the doctrine of the advisability of balancing the budget over the complete cycle. The best way to achieve a balanced budget was to continue heavy outlays until such time as economic recovery should permit revenues to catch up with expenditures. This view was expressed by President Roosevelt in his budget message of January 3, 1936:

> Secure in the knowledge that steadily decreasing deficits will turn in time into steadily increasing surpluses, and that it is the deficit of today which is making possible the surplus of tomorrow, let us pursue the course that we have mapped.

Having accepted the doctrine of priming the pump through the medium of large government outlays, the administration vigorously pursued a policy of public spending and deficit financing. Those sections of the relief and recovery program which were found to be slow in developing and comparatively small in magnitude were scrapped and new instrumentalities for disbursing public funds were established. Thus the FERA program of federal grants to the states was liquidated and the federal works program instituted. It was felt that only by greatly accelerating the volume and speed of government disbursements could processes of real recovery be generated.

A good deal of confidence as to the effectiveness of deficit financing was expressed during the economic recovery of 1935–36. Many held the view that at last an instrument had been found for controlling the fluctuations of the business cycle. With the serious recession of 1937, however, grave doubts began to be expressed as to the ability of the government to prime the industrial pump. For some, the course of events seemed to lead to the conclusion that deficit spending cannot itself start a revival of such a sort that it can go on under its own power after the stimulus of deficit financing has been removed. More emphasis was placed on the compensatory aspects of government spending.

> Such spending may be a stimulus to production, which may be self-multiplying to some extent but not to any significant extent self-perpetuating. In this aspect it may be useful to tide over a depression until other forces initiate a self-sustaining revival.[20]

The compensatory viewpoint seemed to have been accepted by the administration. The ideal of balancing the budget in the near future appeared to have been abandoned. In its place was the suggestion that the balance was destined eventually to appear whenever the national income should have grown to the requisite amount. Until that point, the President urged, government spending would be necessary to compensate for the lack of sufficient private spending. The budget message of January 3, 1939, presented estimates of the revenues that the existing federal tax system would produce at various levels of national income.[21] The inference seemed to be that if we should succeed in attaining a high level of national income, the budget problem would be solved more or less automatically. The inference was, further, that the major concern of the government should not be budget balancing but the raising of the national income to a sufficiently high level. The President, in his budget message, declared:

> We cannot by a simple legislative act raise the level of the national income, but our experience in the last few years has amply demonstrated that through wise fiscal policies and other acts of government we can do much to stimulate it.

FAILURE TO APPLY AND COORDINATE THE FISCAL PROGRAM

On the basis both of its declarations and its actions it would seem that the Roosevelt administration had accepted deficit financing as the keystone of its

---

[20]J. M. Clark, "An Appraisal of the Workability of Compensatory Devices." *The American Economic Review*, 29 (March, 1939, Supplement), pp. 199–200.

[21]Whereas the national income today is in the neighborhood of sixty billion dollars, the President suggested, an increase to seventy billion dollars would result in a national revenue of six billions; with a national income of eighty billions the revenue would be eight billions; ninety billion dollars of national income would contribute ten and six-tenths billion dollars of revenue to the national government.

fiscal policy and as an important agent for effecting economic stabilization. Let us note to what extent such a program was actually carried out from the standpoint of a logical application of the principles of deficit financing.

It is true that a concerted effort was made by the federal government to push a vast amount of money directly into the income stream. But while federal expenditures and deficits increased rapidly, those of the state and local governments remained at about the same level that they were in 1933. There was no tie-up between the federal program and nonfederal activities, even though it was obvious that an expansionist program could have significance only in relation to the total amount of governmental deficit financing.

From the standpoint of pump-priming policy, the important thing is the net addition to the spending power of the community.[22]

Various methods have been employed to measure the net flow of income directly attributed to government activity. But they all show the same thing—that federal income-increasing expenditures, which were at a very low level at the depths of the depression, reached their peak during the recovery years of 1935 and 1936, and were not tapered off until 1937. At the same time state and local governments were making net deductions from the disposable cash income of the community.

There are several possible explanations of why federal income-increasing expenditures were at a high level during the recovery years of 1935–36. One reason which has been presented is that it was a direct outcome of certain political phenomena, which, in fact, make impossible the application of the pump-priming theory in a democracy. Whereas a full acceptance of a pump-priming policy implies the willingness, and the ability, to run counter to the cycle not only on the downswing, but also on the upswing, in a democracy—and especially in the United States—political institutions and traditions make a rapid revision of expenditures and taxes on that pattern impossible. A decrease in the level of expenditures is a heroic task; specific suggestions for economies invariably meet with overpowering opposition. At the same time, a rapid increase in taxation is politically unpopular. The conclusion is, many have claimed, that the second part of the pump-priming theory cannot be applied.

Another explanation, and one which has been urged by a good many government officials as well as economists, is that the degree of recovery which was being achieved in 1935 and 1936 did not justify the contraction of federal income-increasing expenditures. Many millions were still unemployed and business had not yet taken up the slack. This meant either that the pump had not been sufficiently primed or that the government outlays could not be depended upon to set the economy in full motion and were merely filling a gap left by business.

---

[22]Arthur D. Gayer, "Fiscal Policies," *American Economic Review*, 28 (March, 1938, Supplement), p. 98. The above figures of total expenditures and debt are not satisfactory measures of the government contribution to community income. It is apparent that not all government expenditures lead to an increase in buying. "Liquidating expenditures," for instance, i.e., those expenditures which are used to repay debt, may serve a useful purpose in preventing forced liquidation, but do not result in a direct increase in the expenditures of the public. And, of course, when the government spends money that is collected in taxes and would have otherwise been spent by the tax-payer, there is a mere transfer of buying power rather than a net increase.

In either case, this school of thought holds, it was necessary to keep pumping funds into the income stream. On the other hand, it has been suggested that if the government had tapered off its expenditures early in the recovery, the private economy could have forged ahead on its own steam. A conclusion as to whether or not the administration actually followed the dictates of the pump-priming theory can be arrived at, it would seem, only on the basis of the criterion of recovery which is used. If recovery is defined as a period in which the number of unemployed has reached a low level, then a case can be made out for the justification, under the dictates of the pump-priming theory, of the government's action in 1935–36. If, however, the criterion is a general improvement in business sufficient to show that the economy was on the upswing of the cycle, then it would seem that the administration failed to follow the second part of the pump-priming theory.

Conclusions as to other aspects of the Roosevelt recovery program are much less controversial and point to a definite failure on the part of the government to tie all the elements of its program into a consistent whole.

Contrary to the hopes of those who looked to public works as a primary factor in the stabilization of the business cycle, governmental construction, far from following a countercycle movement, followed the course of business prosperity.

Similarly, the developments in the tax structure of the country have not followed the dictates of the countercycle theory, which urges an increase in the "propensity to consume" during depression.[23] On the contrary, the depression brought a sharp rise in the proportion of total revenue raised from indirect taxes weighing on consumption in contrast with the direct taxes applicable to individual and corporate income. Sales taxes came into prominence, as did other taxes weighing on mass consumption. The social security taxes greatly strengthened the general tendency. For the federal government, this was in sharp contrast to the type of tax structure existing during the prosperity era.

All the evidence would seem to point to the conclusion that insufficient attention was given to the effects of the tax structure upon full employment in general, and upon the immediate recovery problem in particular. It would seem that the question of taxes on consumption versus taxes on savings did not receive the attention it deserves as an essential aspect of fiscal policy. Only to a small extent were attempts made to use the tax structure as a regulator of the consumption-saving-investment mechanism. Among these was the attempt to discourage, through taxation, the accumulation of large undistributed reserves, but this proved to be a heavy-handed remedy with unlooked-for repercussions.

WHY FAILURE?

One cannot escape, of course, from the fact that many difficulties stood in the way of successfully translating the countercycle theory into a coordinated

---

[23]The phrase "the propensity to consume" (as devised by Keynes) refers to the proportion of income which the public is prepared to spend on consumption purchases at various income levels. Under the dictates of the pump-priming theory, the tax structure should be designed to increase the propensity to consume.

program. One was the lack of unification in the political setup. The activities of state and local governments tended to run counter to the recovery program of the federal government. Another difficulty was the interference with the program by uncontrollable political developments. Such were the invalidating of the processing taxes by the Supreme Court, and the approval by Congress, over presidential veto, of the immediate payment of the veterans' "bonus." Again, there was the ever-present influence of special pressure groups to prevent the logical and coordinated execution of fiscal policy. To note the furor which arose in the Senate when the administration attempted to reduce loans on cotton is to realize that political feasibility, and not only economic soundness, has shaped the course of recovery policies as well as of other democratic programs.

Possibly our governmental setup is not at all designed for the direction of deficit financing and we must agree with Haig that: "Perhaps, before deficit financing can be made safe for democracy, democracy will have to improve its mechanism so that action will be less influenced by the shortsighted and immediate special interests."[24]

It may be argued, of course, that the countercycle theory was something which existed, in reality, only on the plane of academic discussion, and was used by the administration merely to justify huge expenditures which arose in the main from aims far removed from the promotion of economic stability.

But even assuming sincere intentions on the part of the administration, it may well be asked whether a coordinated and effective program could possibly have been carried out. In face of the apparent dangers of instability and unemployment and the ever-present threat of serious economic crisis, such a question has very real significance for public policy. The answer must clearly be in the negative. The fiscal policy which was adopted was a revolutionary departure from traditional federal financial programs. But neither the institutions nor the fiscal concepts of the period were capable of the rapid readjustments that were obviously necessary.

Any attempt at a change of a social pattern must reckon with long-standing traditions and accepted symbols. This principle is on the one hand the balance wheel of social organization and on the other hand one of its greatest elments of rigidity. The social needs were felt by everyone, but the new slogans which were offered had a queer sound. A *New York Times* editorial of December 27, 1938, well expressed the spirit behind the traditional fiscal point of view:

> There is one objective standard that everyone understands clearly—Federal budgets "annually balanced." Once we depart from that, except under the sheerest necessity, we are adrift on the seas of confusion, for all sorts of ingenious reasons are invented for not going back, and the vested interest in favor of keeping the new situation is enormous.

This paragraph is worthy of careful note. What is wanted, in the first place, is an objective standard which can be clearly understood. The administration was in no position to furnish such a standard; it was groping its way through unexplored regions. An objective standard cannot be evolved until the goal is clear

---

[24]Robert Murray Haig, "Facing the Deficit," *Yale Review*, 25 (Summer, 1936), p. 693.

and steadfast. But, we may ask, is the fiscal criterion the one upon which we can judge a new course of government action? Changes in the institutional structure which are desirable from one point of view may be questionable from another. Of course, "the vested interest in favor of keeping the new situation is enormous." But what of the vested interest in favor of keeping the old? A thoroughgoing change in fiscal policy is certain to engender change in the nature of property relations. Is the financial machinery of government, then, to be geared to the preservation of the status quo? Clearly the nature of our democratic institutions makes such an assumption untenable. And yet, in the realm of the planning and execution of fiscal programs, our traditions and concepts are geared to the assumption of a static role for fiscal policy.

Developments everywhere have made it apparent that governmental fiscal policy is necessarily a mutable thing which tends to change with new political concepts and ruling groups and with new economic conditions. But at all times in modern society—and this point must be extremely clear—fiscal policy functions within a budgetary context. An eminent Swedish economist, in referring to governmental attempts at a solution of the financial problems, recently declared:

> The shortcomings of the new fiscal policy as it has been tested out in various countries during the last depression are, to a considerable extent, to be explained by the fact that this policy was frustrated as a result of being pressed upon a budgetary system which had been built on principles contradictory to this self-same policy. It is, therefore, just at present an important problem of economic engineering to construct a new scheme of legal and institutional regulations for the fiscal households. . . .[25]

The successful application of a countercycle fiscal policy obviously requires careful planning of a coordinated program, and a long-term point of view. It requires, furthermore, a consideration of governmental financial activities at all levels of government, since the important thing is the net result of the impact of the public economy on the private economy. But all these elements were lacking in the recent fiscal program. The budget system was geared to a year-to-year financing of regular, recurring federal services. The budgetary techniques employed were incapable of successfully planning a long-term unified program of deficit financing. There was no single governmental agency, with adequate facilities, to coordinate the whole recovery program and to supply the necessary information. At the same time that the Budget Bureau was busy examining the individual items of expenditure along traditional lines of economy, the President was allocating huge sums entirely outside the budget system. In addition, independent agencies, with powers of obtaining funds and spending, were multiplying at a rapid pace. Although this may have been necessary in view of the need for speed and flexibility, it certainly helped to prevent the development and execution of a unified program.

The question as to whether or not the administration could have been more successful in executing a policy of deficit financing if it had possessed better

---

[25]Gunnar Myrdal, "Fiscal Policy in the Business Cycle," *American Economic Review*, 29 (March, 1939, Supplement), p. 186. Reprinted with permission of the *Review*.

tools of planning and coordination is not, for us, the major issue. We are concerned, rather, with the implications of our recent fiscal and budgetary experience for public policy in general.

THE PLACE OF THE BUDGET IN THE SOCIAL STRUCTURE

We can proceed on the assumption that economic stabilization has become the direct responsibility of the government as the ultimate guardian of the public welfare. Governments today rise and fall largely on their ability (or luck) to satisfy the more important social needs, and this, under existing conditions, means to prevent the ravages of depression. As the problems of stability and security become increasingly crucial issues of political import, it can be expected that governments will be more and more concerned with the successful planning and carrying out of fiscal policies aimed at their solution. The problem of our democracy has become one of retaining popular control over a government which is asked actively to promote economic stability and social security.

In a democracy the chief concern must be, naturally, with the formulation of social objectives and the translation into action of such objectives through democratic means. If the democractic process has meaning and vitality, then popular control must be most effective at the level of policy formulation and in the selection of policy executors. But, at the same time, the agents of the people must be effectively equipped if the social objectives are to be achieved. Essential to the translation of policy into action is a flexible and efficient machinery for the planning and carrying out of fiscal programs. The budget is clearly the instrument most suited to such a task. But there is a serious need for a careful study of possible improvements in the budget process and in budgetary techniques if the successful planning and execution of financial programs are to be assured.

The prevalent ideology which conceives of public budgeting in terms chiefly of control and economy, under the aegis of traditional principles, casts a mist of unreality over the major issues. These are obviously in the realm of social objectives and fiscal policy. Any view of public policy can be reduced to a combination of group interests which, after being identified with the public interest, are offered as the basis for governmental action. Our political debates arise over differences about which parts of the social whole are to be identified with the common welfare. Our democracy is predicated upon the belief that from the clash of diverse objectives and pressures a line of public policy will be established that will advance the interests of a very great proportion of the population.[26]

At the level of fiscal policy, and in addition to the questions of diverse group interests, arise the controversial issues concerning the course which might best meet the social needs. Is a solution of the problems of instability and unemployment to come from within the private economy, left free to solve its own problems? Those who hold to this view insist that although the business cycle is

---

[26]Pendleton Herring, *The Politics of Democracy* (New York, 1940).

inherent in the capitalistic system, the severity and length of the depression period can be minimized if a *natural* recovery is permitted. The state must "tighten its belt" and create an atmosphere of confidence so as to encourage the business community to get their affairs in order and then forge ahead. And a balanced budget is considered essential to such confidence.

Or can the government overcome instability by a long-run, countercycle policy? Under such a policy the government must adopt a program of deficit spending in depression to be offset by surplus financing during subsequent prosperity. This means that annual budget balancing will have to be abandoned in favor of a rough balance over the period of a complete business cycle.

Or, again, is a program based on a large volume of permanent investment necessary to assure the full employment of the factors of production? Such a policy would mean that instead of balancing the budget annually, or even over the period of the business cycle, a progressive rise in the public debt would be the course relied upon to fill the gap left by inadequate private investment.

The mere summary statement of a few of the alternatives of fiscal policy, actual and theoretical, makes it clear that the traditional concepts of government budgeting are predicated on a definite preconception of the type of fiscal policy deemed desirable. A balance between current revenue and all expenditures within the fiscal year is only one of the many possible courses which may be followed. It is of course possible that those who have the mandate of the people may interpret social welfare as best served by such a policy. But, on the other hand, it is just as likely that an alternative policy may be decided upon. Certainly the question of fiscal policy to be pursued cannot logically be decided on the basis of budgetary traditions. Such phrases as "balanced budgets" and "extraordinary budgets" are, under existing conditions, more useful for exhortation than for analysis. Emphasis should be shifted, as Herring suggests, "from the vindication of abstractions to the study of concrete data and to the discovery of administrative devices that will get the job done."[27]

The problem of government budgeting has become one mainly of skill in adjustment. The criterion for judging budgetary techniques and procedures must be the degree to which they aid in successfully planning and carrying out governmental fiscal programs, and not the extent to which there is strict adherence to a preconceived set of principles.

WHAT IS SOUNDNESS?

The question which immediately arises is, does not such a conception of governmental budgeting carry with it implications of constantly changing budgetary policies and techniques, and will not such a phenomenon have serious repercussions on the fiscal soundness of the government? Such a question derives directly from recent financial experience, which has been marked by continually changing governmental fiscal policies, attended by popular fears of the

---

[27]*Ibid.*, p. 414.

implications for soundness. We are, undoubtedly, passing through a transitional stage in our development. The relation of the state to the private economy had not yet been defined. The proper role for fiscal policy in the promotion of stability and security is still an extremely moot point. Under such conditions, the soundness of the fiscal system has particular significance, but, at the same time, soundness becomes a goal whose achievement is extremely difficult.

Two important questions arise in this connection: What is fiscal soundness? And how is the desired degree of such soundness to be achieved? Financial developments throughout the world have made it clear that there is nothing in fiscal reality corresponding to a conception of absolute financial soundness with the implication that one fiscal system is "sound" and another "unsound." This notion can only be defined in relation to a particular fiscal household, and even then merely in a relative sense. The soundness of a fiscal system can be judged, then, only on the basis of the criterion established within the fiscal household. Such a decision becomes a matter of primary importance.

> The degree of soundness to be kept up in a system of public finances being the basic principle of fiscal policy, it must be established by a political decision. . . .
>
> It befits an enlightened democracy not only to make this fundamental decision and to stick to it, but to base it not upon abstract stereotypes of definitions and the meaning of the terms, but upon an economic analysis in rational terms of the effects of a choice of one or another degree of soundness: effects on the trend of total capital formation, on income distribution, on the development during future periods of the tension between necessary taxation on the one hand, and, last but not least, the effects on public confidence.[28]

Once it is clear that fiscal soundness cannot be an absolute concept, but must depend upon individual political decisions, it becomes equally clear that budgetary policy cannot logically be based on a preconceived set of absolute principles, but must be geared to the financial programs adopted in the fulfillment of the basic political decision. The budget, then, can serve financial soundness best by aiding the successful planning and execution of fiscal policy, and by introducing regularity and system into government finance. The important problem is one of getting things done. Under present conditions, frustration is a more serious threat to democracy than any willful act of officeholders.

Certainly, that nation is not sound which adheres religiously to strict rules of budgeting, but lets its land lie waste and its machines idle. Nor does that country assure the democratic way of life if it imposes a thorough system of budgetary controls, but permits its farmers to be forced off their land and its city workers to wait vainly for factories to open. The problems of soundness and control go right to the heart of the democratic process and of the capitalistic system. Principles of public budgeting cannot be treated in a fiscal vacuum, but must be looked at in the context of social needs, political aspirations, and economic conditions. The principles of democratic budgeting must be the principles of a nation seeking to solve certain of its problems through collective action, and using the budget machine as a springboard for such action.

---

[28]Myrdal, *op. cit.*, pp. 186–187.

16

Fiscal Policy at the State and Local Levels

The financial activities of the state and local governments, no less than those of the federal government, must inevitably have an important effect on the national economy. In fact, war finance aside, the subordinate units collectively have always imposed more taxes and spent more money than the central government.

In the fiscal year ending June 30, 1941, before the United States actively entered the war, state and local tax revenues amounted to more than 11 percent of the national income, while in the same period the expenditures of state and local governments amounted to almost 12 percent of national income payments. We can safely assume that, although permanent changes in the public and private economies are certain to result from the war, the states and localities will continue to affect significantly the national economy. Whether they do so favorably or adversely is of utmost importance.

The record of the past is far from encouraging. There are serious limitations on the ability of state and local governments to follow an economically sound fiscal policy. Nonfederal units can be expected to contribute to the stability and progress of the economy only if certain fundamental changes are made in intergovernmental relations and in state and local financial structures.

FISCAL PERVERSENESS

The taxing, borrowing, and spending activities of the state and local governments collectively have been characterized by a fairly consistent perverseness from the standpoint of economically sound fiscal policy. They have followed the swings of the business cycles, from crest to trough. The governments have spent and built in prosperity periods and have contracted their activities during depressions. In the boom of the late twenties, their finances, instead of tempering inflationary pressures, added to the disposable income of the community: inflationary borrowing was expanded and prices bid up in large-scale construction activities.

In the depressed thirties, the finances of these governments had a deflationary rather than an expansionary effect on the economy: expenditures, and especially construction outlays, were severely cut, borrowing was restricted, and taxes weighing on consumption were substantially increased. Table 1 reveals the cyclical character of state and local construction activities and net income-increasing expenditures (i.e., the net additions to, or deductions from, the disposable cash income of the community), as well as the sharp increase in sales taxes (i.e., those taxes which weigh most directly and heavily on consumption). In following a countercycle expenditure program, the Federal government succeeded where the states and localities failed. In tax policy, however, the Federal government joined the swing toward consumption taxes.

Although the information now available is incomplete, it is evident that, in the current inflationary period, state and local governments are adhering to their

TABLE 1.   FEDERAL, STATE, AND LOCAL FISCAL POLICY INDICES, 1928–1939[A]
(IN MILLIONS OF DOLLARS)

Fiscal year ending	Net income-increasing expenditures[b]		Expenditures for new public construction[b]		Taxes on sales	
	Federal	State and local	Federal[c]	State and local	Federal[d]	State[e]
1928	− 77	810	188[f]	2,104[f]	1,054	—
1929	−232	928			1,065	—
1930	388	1,221	307	2,409	1,060	484
1931	2,419	1,291	422	2,156	839	531
1932	1,797	676	460	1,334	739	547
1933	1,809	−705	647	707	961	558
1934	3,460	−1,165	1,380	794	1,404	921
1935	3,568	−657	1,234	616	1,573	1,211
1936	4,374	−450	2,335	881	1,794	1,217
1937	1,114	−244	2,043	845	2,104	1,318
1938	2,225	−321	2,139	1,084	1,935	1,454
1939	3,581	209			1,905	1,475

[a]The measures employed here are extremely rough, but they serve to give a picture of trends.
[b]By sources of funds.
[c]Including work relief.
[d]Includes liquor, tobacco, manufacturers' excise, soft drinks, admissions, oleomargarine, and customs.
[e]Includes gasoline, general sales, liquor excises and licenses, and tobacco excises and licenses. The license taxes would not be eliminated, because for certain years they are not reported separately. Their yield, however, is very small.
[f]Average for 1925–1929.
Sources: Net income-increasing expenditures: Estimates of Laughlin Currie, *Temporary National Economic Committee Hearings*, Part 9 (Washington, May 16, 1939), p. 4011, as revised by Haskell Wald.
    Estimated expenditures for new public construction: National Resources Planning Board, *The Economic Effects of the Federal Public Works Expenditures, 1933–1938*, prepared by J. K. Galbraith (Washington, November, 1940), pp. 17–18.
    Federal sales taxes: *Annual Report of the Secretary of the Treasury, 1941* (Washington, 1942), pp. 416, 484–487. State sales taxes: 1930–1935: Treasury Department, *Collections from Selected State-imposed Taxes, 1930–1935* (Washington, November 30, 1936), Table A; 1936: Tax Research Foundation, *Tax Systems* (8th ed., Chicago, 1940), pp. 351–355; 1937–1939: Census Bureau, Division of State and Local Government, *Financial Statistics of the States*, annual series.

record of fiscal perverseness. State and local authorities are submitting in many instances to the pressure to increase expenditures and to reduce tax rates.[1] Provisions for debt retirement, for the setting aside of reserves, and for the establishment of "shelves" of public works for postwar construction are few and far between—and this in the face of thoroughly sound resolutions and recommendations of the more important agencies representing state and local officials (e.g., the Municipal Finance Officers Association and the Council of State Governments).

ECONOMIC AND INSTITUTIONAL LIMITATIONS

A number of important underlying factors have contributed to this unfortunate record of state and local finance. We must consider these factors to determine what adjustments have to be made if the fiscal household is to be set in order.

Financial Programs in Periods of Prosperity

Fiscal perverseness in boom periods would seem to be due in the main to institutional factors. When treasury surpluses loom, strong pressures are brought to bear for the construction of capital works, on the one hand, and for the reduction of tax rates, on the other; state and local traditions of legislative resistance to pressure groups are far from well established. In addition, a number of state constitutions and local charters require annual balancing of the budget, and thereby prohibit the accumulation of reserves. Limitations on the reduction of expenditures appear also in the form of large outlays for maintenance and replacement, which cannot be cut without impairing essential services (e.g., waterworks, sewers, schools, and hospitals). Moreover, localities in a number of states find themselves saddled with certain mandatory expenditures. A further obstacle to reductions in expenditures is involved in the character of the existing grant-in-aid system. Both federal grants to states and state grants to localities are rigid in their nature and hold out financial inducements for the grant recipients to keep up their expenditures in the aided fields during inflationary periods as well as during periods of depression. Of importance, also, is the fact that states and localities are limited in their ability to accelerate the rate of reduction of debt because the bulk of their bonds outstanding do not have callable features. On the whole, however, under prosperous conditions,

---

[1]There has been a 25 percent decrease in the New York State personal income tax, and another reduction in tax rates is contemplated. Mississippi has also reduced its income tax rates, as has South Dakota. Illinois has lowered its general sales tax rate, while Indiana has reduced the rates of its gross receipts tax. A report by Rosina K. Mohaupt for the National Municipal League reveals that during 1942 cities with populations between 30,000 and 500,000 decreased tax rates, averaging 5 cents per $1,000 of assessed value, from the 1941 levels.

there are few, if any, serious economic limitations to the pursuance by non-federal units of a sound financial program.

Economic Limitations in Depression

The situation in periods of depression is quite different, however. Then, state and local governments are confronted with serious economic obstacles to the carrying out of a countercycle fiscal program. In the face of a strong deflationary movement, most nonfederal units find it difficult to adjust their finances so that aggravation of the downward spiral will be prevented.

The ability of a governmental unit to maintain its expenditures and to add to the disposable income of the community depends fundamentally upon (1) borrowing capacity, (2) availability of reserve funds, (3) ability to obtain funds through taxes which do not reduce substantially the consumption of the community, and (4) grants from a higher level of government.

Municipal Credit

There are strict limitations on the ability of states and localities to borrow in periods of depression. Being dependent, in the main, upon banks and other private investors—whose policies they cannot control—they can obtain funds only when they can meet the criteria of soundness set up in the municipal security market. When tax yields shrink and borrowing becomes increasingly necessary in order to maintain service levels, the private market for municipals is most restricted. Credit can be obtained, if at all, only under unfavorable circumstances—short terms, high interest rates,[2] and stiff conditional requirements (in the form of provisions dictated by private investors concerning economies in expenditure, tax collection procedure, etc.). Most significant is the fact that the states and localities which had been hit the hardest could not obtain credit at all and were forced to default, to slash services, and, in some cases, to resort to the practice of printing scrip.[3]

Certain economic problems connected with nonfederal borrowing should be noted. Basically, for most state and local units, borrowing has the characteristics of the receipt of credit from abroad. Since to a large extent funds must come from institutions and individuals located in other jurisdictions, the payment of interest and repayment constitute a siphoning out of the area of current

---

[2]In 1932, in fact, no less than 78.7 percent of all state and local issues bore rates of 4.5 percent and higher.

[3]In 1932, 697 issues totaling $260 million could not find a market; in 1933, 528 issues with a dollar volume of $212 million failed of sale, including sales by such governments as Buffalo, Philadelphia, Cleveland, Toledo, Mississippi, and Montana. The governments were not shunning the capital market; instead they found access blocked. The establishment of PWA and the liberalization of RFC loans changed the picture substantially and assured a much broader market for state and local securities. It is patent that in the future the national government must stand ready to extend loans to nonfederal units on liberal terms, through an administrative structure which can assure prompt clearance of applications.

revenues, rather than a mere redistribution of income within the community. Unlike the situation for the national government which borrows from its own citizens only, the payment of interest involves a real cost to the members of a debtor state or locality. Moreover, the preferential claims of interest charges and repayment constitute an overhead cost in state and local budgets which, if large, impose a serious element of rigidity and may impair the ability of those governments to support their basic services. In the face of the extremely regressive state and local tax structures, the accumulation of large municipal debts would bring about, through the payment of interest and repayment, an income redistribution with unfortunate consequences. It would constitute a shift of important proportions from the consumer to the bondholder. Such a shift would be undesirable at all times except in periods of inflation.

Of even greater importance from the viewpoint of fiscal policy is the fact that through deficit spending a state or locality can affect the level of income within its area only to a limited extent. The secondary effects of its spending will be diffused; the geographic "leakages" (the proportion of the new income not spent on domestic output) will be very large.[4] Moreover, an individual state or locality can be expected to spend its money on projects which answer its own immediate service needs. It cannot very well adjust its orders for materials in such a way as to obtain a maximum total leverage effect (i.e., the maximum amount of induced investment and consumption). It may, in fact, aggravate maladjustments in the economy. Apparently, then, the states and localities can contribute to an expansionary policy only if guided by and underwritten by the national government. As a practical matter, the responsibility for the stimulation of income and investment must rest with the Federal government, for it alone is in a position to handle adequately the interrelated problems involved in the carrying out of a positive and flexible countercycle fiscal policy.

Prosperity Reserves

A second source of funds for states and localities in depression is that of accumulated reserves. The availability of such funds depends on the foresight of the authorities and their resistance to pressures during the previous period of prosperity. Unless the prosperity period is of sufficient duration, the reserves cannot be expected to be of importance quantitatively. The most that can be hoped for is that they cushion the first impact of the depression and help to stop the deflationary spiral. Two safeguards are necessary. Adequate provision must be made to guard against raids on the reserves in prosperity and against depreciation of values in depression. If the downturn is sudden and severe, the bonds accumulated in the reserves may be dumped on the market, with serious deflationary effects on the market and on security values. This can be avoided if

---

[4]The production of construction materials, especially, is concentrated in a relatively small number of industrial areas. It is also worthy of note that, unlike the situation for large national units, state and local imports do not necessarily create exports which help to sustain employment. There is no adjustment mechanism at that level.

reserves are kept largely in the form of special Federal securities, or if national agencies are directed to purchase bonds offered by the state and local reserves.

State and Local Taxes

In general, limitations on borrowing capacity mean that the ability to add to the expendable income of the community must depend on the yield of nonconsumption taxes. Even so-called nonconsumption taxes are more or less deflationary, partly because they fall to some extent at least on the consumption stream, and partly because taxes *per se* are inherently restrictive. How serious a reduction of consumption is caused by a given tax depends, of course, upon the saving habits of the class of taxpayers upon which the tax falls. Because the bulk of individual saving is made by the higher income groups, estate, inheritance, and highly progressive income taxes constitute a relatively small drain on consumption compared with excise taxes on items which loom large in low-income budgets. Another type of problem, however, arises in connection with the first group of taxes, and that is the possibility of discouraging risk-taking investment at a time when such investment is crucial.

The states rely heavily on consumption taxes. This reliance arises largely from the inadequate yield of other state taxes. Although a majority of states now have personal income taxes, these taxes, with few exceptions, yield relatively little revenue. This can be explained, in part, by the fact that wealthy individuals are concentrated in a few centers, and most states do not have a large income base unless exemptions are extremely low. In 1938, for example, the percentage of incomes of $5,000 and over to total state income payments ranged from a minimum of 2½ percent to a maximum of 28 percent. In 35 of the 48 states, taxable incomes of $5,000 and over amounted to less than 10 percent of total income payments within the state.

Competition among the states limits the steepness of income-tax rates which any one state can impose. A further limitation, especially for the agricultural states, arises from the difficulty of assessing farm incomes. Also, a number of the states do not possess the administrative and legal talent required to administer a modern progressive income tax.

During the thirties, when the income taxes and other cyclically sensitive taxes yielded little revenue, the states—in their desire to secure revenues that would enable them to obtain WPA and social security grants—turned to the least cyclically sensitive and most productive tax base, that is, the transactions base. Finally, the repressive character of the state tax structure is due in no small part to the fact that, in its development, considerations of economic soundness were generally subordinated to political feasibility and to the expediency involved in "plucking the most feathers with the least squawk." Now about 50 percent of all state revenues arise from taxes on sales. If the reliance on taxes that weigh heavily on consumption continues, the state tax structure can be expected to have a restrictive effect on the national economy during periods of depression.

Since localities are restricted in their ability to borrow, the level of their outlays will depend on the yields of the property tax—upon which they are almost entirely dependent—unless they have accumulated reserves or receive substantial grants from the Federal government or from the states. Because a property tax constitutes an overhead cost for individuals and businesses, it deals harshly with those whose incomes contract in depression. With property taxes levied at high rates in most areas, an avalanche of delinquencies can be expected during a period of depression. If a locality should attempt to sustain its outlays by raising tax rates to compensate for the losses due to delinquencies, it will probably increase the number of delinquencies. In a depression, also, the high rates of the property tax tend to have a depressing effect on real estate values and on the rate of private construction.

Grants-in-Aid

Grants from higher levels of government constitute another source of income for states and localities which may enable them to maintain their expenditures during periods of depression. Since most states find their financial resources severely limited in periods of depression, they can do little to aid their subordinate units. Chief reliance must be placed upon the Federal government.

Today most federal-aid acts apportion fixed sums of money among the states on the basis of service need (generally measured by population), and require that the federal grant be matched by state or local funds, usually dollar for dollar. The Social Security Act departs somewhat from this pattern, and authorizes indefinite grants equal to expenditures from state and local funds to meet public assistance costs falling within the limits of the federal act.

Experience has indicated that where a grant is based on a matching or other uniform-ratio basis, the larger per capita grants generally go to the states with the greater economic and financial resources, and the states with the smallest resources as a rule receive the smallest per capita grants. Moreover, while the wealthier states, or those least affected by a depression, can take advantage of federal grants with comparative ease, the states with the least resources, or those hit hardest by a depression, can do so only by burdening their residents with extremely heavy—and generally regressive—taxes, or can do so at the expense of unaided activities. Thus, those governmental units which are most dependent on outside aid, if they are to maintain their services and their income-increasing expenditures, receive the least assistance under the present grant-in-aid system.

Relative Resources and Service Levels

The limiting factors discussed previously have forced state and local spending generally into a cyclical pattern. But the global figures hide significant differences among the various areas of the country. The ability of a nonfederal unit to maintain a high level of services, and to contribute to the disposable income of the community in times of depression, depends on its fiscal capacity, that is, its ability to raise revenue. If we examine a significant index of relative fiscal capacity among the states—that is, per capita income payments to residents—we find extreme variations. For example, in 1940 per capita income payments ranged from $195 to $960, with a national average of $573. The average amounts paid by the states to recipients of public assistance correlated directly with income payments: in November, 1940, the seven states with the highest per capita incomes (over $750) paid old-age benefits that averaged $25.78, while the seven states with the lowest per capita incomes (under $325) paid benefits that averaged $8.84 (even the most generous of these paid only $10.10).[5] The rates of unemployment compensation follow the same pattern: minimum weekly benefits for total unemployment for the seven richest states ranged from $5 to $10; for the seven poorest states the minimum payments ranged from $2 to $5.[6]

Outlays for public assistance are provided in part through grants from the federal government, which cover a large share of the cost. In elementary and secondary education, where the only equalizing factor is state grants to localities, the disparity in service levels among states is most striking: for example, in 1939–1940 average expenditures per pupil (from state and local funds combined) ranged from $30 to $157.[7] In the depression of the thirties the poorer states lowered their education service levels drastically. Between 1930 and 1934, each of the 14 states with the lowest per capita incomes decreased their educational expenditures, and 11 of the 14 had percentage decreases in expenditures per pupil substantially more than the national average (22.2 percent decrease between 1930 and 1934).

Obviously, the poorer areas of the country cannot finance an adequate level of services from their own resources, nor can they maintain their expenditures in periods of depression. In those areas where purchasing power is at the lowest level, the nonfederal units can contribute least to the disposable income of the community.

LOOKING AHEAD

It seems safe to proceed on the assumption that, whatever the rate of economic progress in the postwar period, we shall be faced with serious eco-

---

[5]The richest states, which provided aid to dependent children, paid average benefits ranging from $31.15 per family in one state to $58.50 in another, with an average for those states of $42.92. The range among the poorest states was from $13.69 to $21.30 per family, with an average of $16.69. See Social Security Board, Bureau of Public Assistance, *Distribution of Assistance Payments to Recipients, November* 1940 (Research Memorandum 2, Washington, May, 1941), Tables 2 and 12.

[6]Social Security Board *Comparison of State Unemployment Compensation Laws as of December* 31, 1941 (Employment Security Memorandum 8, Washington, December, 1941), pp. 86–87.

[7]U.S. Office of Education, *Advance Statistics of State School Systems*, 1939–1940 (Washington, May, 1942). A similar discrepancy may be noted in other local service levels. A study of 34 important urban areas throughout the country made by the Children's Bureau of the Department of Labor reveals that in 1940, per capita net expenditures for health and welfare service (i.e., excluding payments by persons receiving service) ranged from $13.32 to $52.86. These 34 cities grouped by regions show that the average per capita disbursement for health and welfare services for the cities in the South was one-third below the average for all areas. Children's Bureau, *The Community Welfare Picture in 34 Urban Areas*, 1940 (Washington, June, 1941), pp. 9, 11.

nomic tensions and the possibility of violent cylical fluctuations. It is imperative, then, that one of our most potentially effective economic weapons—the financial machinery of government—be geared to making its full contribution.

The conclusion seems inescapable that if public finance is to contribute to the progress and stability of our economy, certain drastic revisions must be made in governmental fiscal structures and in intergovernmental relations. Were it not for one factor, a discussion of drastic revisions would definitely be of the ivory-tower variety. That factor is the assurance that political groups cannot hope to retain power, under modern conditions, unless they can successfully deal with the problems of economic instability and individual insecurity. The foregoing analysis would seem to indicate that, if sound, coordinated fiscal programs are to be carried out and if adequate levels of service are to be maintained throughout the nation, there is need for action along several fronts.

Toward Eliminating Fiscal Incapacity

The vicious cycle in which the poorer areas of the country find themselves must be broken. The fiscal incapacity of these areas largely precludes their pursuance of economic and financial programs which would enable them to improve living standards and to meet successfully the onslaught of depression. This is not a problem for the economically backward areas alone; it is the concern of the entire nation. The poverty of undeveloped and exploited areas spreads like infection to other communities. Moreover, when children grow up without sufficient nourishment and medical care and without adequate training, when disease and sickness are high, and when workers are permitted to lose their skills, the whole nation loses in productivity and fails to achieve its potential. On the other hand, growth in one region generally fosters growth all around. To provide economic opportunity for the people of an area and thereby to increase their buying power is to expand the market for goods produced in other areas of the nation and to open attractive outlets for investment. For the areas with inadequate fiscal resources, ability to solve the problems of cyclical fluctuations is contingent on the improvement of economic capacity and the achievement of a better balance in service levels and in purchasing power levels as between different areas of the country. A multiform attack on the problem seems necessary.

1. *Long-term programs of development.* Through the cooperative effort of the Federal, state, and local governments, long-range developmental programs should be undertaken to bring about the effective utilization of land, water, and mineral resources, so that every region may develop as broad a base of economic activities as its natural resources can economically sustain. The planned and intensive development of native resources and markets is crucial for the poorer areas of the country. It is an important key to economic expansion.

2. *Reallocation of certain governmental functions.* The federal government must necessarily assume the responsibility for the adequate performance of public services which are of direct national concern. The responsibility might be discharged either through actual administration or through increased financial participation, together with control over standards of performance.

The reallocation of functions—either administrative or financial—is called for especially in two groups of public services. The first group includes those services that are essential to guarantee healthy, productive individuals and to prevent the creation of permanently underprivileged classes. Among these services fall education, nutrition, child and maternal welfare, medical care, and public housing. Broadly speaking, the provision of an adequate level of such services is necessary to increase the potential income-producing power of areas where low income is attributable to long-standing economic handicaps rather than to the ups and downs of the business cycle. The second group of services includes those whose objective is to relieve the acute forms of human distress associated with extreme poverty. In this category fall social security and relief. The maintenance of an adequate level of payments throughout the country, especially of unemployment benefits and relief, is essential if distress is to be alleviated wherever it may occur and if the purchasing power of low-income areas is to be improved. Only federal administration or a high degree of federal financial participation (on an equalizing basis) can put a floor under these crucial public services.

A reallocation of functions and costs from one level of government to another must inevitably result in a shift in burdens from certain groups of taxpayers to others. This follows from the differences in tax structures leading to varying impacts on the money streams of the economy. Because of the breadth of federal tax bases and the relative progressiveness of the national tax system, a shift of certain burdens to the federal government has much to commend it from the standpoint of equity and economic soundness.

3. *Variable grants.* The grant-in-aid is a convenient tool for achieving a better balance in service levels and in purchasing power between different areas. To achieve greater equalization, distribution of the grants should be based on the needs and resources of the recipient units.

Where, for the services discussed above, a relatively high degree of federal financial participation is preferable—for political or administrative reasons—to direct central administration, such participation should take the form of variable-ratio grants, as opposed to uniform-ratio or equal-sharing grants. The percentage of Federal participation (possibly within a range of 25 to 75 percent) would be related to the significant differences in the resources as well as in the needs and tax efforts of the various states. The Federal percentages would vary inversely, and the state percentages directly, with state resources, possibly measured by average per capita income, which is a rough measure of both resources and needs. Under a plan of this sort, in the states with relatively low resources the increased Federal grant would offset the small amount of funds which such states can obtain through their own tax systems, making it possible for these states to provide the nationally important services at levels of adequacy not much different from those of the states that have larger financial resources.

Where the responsibility for the administration of a service is shared by both the state and its localities (e.g., education) or is entirely a local function, the Federal grant should be conditioned, among other things, on the distribution by the state of grants to localities on a similar variable-ratio basis. This is necessary because differences in resources among the various areas *within* the states are extreme. For example, a recent study of county taxable resources in Ohio revealed that per capita assessed valuation (Ohio law requires 100 percent valuation) ranged from $571 to $1,759. The picture for other states is undoubtedly not far different than that of Ohio. The equalization purpose of federal grants would be defeated, in part at least, unless the states allocated funds to localities on the basis of relative needs and resources.[8]

4. *Local consolidation.* In the case of localities, a better balance of burdens and resources can be achieved through local government reorganization. Generally speaking, inequalities in resources and burdens decrease as the size of the district increases. In rural areas, the problem is essentially one of shifting key governmental functions from the manifold small districts to large county areas. In urban areas, the development of metropolitan governments is of prime importance. It would go a long way toward solving certain of the problems inherent in the present tendency for wealthy families to move to independent suburban districts, leaving the central city with heavy burdens and a small tax base. The formation of such metropolitan areas could be carried out directly in connection with much-needed long-range programs of urban redevelopment. Local consolidation might well be a precondition of Federal grants to states and localities.[9]

Toward Improved State and Local Fiscal Structures

In addition to ensuring greater equalization in burdens and resources, the foregoing proposals, if adopted, would undoubtedly place the nonfederal units as a group in a better financial position than at present. If the federal government were to assume a substantial share of the cost of carrying out the public functions which are of direct national concern, state and local revenues might well be adequate for the remaining responsibilities.

For the localities, the pivotal point would be increased central financial support of public education. In recent years, public school costs have amounted to roughly one-third of total local expenditures. In 1941, for example, local government expenditures on schools were $2,240 million out of a total outlay, exclusive of debt retirement, of $6,730 million. The states contributed $735 million to the localities—or one-third of the educational costs—in the form of grants, while the federal government contributed only $83 million in grants, chiefly for vocational education.[10] If the Federal government were to assume the

---

[8]It is important, of course, to guard against the tendency of freezing uneconomic situations through grants-in-aid, or, for that matter, through public works. The death struggles of decadent communities should not be prolonged.

[9]The reorganization of local governments into logical economic and administrative units is needed also because the carrying out of sound fiscal programs requires a broad scope for planning and for financing, as well as expert administration. Successful reorganization would bring within the scope of local authority an area for which significant plans could be drawn up for such matters as zoning, residential construction, transportation, recreational centers, and, in general, the development of desirable cities and towns.

[10]Of this sum, $61 million were for defense training. Another $30 million were distributed, in loans and grants, directly to the localities faced with special educational problems growing out of the war effort. In 1940, only some $55 million in Federal grants were distributed for public education.

responsibility for roughly one-third of total educational costs, and the states another third, both in the form of equalization grants, the localities as a group would find themselves in a much healthier financial position.

The ramifications of such a shift in burdens are extremely important. For one thing, the poorer localities would be in a position to finance other local services more adequately. For another, pressure on the property tax would be reduced. The property tax has deteriorated in recent years, mainly because of the heavy burden that it has had to bear. Relief of this burden can be expected to result in better administration of the property tax and in fewer delinquencies, and it would help to remove the block to construction activities. The financial position of localities could be improved further through an increase in local sharing in certain state-collected taxes. Complete local reliance on the property tax is both inequitable and economically unsound. It seems advisable that the states share with their localities yields from gasoline and automobile taxes and licenses. Local governments spend large sums on highways and streets;[11] yet they receive little—in many cases nothing—from automobile and gasoline taxes.

Federal assumption of the unemployment compensation program in whole or in part, and some of the burden of relief of employables, would be an important factor in preventing fiscal breakdowns and inadequate assistance to the unemployed and needy in periods of depression.

Tax Reform

Certain changes in state and local tax structures are essential if public finance is to contribute to the progress and stability of the economy in the postwar period. It is necessary to eliminate the tax barriers to interstate commerce as well as the disrupting effects of an irrational assortment of business taxes and of the competition for business enterprises through the use of the tax mechanism. Of paramount importance, also, is a shift away from consumption taxation to income taxation. The personal income tax has shown itself capable of yielding huge revenues in periods of prosperity. If the states were to follow the practice of setting aside reserves in prosperity periods to be used during depression, the pressure to rely on the more stable, but regressive sales taxes would be relieved.

Significant improvements would undoubtedly result from the adoption of a single nationally administered business tax, either a business net income or corporate net income tax. A certain share of the yield—possibly one-quarter or one-third—would be allocated to the states on the basis of the widely accepted "Massachusetts formula" (based on ratios consisting of gross receipts, pay rolls, and tangible property). The advantages which would accrue from the substitution of such a single tax for the present chaotic mass of business taxes are many: (1) the single business tax would reduce enormously the costs of collection and of compliance; (2) it would eliminate the unhealthy competition for business concerns which now exists between the states; (3) it would eliminate certain of

---

[11]In the fiscal year ending June 30, 1941, local government expenditures for highways and streets amounted of $467 million.

the interstate tax barriers and discriminations against foreign concerns; (4) it would permit business enterprises to plan more securely; and (5) it would lessen the burden on private enterprise during periods of financial distress. Additional improvements could be brought about by incorporating into the business tax certain features which would create a favorable basis for the emergence of new private investment; among others, the encouragement of investment in equity capital, the elimination of discrimination against businesses with highly fluctuating incomes, and the granting of tax credits for new investment.

Another measure which can be expected to improve greatly the fiscal structures of the states is the adoption of a system of state supplements to the Federal personal income tax, such supplements to be collected by the Federal government along with its own levies and returned to the states. Such an arrangement would give the states complete independence as to whether or not they use the personal income tax and as to the rates to be applied. It would, however, have a number of important advantages: (1) it would reduce the costs of administration and compliance; (2) it would undoubtedly encourage a much greater uniformity in rates among the states; (3) it would permit the use of the income tax by those states which at the present time do not possess the administrative and legal talent required to administer such a tax; (4) it would enable many of the states to assess more adequately income in kind and farm income generally; and (5) it could be expected to encourage a greater reliance on the income tax.

Credit Policy

If nonfederal units are to be in a position to maintain their essential services and to contribute to the disposable income of the community, state and local credit operations must be facilitated. It becomes incumbent upon the Federal government, with its superior credit standing, to underwrite state and local borrowing. The national government should stand ready to extend loans to the subordinate units at the lowest possible interest rates. This would amount, in principle, to an extension and liberalization of the credit policies pursued by the Reconstruction Finance Corporation and Public Works Administration in the depression of the thirties. The controls involved in the extension of loans to state and local governments could be employed to bring about a greater conformity to national economic policy.

Fiscal Patterns

A reallocation of functions and of taxes which resulted in a larger scope for national fiscal policy would enhance the field for coordinated and flexible financial programs. It seems apparent that the states and localities, with few exceptions, are in no position—economically or institutionally—to follow a flexible countercycle fiscal policy. The most that can be expected—and possibly the most desirable arrangement—is that they stabilize their financial activities. This would involve the setting up of reserves and the advance planning of public works in prosperity to enable them to sustain their expenditures in depression. The states and localities would maintain tax rates in prosperity, and during periods of depression they would refrain from adding to the tax burden. They would borrow in depression, from a federal loan agency as well as from private investors, to fill any gap in revenues that may appear.

The additional responsibilities placed on the national government would make more imperative than ever improvements in Federal finances and administration. Improved management of fiscal policy is urgently needed. Of crucial importance also is a greater degree of decentralized administration. Responsiveness to the needs of the people directly concerned must be safeguarded as much as possible. A federal-state-local commission to advise Congress and the President on matters of intergovernmental relations would undoubtedly make for better understanding and cooperation at all levels of government.

The Question of Centralization

Admittedly, the proposals set forth above would involve certain drastic departures from existing fiscal structures and intergovernmental relations. The indications that such steps must soon be taken are so clear, however, that we have only the choice between trying to plan for this development as wisely as we can or letting it be forced upon us by the pressure of events.

These indications lie partly in the likelihood of a repetition of our experience during the depression of the thirties. The period was characterized by fiscal breakdowns and chaos and severe suffering. It was marked by numerous tax delinquencies in distressed urban and rural areas, a breakdown of the local relief structures, a wild scramble for tax sources with a shift to regressive taxes, and an expansion of certain centrally aided programs at the expense of other governmental functions. It seems inevitable that a repetition of such an experience would compel the national government to assume a major share of the responsibility for combating the depression.

At the present time, under the stress of the war program, the federal government is assuming an ever-increasing share of the responsibility for the performance of governmental services. Not only is it absorbing new functions, but it is stepping in to remedy specific maladjustments and abnormal needs both in individual geographic areas and in individual sections of our economy. The question, then, is largely one of whether or not this trend should be extended, in a planned fashion, into the postwar period.

The prospect of increasing centralization generally conjures up fears of totalitarianism and dictatorship. The obvious lessons of history, however, should not be overlooked. In each instance, during modern times, dictatorship has come as a result of social and economic breakdown. Frustration and chaos are the forebearers of totalitarianism, not centralization. Certainly, the experience of Great Britain, with a unitary form of government and an ever-increasing degree of centralism, does not bear out the fears of those in the United States who see in the increasing importance of the federal government the opening wedge for dictatorship.

Moreover, our traditions of local initiative would not be done away with.

On the contrary, a proper allocation of functions will serve to remove from states and localities the onerous burden of problems which they cannot manage, and to enable them to concentrate on the proper administration of functions of a local interest. A healthy local financial structure is decidedly conducive to civic interest and pride.

V

PLANNING EDUCATION

INTRODUCTION

At the age of 26, Perloff wrote in his earliest article,

> If the democratic process has meaning and vitality, then popular control must be most effective at the level of policy formulation and in the selection of policy executors. But, at the same time, the agents of the people must be effectively equipped if the social objectives are to be achieved.

Training planners as the agents of the people charged with the formidable task of creating a better tomorrow became the focus of his efforts to reform planning education.

Whereas his successes were legion in promoting and reforming planning education—particularly by challenging the tradition that a good planner need only have a thorough acquaintance with principles of design and law and stressing that a planner needed to know above all how the social sciences contributed to the solution of urban problems—there was one failure. The University of Chicago experiment had succeeded in integrating the social sciences into planning education and research, but Perloff was unable to effect a marriage between traditional physical planning and the newer policy approaches grounded in social theory. A potential liaison with the Illinois Institute of Technology refused to materialize, in part because that institution's leading figure was committed to a single design concept (linear, high-rise cities) of only limited appeal. An experiment to test the linkage in practice failed as well, but for different reasons. Hyde Park, a neighborhood adjacent to the University of Chicago campus, was declining in both physical and functional terms. What better opportunity to test whether physical solutions could be influenced by the principles of social sciences to restore its vitality? Bull-dozing was proposed by the University administration; Perloff argued that rehabilitation was a solution better geared to the needs of the residents, while maintaining the fragile town-gown ties of a university community. The alternate to the University's plan called for mixed land uses with a lighted center that would attract activities during both day and night. Alas, the University's insensitive proposal won out, and the hoped-for fusion of the physical with the social never materialized.

Other linkages were more successful. The most notable occurred in Perloff's advocacy of an expanded vision of planning education joined to the realities of

257

planning practice. Six years of directing research at the distinguished Resources for the Future, a private, not-for-profit research institute, provided a fertile background of knowledge. But the translation into action—the overriding criterion that guided his scholarship—required deeper involvement in planning education. In 1968, his move to UCLA as Dean of a fledgling School of Architecture and Urban Planning provided two opportunities: the chance to teach others how to link knowledge to action, and a chance to try, once again, to find a common ground for injecting the design aspects of architecture into the social sciences of urban planning. As he put it in an address delivered at a ceremony convened in 1983 to honor his tenure of a decade-and-a-half at UCLA,

> Both the Chicago and RFF experiences . . . left areas of frustration. Much of this centered on the large gap I perceived between the idea level—where provocative and valuable concepts were being projected—and the world of actual practice. I felt a strong urge to get back into education, where education, research, and practice could all be combined. I was convinced that all three elements had to work closely together. If practice did not reflect both the understanding that was developed in education—and the dreams that were created there—as well as the results of the most advanced research, it would be a pit of nonprogress.

A tour of leading universities offering programs in architecture, urban design, and urban planning uncovered the frustrations others had experienced in forging the unions that conceptually seemed so logical. The practitioners and academics who taught in these three, presumably interrelated, fields guarded their turf carefully, even jealously. Forced integration presented serious problems. Incorporating new areas of inquiry into established fields was resisted. Bridges that in principle could be easily built in fact were never completed, as rivalries stymied progress.

A new school, where time had not balkanized the fields, offered promise, and so the UCLA story began. A fifteen-year career of building that school was, by any measure, a success. The ingredients of the recipe were

> strong core programs for architecture and urban planning, an increasingly strong research base, and research accomplishments, a strong practice arm to help students move properly into the forward-looking practice, ties to the profession and to the community-at-large, and a smart faculty.

What of the future of planning education? To Perloff the challenge involved, as before, building links to related disciplines, incorporating into planning new dimensions whether they are methodologies, substantive fields, or problem areas. In his 1983 address, he expressed confidence that "the pressures of rapidly changing technology and international competition will once again—and very soon—put planning education and research at the forefront of national concerns." Concerns about the quality of the environment and the quality of life in general would rank high on the national agenda. Specifically, the challenges to education in architecture, as well as in planning, would be in the areas of combining technology and design with human needs and aspirations, the unresolved dilemma of merging the physical (whether defined as the man-made or

the natural environment) with the social and economic, and strengthening research and aligning it more directly to action.

The first of the pair of articles reprinted in this part received the commenda-
tion of the editors of the journal in which it appeared as "the most thoughtful
contribution to Planning Education yet made in the United States." Perloff ar-
gues for planning much as others have argued for education in other professions. In brief, he calls for developing basic principles, for strong exposure to the
social sciences, for a solid base of core courses as well as specialized courses in
university programs to produce a "generalist-with-a-specialty," and for tying
education to a strong research component.

The arguments follow two lines of development. It is time to broaden planning education from training in a few skills thought to be relevant: "the shaping
and guiding of the physical growth and land use arrangements of urban communities" and administrative capabilities for jobs in municipal government. "This
article . . . raises the question of what is an appropriate intellectual, practical,
and 'philosophical' basis for the education of city planners and attempts some
tentative answers." As journal articles go, it is a very long piece, for it has large-
scale ambitions. It deals with the past development of the urban (or city) planning field, and just as importantly, with the present and future.

The historical view demonstrates how the faculties of planning programs in
American universities were the perennial Johnny-come-latelies to the field, relying on knowledge transmitted from other fields rather than generating their
own.

> The history of city planning serves to underline very sharply why planning
> education cannot rely on the transmission of existing knowledge and meth-
> ods in a traditional apprenticeship manner, but must be geared to the con-
> tinuing search for new knowledge and methods and the development of a
> basic core curriculum at the heart of planning education. . . . the very
> breadth of the actual and potential intellectual and professional contributions
> makes it evident that a sound planning education cannot be pieced together
> by drawing on a little bit here and a little bit there. Only if planning students
> are required to have a rounded education as a prerequisite for graduate
> training, and if the training of city planners centers about a carefully de-
> signed core curriculum can this surrounding richness be a source of strength
> for city planning education rather than a source of confusion and dilution.

Contrasting the requirements of the profession—not only as they are, but
also as they should be—with the education planners receive, leads to a set of
three guidelines for planning education. First there is the need for a "sound
general education as a foundation for professional education." Second, and
most importantly,

> professional schools must develop and emphasize the fundamental princi-
> ples . . . upon which the professional tasks are based rather than rule-of-
> thumb procedures, and to teach these principles so that they are understood
> in a broad social and intellectual context as well as a problem-solving context.

Finally, there is the need to confront the issues of increasingly specialized
and technical knowledge "by training not the narrow specialist but the gener-

alist-with-a-speciality." Continual experimentation is called for in methods for educating students characterized by "breadth with expertise." Much of this can be done by building bridges to "nourishing" disciplines and fields. The principles form the foundation for more specialized learning at schools and later on the job and for that matter, throughout the remainder of their careers.

The second chapter, "The Evolution of Planning Education," identifies trends in the field since the 1940s, updates materials presented in the first piece, and assesses certain directions educational programs are taking. Perhaps the piece's major contribution is a discussion of the persistent tensions between opposing requirements and demands, between generalist and specialist skills, between technological and humanistic skills, between substantive professional and administrative elements, between concrete current problems and the uncertain future, between scholarly and professional approaches, and between full-time education and continuing education of others. The list of tensions provide planning educators and administrators of collegiate planning programs with a set of scales on which to assess the balance offered in their programs and, implicitly, with a set of goals for their programs to achieve. Given the formidable tensions that direct (and misdirect) the course of planning education, substantial progress has been made and planning education is maturing. "Many of the key *ingredients* for excellence (and social significance) are already in place—such as full-time faculties, well-developed degree programs, research capabilities, and university support." But, concludes Perloff, "the *achievement* of excellence is still somewhere off in the future."

Much remains to be done before the desired state is reached. This includes first, securing "substantial support for planning approaches at state, regional, and local levels, largely through federal support of such activities" (including fellowships and research grants); second, developing stronger intellectual ties to professionals in related, evolving fields, such as policy science, systems analysis, urban economics, and urban law; third, establishing a professional doctorate as the counterpart to the PhD and to put practical education on an equal footing with planning scholarship and research; and finally, the sine qua non of excellence, recruiting the most able into the field.

17

Education of City Planners

Past and Present

INTRODUCTION

City planning[1] in the United States has grown rapidly in scope, in complexity, and in the number of career opportunities the field provides. Almost every city in the United States, as well as many of the smaller urban communities, has established a planning agency or employs private planning consultants. In addition, there are many redevelopment, housing, and urban renewal agencies and citizens' organizations employing trained planners. County and regional planning organizations, at times extending over very large areas, are being set up in every part of the country. An indication of the growth in planning activities is provided by the fact that the number of full-time employees of public planning agencies doubled in the decade after World War II, and membership in the major professional organizations more than doubled. At the same time many new opportunities for planners have opened up as consultants to, or employees of, private corporations undertaking various types of urban-development projects. Planners are being called upon to carry out activities of great variety and difficulty; activities which frequently directly influence the strength of the urban community's economic base and social fabric.

Looking ahead, it seems evident that with the continued rapid urbanization, the increasing complexity of urban life, and an awakening sense among the American people of what our enormous national wealth and productivity can

---

[1]The term "city planning" is used in its broadest sense throughout the paper, that is, referring to planning activities concerned with the entire urbanized area and rural hinterland of broad metropolitan regions, as well as activities centering on small urban communities or the central city of a metropolis. "Urban planning" or "regional (metropolitan) planning" might be preferable terms as far as technical accuracy is concerned, but the term "city planning" has the advantage of wider understanding and traditional usage. The problems of education as related specifically to regional planning will be discussed in a later paper.

accomplish on the urban scene, still greater pressures for, and on, city planning can be expected.

In this context, the education of city planners in the United States is inadequate, both qualitatively and quantitatively.[2] The planning educators themselves are the first to recognize this, and the first to welcome discussions of the problems of planning education. They know that they are not recruiting an adequate number of first-rate students into the university planning schools, that their curricula are not based on fundamentals and rely too heavily on bits and pieces of accumulated wisdom, that they are not contributing enough to the development of planning tools, and that their research—if there is any—is not sufficiently basic and must rely on research scholars trained in other fields.

Since the future of city planning is certain to be greatly affected by the type and quality of education provided in our institutions of higher learning, this is a significant problem for the entire planning profession and not alone for those directly associated with the planning schools. It is a problem also for the colleges and universities of the nation.

THE VIEW FROM THE ADMINISTRATION TOWER: THE DEVELOPMENT OF PROFESSIONAL EDUCATION

It is quite evident that many of the top college and university administrators are confused about planning and education for planners. The planning review committee has recently become almost a fixture of planning education. Administrators at Harvard, Chicago, Columbia, MIT, Florida, Michigan, and elsewhere have turned to that symbol of perplexity, the review committee, only to find—as they undoubtedly already know—that there are no simple administrative or organizational answers to basic educational problems.

Many of the university administrators have shown themselves to be troubled by the controversies that seem to whirl continually about the planning school, by qualitative inadequacies, and by the fact that so many basic educational questions are as yet not even partially resolved. Is planning actually a separate field of study that needs a separate school, or is it an aspect of some other field like architecture or social science? Should it emphasize the design

---

[2]As far as quantity is concerned, a gap between the demand for, and the supply of, trained planners has developed over the past decade and seems to be widening rather than closing. A survey of the present personnel situation (mainly with regard to positions in public planning agencies) was provided by the *Newsletter* of the American Society of Planning Officials of February 1956 (Vol. 22, No. 2, pp. 9–10): "During 1954 we advertised just over 200 positions. During 1955 we advertised 413 positions. According to our records these are currently 265 unfilled planning jobs. It is, of course, difficult to prepare firm estimates of supply and demand since there is a good bit of variation in titles attached to positions concerned with different types of planning tasks and since individuals with planning titles are sometimes involved in activities which have little if any relationship to the planning of urban communities. In evaluating quantitative deficiencies, attention must be given to the fact that currently in the United States there is a general shortage of trained personnel in almost every field.

skills and an applied approach or should it provide a very broad training in a research-oriented environment? And so on. This disturbed feeling about planning education on the part of university administrators is no small matter. Their understanding and support is urgently needed if planning schools are to prosper—or even exist.

The "Natural History" of Professional Education

It seems to me that some useful things can be said by way of clarification concerning the difficulties in which planning schools find themselves—particularly since many of the problems of planning education are basically similar to those which plagued other professions at critical stages in their development.

While each profession has its own special history and development, there are some important common elements which, if analogies are not carried too far, can be highly suggestive in analysing the development of education in a particular profession. In some important respects planning education today is about where medical and legal education in the United States were at roughly the beginning of the century. In the case of medical education, this would be the period before the reforms instituted at the Johns Hopkins School of Medicine, and later the development of other great medical schools, led the way out of confusion and mediocrity. As Dr. Richard H. Shryock points out in his review of medical education,

> Like the arts colleges, American medical schools had long been preoccupied simply with the transmission of learning; and most of them did even this in a superficial manner. . . . A commercial spirit permeated the profession. It is hard to realize, today, that it became easier to gain entrance to a medical school than to a good arts college; that the course in the former was much shorter than in the latter. . . . Medical research was pursued occasionally by only a few individuals.[3]

It took a basic reorientation—which required a new kind of organization, new faculties, and new educational techniques—to bring medical education to a high level of excellence. It took the provision of professional training within a research-oriented environment, emphasis upon the advancement of knowledge rather than merely the transmission of knowledge, the appointment of full-time

---

[3]Richard H. Shryock, *The Unique Influence of the Johns Hopkins University on American Medicine* (Copenhagen: Ejnar Munksgaard, 1953), pp. 11–12. For some interesting parallels in the development of education for the legal profession, see Alfred Z. Reed, *Training for the Public Profession of the Law*, Historical Development and Principal Contemporary Problems of Legal Education in the United States (Boston: Updike-Merrymount, 1921); Sidney P. Simpson, *The New Curriculum of the Harvard Law School* (Cambridge: Harvard Law Review Association, 1938, Reprinted from the Harvard Law Review, Vol. LI, No. 6); and Albert J. Harno, *Legal Education in the United States*, A Report Prepared for the Survey of Legal Education (San Francisco: Bancroft-Whitney, 1953). At the beginning of the century much of the legal education was characterized by the teaching of local and concrete law (as against national and generalized); a "dogmatic" use of textbooks (as against a critical examination of cases or original sources); in many cases, no entrance requirements for students; and a great deal of practitioner-teaching.

faculty members rather than part-time local practitioners, real clinical teaching, the limiting of admission to those who had completed college training (including training in the basic sciences), the lengthening of the course of studies, and the development of post internship training in specialities. Also, it took the assumption of educational leadership by the full-time faculty members.[4]

The amount and type of leadership in the guidance of professional education provided by the university scholars, as compared with the practitioners, may well be an excellent gauge of the maturity and progress of a professional group (even though practitioners have a special, and highly important, educational function to perform in every instance). In the case of city planning, it seems evident that the full-time planning faculty members are not yet providing the type of enlightened and aggressive leadership which is needed to bring education for the city planning profession to a high degree of excellence. But it is worth noting that the problem of leadership has been characteristic of all professions in the earlier stages of their development.

Usually professional education has been pushed into the universities by outside leaders of the profession and the practitioners themselves have provided much of the instruction and have set the orientation of the training curriculum. Only some time later—in some cases, generations later—have the university scholars taken the reins and developed an educational program for the profession which reflects the ideals and resources of the universities, as well as the evolving—rather than the past and current—needs of the profession.

Some of the problems and difficulties of planning education, then, are those which are characteristic of an early stage in the development of education for almost any profession. In this connection we note that courses in city planning were not available in the United States until 1909 and that the first school of planning was established in 1929. Education for city planners is of relatively recent vintage.

Other types of problems and difficulties are quite specific to city planning, and therefore to planning education. Possibly outstanding among these is the confusion that has resulted from the fact that city planning in the United States has been influenced and guided by *two* relatively distinctive streams of development. These two streams have intertwined and in some sense even merged, but each has enough of its own special elements to make the process of merging an extremely difficult one.

One stream of development in the city planning field has been more or less typically professional in character; that is, *the evolution of a separate skill group* (a development similar to that in the case of doctors, architects, and engineers)— here, a skill group concerned with the shaping and guiding of the physical growth and land-use arrangements of urban communities, through the making

---

[4]I was encouraged to include this comparative discussion of professional education when I discovered, in reviewing the educational history of several professions, that some of the reforms which seem so necessary in the education of city planners were precisely the types of reforms which were crucial in raising the educational stature of other professions. This suggested that other reforms and other developments within these professions might be suggestive in looking towards improvements in planning education.

and application of plans and designs covering the location and three-dimensional form of various types of public and private improvements upon the land. Central to this stream of development has been the image of the individual, having met the requirements of a professional society, serving a public or private client by carrying out more or less clearly defined professional tasks. Over time the tasks have been significantly broadened but, within this line of development, the assumption has been that the individual planner must himself learn and absorb the knowledge and skills which the broadened tasks call for. This is a stream of development which began at the turn of the century with the city plans produced by the architects-and-engineers-turned-city-planners, which was strengthened by the formation in 1917 of a professional association (the American City Planning Institute) and which today sets the framework for some of the planning activities and much of graduate planning education.

The other stream of development—which came to be a significant force in the 1930s and which has gained momentum since then—has been *the evolution of an administrative function of planning within municipal government*. This has been essentially a staff advisory function, and increasingly a staff function similar to other staff (or central overhead) functions, such as budgeting and personnel management. The planning function in local government has come to be concerned with activities, such as the programming (scheduling) of public works and improvement projects, analysis of problems related to the overall economic and physical growth of the community, and the making of recommendations as to means (legal controls, incentive payments, etc.) which might be employed to encourage private urban development and redevelopment activities. Central to this stream of development has been the emphasis on an administrative function carried out by an official planning agency, working within the political framework of the municipal government, concerned with certain aspects of all municipal activities (i.e., the overall planning aspects) in the same way that the budgeting office is concerned with the allocation of funds to all municipal agencies or the central personnel office is concerned with civil service administration influencing all or most of the departments within the local government.

The focus in this stream of development has been on a function (rather than on a professional skill) and therefore the emphasis has been on a team effort and on the various skills that the team as a whole—and not any one individual member—must have. Just as the main focus in the other stream of development has been on plan making of a comprehensive sort, the focus in the latter stream has been on accomplishments in an administrative and political setting.

As suggested above, these two lines of development have crisscrossed, intertwined, and in some ways merged. Thus, the separate-skill-group development has involved a broadening conception of the professional skills required for city planning to include understanding and ability in the administrative-political realm. It has become quite widely accepted that the professional planner should have some training in administration and that he should seek to develop an understanding of politics as soon as he possibly can. On the other side, the administrative-political stream of development has involved the establishment of skill requirements in the recruitment of persons into official planning agencies, which has ensured that most of those holding public planning posts have had training in the separate-skill-group tradition. This intertwining reflects the fact that city planning in the United States, in its public form, has been developing as a governmental function which joins together *general staff activities* (concerned with integration and balancing of municipal government operations, for example, through capital-improvement programming) and *substantive activities* concerned with guiding urban physical development (for example, through the preparation of master plans and the application of zoning and other controls to carry them out).

All this, however, is still in a relatively early stage of evolution and it is difficult to see all the implications. Thus, it is inevitable that discussions of city planning and of planning education should sometimes take the first (separate-skill-group) stream of development as the framework and stress what the professional planner has to know and be trained in; at other times, to refer to the administrative-political line of development and stress the team requirements; and still at other times (but, as yet, only rarely) to consider the implications of both lines of development and of the potentialities inherent in them.

A Look at History and Trends

A review of the main facets in the development of city planning is instructive in several ways. It serves to bring into focus the impact on the city planning field of a dual (instead of a uniform and consistent) line of development. Also, it is suggestive of the direction which planning education should take if the latter is to turn the dual development into a source of strength rather than a cause for division and confusion.

This paper is intended as a contribution to the discussion of planning education which has been under way for some time in the planning journals, conferences, and elsewhere. It raises the question of what is an appropriate intellectual, practical, and philosophical basis for the education of city planners and attempts some tentative answers. It highlights certain guidelines which can be drawn from an examination of the main facets in the development of the field of city planning and of planning education—past, present, and future.

THE DEVELOPMENT OF THE CITY PLANNING FIELD

City planning in the United States has gone through several stages, each of which has had its own special characteristics. (The main features of the various stages are described in Appendix A, and landmarks in the history of city planning are briefly described there.) During the 60-some years since the beginning of the modern city planning movement in the United States (usually dated from the Chicago World's Fair of 1893), the functions of city planning and of the persons called planners have changed significantly. In an important sense, however, the most striking feature of the history of city planning has been what might be called its "cumulative" characteristics, the fact that the planning field has been broadened continuously as the scope for municipal government activities has grown and as various movements, ideas, professions, and studies have come to have an influence on city planning.[5]

Not unexpectedly, the course which city planning took was quite directly related to the environmental context within which planning functioned—the social attitudes, the prevailing view of the appropriate scope for governmental activity, the types of groups which wielded economic and political power. And the training of planners, in turn, reflected the professional view of the kinds of skills needed by those carrying out planning activities.

The Earlier Phase: The Role of the Architect, Landscape Architect, and Engineer

In this framework, it is instructive to note some of the "whys and wherefores" of the role of the architect, landscape architect, and engineer during the early period (the Chicago Fair of 1893 to World War I) precisely because this early history has profoundly influenced the entire development of city planning.

The latter part of the 19th century and the early part of the 20th was a period in which the accepted scope for municipal activity was defined in limited terms and when extensive public control of private property was next to inconceivable. At the same time, however, many people were anxious to avoid the worst features of industrialization and urbanization: the ugliness, crowding, and lack of public facilities. Also, there was a reaching out for status and symbols of achievement on the part of rich and powerful individuals and groups, particularly in the larger cities, through the creation of urban "monuments," such as civic centers, park systems, and broad thoroughfares—("I am a citizen of no mean city."). The civic improvement organization and the commerce club, sponsoring activities designed to improve the appearance and amenities of cities, grew up and flourished. Here was a context within which the "city beautiful" concept could be expected to emerge and within which the need for the planning of public improvements and park systems could become accepted and acceptable.[6] The architects and landscape architects could undertake the planning of civic centers, park systems, and thoroughfares as an extension of their established activities.

---

[5]In this respect, the city planning profession in the United States has followed a quite different course than has the town and country planning profession in Europe and elsewhere in the world. Outside of the United States, with some variations (as in Canada and Australia), the planning profession has in the main limited itself to physical planning and in very large part to the civic design aspects of such planning. For an excellent brief description of the major characteristics of the planning profession and of planning education in the United States and abroad, see Frederick J. Adams, "The Status of Planning and Planning Education," *United Nations Bulletin on the Education of Planners* (Mimeographed 1956). A description of programs provided by planning schools and an outline of the historical development of planning education in countries throughout the world is provided in the bulletin published by the International Federation for Housing and Town Planning, *Education in Town Planning: An International Survey* (The Hague, Netherlands, 1952).

[6]Although the drive for civic improvement was strong enough to get a great number of plans on paper it was not strong enough to get very many projects built.

A similar logic appears in the further development of planning in the 1910s and 1920s. The increasing rapid urbanization, with its accompanying congestion and demands on public and private services and facilities, focused attention on problems of traffic and transportation, sanitation, and a wide range of public improvements. Add, further, the high value placed on the efficient functioning of cities by a controlling business community that had come to think of efficiency in government as "good business," and one can understand why the "city practical" concept should have developed and why there should have been a receptivity for the ideas and skills of the engineers as well as of the architects. These professionals were the experts in construction and efficient functioning; it is hardly surprising that they should have come to the forefront in an age of building.

It is a matter of no small importance that many members of these professions were men of skill, imagination, and vision. The new planning activities were not foisted upon them. Certainly, their skills fitted them for the key planning tasks *as then seen*, but they themselves were the ones who developed city planning as a new professional field and who laid the foundations at each stage for a continually broadening view of planning and what it should attempt to achieve. Thus, even in the earliest period, some of the plans demonstrated the inherent logic of public control of certain private activities, as in connection with transportation and traffic, and the need for the extension of the common law of nuisances. Daniel H. Burnham could say as early as 1909, in his *Plan of Chicago*, "It is no attack on private property to argue that society has the inherent right to protect itself against abuses."

Until the end of the 1920s education for city planning as such was quite limited. Most training took place on an apprenticeship basis in the offices of planning practitioners. The first formal university training in city planning was not introduced until 1909, and then only as a few separate courses given to students of landscape architecture. Training in architecture, landscape architecture, and engineering was then seen as adequate for the planning tasks. Not until 1923 was city planning accepted as a graduate specialization, and then only in one department in one university (Harvard). Instruction was carried out entirely by planning practitioners.

The establishment of a separate school of planning (at Harvard University) in 1929 marked, after a full generation of planning activity, the recognition, at least on the part of some practitioners and educators, of the need for separate teaching facilities for city planning.

Laying the Foundation for a Broad View of Planning

One cannot examine the Chicago Plan of 1909, or read the papers given at the early national planning conferences or the early zoning reports, without being struck by the breadth of conception and the far-reaching vision of many of the planners of the period.[7] Thus, almost from the very start, the stage was set

---

[7]John M. Gaus, *The Education of Planners* (Cambridge: Harvard Graduate School of Design, 1943), p. 8.

for the constant widening view of the planning field which has taken place since then. Over the years there came in fairly quick succession a whole set of additions to the conception as well as the practice of planning. From (1) an early stress on planning as concerned chiefly with esthetics, planning came to be conceived also in terms of (2) the efficient functioning of the city—in both the engineering and economic sense; then (3) as a means of controlling the uses of land as a technique for developing a sound land use pattern; then (4) as a key element in efficient governmental procedures; later (5) as involving welfare considerations and stressing the human element; and, more recently, (6) planning has come to be viewed as encompassing many socioeconomic and political, as well as physical, elements that help to guide the functioning and development of the urban community. Similarly, from a tendency to focus on the isolated project (the civic center, the lake front), the point of view and, to some degree at least, the function of planning has been enlarged to encompass the whole city, then the larger metropolitan community, then the broader region, and here and there there has been demonstrated an awareness of the intimate and vital relationship of the city to other cities, and to the region, the state, and the nation.

It is certainly true—and one is justified in stressing the fact—that much of this broadening has not been really absorbed as yet, that it is often quite superficial, that there is a continuous falling back on the narrower purely-physical-and-isolated-project point of view. But it is at least equally important to observe that there has been such a broadening, and that the slipping back tends to become less and less frequent and not quite as far back, as time goes on. I stress this point as background for the view which I will develop later, that the planning schools need not be nearly as cautious and apologetic as they have been about broadening their planning curricula. This would, in fact, only parallel the actual development of the planning field, and not be the startling innovation that some planning educators seem to think. But before discussing the current situation, it would be helpful to round out the historical story.

The Role of the Lawyer and the Social Scientist

The lawyers were the first professional group, outside of the architects, landscape architects, and engineers, to take a significant part in city planning, both practically and conceptually. By the time of the first World War, a number of lawyers were already devoting their main attention to city planning, and several lawyers were among the small group of professional planners to form the American City Planning Institute in 1917.

Practicing lawyers, as well as legal scholars and the courts, laid the foundations for what were to become the major legal tools associated with city planning—zoning and subdivision control—through the development of legal concepts centering on the police power and eminent domain.[8] They also figured prominently in the erection of a legal framework for city planning in the United

---

[8]Edward M. Bassett, *Zoning* (New York: Russell Sage Foundation, 1936); Alfred Bettman, *City and Regional Planning Papers* (Cambridge: Harvard City Planning Studies #13, 1946).

States through the statutes of the individual municipalities (mainly zoning ordinances)—and through state enabling legislation—particularly the extremely
important "model" enabling legislation for city planning and zoning promul-
gated by Advisory Committees of the U.S. Department of Commerce in the
1920s. A small but highly influential group of lawyers—men like Edward Bassett
and Alfred Bettmann—also served actively on planning commissions and on
special study groups, and in other ways played an important role in city
planning.

The history of the development of zoning and other legal tools which came
to be so closely associated with city planning illustrates rather well the flexible
manner in which city planning in the United States drew on, enriched, and gave
direction to a variety of movements and conceptions relating to urban development (provided that these were in tune with the times, i.e., provided they fitted
into the prevailing socioeconomic-political environment). Zoning could, of
course, be accepted as a tool not only of orderly urban growth but for the
preservation and increase of property values—undoubtedly a crucial factor in its
relatively early adoption.

The social-environment element perhaps also played a significant part in
the rather late incorporation into city planning of the approaches, techniques,
and personnel from the social sciences. The social scientists began to probe into
urban questions at a fairly early stage. By the time of World War I, Professor
Richard T. Ely and his colleagues and students at the University of Wisconsin
were already deep into the problems of land economics, including urban land
economics. Ely's monumental treatise on *Property and Contract* was published in
1914.[9] By 1925, Ely's Research Institute could sponsor a journal devoted to
problems of land and public utility economics. In the 1920s also, significant
advances in the study of the urban community were made through the research
of social scientists at the University of Chicago, men such as R. E. Park and E. W.
Burgess in sociology, Charles C. Colby in geography, and Charles E. Merriam in
political science.[10] At other universities as well the social scientists were making
available a body of detailed knowledge about the city and developing insights
and techniques of great potential value for city planning.

But the social scientists who were concerned with urban questions tended
to emphasize disturbing social and economic problems—such as slums and
inadequate housing, social disorganization in the urban communities, and inadequate public services and facilities, speculation and abuse of land—matters
which in the 1910s and 1920s were as yet generally deemed to be largely outside
the scope of legitimate municipal government activities (although some municipal reform legislation, e.g., with regard to tenements, were already on the
statute books). As Robert Walker suggests:[11]

---

[9]Richard T. Ely, *Property and Contract* (New York: MacMillan, 1914); also Richard T. Ely and
   Edward W. Morehead, *Elements of Land Economics* (New York: MacMillan, 1924) and
   Richard T. Ely and George S. Wehrwein, *Land Economics* (Ann Arbor: Edwards Brothers,
   1928).

[10]For a review of the work of the Chicago social scientists during the 1920s, see T. V. Smith
   and Leonard D. White, eds., *Chicago: An Experiment in Social Science Research* (Chicago,
   University of Chicago Press, 1929).

[11]Robert A. Walker, *op. cit.*, p. 35.

The leaders of the planning movement made an invaluable contribution to good government and to the acceptance of the planning idea between 1920 and 1930. Consultants, members of planning commissions, and civic leaders in private organizations argued the need for planning in city government on countless occasions, gradually arousing public interest and bringing about the creation of official planning agencies in practically all the important cities of the country. On the other hand, the sources of the strongest support for planning [in the 1920s] were not those from which one would anticipate serious agitation for a frontal attack upon slums, poverty, disease, and other municipal problems then being glossed over by urban governments.

It was not until the depression of the 1930s had altered both social attitudes and the accepted fields of municipal government activity that city planning quite seriously began to draw on the social sciences.[12] In the depression years, the planning agencies expanded their efforts to encompass a much wider field than public works and zoning. The planning commissions, responding to the stimulus of available federal funds, entered energetically into planning for slum clearance and housing. Incidental to the preparation of applications for housing projects, they collected data on such phases of city life and government as crime, disease, income, industry, the cost of rendering municipal services, and tax delinquency. Increasingly, social science materials and methods and social scientists came to play a significant role in city planning.

Administration to the Forefront

The depression not only focused attention on social problems, but also highlighted questions of administration and organization.[13] Interest in efficient government and in management had at an early stage come to have some influence on city planning, but it was not until official public planning agencies had undertaken the city planning function and displaced the private civic organizations, and not until the study of public administration had gained some stature, that questions of administration and governmental organization in city planning received active and detailed consideration. Thus, for example, the Urbanism Committee of the National Resources Committee was composed chiefly of administrators and students of administration. Their famous report, *Our Cities: Their Role in the National Economy* (1937), as well as their supplementary report, *Urban Government* (1939), seriously probed the problems of planning organization and administration. Also, over time, an increasing number of un-

---

[12]A notable exception was the *Regional Plan of New York and Its Environs*, which was prepared under the direction of a committee organized in 1922 and which was published in 1929. The plan comprised a series of survey volumes which dealt with problems of population, industry and economic development, land values, government, public services and facilities, and metropolitan growth and arrangement, which made substantial use of social science knowledge and techniques. The Regional Plan, however, stood alone in the city planning field in this respect. Together with the establishment of the first planning school, the Regional Plan symbolized the transition from the earlier historical phase in city planning to the modern phase.

[13]An extremely useful discussion of the problems of planning organization and administration is provided in Walker, *Op. cit.*, particularly Chapters 4–7.

versity-trained public administrators joined staffs of city planning agencies. They brought with them definite ideas about the need for integrating the planning agency more closely with the structure of local government.

But it was, undoubtedly, the force of circumstances which brought to city planning what amounted to a new line of development, a new dimension. Municipal officials, as well as students of public administration, came increasingly to see that the city planning agency could perform many quite practical administrative tasks which would help to solve pressing problems, especially when there is much to do and few funds to do it with. The preparation of informational reports of all sorts, capital-improvement programming, and capital budgeting came to be ongoing activities of many of the municipal planning agencies. This movement toward planning as a staff activity gathered so much momentum after World War II, in fact, that questions have been raised as to whether the main purposes of urban planning were not being lost in the pressure of short-term administrative activities. (This problem is discussed at a later point.)

The 1940s and 1950s

World War II and the postwar era accentuated the changing orientation of planning which came into being during the depression. The planning of housing for war workers and the preparation during the war of a "shelf" of local public works plans in the event of a postwar depression focused attention on the economic and social elements of planning. This was true also of the rapid population and industrial changes which took place during World War II and which continued in force in the postwar period. One consequence was to make more clear to local communities that useful physical planning can proceed only on the basis of adequate information about the economic and industrial foundation upon which they rest. Thus, a number of city planning commissions undertook studies of the economic base of their communities.

During the past decade—in part at least, as a consequence of the federal aid made available for public housing, urban redevelopment, and urban renewal—city planning has become increasingly concerned with the social and economic aspects, as well as the physical aspects, not only of housing and slum clearance, but of many features of the urban scene. A new appreciation has been developing of the human elements in city development and city planning.[14] Also, attention

---

[14]Walter H. Blucher, former executive director of the American Society of Planning Officials, aptly characterized the changing approach to city planning in the following terms: "In the early part of this century, the emphasis in city planning was on the city beautiful. During the twenties, it was on the city practical. Today, the emphasis is on the human beings who populate a community. The city is intended to serve humans; humans are not intended to serve the city (although they do have a duty and a responsibility to the city as a governmental unit). With these changes in attitudes, could the theory and practice in planning have stood still?" "Has the Technique of Planning Changed?" *Newsletter, American Society of Planning Officials* (April 1949), p. 33. In his editorials in the ASPO Noewsletter, Blucher for many years provided a lively current record of events, ideas, and controversies in the city planning field, and himself provided many valuable suggestions.

has been turned to the problems of making large-scale planned developments attractive to private capital, particularly in connection with redevelopment and renewal projects. At the same time many new opportunities for planners have opened up as consultants to, or employees of, private corporations undertaking various types of urban-development projects, including the construction of entire new cities on open land.

Looking back over the history of city planning, it becomes clear that both the term "planning" and city planning activities have served extremely useful social ends. Planning—as an approach, a symbol, and an activity—has helped to bring to the forefront, and into the consciousness of governments and of the general public, the importance and desirability of being concerned (operationally) with relationships among people, physical objects, and ecological forces; of trying to see things whole; of setting goals and of trying to figure out the best ways of achieving them; of trying to coordinate and integrate the different kinds of physical improvement and development activities carried out by the government; of aiming at and working towards a better future. Looking at planning, as a social historian might, it may be seen as a *response* to man's reaching out for meaningful unities in his community life, as well as a response to man's need to dream.[15] Thus, at least in the United States, a dynamic relationship has developed between city planning as an idea and an activity, on the one side, and, on the other, the broadening popular view of municipal government responsibility and the more widespread acceptance of the need for consciously working toward an improved urban environment.

THE DEVELOPMENT OF PLANNING EDUCATION

The various phases in the education of city planners followed quite closely the development of the city planning field itself. This can be seen by relating the educational background of planners to the different phases in the history of city planning.

As will be noted, city planning in the United States has developed through a series of additions and extensions, continually absorbing new techniques and adding new tasks. This "absorptive" quality has been true of planning education as well. At most planning schools, three-dimensional design and site and project planning from the beginning were the central elements in the training of planners. Most of the teaching and most of the student work centered about the drafting board.[16] Somewhere along the line, social science subjects were intro-

---

[15]In this respect, of course, planning shares a common role with philosophy and community action (among others).

[16]It is not surprising, considering the long period during which the physical and design aspects of city planning were predominant, that the earlier city planning curricula should have centered on design and project planning and that professionalization should have jelled more or less around this phase of city planning. Yet 1929 saw the first planning school established. This was the year when the *Regional Plan of New York and Its Environs* was published, with its sophisticated use of social science materials and techniques and with its broad conceptions of both the planning tasks and the area over which urban planning should extend. It wasn't until the 1940s that university planning education really caught up with the Regional Plan of New York.

duced into the planning curriculum—for example, some land economics—and social science students began to take degrees in planning.[17] Later, the regional aspects of urban planning, began to be considered. And later still (at a few schools) some serious research work was undertaken and planning students were encouraged to do research themselves. Five of the 22 planning schools which were in existence in 1954—when Frederick Adams published his survey of planning education—(all of them started in the 1940s) were organized through the stimulation of social science departments and tended to put at least some emphasis on the social sciences. These schools have also led the way in organizing research programs in problems of urbanism and planning.

The overall educational picture is, then, one of gradual assimilation of social science, regional aspects, and research into planning curricula—but always with a considerable lag. In general, it has only been long after the practitioners found themselves ill equipped to undertake tasks thrust upon them (tasks such as population and migration analyses, regional economic surveys, and the development of programming and capital-budgeting techniques) that the universities responded with changes in their existing training programs or initiated new planning programs. On the whole, planning education has tended to follow somewhat haltingly after the march of practical events, rather than to anticipate needs and to develop new knowledge and methods. Also it should be noted that in only two or three planning schools has the assimilation process gone very far to date. Most of the planning schools have as yet gone very little beyond urging students to take some courses in the social sciences or to refer in lectures to the importance of looking at regional factors in urban planning.

The training of city planners at the universities has until quite recently been mainly in the hands of planning practitioners—men who devoted much of their time to private practice while they were teaching, or who considered themselves to be *transmitting* to students know-how they had acquired in long years of practice. Until the last decade or so, planning education, thus, has been essentially an extension of the field of planning practice. Teaching by practitioners had special import stemming from the fact that these men had, with few exceptions, been trained in architecture, landscape architecture, or engineering. There was a strong tendency to depend on familiar tools and approaches (such as heavy reliance on the drafting board) merely because they were familiar and not because careful evaluation had shown them to be effective as educational techniques in city planning training. Also, in an earlier period the technical requirements of the planner were rather rudimentary and, at the same time, the individual planning consultant led a somewhat tenuous existence, so that it was not surprising that the practitioner glided back and forth between planning and his mother trade.

---

[17]The entry of social science students into planning has been gaining momentum. Frederick J. Adams reports, in his *Urban Planning Education in the United States* (p. 15), that in the school year 1951–52, in the 19 schools with graduate programs, 34.5 percent of the students registered received their undergraduate training in one of the social sciences. (38% of the students were from architecture or landscape architecture, 11% from engineering, and 16.5% from other fields, including the humanities).

Since World War II, as city planning became more firmly established as a separate profession, and a graduate planning degree became increasingly a requirement for both public and private planning positions, the planning schools have begun to rely more heavily on full-time faculty members. In some cases, however, the qualitative gains have been questionable. A full-time teacher who falls back on the transmission of bits and pieces of practical wisdom is likely to be less effective and useful than an able part-time practitioner-teacher who can bring his students into intimate contact with practical work in the field.

The important criterion—in planning education, as in other professional education—is, of course, whether the faculty members are individuals whose careers are devoted to expanding the knowledge, principles, and methods of the

TABLE 1.   STAGES IN THE EDUCATION OF CITY PLANNERS

Historical phase	Educational background of city planners
Earlier Phase: 1893 (Chicago World's Fair) to World War I	
Main focus on "City Beautiful"	Architecture or landscape architecture
Earlier Phase: World War I to late 1920s	
Main emphasis on public-works and land use planning (the "City Practical").	Architecture: landscape architecture; civil engineering; law (in a few cases): a few planning practitioners with one or more courses in planning (taken in schools of architecture and landscape architecture).
Modern Phase: 1928–29 to 1939	
Greater attention to social problems; city planning increasingly becoming an administrative (general staff) function in municipal government. Planning schools established at Harvard (1929), MIT (1935), Cornell (1935), and Columbia (1937).	Architecture; landscape architecture; civil engineering; law or social science; city planning (as such)—very few: many planning practitioners with some courses in planning; a few with degrees in planning.
Modern phase: 1940 to present	
Increase in scope and areal extent of planning activities; importance of federal aid, particularly in urban redevelopment and renewal. 18 planning schools established between 1941 and 1952.	Planning; architecture; landscape architecture; civil engineering; law or social science: most planning practitioners with some training in planning; many with degrees in planning[a]

[a]In October 1952, there were 538 alumni of planning schools, 431 of whom had graduate degrees in planning. A much larger number, of course, had taken courses in planning schools. Frederick J. Adams, *Urban Planning Education in the United States* (Cincinnati: Alfred Bettman Foundation, 1954), p. 17.

field, rather than merely to transmitting knowledge and methods already widely employed.

The history of city planning serves to underline very sharply why planning education cannot rely on the transmission of existing knowledge and methods in a traditional apprenticeship manner, but must be geared to the continuing search for new knowledge and methods and the development of a basic core curriculum at the heart of planning education. As indicated above, the very functions of city planning have been changing at breathtaking speed, with major changes taking place not in a matter of generations, but in a matter of a few years. The students being trained today must be prepared for many such changes during their working lifetime.

Also, an examination of the history of city planning highlights the extent to which planning has evolved by drawing on the knowledge, methods, and personnel from a large number of professions and academic disciplines. Appendix B outlines some of the intellectual and professional contributions to, and influences on, city planning. Even a bare outline of these contributions and influences suggests the richness of the sources from which city planning has drawn or is now beginning to draw. But the very breadth of the actual and potential intellectual and professional contributions makes it evident that a sound planning education cannot be pieced together by drawing on a little bit here and a little bit there. Only if planning students are required to have a rounded general education as a prerequisite for graduate training, and if the training of city planners centers about a carefully designed core curriculum, can this surrounding richness be a source of strength for city planning education rather than a source of confusion and dilution. This question is discussed in some detail at a later point.

SOME TRENDS AND THEIR IMPLICATIONS

The main concern of city planning and of planning education must, obviously, be with the evolving situation and with the near- and longer-run future. Special attention might well be paid to the trends which are likely to have a far-reaching and profound influence on planning. It is not a question so much of "looking into the future" as it is a question of not overlooking fairly well established trends and developments already on the horizon.

A Great Age of Urban Building and Rebuilding

A trend which is certain to have a profound influence on city planning and city planners is the impressive continuing increase in our national wealth and income—that 3 percent compounded, annual rise in Gross National Product. This increase, joined with our great scientific and technological progress, suggests a future of greater opportunites for better family and community living.[18]

We look forward to more family income and leisure. Projecting what is

---

[18]Assuming that we have the wit and good luck to avoid both serious depression and war.

happening now, we can see that city planning is likely to be influenced by the changing attitudes and activities of urbanities; including

- a greater sensitivity to the environment of family activities
- greater participation in, and use of, cultural activities and facilities
- ever-increasing demand for recreational facilities
- greater demands made on public services and facilities, including greater use of the highways by multicar families
- insistence on a wide choice of alternatives in community environment and living patterns, so that satisfactory living can be achieved at every stage of the life-cycle

It may well be that the American people are only now beginning to sense what our great national wealth and productivity can accomplish on the urban scene. Some important lessons are being learned: for example, that because of the peculiarities of our system of public finance, the federal government may have to supply much of the funds for urban construction and reconstruction,[19] that a public-private partnership (as in urban redevelopment) can be remarkably effective in getting things done, and that more can be accomplished through positive developmental planning than through negative controls.

What are the implications for planning? One of the most important is the likelihood that there will be more and more individual urban development projects—new subdivisions and new towns (the Levittowns and Park Forests of the past decade are in all likelihood only the beginning), many slum clearance and redevelopment projects, many neighborhood renewal projects, and similar individual developments. And these will have to be planned as separate projects (even if in a larger context), in detail and in three-dimensional terms. Some of these are being, and will continue to be, planned by public agencies, but many are likely to be planned by private consultant firms. What kind of planners will these private consultants be? Will they have a sense of public responsibility? Will they be individuals of depth or narrow technicians? Imaginative, creative solutions to the problems of modern urban living will be at a premium. Will planners in both the private and the public realms be among the foremost groups in providing such solutions? Will private and public planners have a common base of training and a common language so that they can achieve an effective type of public-private cooperation? Here is a great challenge for the United States planning schools.

The other side of the coin may well be that the very number of individual projects being carried out will highlight the importance of comprehensive planning on a regionwide basis as never before. It may well be that we can look forward to an ever-increasing appreciation of the need for planning for orderly urban development, with very lively (meaning, politically conscious) concern on the part of urbanites as to just what is being planned for and against.

---

[19]This topic is discussed in the next section.

More Federal Activity in the Urban Field

Another trend worth noting is the increasingly important role of the federal government in urban planning and development. Both the scope and size of federal contributions to urban communities have been increasing. Federal aid for roads, certain types of waterworks, hospitals, housing, and slum clearance have been important in metropolitan development for some time, while financial assistance for redevelopment and urban renewal as well as for community planning, metropolitan studies, and demonstration projects are highly significant postwar phenomena.

The trend suggests that federal aid to urban communities can be expected to increase significantly, particularly considering the superior fiscal capacity of the federal government. Substantial federal assistance for the construction of schools is just on the horizon. There is a strong likelihood that the federal helping hand will be extended to other public works as time goes on. It isn't too hard to imagine that once the variety of national grants to cities proliferates, the aid may be packaged into a general federal grant for "urban public facilities."

The increase in federal financial assistance to cities can be expected to be accompanied by stricter and more seriously enforced federal provisions as to the type and quality of community planning which must be under way before a city can qualify for federal aid. National aid to assist communities in their planning is already established, and grants for this purpose are likely to increase in amount and scope. It does not seem too far fetched to assume that in the not too distant future the federal government may establish a Department of Urban Affairs (Urbiculture?) or inaugurate something resembling an *urban extension service.* Through such a service, the most advanced technical know-how might be brought to cities by specially trained federal personnel—"urban extension agents."[20]

With the overwhelming majority of the American people living in urban communities (for example, it is entirely possible that by 1975 the urban population may be some 70 percent or more of the total population of the country), there seems a very strong likelihood that urban problems will increasingly be of direct national concern and increasingly be conceived in national terms. How far away are we from the time when national politics will be largely urban politics, when the major parties will be concerned mainly with vying for the city vote? How long will it be before the national government openly recognizes metropolitan resources as among the most important resources of the nation?

What are the implications of this? Certainly, one can expect more and more attention to be given to the city-region (i.e., the entire area of urban dominance) as the focus of urban studies and ultimately of urban planning.[21] Can the federal government long continue to act as though the local neighborhood was its

---

[20]Such a service, or federal aid in general, would in no way replace the need for fiscal reform which would permit municipalities to obtain a more adequate share of public revenues. Cities must be in a position where they can do most things for themselves; federal aid and special services should be no more than useful supplements.

[21]See the suggestive article by John R. P. Friedmann, "The Concept of a Planning Region," *Land Economics,* Vol. 32 (February 1956), pp. 1–13.

natural focus of interest? For the moment this is the most readily accepted approach, but once federal interest in the urban field becomes more firmly established, the federal government is likely to turn its attention to the matters which are more directly of national interest—for example, urban-agricultural relations at the urban fringe and the whole problem of metropolitan structure, industrial location and movement of materials and products, the urban communications and transportation network, the optimum use of public utilities, and so on. One can expect large numbers of persons to be concerned with these questions both within the federal government and within the urban communities. The planner who deeply understands city-regional relations, intercity relations, and urban-federal relations is likely to be much in demand.

Another implication would seem to be that important opportunities will be opening up for skills which are not yet in large demand in government service—for example, the urban and regional research worker (the population expert, the "human ecologist," the industrial location expert, the economic-base expert, etc.); the metropolitan planner (particularly expert in matters of regional structure, regional economy, etc.), the urban-planning analyst (who already has a significant role in the federal programs).

Will the planning schools supply these skills?

The Growth of Departmental and Other Agency Planning

More and more persons carrying out planning tasks are employed by municipal agencies other than a planning commission. Not only is an ever-increasing amount of planning done by housing, redevelopment, and urban renewal agencies, but many planning activities of an important nature are carried out by planning units within city boards of education, departments of public works, departments of health and sanitation; and so on. This is certainly all to the good, since it would be unfortunate if departmental functions of the municipal government were carried out without attention to the orderly development of capital improvements and without programming of major departmental activities, or if redevelopment and renewal programs were carried out without careful attention to project land uses, project design, etc. But this raises some important questions.

How well equipped are the present city plan commissions and their employees to bring the many separate departmental plans and programs into meaningful overall plans and programs? Are planners in the central planning office carrying out what is supposed to be one of their key jobs—that of assisting in the executive task of coordination and integration—or are they actually far removed from the planning as well as the operations of the various municipal agencies?

The requirements are easy to state. The planners within the city plan commission should be fully aware of the fact that the work of their agency is only a part of the whole planning function of the city government; that one of their most important jobs is that of helping the municipal officials to evolve a framework for departmental and other planning (long term objectives, strategy, standards) and to help in coordinating and integrating the many separate planning

TABLE 2.   SOME GOOD AND BAD FEATURES OF TWO APPROACHES TO CITY PLANNING

The approach involving a semi-independent planning commission concerned mainly
with a long-range master plan

Undesirable form	Desirable form
The Master Plan: viewed mainly as a series of maps and drawings, presenting a static (more or less, once-for-all) view of the future of the city. Inflexible and basically inapplicable.	The Master Plan, periodically revised, seen as focusing attention on the longer-term problems and the longer-term development of the community; setting up generalized goals, a general strategy of development, and broad standards for the day-by-day activities. The Plan accepted officially by the legislature at each major revision.
Emphasis in the planning: on the grand design, with a concentration on dominant physical features—the thoroughfares, park system, and the public facilities, and on specific land-use designations for every part of the city. Little, if any attention to the dynamic and continually-changing forces which determine urban development.	Emphasis on (1) the strategic features in urban development, such as the "activity" centers (industrial, commercial, recreational) and the highway system (consciously setting a sensible pattern for urban expansion); on (2) standards for individual development projects (both public and private); and on (3) fitting departmental programs into a coherent pattern.
Independence of the planning commission achieved through its organizational position and, in general, its removal from the mainstream of politics and municipal administration—and for that reason, the planning largely ineffectual and unused. Stress on the independence feature.	The basic approach, at its most sensible, suggests a view of planning as concerned with the more basic and longer-range questions rather than the more immediate matters having temporary political import; also suggests the desirability of placing a high value on the contributions of the expert and the creative planner—within a democratic and responsible framework.

The approach involving an official planning agency serving as a staff arm
of the chief executive

Undesirable form	Desirable form
Closeness to politics forcing the planning agency to work on problems and to sponsor programs which have temporary political significance rather than any longer-range importance; the main criterion for planning activities being that of pleasing the "powers that be."	The planning agency in the mainstream of political and administrative activity so that plans and programs get carried out, but the chief executive relying on the planning agency to provide a framework for all improvement programs and development activities without getting involved in the short-run partisan activities.

(continued)

Undesirable form	Desirable form
The planning agency carrying out routine administrative tasks, which are mostly busy work carried out without significant reference points or in a vacuum, such as continual zoning changes, "quickie" studies, and reports on small-project plans.	The activities of the planning agency centering on a few clearly defined functions, such as the periodic revision of the master plan and the annual preparation of a capital budget and revision of a longer-range financial plan. The activities would involve regularized tasks, parts of which can be made routine—thereby using less expensive and more readily available skills.
The planning agency, as a staff unit, "coordinating and integrating" the programs of the various municipal departments where they involve the physical development of the city, but having no general framework by which to judge and merely trying to substitute one judgment for another (and generally more expert one).	The planning agency providing a framework for the programs of the individual departments—in the form of master-plan standards and strategy—so that departmental programs can be geared to these in the first place and so that there are definite criteria for judging the recommended programs of the operating departments.

activities of the government—that is, bringing the plans of the individual operating departments into "harmonious adjustment." Ideally, the city plan commission should have both the interest and talent to strengthen the planning role of the operating departments; to encourage, stimulate, and guide departmental planning. Also, both the planners within the central agency and the departmental planners should understand each other's problems, approaches, and techniques. If all the planners involved in the specialized tasks of the individual departments have no understanding and little interest in the central tasks of the city plan commission, then the job of integration becomes next to impossible.

Here is a real challenge for the planning schools. In the first instance, they must attract to their courses the individuals who are likely to do the departmental planning—the public health officer who is interested in administration, the engineer who is interested in highway planning, and similar individuals—so that they take training in planning as well as in their fields of specialization. And at least equally important is the need to provide a common core of training so that both the persons who will be the central planners and those who will be the departmental planners and the planning specialist-consultants will have had a significant common experience and will tend to speak the same language. The latter is particularly important since in actual practice, planners tend to move about rather freely from one type of planning position to another.

Planning as a General Staff Activity

One of the most important of the trends worth noting is the changing form and function of municipal planning activity.

City planning has been getting away from the earlier approach—which involved a semi-independent "nonpartisan" planning commission, set up in a vague advisory capacity, concerned mainly with sponsoring a long-time, mapped physical master plan as drawn up by a consultant and with preparing and executing detailed zoning and subdivision regulations. Serious criticism was levied against this approach, and justifiably; this type of planning was removed from the people and lacked democratic support; it was outside the mainstream of political action and municipal administration; it was essentially static and could not keep up with the rapid pace of urban development. The campaign to bring planning into the center of things has, in many instances, been largely accomplished. The public planning agency is becoming a more integral part of the municipal government machinery, and is likely to become even more so in the future.[22]

As desirable as this development may be, it brings in its train a number of serious problems. Thus, for example, direct contact with the current political problems of the city government has had a significant impact on the work programs of the planning agency. The load of day-by-day routines and crises has steadily increased, thus reducing time available to the staff for long range planning studies and for the design of alternative solutions for the basic urban problems. With the additional administrative and political duties, planning agencies have found it necessary to contract with consulting firms for more and more of the basic planning studies as well as for specific project design. Goodman, in an article analyzing the current functions of official planning agencies, estimates that today "only about 30 percent of the effort of typical planning agencies is spent on matters that are removed from day-to-day referrals or services. The remaining 70 percent is absorbed in short-term operations."[23]

It is not enough merely to point out that the city planning agency should be a staff arm of the chief executive—this is already clearly the organizational direction of city planning; the *kind* of staff work to be done and the manner in which it is to be done are the issues for the future. And these issues are, of course, of direct significance for planning education, since what is involved here is the question of what the planner in a public planning agency is going to be doing on the job, and the type of training he will need.

On the whole, too much emphasis has been placed on the appropriate organizational place for public planning activities and not nearly enough atten-

---

[22]The current status of the plan commission is described by Mr. Perry L. Norton, Executive Director of the American Institute of Planners, in a clear and insightful manner in a recent paper given at a seminar on planning education, held in Puerto Rico, "Comments on Papers by Sir William Holford, Professor Frederick J. Adams, and Dr. Peter Oberlander" (Mimeographed, March 13, 1956). That this is a normal enough development has been stressed by Robert A. Walker (*Op. cit.*, p. 134). He points out that practically all existing municipal functions—including police, fire, public works, health, and welfare services—have gone through a period of being administered by an independent board and have only gradually been assimilated into the administration hierarchy of city government.

[23]William I. Goodman, "The Future of Staff Planning," *Journal of the American Institute of Planners*, Vol. 22 (Winter 1956), p. 27.

tion has been given to the questions of what is a sensible *administrative approach* to public planning and what is the appropriate *content* of such planning. In terms of political-administrative arrangements and in terms of the content of planning activities, there are sound aspects to the older planning approach as well as unfortunate and fruitless features. On the other side, the newer approach opens up the highly undesirable possibility of a short-sighted, day-to-day patchwork of activities. If city planning is to be truly effective, organizational arrangements and administrative techniques must be worked out which will tend to retain the best features of the more traditional approach while shifting public planning activities to a sound staff basis.

By overstating differences somewhat, the major features of both the more traditional approach (involving a semi-independent agency concentrating on a long-term master plan) and of the newer approach (involving the planning agency as a staff arm of the executive)[24] can be shown to have *both* an undesirable and a desirable form.

What emerges especially is the need for chief executives and political leaders of municipal governments to learn to use staff work, and specifically planning staff work, with some effectiveness. This is likely to take some time under any circumstances, but probably much less time *if* the city planners themselves have come to understand what is desirable—through appropriate university training as well as on-the-job experience. They can then, at least, advance a desirable pattern when the circumstances are favorable for organizational and administrative improvements.

Another Trend: The Growth of Urban and Regional Studies and Specializations

I have already referred to the various types of social science studies and research activities which have influenced city planning. It is worth noting also that simultaneously a group of specialists have been trained, within different academic disciplines, who are expert in various phases of urban living and metropolitan development.

Thus, members of the sociology departments of universities in the United States are not only carrying out studies which provide information and developing techniques of great importance for city planning, but are also training urban sociologists, demographers, and human ecologists, and other specialists who might conceivably play an important professional role in city planning. Similarly, political science departments are training public administrators and others who could become even more important in city planning than they already are. Economics departments and business schools are providing land economists, experts in regional economics and aggregate economics (income, input-output,

---

[24]A forceful case for this general approach is presented by Charles S. Ascher, "City Planning, Administration—and Politics," *Land Economics*, Vol. 30 (November 1954) pp. 320–28. The best known case for an independent position for the municipal planning agency has been presented by Rexford G. Tugwell, "The Fourth Power," *Planning and Civic Comment*, Vol. 5 (April-June 1939).

economic-base studies, etc.), students of industry, transportation, and market-ing, and others. Departments of geography are training urban geographers, transportation experts, resources experts, and other specialists with know-how in the urban and regional fields. Similarly, there are property lawyers, specialists in laws regulating land uses, and others from the legal profession; cultural anthropologists from anthropology; social psychologists and others from psy-chology; and so on.

While more and more of these specialists have been seeking and finding employment in city planning, entrance of these groups into the planning field is still fairly limited. Here, again, is a great challenge for the planning schools—a challenge which, with only two or three possible exceptions, they are not meeting.

The city planning field has been developing in such a way that there is an ever-increasing need for skills of the type represented by the specializations referred to above. To take full advantage of the potentialities inherent in this situation, however, two requirements would have to be met. One is to attract some of the very ablest of the individuals in these specialist groups into the planning field. This can be done most effectively at the university level, before they have finally decided on their career lines, rather than by planning agencies after they have been graduated. Only a planning school which has academic status, a broad-gauge program with many interdepartmental ties, and an impor-tant program of research, can hope to attract such people. The other require-ment is that once it has attracted them, the planning school should be in a position to provide a significant training program in planning with a relatively small number of courses and workshops. Since planning studies would be a minor for these people, they cannot be expected to neglect their other studies to take a long period of training in planning. An extension of time for the total program of graduate studies is, of course, an attractive solution—but extremely difficult to apply in reality.

Another point which should be made in connection with these specialized skills is that *recruitment of able persons from these groups might well be one of the most important steps in any program aimed at solving the current shortage of personnel in the planning field*. Almost any other relatively short-run solution of the supply prob-lem would tend to involve a lowering of standards in one form or another. It is better to recruit able specialists possessing skills that are much needed in city planning, than it is to bring in poorer "general" planners—or rapidly and con-tinually to upgrade partially trained and inexperienced "general" planners (so that they perform about as well as unseasoned wood in a frame structure). Experience has shown that many members of these specialist groups tend to be attracted to city planning once they have come into contact with it. If they can be provided with a relatively brief *core training* in planning, they would make excel-lent recruits for both the public agencies and the private consultant groups.[25]

---

[25]Those who are acquainted intimately with these specialist fields, as well as with city planning, tend to feel that the fields provide excellent preparation for a career in city planning, in both a specialist and in a general-planning role. Professor Howard K. Menhinick, head of the planning school at the Georgia Institute of Technology, high-

The great reservoir of skills and talents available in these city-oriented fields is a significant *resource* for city planning, a resource which is as yet largely untapped. The effective use of this resource should become a first-order-of-business for the planning profession and, more particularly, for the planning schools.

FOUNDATIONS OF EDUCATION FOR CITY PLANNERS

The progress of a profession usually depends upon many factors. Key among these is the extent to which the profession comes to base its techniques of operations upon principles rather than rule-of-thumb procedures or simple routine skills.[26] The more complex the problems with which the practitioners have to deal and the greater the variety of situations which they can expect to encounter, the more inadequate becomes the apprenticeship system of education—whether the "master" transmits his accumulated knowledge in a classroom or directly on the job. The major task of professional education thus becomes one of developing and advancing the basic principles to be used in the profession and providing an integrated set of learning experiences which would permit the student, in essence, to rediscover these principles himself and learn to apply them in a problem-solving setting.

The progress of a profession would also seem to depend on the ability of the practitioners to relate themselves effectively to the broader social and intellectual context within which they are functioning. Thus, a sense of social responsibility (or what some would call a code of ethics), high standards set and accepted for research and articles in professional journals, and an ability to exchange ideas to work effectively with people from a variety of fields—all these, and similar elements, tend to determine the stature and the status of a profession.

---

lighted this point through the publication of an ingenious series of leaflets prepared by experts from various fields. Here are some of the comments of several of the experts.

Attorney Norman Williams, Jr.: "Lawyers have always player a prominent role in the development of urban and regional planning, and legal training provides several important advantages as a background for graduate study and a career in city planning."

Economist Alvin H. Hansen: "There seems . . . to emerge an attractive career in city planning for competently trained economists primarily interested in economic policy and community progress."

Sociologist Edwin S. Burdell: "Planning in a democratic society includes as much the organization of the community and the body politic, the means of mass communications, and the legislative and administrative processes as it does the specific physical solutions. In this whole process the sociologist can play a vital and creative role."

Other representatives from the social sciences were from business administration, geography, and public administration. Represented also were *architect* Henry S. Church-ill, *Civil Engineer* Harland Bartholomew, and *Landscape Architect* S. Herbert Hare, and their statements about their fields as a preparation for city planning are equally as pert inent as the statements of the social scientists. However, I assume that it is not necessary at this stage to argue the case for using specialists from these fields in city planning.

[26]For a useful discussion of this and other characteristics of a profession which set the fundamental tasks of professional education, see Ralph W. Tyler, "Distinctive Attributes of Education for the Professions," *Social Work Journal*, Vol. 33 (April 1952), pp. 55–62.

One other point should be added. As a profession expands its knowledge and skills, it finds that it must develop specialists of all types if the profession is to make optimum use of the expanding know-how and if it is to speed the development of additional knowledge and skill.

These requirements for progress in turn suggest certain requirements with regard to professional education—for city planning as much as for other professional activities. (1) The need for a sound *general education* as a foundation for professional education. (2) The need for professional schools to develop and emphasize the fundamental *principles* upon which the professional tasks are based rather than rule-of-thumb procedures, and to teach these principles so that they are understood in a broad social and intellectual context as well as in a problem-solving context. And (3) the need to cope with the problems of increasing specialized knowledge and techniques by training not the narrow specialist but the *generalist-with-a-specialty*.

These might well be the guiding principles in the education of planners. Using such a standard, it seems evident that planning education in the United States has a long way to go before it can hope to provide a sound background for effective professional performance. I would like to refer briefly to what might be the basic requirements if the planning schools are to provide good professional education.

Requirement #1: General Education

First, the planning schools should require a general education at the college level of all those who will enter the field as planning professionals.

Reference to a "general education" does not imply any specific set of courses or even a specific approach to education. As a matter of fact, different colleges and universities use the term to cover what is in effect a wide variety of educational programs. But there are important elements of agreement as to objectives and even program; thus, for example, general education is taken to include bringing the student into contact with the major academic fields (the biological, physical, and social sciences, and the humanities) as well as with certain tools of communication and thought such as English, foreign languages, and mathematics. It is agreed that the emphasis should be on the learning, thinking, and problem-solving processes so that, among other objectives, the student is provided with both materials and procedures for continuing life-time learning.

From the standpoint of planning education, interest centers of course on the student having a broad *foundation* for training in city planning. A liberals arts education in the better colleges and universities would seem to meet the key requirement. Where the undergraduate curriculum in the college involves a great deal of specialization, however, much can be said for incorporating an undergraduate program in planning—essentially as a technique for broadening the educational base of those who want to become professional planners.[27]

---

[27]The inherently broad character of training in planning is given as one of the major reasons for the desirability of undergraduate education in city planning by Lloyd Rodwin. "The Achilles Heel of British Town Planning," Appendix A of *The British Towns Policy* (Cambridge: Harvard University Press, 1956), pp. 196–97.

The major problem today arises in the case of students wishing to enter a graduate program in city planning whose undergraduate training is limited almost entirely to architecture, landscape architecture, or engineering. Here I would applaud Professor Frederick Adams' statement, in his report *Urban Planning Education in the United States*, to the effect that:

> The pattern now prevalent of superimposing two years of graduate work on to a four or five-year course in a field other than planning (say, architecture or engineering) is open to serious question unless specific requirements in . . . general education are insisted upon at entrance to the graduate program or made additional to the two years of professional studies. In any event, every effort should be made to bring about greater coordination between the undergraduate and graduate curricula for those wishing to enter the planning field.[28]

A great deal of educational know-how and imagination would be involved in working out programs in general education for students with undergraduate degrees in applied fields. A planning school would be well advised to try to obtain the assistance of professional educators—and especially those with substantial experience in the field of general education—in outlining programs for such students.

Requirement #2: A Planning Core

The planning schools of the country should make a major effort to develop a sound *planning core* in their training programs. It may well be that this is the most important single requirement in the field of planning education at the present time. A deliberate effort must be made to speed the development of general principles of city planning (in terms of substantive materials, hypotheses, and theories) as well as the development of basic methodology of planning. These basic principles and methods or techniques should make up the heart of the training program in planning—or, more accurately, should form the *foundation* for more specialized training in planning and for the continuing process of learning which should take place on the job.

A core program of training, which is developed specifically as the foundation for effective problem solving and life-time learning in a given professional field, obviously cannot be made up of a series of survey courses, or cram courses, or any other potpourri of courses. And this is as true of planning as of other professional fields. City planning has much to learn from other fields of study, but a sound planning education cannot be provided by exposing students to bits and pieces of many subjects, given in the different departments and schools, as is done today by many of the planning schools. They should, of course, take courses—possibly a substantial number of courses—in other departments and schools, but these should be directly *integrated* into his basic training or specialized training, and not be merely a matter of "coming into contact" with a field which is "related" to planning. To say that planners should

---

[28]*Op. cit.,* p. vii.

have "broad education" is not to mean that their education must cover everything, since that can be done only in the most superficial way, if at all.

A core program should center about the basic principles and methods of planning (which, one soon finds, are quite limited in number and scope). It should permit or encourage students to rediscover the validity of the basic propositions by painfully struggling through the hypotheses and validating them—since this is the only way they will really come to understand them and be able to use them. Similarly, they should learn to use the basic methods by employing them in a problem-solving context. It is the thinking through and working through that is at the heart of the learning process, but of course students must be provided with some materials (or intellectual building blocks) to work with—basic substantive materials, propositions, and techniques that others have worked out and that students can build upon. The core program should serve other purposes as well. It should make it possible for students to become acquainted firsthand with the primary materials and primary sources. It should enable them to come to understand various kinds of interrelationships— among problems, subject matter, specialists. It should help to develop in their basic attitudes and approaches to the planning field (such as a sense of social responsibility, appreciation of the possibilities and importance of creative solutions, humility as to what one person can know and what one group can accomplish and willingness to turn to others for help, to mention a few). In other words, the core program should provide a good sound base on which advanced, more specialized, and life-time planning education can be built.

This is not to suggest that the core program is the whole of a desirable curriculum in planning. Within a two-year graduate program in city planning, for example, no more than one year would, I should think, be devoted to the core as such (although certain of the objectives would, of course, permeate the whole training program). The noncore courses would tend to be planning courses of a more detailed and specialized variety as well as courses in other departments. These noncore courses can be expected to make up an important part of any curriculum, but they should—ideally—be the "superstructure" on a foundation of a planning core.

The planning core, if it is well conceived in terms of fundamentals, should serve almost equally well the educational needs of planners whatever their career lines—whether they will work for public planning agencies, or will come to be consultants chiefly working under contract with official agencies, or will serve mainly as consultants to private construction firms or other private units. All of them must be well trained in the basic principles and methods; all of them must have a common language since they will have continual work contacts; all of them should share the responsibilities of the profession—as profession, and should also share certain attitudes, particularly as regards public responsibility and public service.

Some concrete suggestions concerning the possible content of a core are set down in Table 3. I would like to stress the point that this is meant to be suggestive, rather than a specific proposal.

One of the main objectives of the suggested core program is to provide a technique for bringing together into a fruitful amalgam the two streams of devel-

TABLE 3.   ILLUSTRATIVE CONTENT OF A PLANNING CORE CURRICULUM

Outline of Key Elements Involved:
  I. Basic knowledge: hypotheses, theories, principles: main focus on:
      A. The planning process
      B. Urbanism and the urbanization process
      C. Physical elements of planning
      D. Socioeconomic elements of planning
 II. Basic methods and tools:
      A. Analytical
      B. Design
III. Problem-solving experiences: case studies, individual problems, group workshop
      problems.

  I. Basic knowledge. The four main foci represent the manner in which the core
     knowledge is usually organized; planning core courses would not necessarily be
     organized along this line.
     A. The Planning Process: some key topics—
         1. How planning fits into the decision-making and operations of private and
            public organizations; staff & line functions, policy formation and administra-
            tion, etc.
         2. Steps in the planning process: analysis of each step in terms of the
            organizational context and societal contexts (e.g., role of public, legislature,
            executive, staff offices, and line offices in establishment of goals, in choosing
            among alternative means, etc.)
         3. Major decision-making groups affecting development of urban community:
            characteristics of these groups and how they are and can be influenced (e.g.,
            the private builders, sub-dividers and bankers, construction unions, indus-
            trialists making location decisions, and so on).
         4. Uses and limitations of knowledge in planning: facts and values; functions of
            research and judgment.
         5. Standards, requirements, and priorities in planning.
         6. The organization of a public planning agency: alternative possibilities; rela-
            tion to municipal departments; the nature of planning staff work; possible
            lines of communication with public, legislature, executive.
         7. The nature of planning decisions in private units concerned with urban
            development.
     B. Urbanism and the urbanization process. The focus is the urban community and
        its development. Should provide a view of urbanization as a dynamic process
        related to developments in the economy, in technology, in social organization,
        etc. Some key topics—
         1. Historical development of cities; factors determining location, form, growth
            or decline.
         2. Relation to economic system: economic functions, relations to regional and
            national economy, economic base, interurban flows.
         3. Population growth and the pattern of movements in, into, and out of cities.
         4. Role of technology in urban development; forces involved in application of
            known technology, implications of new technology.
         5. Metropolitan structure: land uses under different types of urban organiza-
            tion, location of activity centers, nature of circulation systems linking areas.
         6. Municipal and metropolitan government: forms and functions, trends in
            governmental changes and forces behind them; influence of government on
            urban development—past, present, and future.
         7. Efforts to plan and control the environment, from ancient times to present:
            varying goals and objectives, role of various power groups, how man has
            organized to influence the environment, what has been legislated (what

(continued)

TABLE 3.   (*Continued*)

---

problems have urbanites been most interested in solving) and what types of
tools have been used. In general, what can be learned from the efforts of the
past and present.

C. Physical elements of planning. The focus is the three-dimensional city, and
movement of persons and things.)

1. Understanding the physical environment of the urban community: role of
   natural resources and physical factors in location, form, land use, density,
   and growth; land, water and other requirements of urban uses as compared
   to agricultural, recreational and other uses; potentialities of changes in
   physical features and physical limitations of a given environment, etc.
2. The theory of city form; major elements in the three-dimensional city.
3. The major determinants of land use in the urban community and the
   principles of planning for land-use requirements, in alternative forms.
4. Key principles of intra-urban and interurban movement; transportation as a
   factor in urban growth and urban structure.
5. Utilities and facilities: interrelationship, location and design; the criteria of a
   well-serviced community.
6. Shelter in its various forms: the implications of current standards; the
   potentialities of existing and new technology; the context of shelter.
7. Esthetics: basic elements, changing popular taste, the social role of the
   designer and planner; the nature of creativity.

D. Socioeconomic elements of planning. The focus is society and human behavior
as it relates to planning in the urban community. Not a survey of the social
sciences, but certain basic knowledge and approaches of these disciplines from
the point of view of the planner and the problems he deals with, rather than
that of the specialist in the discipline.

1. Culture and personality: key factors in human behavior as they touch upon
   such matters as decision making, goals implicit in the culture, types of
   controls which tend to be resisted. types of problems for which solutions are
   collectively sought.
2. The nature of social institutions, particularly those geared to the solution of
   social problems, to reform, and furthering of special interests.
3. Economizing: the basic principles of deciding, in both public and private
   decision making, among alternatives on the basis of costs and return (e.g.,
   cost-benefit analysis in the evaluation of public works).
4. Power structure and power use in the community as it influences urban
   planning.
5. Social engineering: the potentialities and limits of planned, rational action;
   the nature of social control.
6. The type of knowledge about urban phenomena and rational group action
   which the social sciences can provide, and how one can tap this knowledge.

II. Basic methods and tools:
A. Prerequisite: training in statistics, and in maps and aerial photographs.
B. Analytical methods and tools:
   1. Preparation and uses of physical survey and social survey in planning.
   2. Other techniques for analyzing current and evolving situation: e.g., eco-
      nomic-base study, industry linkage and impact studies, techniques for
      analyzing traffic movement, etc.
   3. Use of models: mathematical, statistical, three-dimensional.
   4. Projection and prediction; dealing with uncertainty.
C. Design methods and tools:
   1. Study of the key design features of cities, from ancient times to present, and
      of the basic techniques behind them.

(*continued*)

TABLE 3.   (*Continued*)

---

2. Design considerations in site planning.
3. Basic elements of project design for different purposes (residential, commercial, industrial, civic, etc.); the development project under different circumstances (on new land, clearance and redevelopment, renewal—including rehabilitation and remodeling).
4. Design elements in the neighborhood, the local community, the total urbanized area.

III. Problem-solving experiences:
   A. Use of case studies and of hypothetical problem wherever applicable, as a means of having the student work through principles and basic methods himself.
   B. Student workshops, applying planning and other knowledge and methods to the solution of planning problems and the preparation of plans. Workshop activity directed at learning to work in a problem-solving context, learning to divide up tasks so that they become manageable, learning to use research in the analysis of problems and in the search for solutions, learning to measure the costs as well as the benefits of alternative solutions, highlighting the types of expertise needed in planning and how to obtain help and, in general, development of attitudes and approaches to the planning field.

---

opment which have characterized city planning in the United States. Such an amalgam would mark the evolution of a new type of city planning profession (in fact, of a new type of profession)—one which combined effectively general administrative-political know-how and a spirit of public service together with substantive skills related to the physical-socioeconomic development of urban communities.

The content of the core curriculum must develop out of the requirement that the planner should learn to deal effectively with complex, relatively aggregate elements and interrelationships in the highly dynamic context of the evolving urban community. The planner is usually concerned with complex phenomena—such as the relation of homes to places of work and recreation—and with the physical, psychological, social, economic, and political aspects of any problem or situation, and not just one aspect. He cannot retreat to *ceteris paribus* (all-things-being-equal) assumptions, as can the theoretical scholar. A fruitful way of learning to deal with aggregates and interrelationships is to learn to relate problems to a useful "reference system" or subject "cluster." Four such clusters make up the parts of the illustrative core curriculum presented in Table 3.

The table is intended only to highlight some key features of a planning core, and is meant to be only illustrative. A great deal of conscious effort on the part of many planning scholars and practitioners will be required before a really sound core based on planning principles and basic methodology can be developed. At this stage in the development of the planning profession, research by faculty members of planning schools on core subjects will advance the planning field more than will research on peripheral and highly specialized aspects of planning.

Even assuming that very rapid progress can be made on working out basic planning principles and methods, through a concerted and coordinated inter-university effort, it still cannot be expected that a uniform system of core courses will be established at all the planning schools—nor would it be desirable that this be done. There are many ways of opening up vistas for students through which they can come to understand, and learn to use, basic principles and methods, and it is highly desirable that various schools experiment with different approaches to the development of a core program. However, it *is* extremely desirable that methods of evaluation be devised so that the elements of strength and of weakness in the teaching program at each school can be known and improvements made over time. There are many ways of providing for such evaluation.[29]

One other point. Not only is the development of a planning core essential for the training of city planners, but the planning core may well be a lever which would make possible the absorption into city planning of a large number of specialists from other fields. A real challenge for the planning schools is to develop a planning core which is so attractive that able students from all over the university take the core courses and become potential recruits for city planning jobs.

Requirement #3: Specialized Training

The final point suggested by a review of the key elements of professional education concerns specialization. Professional specialization appears to be inevitable, in planning as in other fields.

There is a strong tendency in certain of the planning schools today to attempt to train *the* planner. This stems from the feeling by the faculty of these schools that a unique type of training of a generalist character is essential. Looked at in terms of the historical development of the planning profession, this approach can be seen as a rather natural—*and healthy*—reaction to the earlier educational background of city planners (which consisted of training in architecture, engineering or other specialized fields, with, at best, only a few miscellaneous courses in planning). It has been important to establish that while in the past, when public works and land use controls were almost the entire preoccupation of city planners, able individuals with nothing but a specialist background could perform effectively in the planning field, today the highly complex tasks of city planning call for graduate training in urban planning as such.

---

[29]One method which I believe might be effective would involve an annual contest for the best solution of a common workshop problem drawn up by a Contest-and-Evaluation Committee composed of experienced educators and practitioners. The students in the second-year workshop in each school would spend a specified period of time in working out a solution for the common problem distributed by the committee. These would be judged by the committee and a prize awarded to the best solution. In addition, the committee would set down detailed comments on each of the group solutions, pinting to good and strong elements of the solution. These comments should be helpful to the faculty of the various schools in coming to see gaps and weakness in their students' preparation. The committee should be changed frequently not only to avoid burdening one group but in order to get a variety of approaches represented over time.

Architecture, engineering and other applied fields, it is felt by most planning educators, may themselves be of technical assistance to city planning, but training in these fields involves materials, approaches, and methods which are substantially different from those involved in urban planning. Such specialist training, in reality, requires retraining if the individual is to be a good city planner.

Thus, the association between separate training in city planning and generalist training—or the training of *the* planner—may well arise from the conscious or subconscious need to set off planning training as such from specialist training in the applied fields as preparation for city planning careers.

It may be that this type of emphasis is still needed in order to firmly establish the separate and distinct character of the city planning field. But a better approach might be one less concerned with symbols and contrast and more concerned with the realities of quality. Such an approach would involve a conscious effort to bring about general improvement in the education provided in the planning schools. There is no better way of advancing the status of a profession than by the excellence and expertise of its specifically trained practitioners.

From this standpoint, I believe that it is a mistake for the planning schools to attempt to train *the* planner. At best, they will train individuals who will ultimately do well as top administrators, but will have had tough sledding in the early stages of their careers. At worst, they will train amateurs instead of professionals.

Given the complexity of modern city planning, some degree of specialization seems inevitable. But there are different approaches to specialization and different degrees of specialization. It is one thing to put young persons into a specialized field from the very beginning of their college training and never provide any opportunities for a broadening experience. It is a very different thing to provide special advanced training to students who have had varied backgrounds provided by a general education and a well-developed planning core program. The objective for planning education is, I think, clear enough. It is to provide *expertise with breadth of outlook.* This can be done by encouraging students to build a "planning specialization" through a carefully devised program to meet their special needs and aptitudes after completing general educations and planning cores, or in parallel to these. (Specialized studies might quite effectively be taken at the same time as the more generalized studies.) I would call a person who has had this type of education a generalist-with-a-speciality, as contrasted with either the "pure" generalist or the specialist as such.

The key criterion is, of course, which type of university training will provide the best foundation for the important and long period of learning which will take place on the job. There is much to be said for training that permits individuals to make significant contributions through his advanced knowledge of an important special field, as well as through their abilities to handle a wide variety of problems well. Professor C. R. Van Hise expressed this idea effectively, in his much quoted AAAS speech, when he said: "No man may hope for the highest success who does not continue special studies and broadening studies to the end of his career."

A planning specialization can most effectively be developed on the basis of a full program of training—undergraduate as well as graduate. Thus, for example, planning students who have had substantial training in the social sciences as undergraduates might well take some advanced courses in statistics, population and human ecology, and survey techniques while taking their planning core as well as later, and then do a special piece of research on *social survey for planning*. Thus they would develop, in a logical sequence, a useful specialization which will stand them in good stead in their planning work. Similarly, planning students with undergraduate degrees in civil engineering might take advanced courses in subjects dealing with transportation during and after their planning core training, thus developing a specialization in *transportation planning*. Other needed planning specializations can be developed in a like fashion. Ideally, the specific planning specialization taken by a student should reflect: (1) the evolving needs of the planning field; (2) the interests and aptitudes of the student; (3) the educational background of the student; and (4) the areas in which the university can provide specialized training of a high order.

It is extremely difficult to achieve the goal of breadth combined with expertise unless *the planning schools themselves* concentrate on one or a very few elements within the complex planning field. This is not to suggest that other elements should be neglected—far from it. The core elements must be taught, or the educational program would be incomplete. But I am firmly convinced that planning education will make genuine progress only when the various planning schools concentrate on those elements in which they have unusual strength all around.

What the appropriate concentration for a planning school might be would depend, of course, on its special areas of academic strength as well as on the nature of the tasks planners are called upon to perform—plus continual *experiments* in methods of training students characterized by "breadth-with-expertise." In the case of the very largest and strongest universities, more than one kind of concentration might be feasible, but the number of concentrations is not nearly as important as is the effort to be absolutely first-rate all around in whatever fields are taught beyond the planning core. Illustrations of the kinds of concentrations which might be appropriate for various universities are:

1. Three-dimensional urban design (civic design, community architecture)
2. Construction and movement (planning of transportation, housing, urban utilities and facilities)
3. Planning administration and planning law
4. Socioeconomic analysis and research
5. Regional analysis and planning (the relation of the city to the larger region, to other cities, and to the nation; industrial location; regional economic base, etc.)

Thus, for example, planning schools located in technical institutes might be expected to concentrate on the first and/or the second of these to take advantage of their special strength, while a school in a university with a great social science faculty might focus on socioeconomic research and analysis, or on planning administration, or on regional analysis, or on all three. But whatever the area of concentration, each planning school should be in a position to offer a strong, rounded core curriculum. Otherwise it has no right to offer graduate degrees in planning.

If a planning school can cover everything and still be *absolutely first-rate*, it would have every justification in claiming to provide "a complete training in city planning." (It should still, of course, encourage its students to develop a planning specialization for themselves.) However, if a planning school does not have the resources to be *absolutely first-rate* in all city planning fields, then it should consider very seriously the possibility of achieving higher quality by some form of concentration.

It might be objected that a development of the type suggested here would really be retrogression and that planning would once again tend to be a mere adjunct of a school of architecture or engineering or social science. If this were to be the consequence, then it would be retrogression indeed. Note, however—and this is the heart of the whole matter—that I have strongly stressed, throughout, the importance of a general education as an absolutely essential foundation and of planning training that centers on a very carefully worked out planning core. Both of these elements were missing in the earlier period when planning *was* a mere adjunct of a school of architecture, landscape architecture, or engineering. Now, to go to the other extreme and remove planning education entirely from the academic and professional fields which nourish it, is just as much of a mistake.

The history of city planning and of the forces which have influenced it suggest strongly that the very nature of city planning is such that it can gain the most by continually nourishing itself by intimate contact with related fields of study and of endeavor. It can do this best *not* by trying to encompass everything (on the very surface, a foolish task), but by having as practitioners persons who are generalists-with-specialities and who form a natural bridge to the other nourishing fields.

The larger public planning agencies, particularly, need planners with substantial knowledge and skill in the major areas of planning if these agencies are to get optimum returns from the various specialists who are recruited into the planning agency. Thus, for example, a planner with strong training in three-dimensional urban design can normally be expected to work more effectively with the design technician than can the complete generalist, just as the planner who has developed a specialization in social survey for planning can work effectively with the demographer brought in for a special study. Another way of putting it is that the generalist-with-a-specialty is a natural link between the administrators at the top of the governmental hierarchy and the various specialists who come from other fields.

A really effective and *expert* team can be built to carry out the planning tasks by bringing together (1) planners with some specialized know-how, (2) specialists with some training in planning, (3) technicians to handle the purely physical tasks, and (4) individuals who do not fall into any particular category but because of special attributes of talent and inclination can serve effectively on a planning team. (There must always be room in planning for the genuinely creative talent, whatever its background.)

Tasks of Leadership

There seems to be a direct relationship between the maturity and progress of a profession and the amount of educational leadership provided by the full-time university scholars who devote themselves to the advancement of the field. I am convinced that the progress of the city planning profession during the next generation will depend to a significant degree on the extent to which the university educators can and do exert genuine leadership in planning education. This would involve advancement in a number of key areas:

1. *Recruitment:* The progress and the status of the planning profession is tied to the caliber and characteristics of the individuals who enter and stay in the city planning field. Leadership on the part of the planning schools in this area is urgently needed. The quality of the schools themselves is of course a crucial factor in recruitment: the attractiveness of the training program, the quality of the teachers, the interest aroused by the research activities, and the excitement generated by the planning schools in the academic world—all of these have a great deal to do with the number and caliber of students attracted into planning. Beyond this, the schools might contribute importantly to making potential recruits aware of, and interested in, the opportunities available in the city planning profession. There is a potentially great and rewarding field of endeavor here, and outstanding men and women must be challenged to enter the field and themselves make it possible for the potentialities to be achieved. There is an essential prior task of analyzing carefully and developing an understanding of the characteristics and aptitudes needed if an individual is to function well in city planning, and of the places (types of schools, academic fields, specific activities) where such characteristics and aptitudes, as well as potential interest, are likely to be found.[30] Recruitment, to be effective, must be purposeful and pinpointed.

---

[30]In a letter to the author (August 31, 1956) Mr. Dennis O'Harrow, Executive Director of the American Society of Planning Officials, underlined the importance of this type of study and analysis. He wrote:

"Dr. Edwin Burdell suggests that we must solve the shortage of planners (and of other professions) by recognizing and training a subprofessional group. In all of the professions there will always be a limited number of persons who have the time, finances, and ability—especially ability—to complete a full course of training. Therefore we should consciously seek to set up courses and training for this subprofessional group. In medicine this group includes, of course, lab technicians, dental assistants, and practical nurses. In engineering it would include drasftsmen, computers, surveyors, etc.

"From this beginning I would go on to say that perhaps we need some very careful management surveys of the activities in planning offices to determine how we can best train and supply subprofessional help to take care of the overwhelming problem of day to day planning administration. As every planning practitioner knows, all the creative planning that he can sandwich in between the demands on his time for zoning variances, subdivision review, house numbering, street naming, and so on, will amount to practically nothing unless he has a much larger budget and staff than he can muster from the present and future supply of fully trained planners.

"And of course the matter of native intelligence and ability is quite important. There are many more persons competent to handle routine administrative problems than there are or ever will be to do creative planning. A good many of these less creative persons are even now in top jobs in planning staffs.

2. *On-the-job training:* The planning schools will have to come to play a central role in education beyond formal university training. A number of the larger public planning agencies have encouraged staff members to continue their studies and some have organized on-the-job training programs. To date, most in-service training programs have tended to be intermittent and fairly limited in scope. Educational leadership on the part of the planning schools would, certainly, involve assistance in the organization of regularized on-the-job training programs, supply of study materials, and provision of some of the teaching personnel.

3. *Whole-life education:* The question of encouraging life-time learning, that is, of facilitating a continuing growth in knowledge, skills, and breadth of vision, is critical for educational leadership. There are many activities that can contribute to this general objective. Planning schools can encourage (and, in the first place, inspire) graduates to write for professional journals and to search for new knowledge and new methods in carrying out their tasks. They can sponsor summer sessions and special conferences and in other ways provide opportunities for practitioners to come *directly* into contact with new ideas, new methods, and new points of view. They might work to make the annual conferences of the professional organizations a useful educational device (as well as a meeting ground and a market place). They might do a great deal to contribute to the educational value of the periodic meetings of the local chapters of the professional societies and, even more importantly, to recruit local practitioners to assist in many ways in various educational tasks. In general, the planning schools must become concerned with planning education in the broadest sense.

4. *Research:* The crucial present need is, as suggested earlier, the development through research—as well as in other ways—of the general principles and basic methodology of planning (concretely, in terms of evolving a sound core program). Close behind in importance comes research in significant new fields, the experimental areas. Both of these types of research (which will often tend to be interrelated) are needed not only to advance knowledge in city planning, but also as an important way of attracting really first rate people into the planning field, as teachers, research workers, and practitioners.

5. *A Program to Speed Educational Progress:* The abler and more sensitive practitioners and academics are aware of a changing of directions, of exciting new opportunities just on the horizon, of the profession's glaring limitations that hinder progress. This may well be a situation not unlike the one when, in 1928, members of the planning profession and educators called a special conference to consider problems of planning education and research. Out of this conference came the first planning school in the United States and the start of a new era for the profession.

Today, as then a great thrust forward in planning education is possible and called for. It will undoubtedly take the development, through the joint effort of leaders of the profession and university personnel, of a carefully worked out

---

"I don't think we really know much about the duties, aptitudes, and quantity of personnel needed in the subprofessional group. I think this whole field could stand a great deal of study and investigation."

program to speed progress in planning education, and possibly the winning of foundation support to help finance certain aspects of the program. Leadership by the planning schools in the design of such a program may well signalize the assumption of educational leadership by the university scholars. This would certainly be a development of great significance for the future of city planning.

APPENDIX A

SOME LANDMARKS IN THE HISTORY OF CITY PLANNING AND OF PLANNING
EDUCATION IN THE UNITED STATES[1]
EARLIER PHASE

Chicago World's Fair (1893) to World War I

*Main Focus on "City Beautiful"; City Planning Instruction Limited to Lecture Courses
in a Small Number of Landscape Architecture Schools.* The *modern* city planning
movement in the United States is usually thought to start with the Chicago Fair.[2]
Major emphasis was on esthetic considerations, but there was a growing
awareness of social problems. Plans dealt mainly with civic centers, parks,
streets, and transportation. They were sponsored by civic improvement organizations and prepared by consultants drawn chiefly from architecture and landscape architecture.

1893 Chicago World's Fair inspired civic efforts to improve the physical features
of cities. Other civic movements coincided with the ferment stemming
from the Fair and influenced city planning, for example, the movement
concerned with parks and natural areas (Charles Eliot's inspiring plan for
the development of the Boston metropolitan park system was prepared in
the early 1890s), the municipal reform movement, the home rule movement, and the settlement house and related movements which brought
attention to slums, congestion, and similar social problems.

1902 Preparation of a revised plan for Washington, D. C., based on the original
L'Enfant Plan, by a committee of three architects and a sculptor who had
been associated with the Fair.

1905 Organization of the National Association of Real Estate Boards, which,
together with associations of private builders, bankers, and similar groups,
has had a continuing influence on the course of city planning.

1907 Creation of first official city planning commission (in Hartford, Conn.).

1907 Publication of the *Pittsburgh Survey*, the first systematic city survey; included information on working conditions, housing and living conditions
generally, hospital and other institutional needs of the city, and related
questions.

1909 First National Conference on City Planning, sponsored by groups interested in better housing and sanitation, as well as by the professional

---

[1]No attempt has been made to trace European and other outside influences, largely in the
interests of brevity, even though in many instances these have been extremely important.
The various periods cannot, of course, be set off sharply. Changes were gradual and there
were important variations among the cities in stages of development as far as planning
was concerned.

[2]Of course, American city planning goes much further back, at least as far back as 1682
when William Penn laid out the checkerboard street system for Philadelphia.

societies of architects and landscape architects. The National Planning Conference—focal point of the organized planning movement—was actually organized in 1910 under the leadership of the architects and landscape architects.

1909 *Plan of Chicago,* sponsored by Commercial Club of Chicago, prepared by Daniel H. Burnham.

1909 Introduction of a lecture course on city planning at Harvard University for students in the department of landscape architecture. Shortly thereafter Charles Mulford Robinson introduced instruction in city planning into the landscape design curriculum at the University of Illinois.

1911 Publication of the *City Plan for Rochester,* prepared by Olmsted and Brunner, and George Kessler's *City Plan for Dallas,* together with the earlier *Plan of Chicago,* marked extension of the scope of city planning to a wide range of public improvements and to privately owned transit and transportation.

World War I to Late 1920s

Main Emphasis on Zoning and on Public-works and Land-use Planning (the "City Practical"); Instruction in City Planning in Schools of Landscape Architecture and Architecture. City plans—usually referred to as "complete master plans"—were sponsored by semi-independent official city planning commissions (by the early 1920s there were almost 200 planning commissions), and prepared in the main by consultant firms. Plans usually treated streets, transit and other transportation, central business districts, public buildings, parks and recreation, "civic art or civic appearance," zoning and subdivision control. Emphasis was on the physical layout of the community, with detailed attention to the engineering and financial considerations (the "City Practical").

1916 First comprehensive zoning ordinance, adopted by New York City.

1917 The American City Planning Institute was created, marking claim that practitioners considered city planning a separate profession.

1923 Wichita Plan, prepared by Harland Bartholomew and Associates, followed by the Memphis Plan (1924) and others typical of the period.

1923 The Department of Landscape Architecture at Harvard University introduced a graduate program leading to the degree of Master of Landscape Architecture in City Planning.

1924 Start of an extensive series of social science researches into the city and its problems at the University of Chicago under the auspices of the Local Community Research Committee (later the Social Science Research Committee).

1925 First plan (Cincinnati) to be officially adopted by the city council of a major city.

1925 Inception of "The Journal of Land and Public Utility Economics" (now "Land Economics") organ of the Institute for Research in Land Economics and Public Utilities founded by Professor Richard T. Ely of the University of Wisconsin.

1926 Publication of the last edition of *A Standard City Zoning Enabling Act* and in

(1928) of *A Standard City Planning Enabling Act*, prepared by Advisory Committees of the U. S. Department of Commerce. Both have greatly influenced state enabling legislation permitting municipalities to plan for and control the uses of land within their corporate areas.

1926 Supreme Court upheld comprehensive municipal zoning in a case brought from Euclid, Ohio—*Village of Euclid v. Ambler Realty Co.*, 272 U. S. 365 (1926), providing the classic statement in the field of zoning.

1927 Radburn Plan adopted; first American "garden city" planned in an effort to achieve benefits of an integrated community; included planned use of the superblock with open space at the center and cul-de-sacs. In part, reflected the influence of Ebenezer Howard's *Garden Cities of Tomorrow* (London: S. Sonnenschern, 1902; First published in 1898 under the title *Tomorrow: A Peaceful Path to Real Reform*) and the ideas generated by the Garden City Movement.

1927 The pace of construction influenced the role of city planning in the 1920s. Around 810,000 housing units were constructed in urban communities during 1927, the peak of the housing boom. Some 6,400,000 housing units were constructed during the decade of the 1920s.

THE MODERN PHASE

1928–29 Transition

The following marked the culmination of developments of the earlier phase in the history of city planning and the beginning of the modern phase.

1928 Conference on instruction and research in city and regional planning under the joint sponsorship of Columbia University and the Committee on Regional Plan of New York and Its Environs. Stressed the desirability of developing separate teaching and research facilities for "city of regional planning."

1929 Establishment of first school of city planning, at Harvard University, with the financial assistance of the Rockefeller Foundation. Provided a three-year postgraduate course leading to a degree of Master in City Planning.

1929 Completion of the influential *Regional Plan of New York and Its Environs*. Emphasis was on economic, population, and governmental problems as well as on the more usual physical elements; also detailed consideration of the broader region as well as the core city.

The 1930s

Increasing Attention to Social Problems in City Planning: Larger Role of Federal Government in Urban Affairs; Separate Graduate Training in City Planning. City planning in the 1930s was dominated by social and economic surveys and by housing and slum clearance projects, almost all carried out with some federal aid. It was strongly influenced by the activities of federal agencies such as the Federal Housing Administration, the United States Housing Authority, WPA and PWA, and was aided by the National Resources Planning Board and its predecessors. As compared with earlier planning there was greater interest in economic and social problems, including the problems of the "lower third," and in administrative problems relating to planning.

1930 Publication of "Harvard City Planning Studies" begun.

1931 The White House Conference on Home Building and Home Ownership. Publications of the conference were widely used in schools and had an influence on planning and housing thought.

1933 Establishment of the National Planning Board successors: National Resources Board, 1934–35, National Resources Committee, 1935–39, National Resources Planning Board, 1939–43 which encouraged and helped city planning in many ways.

1933 Inauguration of a five-year course leading to the degree of B. Arch. in City Planning in the School of Architecture at the Massachusetts Institute of Technology.

1934 First "real property inventories" and housing and urban-blight surveys. Also start of housing and slum clearance projects carried out with federal aid.

1934 Formation of the American Society of Planning Officials. Its slogan: "To Promote Efficiency of Public Administration in Land and Community Planning."

1935 Start of M.I.T. graduate program in city planning, leading to a Master's degree; followed shortly thereafter by the establishment of planning schools at Cornell University (1935), with the aid of five-year grant from the Carnegie Corporation, and at Columbia University (1937).

1936 Over 900 official city planning commissions in existence; as well as over 500 county and metropolitan planning agencies. (The latter increased from 85 to 506 between 1933 and 1936.)

1937 Publication of *Our Cities: Their Role in the National Economy*, report of the Urbanism Committee of the National Resources Committee. Emphasized social and economic problems; relationships between the city, the state, the region, and the nation; need for federal assistance to lower units of government; and the desirability of a broad view of the functions and potentialities of planning.

1937 Publication of the report of the President's Committee on Administrative Management; was influential in advancing the view of planning as a general staff function directly helping the chief executive. (Robert A. Walker, in his book *The Planning Function in the Urban Government*, 1941, applied this concept to planning in municipal government.)

1938 New York City Planning Commission, under a new charter, began to operate under the broadest powers granted to any planning agency, including: adoption of a master plan, custody of city map, initiation of changes in zoning ordinance, and preparation of a capital budget which could be altered only by a three-quarters vote of the Board of Estimates.

1940 to Present

Increase in Scope and Areal Extent of Planning Activities; Importance of Federal aid, Particularly in Urban Redevelopment and Renewal Rapid Increase in Number of Planning Schools. During World War II, city planning agencies provided some spot assistance to operating officials and, in some cases, prepared postwar public works plans. Since the war, plans in the larger cities have been prepared by technical staffs of official planning agencies with the help of consultants; plans in smaller towns have been chiefly prepared by consultants. Activities of most planning agencies have been focused on zoning and subdivision control (taking 25 to 50 percent of staff time), public housing, redevelopment and urban renewal and transportation, with increasing importance attached to capital programming. There has been a great increase in planning activities carried out by private development companies, and by municipal public housing, redevelopment, and renewal authorities. Also there has been a large growth of citizens' groups interested in improvement of urban environment and neighborhoods. The number of degree-granting planning schools has increased greatly since 1940, but the number of graduates has fallen short of the job opportunities in the field.

1941 Publication of *A Handbook on Urban Redevelopment for Cities in the United States*, by the Federal Housing Administration, anticipating expansion of redevelopment activities with federal assistance.

1941 Establishment of three planning schools in one year (at the University of Michigan, Illinois Institute of Technology, and University of Washington), marking the beginning of the recent rapid growth in separate professional training for city planning. In 1944, a planning program was established at the University of Wisconsin and in 1946 programs were started at the University of North Carolina and at Michigan State College.

1946 Beginning of Pittsburgh Golden-Triangle redevelopment project which served to emphasize the possibilities of urban planning and redevelopment and to inspire many community undertakings as well as many unfulfilled grandiose plans.

1947 Establishment of University of Chicago's Program of Education and Research in Planning, with emphasis on the social sciences, on research, and on regional considerations in planning. In the same year, planning schools were started at the University of Illinois, Rutgers University, and the University of Texas.

1947 Report on "The Content of Professional Curricula in Planning," drawn up by the Committee on Planning Education of the American Institute of Planning and adopted by the Institute, expressing something of a consensus of the more advanced professional view on planning education.

1947 First occupancy of Levittown, New York, followed by first occupancy of Park Forest, Illinois (1948), marking the beginning of the postwar "new town" mass-built housing boom. The development of new communities on a large mass-built scale, which had had important beginnings before and during World War II (e.g., Oak Ridge, Tennessee, Midtown, Oklahoma, etc.), gained momentum after the war.

1948 The University of California established a planning school, as did the University of Oklahoma and the University of Florida. This was followed by the establishment of planning programs at Iowa State College (1949), Yale University (1950), University of Pennsylvania (1951), the Georgia Institute of Technology (1952), and the University of Southern California (1955).

1949 The National Housing Act of 1949, providing funds for public housing and redevelopment, and reaffirming principle that federally aided urban developments, whether undertaken as publicly owned units or as private redevelopment projects, should conform to a planned program for the entire community.

1954 The National Housing Act of 1954, introducing the "urban renewal" concept which includes neighborhood conservation and rehabilitation as well as redevelopment. A "Comprehensive Community Plan" is mandatory and a "Workable Program" is required for an urban area to qualify for federal financing. The federal government offered, under Sec. 701, to make money available, on a 50–50 matching basis, to state planning agencies for planning assistance to municipalities under 25,000 population and to official state, metropolitan or regional planning agencies for planning work in metropolitan and regional areas. The 1956 Act broadens this section to include planning assistance to municipalities and counties of 25,000 population and over which are declared by the President to be "disaster areas."

Sources: Thomas Adams, *Outline of Town and City Planning* (New York: Russell Sage Foundation, 1935); Robert A. Walker, *The Planning Function in Urban Government* (Chicago: University of Chicago Press, 1941, revised edition, 1950); John M. Gaus, *The Education of Planners* (Cambridge: Harvard Graduate School of Design, 1943); Frederick J. Adams, *Urban Planning Education in the United States* (Cincinnati: Alfred Bettman Foundation, 1954). Walker, particularly, gives an excellent account of the development of the modern planning movement in the United States. Adams provides a full picture of the situation in city planning education as of 1954. Because of the ready availability of such recent data on planning schools, it did not seem necessary to provide detailed descriptive materials on planning schools in this paper.

APPENDIX B

THREE-DIMENSIONAL URBAN DESIGN

Architecture, landscape architecture, art (and related fields) have some concepts concerned with civic design and community architecture.[1]

1. The concept of an appropriate goal for design and planning as being a physical environment which is esthetically and in other ways humanly satisfying, imparting a sense of wholeness, and providing for changes in keeping with the changing needs and values of the civilization.
2. Site planning and project design as the design of spaces and structures within integrated units (projects) which meet biological, technical, economic, social and psychological requirements and demands.
3. The spatial and three-dimensional elaboration of the concepts of the new town, the garden city, the neighborhood unit, the superblock and organized use of open space, giving specific (and inspirational) content to generalized concepts.

FUNCTIONAL EFFICIENCY

Functional efficiency is the most efficient and economical overall arrangements for home and work activities, for movement of people and things, and for public facilities and utilities. The concept of engineering and planning as seeking to produce social end products at lowest possible cost.

LAW

Planning as an aspect of the legal structure of the social system; development of the concepts of police power, eminent domain and related concepts involving public regulation and control of property and land use.

---

[1]There is no uniformly accepted term which can be employed to represent the contributions of those concerned with the design elements of the urban community, including the landscape architect, the architect, the student of fine arts, and the art historian, as well as the planner. The term "civic design" is widely and traditionally employed, particularly where a strong esthetic emphasis is involved. "Community architecture" is a descriptive term employed by Clarence Stein, evidently intending both to convey the architect's claim to the field and to distinguish large-scale urban design from the design of individual structures (with the quite different skills involved). The term "physical planning" is sometimes used to connote urban design, but it is also used—at the other extreme—to cover all of city planning, and for that reason is an especially confusing term.

Because of the special creative element in urban design, the contributions in this area have had more of a content (and inspirational) aspect, joined with the intellectual concepts, than in the case of the other items listed in this table.

POLITICAL SCIENCE, PUBLIC ADMINISTRATION, AND MANAGEMENT

1. The concept of planning as an activity directly influenced by the power structure of the community.
2. The concept of planning as increasing the efficiency and economy of government; also, planning specifically as a general staff function.
3. Scientific management and more recently Operations research: integration of specialized operations and functions into a comprehensive whole on the most efficient possible basis, through scientific analysis of operations, scheduling and smoothing of flows, and optimum arrangements. (There has been an intermingling of ideas and influences concerning management in industry, military branches, and government.)

SOCIAL SCIENCE RESEARCH

1. Geographic and ecological studies of land as related to natural influences and to man and his works; development of techniques of land use analysis.
2. Land economics, including studies of supply and demand factors in the use and development of land and improvements and of property market behavior and what it takes to control such behavior.
3. Economic studies (economic base, industrial location, markets, etc.) have provided information, tools and techniques for planning, and have highlighted the importance of (a) weighing costs and benefits of alternative proposals, (b) of strengthening the economy of the community, and (c) of considering the relationship of cities to other parts of the economy.
4. Studies of policy formation and decisionmaking in government organizations.
5. Social survey, including concept that city planning must be based on a thorough understanding of the total city and the dynamic social forces at work within the metropolis, (e.g., population movements, migration, and other forces coming under the heading of human ecology).
6. Psychological and social studies of individuals and small groups; development of techniques for getting an understanding of individual and group needs, wants, aspirations, actions and reactions.
7. Communications research, action research, human dynamics, and other studies concerned with ways of reaching people, getting them involved, and getting things done have opened new vistas for ways of achieving effective planning.
8. Studies and activities concerned with specific urban social problems, particularly housing, crime and delinquency, education, health, and welfare.

GOVERNMENT FINANCE

1. Municipal finance concepts, and particularly the capital budget, the long-range financial plan, the programming of individual projects, and in

general the view of physical development and other planned activities as having a budgetary-cost consideration as well as space and time dimensions.

2. Fiscal policy ideas, and particularly the notion of planning with an awareness of the business cycle.

REGIONAL ANALYSIS AND PLANNING

1. Metropolitan planning and functions; ideas concerning the planning and operation of specific activities on a metropolitan basis and the value of metropolitan (regional) planning organizations. Also, metropolitan government—the emphasis on the desirability for adjustment in governmental structure to meet the physical, economic, and social realities.
2. The concept of the region as the basis for planning, in a variety of forms: for example, the "natural region," the city-region (the region as the area over which the urban influence extends), and other concepts emphasizing the importance of viewing the city in a broad context.
3. Regional analysis, providing concepts, information, and tools being increasingly employed in city planning—for example, regional input–output analysis, industrial location studies, regional resource analysis, area income studies, etc.
4. Concepts relating to state and regional economic development, and particularly the relation of city planning and development (e.g., industrial sites, adequate homes for workers, transportation) to the effort to strengthen the economy of an area. More generally, concepts concerning the relationship of urbanism to economic development.

PLANNING FOR SPECIFIC GOVERNMENTAL FUNCTIONS

Knowledge and skills developed in particular fields have influenced city planning in general, as well as the other way round, although the relation between city planning commissions and city departments is still on the fuzzy side. Possibly most important have been the influences stemming from the ideas and methods developed in departmental planning and operations of urban and inter-city transportation, schools, health, parks and recreation, and agricultural land use planning and zoning at the urban fringe.

18

The Evolution of Planning Education

It is difficult to come to grips with the major issues involved in American planning education unless they are viewed within the context of what is happening in planning practice, as well as within society at large. Also, to understand the current situation, we must see it against the background of what has happened during the past few decades and what the near future seems to hold. To develop a meaningful picture of the state of the art of planning education, I have found it helpful to sketch out the relationship of planning education to two key contextual elements: (1) major social trends and governmental programs, and (2) planning practice, over a reasonably long period of time—from 1940 to the present (1974) and projected forward fifteen years.

PLANNING AND SOCIETY: A HALF CENTURY OVERVIEW

My approach has been to set within time sequences, starting in 1940, what seem to have been the major trends and developments within the nation generally and within planning practice and planning education specifically, and to conjecture what these trends and developments are likely to produce in the next decade and a half, roughly by 1990.

The point of the exercise is to obtain an overview of the evolving picture and an impressionistic image of the key relationships. While there are some serious limitations in such a broad-brush approach, such as loss of detail and, to some extent, loss of accuracy,[1] it does have the merit of spotlighting some suggestive relationships—or, at least, juxtapositions—which, in turn, serve to raise some pertinent questions. It would be helpful visually if the three areas—social trends, planning practice, and planning education—could be seen together, but this involves some reproduction difficulties, and so they are presented on three

---

This chapter was written in collaboration with Frank Klett. I received valuable suggestions on an earlier draft of this paper from John Friedmann and Peter Marcuse, as well as other colleagues at UCLA, and from William L. C. Wheaton, Don Foley, and other faculty members at Berkeley.
[1]In selecting material for inclusion in the overview, many aspects had to be overlooked in the interest of clarity and brevity, including questions of the relative importance of various trends, conflicting trend lines, and the more volatile economic and political developments and events.

different figures. Even so, the parallelisms and imbalances jump out at us. Some that I feel are especially pertinent provide the background for discussion in this chapter, including:

1. The imbalance between the very powerful forces bringing about extremely rapid urbanization and great changes in skill requirements and in the nature of urban activities, on the one hand, and the weak and limited response to these developments by the national government on the other. (See Figure 1.) We are reminded of this fact when we note the titles of major governmental programs in the urban realm. In the face of the most far-reaching changes in life patterns brought about by advancing technology, increasing affluence, and the massive movement of farm families, including blacks, to the cities during and after World War II, the federal government's initial responses were extremely limited: mortgage insurance and urban renewal, followed long after ("long" given the pace of development) by limited social and human resources programs.

Planning practice and planning education of the 1940s and 1950s paralleled this limited response. In fact, one can go further and suggest that the profession in general reflects the relatively narrow, reluctant approach to planning of recent decades.[2] This is hardly surprising, since professions can be expected to reflect their role in the society at large.

A not unreasonable interpretation of the reluctant approach to planning is that Americans have wanted to have the results of good planning in terms of a better environment and more orderly life, but in many cases have been unready to pay the price in terms of limits that planning might impose on moneymaking and of necessitated changes in life patterns—except when conditions become intolerable or when life patterns are seriously challenged by uncontrolled change.

One may conjecture what planning practice and planning education would have been like during these decades if the federal government had retained and strengthened the National Resources Planning Board, instead of abolishing it during the war, and had attempted seriously to prepare for, and cope with, the great and vital changes taking place in American urban life.

2. Along the same lines, we may note the imbalance between the *technical* and *socioeconomic* natures of the driving forces behind the national changes of the post-World War II period and the traditional response—practically and educationally—that was largely *physical* (geographic and design) and *financial*. For example, social planning does not appear as a a central tendency,—that is, an activity of some significance—until the mid-1960s, when the social pathology resulting from the changes underway was already overwhelming. (See Figure 2.) Adequate attention has yet to be given to the role and impact of technology, as central to planning practice and education. Here is an outstanding example of the sociologist's "social lag."

3. The parallelism between what the federal government supported in its

---

[2]Probably the word "reluctant" is as good a descriptor as any of the way planning has been regarded in the United States, compared to, say, the professions of medicine, law, and engineering.

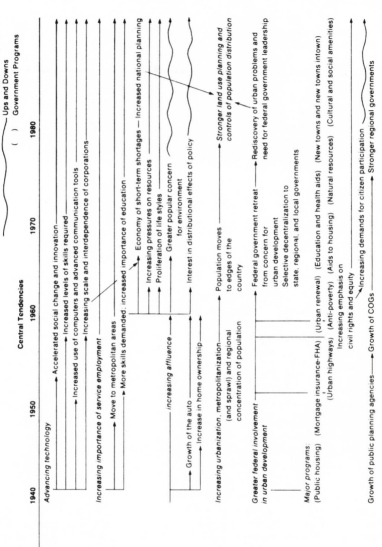

FIGURE 1. Social trends and government programs: impacts on planning.

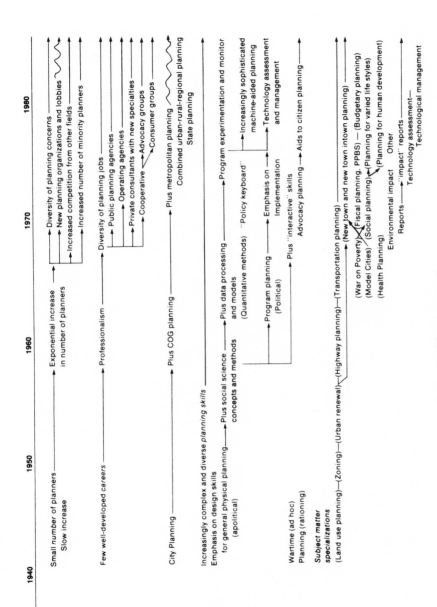

FIGURE 2. Planning practice.

urban programs and the emphases in planning practice and in planning education is obvious. That planning practice was so deeply tied to national urban programs is a reflection of the fact that, until recent years, most planning practitioners worked either for public agencies which were in no small part dependent on federal funds or for private consultant firms where most of the work was related to the national programs; the latter being a typical private enterprise demand–supply phenomenon. Planning education, which until recently has been largely professionally oriented, was logically enough trying to supply the manpower needed for these programs.

The situation has begun to change as planners have been moving into new activities that are less directly tied to federal grants. There is anticipation (which may turn out to be groundless) that, with some version of revenue-sharing adopted as a major form of intergovernmental transfer, more initiative and decisions will be lodged at the state and local levels with planning emphases in new directions, such as criminal justice, environmental controls, and budgetary and financial planning. Guidance for program experimentation and program monitoring also seems likely to gain importance, but here, it is well to note, planners have been slow in responding to what may be an important change in approach for governmental programs.

4. It is apparent that during the period covered by the figures, planning has grown in numbers, overall strength, and acceptance—the latter occurring because there were somewhat greater political and economic payoffs available. This clearly reflects the rapid urbanization, the greatly increased complexity of urban life, the severe problems of the inner city, the sprawl, the degradation of the environment, and the many other changes between 1940 and the present. As noted, this resulted in an exponential increase in the number of planners, the establishment of urban planning as an accepted professional career, and an increase in the diversity of planning jobs. These changes, in turn, provided a fertile ground for the growth of planning schools and of planning education in general. (See Figure 3.) Yet, as noted earlier, the governmental programs and the planning related to them, while quite substantial in quantitative terms, have been established within narrowly conceived boundaries that are far removed from a view of planning as helping to provide a base for guided social change. Against this background, and in spite of the very strong thrust that had been generated, there was no great surprise attached to the fact that the second Nixon Administration—in fact, the end of the first—signalled a freeze and dismantling of federal urban programs and an official turning away from planning toward management. It is not easy to predict whether this is a temporary phenomenon, a Nixon administration aberration, or a longer term flattening out in the growth of planning.

Clearly, planning in the United States is not all that firmly based. Planning practice and planning education have to continue to justify themselves, to gain greater understanding as well as acceptance. But how is that to be accomplished? By trying to raise the professional standing of the field (the route of most professions)? Or by drawing more and more concerned individuals into the planning act? Should planning opt for greater excellence—a relatively small cadre of professionals who are highly regarded because they are better at certain

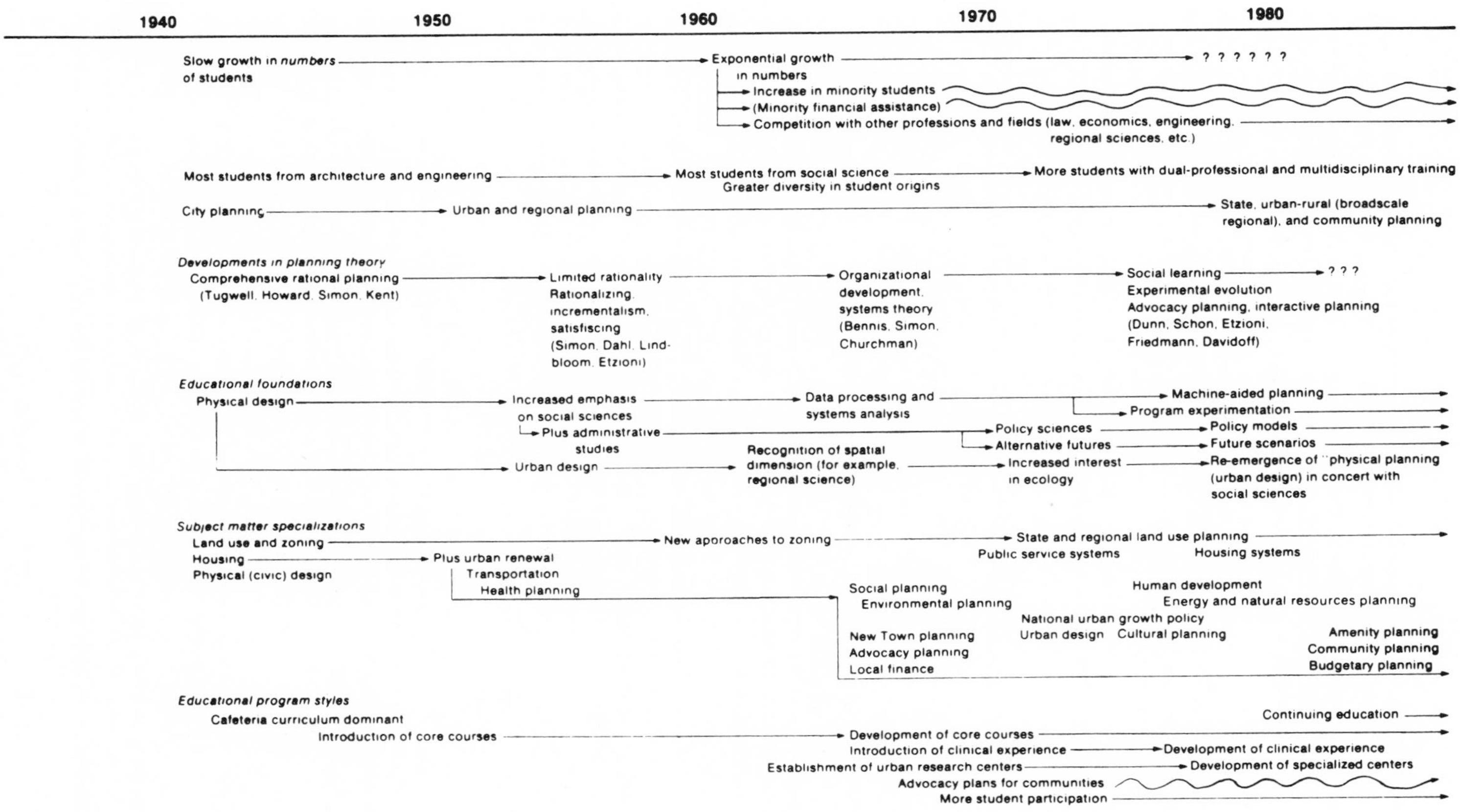

Figure 3. Planning education.

1940 — 1950 — 1960 — 1970 — 1980

Slow growth in numbers of students → Exponential growth in numbers ? ? ? ? ?
→ Increase in minority students
(Minority financial assistance)
→ Competition with other professions and fields (law, economics, engineering, regional sciences, etc.)

Most students from architecture and engineering → Most students from social science → More students with dual-professional and multidisciplinary training
Greater diversity in student origins

City planning → Urban and regional planning → State, urban-rural (broadscale regional), and community planning

Developments in planning theory
Comprehensive rational planning (Tugwell, Howard, Simon, Kent) → Limited rationality. Rationalizing, incrementalism, satisficing (Simon, Dahl, Lindbloom, Etzioni) → Organizational development, systems theory (Bennis, Simon, Churchman)
→ Social learning
Experimental evolution
Advocacy planning, interactive planning (Dunn, Schon, Etzioni, Friedmann, Davidoff)
? ? ?

Educational foundations
Physical design → Increased emphasis on social sciences
→ Plus administrative studies
→ Urban design
→ Data processing and systems analysis
Recognition of spatial dimension (for example, regional science)
→ Policy sciences
Alternative futures
→ Increased interest in ecology
→ Machine-aided planning
→ Program experimentation
→ Policy models
Future scenarios
→ Re-emergence of physical planning (urban design) in concert with social sciences

Subject matter specializations
Land use and zoning → New approaches to zoning → State and regional land use planning
Housing → Public service systems → Housing systems
Physical (civic) design
→ Plus urban renewal
Transportation
Health planning
Social planning
Environmental planning
New Town planning
Advocacy planning
Local finance
→ National urban growth policy
Urban design   Cultural planning
→ Human development
Energy and natural resources planning
→ Amenity planning
Community planning
Budgetary planning

Educational program styles
Cafeteria curriculum dominant → Continuing education
Introduction of core courses → Development of core courses
Introduction of clinical experience
Establishment of urban research centers
Advocacy plans for communities
More student participation
→ Development of clinical experience
→ Development of specialized centers

FIGURE 3. Planning education.

activities than anyone else, or should it attempt to broaden its scope so that it becomes an *accepted* integral part of a broad range of public and civic activities? These questions pose some nice dilemmas for planning, particularly since it difficult to establish the appropriate criteria with which to make any judgments. It is even more difficult to know whether or not this decision can be made within the profession.

Other difficult issues for planning education arise as we try to make sense out of the observable interrelations among social trends, developments in planning practice, and developments in planning education, particularly as we project these interrelationships, including their many fuzzy and conflicting aspects, into the future. Before examining some of these issues, it is helpful to take a closer look at the state of planning education and how it got where it is today.

THE STATE OF PLANNING EDUCATION

Students. There were some 5,000 students enrolled in planning schools in 1973, about 4,000 of them in full-time programs, according to the annual ASPO School Survey. (Corby and So, 1974) Of the total, 1,000 were enrolled in a bachelor degree programs, some 3,700 in master's degree programs, and about 300 in PhD degree programs. Startlingly, the 5,000 students in planning education in 1973 compare with just under 1,000 in 1963 (and under 600 in 1958), a truly phenomenal growth in a very short time—reflected in the trends noted in the figures. In 1973, there were 54 schools offering advanced degrees in planning compared with 28 in 1963, a doubling in just about a decade.

The proportion of minority students enrolled in planning schools is now roughly in line with their proportion in the population. In 1973, blacks comprised 13.3 percent of students enrolled, while other minorities made up some 3.7 percent. This is in drastic contrast to the situation just a few years earlier. Only nine blacks were reported to have received planning degrees in 1968 (amounting to 1.5 percent of the total degrees granted), as compared to 157 in 1973 (or 12.1 percent of the degrees granted). The number of females has also increased substantially. Women received 18.9 percent of the planning degrees granted in 1973, compared to 7.5 percent five years earlier.

Planning schools currently face a serious problem in financing needy students, due to cutbacks or leveling off in both foundation and government grants for student support. As the ASPO Survey points out, there is some fear that planning schools may soon be filled only with the affluent.

Todays planning students come from diverse backgrounds and have a wide variety of skills. Because the field of urban and regional planning has changed so rapidly and has not yet been firmly defined or grounded in established skills, it is difficult to specify knowledge and skill prerequisites. Students often enroll in planning without even minimal acquaintance with such basic areas as mathematics, statistics (quantitative methods), economics, sociology, or politics. Providing a basic grounding in these fields in a two-year master's program seriously eats into the advanced training that can be made available to such students. Also, because faculty time is used up in the process, the better trained students are also denied the more advanced education that might otherwise be made available. This question is clearly tied to the larger issue of whether planning education should seek excellence by emphasizing the training of a relatively limited number of well-prepared professionals or whether it should broaden the scope, even more than at present, of those who enter and practice in the field—seeking representativeness rather than excellence.

Subject Matter Specialization. Planning education has paralleled or closely followed trends in planning practice and government programs in its subject matter specializations. For example, as soon as federal programs and practical demand called for social planners, they were produced, including health planners, education planners, poverty program planners, and others. Environmental planners began to be trained shortly after the demand became apparent. But while reaction time has been short, quality is another matter. The making of a soundly educated social planner or environmental planner or transportation planner takes resources, time for training, strong interdisciplinary ties, and sustained program development which are beyond the means of all but a small handful of schools, and even for these, the early graduates are sent out quite poorly prepared. A highly responsive educational posture involves high costs.

Another question is raised by high responsiveness. Has planning education during the past decades led, or has it merely followed changes in federal programs and in planning practice? The answer is that planning education has led significantly in at least one realm: in appreciating the importance of treating urban problems in a broad regional context rather than in the more narrowly defined jurisdictional framework which has characterized federal programs and most planning practice. Urban *and* regional planning had become a relatively common title for programs in planning education even before the 1950s. Interestingly enough, while metropolitan regional considerations tended to permeate analytical aspects of planning education, only a few have emphasized the important programmatic implications of the regional approach by concentrating, to at least some extent, on environmental and natural resources considerations. Most planners and planning educators discovered the importance of these considerations only when the environmental impact statement became a federal government requirement and the so-called energy crisis appeared. For the most part, a deep appreciation of the importance of natural resources to urban and regional planning is still somewhere off in the future.

Among the subject matter specializations, I do not know of any instances where a sizable proportion of planning schools focused on training for a specialization before it had been encompassed by a federal government program or by local programs with federal financing. However, this is based on limited available materials and a general impression rather than an exhaustive study of planning education programs. I should stress that there are isolated instances of leadership (or anticipation—or foolhardiness, depending on how one regards the matter) in different subjects at different schools at different times. But we are concerned here with *central tendencies*, therefore, it is more appropriate to describe planning education as characterized by rapid response to established demand—but also to some extent, lag—rather than by *leadership*.

The need for leadership in planning education stems from the fact that it takes years of hard work and substantial resources to develop a viable training program so that graduates are able to handle a newly established governmental effort with expertise and profound knowledge—as would have been desirable when the call went out for social planners, environmental planners, and now energy planners.

Merely to list the many specializations which came to the forefront in the past three decades and those that may do so in the near future—as is done in the figures—is to raise the question of the extent to which planning education can focus on the training of specialists. Here it is interesting to note that a number of the major planning schools, as well as some of the smaller ones, have been converging on a single solution; namely, the development of a limited number of broad concentrations or subprograms which encompass several more narrowly conceived specializations—what might be interpreted as a middle ground between fullfledged generalist training and highly specialized training. Deciding on the appropriate concentrations within a planning education program then becomes a matter of the greatest importance since that will influence the timeliness (in terms of societal demands) of the training and the effectiveness of the specialization. The following are examples of areas of (policy) concentration at various universities:

1. *Urban-regional planning,* encompassing the principles of urban development and location, national urban growth policy, and developmental planning in less developed countries;
2. *Public service systems,* including systems analysis and evaluation and encompassing such fields as transportation, education, and health;
3. *Environmental planning and management* (or *land use planning*), combining ecological, economic, and design considerations;
4. *Scoial policies planning* (or *housing and community development*), including problems of poverty and race, social analysis techniques, community planning, and the like;
5. *Urban design* or *environmental design,* combining traditional design approaches and social science and systems analysis concepts and methods.

The subject matters vary somewhat among the different schools, but the basic approach is similar and, I believe, signals an important element of maturation in planning education.

Educational Program Styles. Another element of maturing in planning education has been the move away from the almost universally used cafeteria curricula of the 1940s and 1950s—a little bit of everything the planner ought to know—to a concern with a *core* or *basic* curriculum, pioneered by the University of Chicago planning school in the late 1940s and early 1950s and widely adopted in the later 1950s and 1960s. The development of core knowledge and methods is, of course, key to the development of any area of study; for a professional field, a substantive core is its raison d'être to exist as a separate field.

Examining the catalogues of the major planning schools (not an entirely satisfactory method, since course titles can be misleading), one gets the impression that the various schools have defined the core somewhat differently, but that there is substantial agreement on including: (1) interaction of social, economic, spatial, and political aspects (how the urban system works and is changed); (2) planning theory; and (3) planning methods, including some emphasis on quantitative and design methods.

It should be noted that there is disagreement within the planning field on the validity of the core concept in training programs, with some planning schools taking the position that given the broad scope and rapidly changing nature of the planning field, it is impossible to pinpoint exactly what should go into the core. My own view is that educators cannot really sidestep this question, since they are defining the core when they advise students to choose certain courses and when they choose areas for field or general examinations. It is better to have the choices made consciously, through continuous faculty study and debate, than to hope that somehow the student acquires the needed basis for a lifetime of practice and learning. The concept of training planners for any and all possible futures by emphasizing basic education and student selection of areas of specialization or concentration can carry us only so far. Ultimately the educators of planners, like educators in other professional fields, must accept responsibility for the emphases in education, that build the necessary foundation of knowledge and skill to train students for both effective practice and future learning.

There has been some progress in each of the areas normally encompassed within the planning core. In recent years, there has been a substantial amount of work in translating knowledge on how the urban system works (particularly in the economic and legal realms) into materials for the training of planners. Planning theory is still largely derived, as Friedmann and Hudson have pointed out (1974), but there have been highly significant contributions by planners from the earliest period covered (Tugwell, Howard, Kent) to the current period, when decision theory, advocacy planning, interactive planning, and social learning have come to the forefront. Planners still have some distance to go before they begin to dominate their own field intellectually, but the signs of early sprouting have begun to appear. Planning methods also are still largely derived, but new syntheses and new uses of older methods are beginning to be fairly significant contributions of the planning fraternity, as with regard to systems analysis, programming, social indicators, and regional reporting.

Planning research as an integral part of planning education, gingerly pioneered in the early postwar years at a few schools, blossomed in the 1960s with the development of major urban research centers closely associated with planning schools or located within them. A list of the research studies turned out by the faculty of any of the seven or eight major planning schools (that is, those with a sizable full-time planning faculty) suggests that the output is beginning to be impressive. The future of the planning field will depend in no small part on the quality—and timeliness—of future planning research. The field will have genuine credibility when policy leaders and concerned citizens look to the planning literature not only to understand what is going on in urban and regional development, but also to learn what best might be done about it.

Planning research provides an important tool for coping with the problem of preparing students for specialized activities without trying to provide special training programs for every conceivable area of interest. Students with an established interest which is more particularized than the educational area of concentration provided in their schools can satisfy this interest, in part at least, by being exposed to research in that field. For example, a student whose concentration focuses on public service systems but who has a well defined interest in urban transportation can learn a great deal about the subject by doing transportation research under the supervision of a faculty member knowledgeable in that field. At the same time, he may take several courses in transportation in various departments throughout his campus. This is one of the many reasons why a strong research program is key to a soundly based program in planning education.

Fieldwork and Public Service. Exposure to planning practice before or during planning study is widely thought to be an essential compnent of planning education. Most of the major planning schools have a fieldwork requirement, often a three-month summer internship or its equivalent.

During the hectic and socially conscious days of the later 1960s, an additional ingredient came to the forefront—the desirability of exposing students to some form of service to the community as part of the training program. Community-service centers of various types were launched during this period at many planning schools, and student-sponsored efforts were commonplace. Unfortunately, most of these efforts did not last, either due to organizational weakness, lack of adequate resources, or loss of community spirit among the students and faculty.

Convinced that both fieldwork and community service are valuable ingredients of planning education, UCLA is experimenting with a practice arm, the Urban Innovation Group (UIG), as a way to help students meet their fieldwork requirements. The practice arm is organized as an off-campus nonprofit corporation which undertakes community projects under contract and provides payment to both students and faculty for carrying out the projects. Thus, the students are exposed to practice under the supervision of faculty members, very much in the style of teaching hospitals. (In fact, we use the terms "interns" and "residents" to make it easier for others to understand what we are doing.) A related practice arrangement, but one with unique features of its own, the Buffalo Organization for Scientific and Technological Innovation (BOSTI), is functioning at the State University of New York at Buffalo. Where the local planning infrastructure is unusually well developed (such as in the Boston-Cambridge area), students can generally have apprenticeships when they want them, and the pressure for university-sponsored forms of practice training is not as strong. Apprenticeship, however, lacks the advantage of faculty supervision. With more experimentation in provision of practice training, we will soon be able to more clearly delineate what different forms can accomplish in meeting the important fieldwork–community-service objective.

OPPOSING REQUIREMENTS AND DEMANDS

One valuable feature of looking at planning education in an evolutionary mode is that we become aware of the persistence of certain issues, as against the more transitory developments. When we focus on a subject as complex as planning education at one point in time, particularly the current period, it is all too easy to be caught up in the problems that seem to loom particularly large and to seek a formula for solving them, usually through organizational or institutional changes. It is something else again to grasp that we are observing issues or tensions that are built into the system; that they can not be "solved" but can only be resolved for a given time and place and circumstance.

Both the present and future of planning education can be fruitfully discussed in terms of the continuing tensions between certain opposing requirements and demands. I would put into that category the tensions:[3]

1. Between the need for generalist skills and the need for specialist skills
2. Between the advantages of developing high level technical skills in planning students (and thus competing with strong technical groups, such as operations researchers) and the desire to see planning in a humanistic (and holistic) mode
3. Between stressing professional elements (content and product) and administrative elements (process)
4. Between strongly focusing on current urban problems (making planning essentially a practical problem-solving field) and focusing on the much more abstract and uncertain possibilities of the future (present versus future orientation)
5. Between scholarly and professional approaches (emphasizing research or practice)
6. Between emphasizing education of highly selected full-time graduate students and stressing education of a broad spectrum of students, including continuing education and the training of citizen planners

These are among the most important issues with which planning educators, and the planning profession in general, must cope today; we will confront the same issues in years to come. To illustrate the kinds of questions involved, I will briefly discuss three of these tensions.

Generalist versus Specialist Skills

One can readily stress the great impact on our society of advancing technology and other forces. They have made planning problems—like most other features of our lives—inordinately complex and specialized, stressing the planner's need for specialized know-how and capabilities. Or, one can point to the fact that where specialists do the planning in a complex societal situation (as in the case of urban highway and freeway planning in our large cities during the 1950s and 1960s), the results can be disruptive and even disastrous, thus stressing the need for generalist, humanistic approaches to major planning problems. (Or one can even be thoroughly frightened of the impact of specialist "tech-

---

[3]These are not mutually exclusive, but represent major issues in the field as usually discussed.

nique" with Ellul, 1964, and resist the forces making for complexity and standardization.) But given the fact that the issue is built into our basic system, it is not helpful—at least not operationally helpful—to stress only one element of the equation, unless you are ready either to buy efficiency at any cost or to move backwards into time (a neat trick that we know little about).

What I have come to see as the practical problem for planning education is to *give content* to the normally vague idea of generalist education as well as to provide specialist know-how and skill to students without turning them into tools of technique, narrow individuals who do not see the societal context of what they are doing.

The need for strengthening generalist education suggests the great importance of developing solid courses in planning theory which get at the human problems of planned change and which involve students in probing the moral underpinning of our present society and alternative future societies. Those who worry that the latter would turn us into amateur moral philosophers need to ask themselves whether they prefer that the great moral issues involved in planned change should remain hidden from view or whether it is better that we at least try to make them explicit.

On the equally tough question of providing specialist know-how and skills to students without turning them into mere technical pawns—who might become rapidly obsolete because of the narrowness of their specialty, I have already pointed to the present approach of the major planning schools, involving broad areas of concentration rather than a large assortment of narrow specializations, as a seemingly effective practical solution. I have, in addition, suggested the useful role of research in strengthening the specialization side of the equation. It might also be noted that fieldwork, particularly under faculty supervision, provides yet another possibility for strengthening specialist training without making it the focal point of a planning student's education.

One of the major developments in planning holds out the promise of helping clarify the demands of generalist and specialist education. This is the diffusion of planning approaches beyond the traditional urban fields into all kinds of national, regional, and local activities, as well as into corporate practices. If planning education responds to the opportunities involved in this type of diffusion, as Branch has pointed out (1962, 1966), the generalist, or core, element in planning education would necessarily be greatly strengthened, while at the same time, the varying requirements for the different *realms* of planning would be more evident than they are when the focus is only on urban planning. Skill requirements would also be substantially raised.

Scholarly versus Professional Approaches

Looking at planning education as it has evolved over time, it is evident that it has been following a pathway already traveled by most, if not all, of the professional fields in moving toward scholarly approaches and away from a purely professional or practice emphasis. The usual changes have taken place: from part-time professionals as teachers to full-time scholars as the faculty; from mostly part-time students to mostly full-time students; from an emphasis on studio teaching to more theoretical and methodologically oriented courses.

But drawing further on the history of other professions, we might also note that there is a general tendency to overdo the shift away from practice toward scholarship (often on the pragmatic grounds of a research-oriented faculty taking over from old fashioned practitioners and bringing their own kind in, to the exclusion of the others). There tends to be a cost involved in this throughgoing shift, as students are increasingly badly prepared for practice and as teaching and research are glorified at the expense of doing a first rate job in the field.

Again, as in the generalist–specialist issue, the major problem for planning education is to give content to the "empty-box" terms—here "practitioner" and "researcher" or "scholar." Practitioners can be, and should be, as up-to-date and as able in their particular realm as are the scholars in theirs. They should also know the new significant research that is applicable in the field and the new language associated with it. At the same time, practitioners should be able to bring something special to the students that the scholars cannot. They should not be out-of-date because they have been too busy with their practices to keep up. On the other side, planning researchers or scholars should not be aping the discipline oriented fields and grinding out research that could just as readily be done by economists or sociologists. This type of faculty member cannot possibly have much in common with the planning practitioner. Rather, *planning* scholars should be breaking new ground in strengthening concepts and methods needed to carry out planning tasks. With this kind of faculty the inherent tension between scholarly and professional approaches can be a fruitful kind of tension. The practitioners-to-be among the students would acquire a more-than-superficial view of what research can do for planning practice because of their close contacts with the research oriented faculty, while the researchers-and-scholars-to-be would be challenged to help solve the real problems of planning practice because of their contact with respected practitioners. This happy state is not easily achieved, but it is clearly a desirable one in a planning school that aspires to educate planners who will make a difference to the field after they graduate.

One of the important possibilities on the horizon to bring about this desired state is the development of the *professional doctorate* in planning, a degree parallel to the planning Ph.D. While the latter would continue to be geared to training teachers and researchers, the professional doctorate would make it possible to train advanced practitioners. Graduates with this degree should be able to do high-level research, as well as the more traditional practice activities, in preparation for flexible careers in planning. Also, such graduates, after some years of practice, would be logical candidates for teaching positions in planning schools—along the lines discussed above—even though they might not have specifically trained for practitioner-teaching roles.

Technical Elite versus Mass Planning Education

This is the tension between limiting planning education to highly selected, top-level, full-time graduate students and providing training to a broad spectrum of students. The spectrum might be considered to encompass: (1) the acceptance of graduate students with less than top-level academic standing, (2) undergraduate education, (3) continuing education, for planners already in the field, and (4) training for citizen planners.

This is an issue of societal import, rather than simply an internal planning education issue, for its resolution can be expected to have a substantial impact on how planning is regarded in the society at large *and* the kind of planning education that will be provided. The issue is: who is to plan for our society? Is it to be a highly trained technical elite; a middle range, broadly based but still technically oriented, group; a socially representative technical group which can handle planning tasks in every kind of American community, minority as well as majority; or are we to rely largely on citizen planners?

Looked at over time, it is evident that the planning field, like every other field that has taken on the coloration of professionalism, has been relying more and more on technically trained persons. Thus, for example, ads for planning positions increasingly specify graduate education in planning or closely related fields. One thing that is significant here is that a planning education as a prerequisite tends to be specified only if high level expertise can be relied on in the planning graduate; otherwise, a specialist from another field will be asked for. When we examine ads for planners, it becomes apparent that in the different planning areas (housing, environment, land use, social, economic development, energy, and so forth), different weight is given to experience as against education and the relative assurance felt about the adequacy of *planning* education as such. On the latter point, the importance of an appropriate design for the various fields of concentration in planning education becomes apparent.

It is unlikely that, with the increase in societal and technological complexity, less technical background will be demanded of planners than at present, no matter how much stress is placed on community involvement in planning. This suggests the following conclusions.

First, we should not rely on untrained community persons to try to offset narrowly trained technicians in order to achieve community-oriented, humanist planning. Rather the aim must be to provide a generalist and morally conscious base for technically trained planners, so that the planners themselves can be relied on to seek a humane kind of planning. On the other side, citizen planners—community persons who will take an active part in planning decisions—must be brought strongly into the act and educational techniques must be developed to provide at least a minimum technical grounding for such persons.[4]

Second, while it seems evident that minority planners are urgently needed in the field because of the special insights and feelings they bring to planning tasks, and because of their greater acceptance in certain areas and situations, it will not do to bring into the field minority persons who do not have the necessary background and capacity. It would not be helpful to create second-class planners. Planning schools must make special efforts to recruit able minority students and must provide the financial assistance most of them need.

Finally, it has already been established that there are many openings for paraprofessionals in planning and that in some areas of planning, advanced training is not as useful as practical experience. Thus, there is substantial scope

---

[4]The ASPO publications addressed to the problems faced by planning commissioners are an appropriate start in this direction, as is the research at some planning schools on effective ways of involving community persons in planning decisions.

for undergraduate training. There were 1,000 students enrolled in bachelor's degree programs in 1973, one-fifth of the total planning school enrollment. However, given the increasing complexity of the field, it may be that individuals with only undergraduate training in planning may find themselves severely handicapped at later stages in their careers. This underlines the desirability of giving more attention to continuing education in planning (for those already in the field) than has been the case in the past. Continuing education is important not only for those whose training was limited to an undergraduate program, but for those with advanced training as well, given the rapid rate at which the planning field is changing and the more rapid rate of change that can be expected in the future.

CONDITIONS FOR EXCELLENCE

Granted the need for a broad spectrum of planning education, can the planning schools undertake to meet such needs themselves, and can they do so without jeopardizing their search for excellence in advanced training? The answer lies largely in the organization of the universities themselves. Undergraduate and graduate training are compatible, given the well-established structure of undergraduate and graduate education at most universities. The story is different with regard to continuing education and education of citizen planners, where there is limited experience and more failure than success. I believe that only a detailed study which can look closely at both demand and supply considerations can provide a useful answer here. A quick review of the past reveals little, since most efforts in these directions have been limited in scope and carried out without basic institutional changes to meet the particularized needs of continuing education and citizen-planner education. It will probably take significant changes in university organization or the use of new instrumentalities to meet these needs adequately.

We are dealing with a field whose own uncertainties and weaknesses reflect the reluctant, almost schizophrenic, view of planning held by society at large. This hesitant approach to planning cannot be expected to disappear quickly, however, given the ever greater rate of social change and the increasing pressures on our resources and environment, planning is likely to gain in importance over the longer run—even if there are nerve-shattering ups and downs and some rather drastic changes in what is demanded and what is accepted.

Planning education is itself maturing and beginning to take recognizable form, with planning schools developing along fairly similar lines. Many of the key ingredients for excellence (and social significance) are already in place— such as full-time faculties, well-developed degree programs, research capabilities, and university support, but the achievement of excellence is still somewhere off in the future. Let me very briefly outline what I see as the conditions that must be met if planning education is to achieve a state of excellence.

1. Generation of substantial support for planning approaches at state, regional, and local levels, largely through federal government support of such

activities. However, the new federal role will have to be different than the detailed interventionist role of the 1960s, with much greater local and state control of the substance of planning. Planning is essentially a public field, and it can attain excellence only if there is broad appreciation of what it can accomplish to help achieve societal goals. A corollary is federal government assistance to planning education through provision of fellowships and research grants. Planning is in the same position and has needs similar to other public fields, such as public health and public administration.

2. Development of more powerful intellectual links to professionals in evolving related fields who are achieving excellence, including policy analysts in the new field of policy sciences (analysis and design), system analysts and operations researchers, and urban economists and urban lawyers.

3. Establishment of a professional doctorate parallel to the PhD degree to place, both practically and symbolically, high-level practice education in lock-step with planning scholarship and research. This should help assure that there is no second-class education in planning.

4. Recruitment of evermore able individuals into the field. This is, of course, a sine qua non of excellence. There is no shortcutting here. There are the continuous hard tasks of obtaining scholorship money, fighting for university support, innovating educational approaches, and recognizing and rewarding excellence in all the important aspects of the field.

Finally, it is well to note again that planning education has not yet really come to grips with the implications of the built-in tensions of the field. I have suggested needed areas for further probing. There is much more that needs to be done.

REFERENCES

Alonso, William. "Beyond the Inter-disciplinary Approach to Planning." *Journal of the American Institute of Planners* 37 (May 1971).

Beckman, Norman. "The Planner as a Bureaucrat." *Journal of the American Institute of Planners* 30 (November 1964).

Bolan, Richard. "Generalist With a Specialty—Still Valid? Educating the Urban Planner: An Expert on Experts." Pp. 373–388 in *Planning 1971*. Chicago: American Society of Planning Officials.

Branch, Melville C. *Planning: Aspects and Applications*. New York: John Wiley & Sons, 1966.

Branch, Melville C. *The Corporate Planning Process*. New York: American Management Association, 1962.

Brooks, M. P. and M. A. Stegman. "Urban Social Policy, Race and the Education of Planners," *Journal of the American Institute of Planners* 34 (September 1968).

Cockburn, Cynthia. *Opinion and Planning Education*. CES 1, p. 21. London: Centre for Environmental Studies, August 1970.

Corby, Linda and Frank S. So. "Annual ASPO School Survey." *Planning: The ASPO Magazine* 40 (January 1974).

Denbow, Stefania and T. Nutt. "The Current State of Planning Education." *Journal of the American Institute of Planners* 39 (May 1973).

Ellul, Jacques. *The Technological Society*. New York: Vintage Books, 1964.

Erber, Ernest. *Urban Planning in Transition*. New York: Grossman, 1970.

Friedmann, John and Barclay Hudson. "Knowledge and Action: A Guide to Planning Theory." *Journal of the American Institute of Planners* (January, 1974).

Gold, Harry. *The Professionalism of Planning.* University of Michigan: Unpublished PhD Dissertation, 1965.

Osterman, Paul. "The Shape of the Profession: An Initial Report on the Alumni Survey." MIT Department of Urban Studies and Planning. *Alumni Newsletter,* (Winter Issue 1972–73).

Peattie, Lisa R. "Teaching and Learning for Planners." *Journal of the American Institute of Planners* 35 (January 1969).

Perloff, Harvey S. *Education for Planning: City, State and Regional.* Baltimore: Johns Hopkins Press, 1957.

Planning Education, Special Issue. Journal of the American Institute of Planners 36 (July 1970).

Planning/Network. "The Quality of Planning Education." Summary of Hearings, Los Angeles, Cal., April 10–11, 1973.

The Status of Planning Education, Special Issue. Planning: The ASPO Magazine 38 (September 1972).

Susskind, Lawrence. "The Objectives of Planning Education Re-Examined." *Planning: The ASPO Magazine,* Selected Papers from the ASPO Planning Conference, New Orleans, March 27–April 1, 1971.

Webber, Melvin M. "Comprehensive Planning and Social Responsibility: Toward an A.I.P. Consensus on the Profession's Roles and Purposes." *Journal of the American Institute of Planners* 29 (November 1963).

Willis, Sydney. "Planning Education: A Balanced Role." In *Urban Planning in Transition,* edited by E. Erber. New York: Grossman, 1970.

VI

STAGES IN A CAREER IN PLANNING

An Autobiographical Fragment

THE COLLEGE YEARS

By the time President Franklin D. Roosevelt's remarkable "One Hundred Days" had come to an end, I had decided on my future career. I would devote my life to working on those policy issues important to the solution of society's most critical problems. Planning was being discussed as a key ingredient of any concerted attack on the nation's problems—particularly by the members of the President's "brain trust," Raymond Moley and Rexford Guy Tugwell, as well as by the Secretary of the Interior, Harold Ickes—and I was intrigued by the logic of laying out a planned future course. However, it was some time before I could grasp how the planning mechanism might be used to advantage in a democratic country.

I had just finished my first year in college, and following the New Deal activities was a heady experience. During the early 1930s, the nation was sinking deeper and deeper into depression; suffering was widespread. Even those of us who were lucky enough to escape the worst features of the Depression could not help but be deeply touched by the suffering and despair symbolized dramatically by unemployed men selling apples in the street at 5 cents apiece. Fear *was* everywhere. The New Deal's bold attack on the many problems facing the nation and Roosevelt's inaugural declaration—"We have nothing to fear but fear itself"—were indeed inspiring to a young college student.

Given my career choice and the nature of the issues that were shaping the nation, I decided that my best course was to train in economics and government, or political economy, as so many of the critical issues are economic in nature and government would inevitably go through profound changes in coming to grips with the problems facing it. I decided to transfer from the college and general education course to the Wharton School of Finance, at the University of Pennsylvania, which was centrally concerned with economics and government.

I soon discovered that economics and government were vast terrains and

327

decided that it was the better part of wisdom to focus my attention on one or two themes that logically brought the two fields together. Thus, I chose to concentrate on business cycle policy and on government finance, the latter inevitably strongly related to the former.

My studies in governmental finance introduced me to the complex and important problems being faced by states and localities. The very efforts of overcoming the Depression and maintaining the most critical services were being frustrated by severe governmental finance problems. Here were my first contacts with the problems of housing and city planning, but I saw them then through the very special lens of financing governmental activities.

Economic theory with regard to depression and unemployment was in total disarray, paralleling the floundering of the Roosevelt Administration and its attack on these problems. The roles of budget balancing, of monetary and fiscal policy, and of the gold standard were all being vigorously debated without any clear directions for action.

A number of the Wharton faculty discussed at some length what various European countries were doing with regard to the major issues, and I came to feel that it was important for me to learn, firsthand, about the more interesting attempts to deal with societal problems. I had come to an agreement with my father that I could use the money he would have provided for my fourth year of college to travel in Europe; the remainder would come from my own summer earnings and some small amounts I earned by writing for newspapers and magazines. I managed to get my bachelor's degree in three years and then took off, very close to my 20th birthday, for an eye-opening 15 months in Europe.

LEARNING FROM EUROPE

I had decided to attend the London School of Economics, whose faculty had a worldwide reputation, mostly for work in the areas in which I was concentrating. The London School of Economics at that time was a truly remarkable place with a faculty that ranged from Frederick Hayek on the right to a number of faculty members close to the left wing of the Labor Party. I was particularly anxious to work with Harold Laski, who seemed to me the most exciting political scientist of the day, and with Hugh Dalton, who was probing the issues of government finance with regard to an act creating public programs aimed at dealing with the problems of depression and unemployment.

When I told Laski and Dalton that I wanted to do some research under their guidance which would give me an in-depth view of how the British governmental institutions functioned, they immediately put me to work researching the issue of rating (taxing) empty properties. It turned out that this subject had engaged the attention of Parliament on several occasions since it was first established that empty properties were not to be taxed, and that the issue would be coming up once again in Parliament in the near future. The assumption was that, if I came up with any materials that could be useful to the arguments of the Labor Party—making the case for taxing such properties—that would be all to the good. At a minimum, it would be a good entrée for learning about British local government and the nature of the nation's entire taxing system.

By midwinter, I had prepared a substantial report with the grandiose title of "The Social and Economic Aspects of the Rating of Unoccupied Properties" and a subtitle, "With a Survey of Local Taxation in England and Other Countries." As part of the research, I had sent a short questionnaire to every local government in England and was astonished that I got a response rate of over 80 percent. I suspected that the local financial officers were pleased to find that someone was interested in what they were doing. Thus, I was able to get together reasonable estimates of the cost to the local governments of servicing empty properties, particularly fire and police services, as well as the indirect benefits which came from such local activities as town planning, public lighting, and administrative services that added to the value of the properties. My report included long sections on the issue of equity and taxation and on the logic of the division of responsibilities among the various government levels.

Laski and Dalton were delighted with the materials, and I had the very exciting experience of sitting in the V.I.P. visitors' section of Parliament and listening to some brilliant presentations by several members of the Labor Party constantly referring to the materials I had provided. It was certainly enough to convince me that I had made a good career decision. There was important work that could be done by providing knowledge for formulating policies to cope with the nation's problems.

Although many of the courses that I was taking at the London School of Economics provided comparative materials on what was happening in the rest of Europe and elsewhere in the midst of the worldwide Depression, I was extremely eager to see for myself. But it was not at all clear how I might accomplish that.

Suddenly, later in the year, through a strange twist of fate, just such an opportunity fell into my lap. I met the editor of a European news agency headquartered in Vienna at the home of one of my British friends. At a dinner party attended mostly by businessmen of some standing, the conversation came around to the coming 1936 election in the United States. Everyone who spoke agreed that President Roosevelt would be soundly defeated; after all, all the major newspapers that they came across clearly said as much. With some trepidation I entered the conversation to suggest that the newspapers did not really represent the American voter's views and that indeed Roosevelt was likely to win handily.

After the dinner, the visiting editor asked me if I was interested in recording what I said as a feature story. His agency supplied such feature stories for newspapers across Europe, and he thought there would be substantial interest in the views that I had expressed. After several newspapers had accepted my article (and I had recived what seemed to me then a very handsome check), the editor asked for other stories. His offer, better than anything I could have anticipated, gave me an opportunity to visit the countries in which I was interested, the access to the people who could give the information I was looking for, and the financial support needed to make it all possible.

My first stop was Paris. The Leon Blum government had just come into office through the formation of a "popular front." After a series of ministerial crises, the government had launched a series of programs similar in their intent and general nature to those undertaken by the New Deal in the United States. Through my press credentials, I was able to interview a number of the top members of the government to learn about their intentions and the difficulties they were experiencing. I was struck by the fact that before very long each of the government officials I was interviewing came around to the severe difficulties they were encountering in trying to carry through their programs. They spoke of the ability of the private bankers to sabotage their financial programs and of the widespread lack of compliance.

Although I was well aware of the roadblocks that the New Deal government had encountered, this was clearly in a different league. I got a clear sense of a highly fragile society and came to understand why the government was incapable of taking firm action in the face of the Nazi's infringement of the earlier treaties. I was beginning to learn the valuable lesson of how hard it is to bring about social reforms and to achieve greater equality in the face of bitter opposition from vested interests. I was to see this lesson underlined many times over in my later career.

I had hoped to get some deeper understanding of the Fascist regimes in Germany and Italy in that summer of 1936. But I quickly came to see that it would take a long time, with terrifying risks, to delve into the workings of those governments. My journalistic credentials stood me in good stead but, although I was able to see some of the high government officials, I obtained only a carefully honed propaganda line. The story clearly lay elsewhere but I was not at all equipped in language or background to handle the job well.

In Italy I did get to see Count Galeazzo Ciano, Mussolini's son-in-law, who became Foreign Minister in June 1936. What I got from him was the party line justifying Italian intervention in the Spanish Civil War against the Democratic Republic and in favor of the insurgents. I came out of these countries as I had come in, with a loathing of what they represented and a much more vivid appreciation of how critical it was for democratic governments to overcome severe social difficulties before those difficulties succeeded in undermining the very basis of government. Whereas intellectually I did not need this additional exposure, the emotional factor in firsthand contact was to stay with me forever.

There was another lesson that I was to learn. Like just about everybody else, I immediately fell in love with Paris as a city—indeed, a City of Light. I had already come away from London with a profound appreciation of the beauty of its many broad streets and squares but even more of the vital life of the streets. I had found living there a sheer delight from the aesthetic standpoint and had had the good fortune to meet a number of town planners and to learn about the efforts being made to maintain and enhance the livability of that great city.

Now I found myself truly overwhelmed by the beauty of the even more startling boulevards and squares of Paris, but I was soon to discover another part of the city parallel to what I had found in London. The main streets were just as ugly, dirt was just as real, and it did not take a very creative imagination to grasp the stifling effect that such quarters would have on the people living in them. However, it seemed to me these conditions were a built-in part of a larger social malaise, and I wanted to concentrate on what seemed to me the more critical issues of government organization and policy. I stored the urban issues for later attention but, by the time I left Europe, I knew that urban issues were a key part of the larger mosaic of social problems.

I had long had a special interest in the collective settlements (the kibbutzim) of what was then Palestine, and now I decided to learn more about them and to write about the experience. Through a friend, I was able to get an invitation to spend several weeks in one of the most advanced of the settlements in the Emek Valley. This trip in the summer of 1936 turned out to be quite an adventure and excellent material for a series of articles.

We agreed that I was to be treated as one of the settlers so that I could get a close-up view of life in a kibbutz. The night after I arrived, I found myself, along with the other young persons of the colony, trying to put out fires which had been set by Arab infiltrators in the orange orchards. This violence reflected an escalation of the tensions which had long existed between the Arabs and Jews in Palestine. We were putting out the flames under the rifle fire of the infiltrators— not exactly a comfortable position to be in. For several evenings thereafter, I found myself taking turns manning the periphery of the settlement. This was not exactly what I had bargained for, but it was a remarkably good source of story material.

In spite of the unusual circumstances, I could get a strong sense of what life on a collective settlement was like, and I came away full of admiration for both their philosophical underpinning and their highly intelligent organization of the whole effort. However, I also discovered that this was not exactly the kind of life that I would prefer, nor did I think that it could play an important part in America's social life.

In the Near East, I also visited several of the Arab countries, including Egypt, Lebanon, and Syria, then in the throes of colonial struggles and frequent governmental crises. There was so much to be absorbed. I was beginning to get a deep gut feeling about the importance of culture and tradition in the way nations went about solving their own problems—lessons which were later to stand me in good stead as I began to work seriously with the problems of developing areas in later years.

THE YEARS AT HARVARD

My overseas journey ended when I decided that it was time to return to the United States and enter Harvard University for graduate studies. I had chosen Harvard for the same reason that I had gone to the London School of Economics. Its faculty was deeply involved in the important socioeconomic issues of the day; and the ideas that came out of Harvard, it seemed, were important to what was actually taking place in the national, state, and local governments of the United States. I was admitted to Harvard with a fellowship, and I was to spend the next four years there.

My stay in Europe had convinced me more than ever that I wanted to continue my training in economics and government. I had watched the New

Deal's fumbling efforts to come to grips with the deep depression and high unemployment as well as the parallel efforts in some of the countries in Europe, and I wanted urgently to take part in the creation of knowledge which would permit a nation to solve such urgent problems. The faculty in economics and government was particularly distinguished.

Professor Harold Laski, my mentor at the London School of Economics, had admonished me to take full advantage of Harvard's resources, to reach out far beyond the required courses, and to get to know the many exciting intellectual developments that were taking place at that great university. To get me started, Laski had written a very warm letter of introduction to Felix Frankfurter at the Harvard Law School to let me audit his course and to guide me to other courses at the law school and elsewhere. I discovered, when I met Frankfurter, that he did not believe there was much value in auditing "foreign" courses; but he was happy to let me "waste my time" sitting in on one or another of his courses.

I soon discovered that Frankfurter was quite correct in his judgment and that studying in two fields, economics and government, was quite enough to absorb all my energies. However, I followed Laski's advice to take advantage of the rich resources at Harvard by listening to some of the great figures there, including particularly Towne and Landis (the latter in the new field of tax law) as well as Frankfurter in the law school. I also spent many hours getting to know the activities at the School of Fine Arts. City planning was then being taught in individual courses in the landscape architecture program.

Shortly after I began my studies at Harvard, there was a lucky turn of events. The Graduate School of Public Administration was organized, with a generous grant from Lucius Littauer, specifically to concentrate on government policy in administration. (As a result, Harvard had the first school of public policy. It was followed by a host of others across the country after World War II.) In addition, a new Ph.D. degree program was announced in political economy and government, and permitted students to combine work in both fields. It was as if the program had been tailored to my study interests. I was admitted to the Littauer Center and to the joint degree program and was to receive their first Ph.D.

The organization of the school encouraged faculty to develop new courses on governmental policy across a broad spectrum. However, theory was far from neglected; in fact, it was quite dominant. Joseph H. Schumpeter lectured on his theory of the centrality of entrepreneurship and investment in a capitalist system. Wassily Leontief presented input–output analysis as a powerful planning tool. His theory and techniques were later to be employed both in the Soviet Union and in the United States, a unique development.

I found a number of the courses in public finance of substantial value, but of particular interest to me—as to many of the other Littauer Fellows "preparing for the government service"—was the seminar in fiscal policy given by Alvin H. Hansen and John Williams, the latter also serving as President of the New York Branch of the Federal Reserve System.

The general theory of John Maynard Keynes provided a powerful rationale and relatively unambiguous approach to overcoming the Depression. Hansen became one of the nation's strongest proponents of the Keynesian approach.

The Hansen-Williams Fiscal Policy Seminar became the focus of new thinking about business cycle policy and the techniques needed to manage counter-cyclical policy.

For example, Hansen was arguing that the severe downturn of 1937 was due to the fact that the new governmental programs, and particularly Social Security, were drawing off more funds from the economy than contributing to it. Substantial attention was devoted in the seminar to improving flow-of-funds measurements. In fact, the seminar highlighted the great importance to economic planning of carefully measuring the most important economic indicators. Kuznets's work on national accounts was elaborated and extended.

Given my strong interest in both economics and government, it seemed natural for me to focus my Ph.D. dissertation on the national budget, where economics and government come together most powerfully and most significantly. Hansen chaired my Ph.D. dissertation, and I worked closely with him. He sent copies of the final product entitled "Modern Budget Policies" to members of the Budget Bureau in Washington, and I later learned that it had been widely read within that agency.

Hansen was working as a consultant to the Federal Reserve Board and regularly commuting between Cambridge and Washington. As the nation headed toward war, Hansen agreed to shift the scene of his activities to Washington and invited me to join him there. However, since it would be awhile until he set up his staff on a continuing basis in Washington, he suggested that, because I had an interest in an academic career, it would be sensible to get some teaching experience.

I was offered a position at the City College of New York (CCNY)—I suspect largely through his recommendation—and I taught undergraduates for a year at that remarkable institution. The students were unbelievably bright, politically conscious, and highly inquisitive. It was a wonderful place to learn the teaching game, like being thrown in deep water to learn to swim. In my courses, I relied heavily on concepts and methods learned at Harvard, and I considered my year at CCNY as an extension of my graduate teaching. It was not until I later went to Washington, however, that I could begin to make contributions to knowledge on my own.

THE WASHINGTON YEARS, 1931–1943

I spent some two-and-a-half years in Washington at the Federal Reserve Board as Alvin Hansen's assistant. The Board had invited Professor Hansen to establish a full-fledged staff to work on problems of wartime finance and monetary policy and postwar problems. It was widely accepted that planned approaches to the generation and allocation of sources and goods would be needed during wartime and that some planned provisions would have to be made to avoid a postwar depression. Hansen's sympathy for planned approaches (although not of highly centralized planning) fit the needs of the period, so that Hansen was able to play a substantial role in Washington affairs.

Hansen's main interest was in preparing for postwar recovery. He felt that there was a fairly high probability of a depression following World War II and that it was essential for the future of the nation to prevent any severe downturn in the economy. He had an uneasy feeling that the nation's social fabric might not be able to withstand a really severe depression after the great trauma of the 1930s and the high prosperity of the war years.

Hansen had brought together a small staff mostly made up of his former students, and was anxious to encourage fresh ideas and the invention of new approaches. Thus, each member of the staff was invited to write on those features of the postwar world that interested him the most. At the same time, each of us was given assignments to work on some of the problems of the wartime economy as various public agencies invited Hansen's suggestions. We looked into ways of coping with some of the immediate problems, particularly in regard to fiscal and monetary policy, and some tricky pricing and financing questions as in the handling of energy stocks. It was simulating and demanding to spend two or three days on a very urgent immediate issue and then return to writing about the postwar world—actually, my greatest lesson in how to do research.

Hansen had evolved a scheme for dealing with the postwar period involving planned large-scale investments in the development of natural resources and in the building and rebuilding of urban communities in the context of national, state, and local finance and economic policy. Hansen wanted first to work out the conceptual bases for this approach and then to encourage legislation and the establishment of organizations to bring the ideas to reality.

My first assignment was to prepare a case for a large-scale program of river basin development. This work was followed by a substantial study of state and local finances, as it was evident that such financing under current arrangements exacerbated business cycles rather than mitigated them. I also worked closely with Guy Greer, who was preparing the case for a large-scale program of urban redevelopment including the methods that would make such a program feasible. This work had an important impact on the urban renewal legislation that was to come later in 1949. I could not have imagined a better start for a planning career even if I could have willed whatever I wanted into being. It provided a remarkable overview of developmental programs in our complex federal system, incorporating every level of government and particularly involving the great art of thinking and planning ahead.

It also provided opportunities for working closely with the major planning agencies of the time, including the National Resources Planning Board during its last years in existence; the private, not-for-profit National Planning Association (which was so important at that time in fostering the view that the nation should look ahead to its future); the Federal Reserve Board; the Treasury; and last, but not least, the Tennessee Valley Authority. It exposed me to all those phases of planning to which I would devote my life's work, including a national economic policy, national urban policy and national, state, and regional policies for the development of the nation's resources.

I spent the next years in the army, first as infantryman and then after the European war had ended as a member of the army's information service, which took over supplying news in the U.S. sector from B&B, the German news agency. It was highly instructive for me to get a close-up view of the problems of military government in a conquered nation and of the first stages of the reconstitution of the German society and economy.

When I returned to the United States in the winter of 1946 I discovered that I was uncomfortable because of the freezing that my feet had suffered during the Battle of the Bulge. Instead of going back to work in Washington, as attractive as that was, I discovered that Puerto Rico was looking for a development economist who might help them with their new developmental program, "Operation Bootstrap." I was invited to go to Puerto Rico and thus began another phase of my planning career—another very lucky phase. It was certainly lucky to have an opportunity to work on a program of planned development in the pleasant, mild climate of the Caribbean.

TWO STAYS IN PUERTO RICO

An arrangement was made for me to work out of the University of Puerto Rico through the Institute of Social Science headed by Clarence Senior, an outstanding American sociologist. This arrangement, it was explained, would give me maximum freedom, including freedom from too close a political overview, and would permit me to escape the day-by-day assignments which might have come to me if I were stationed in one of the government agencies. I was soon to discover how my job came about and what I was expected to do.

As soon as I was settled in, Luis Muñoz Marín, the leader of the government, invited me to attend a meeting of his cabinet. I was immediately impressed with his personality and charisma and his very attractive, mostly young, cabinet. Muñoz explained that immediately after World War II they had launched a very ambitious development program to lift the island "by its bootstraps" into a new era. Some months before the meeting, Muñoz had asked his cabinet to prepare materials on the activities within each of their agencies to provide a coherent, organized basis for starting Operation Bootstrap. All of them had compiled materials, amounting to some two dozen thick, book-sized reports. They felt overwhelmed by this copious material and did not quite know what could be made of it. It had been decided that someone from outside with a fresh point of view might be able to bring all of this material together into a coherent report as a blueprint for future activities.

It took me some time to get over the shock of realizing the enormity and complexity of the task that had been given to me, but it was certainly a meaty assignment. I spent the next week going through the materials, frequently calling on Clarence Senior for explanations and guidance. Senior turned out to be a storehouse of knowledge about Puerto Rico with a very sensitive appreciation of the island's politics. He had the sociologist's capacity of seeing the whole picture with a human interest in the personalities and special features of the Puerto Rican culture.

After a careful review of the materials, I decided it would be wise to start from scratch. Even the statistics that were provided had to be revised in almost all cases because the classifications used were not appropriate to designing a development program.

I also felt that it was important to put the island's efforts into proper perspective, because no small part of the program's success would depend on decisions made in Washington and those made by private firms on the continent. Thus, I undertook to outline enough of the history of Puerto Rico and the background of the current effort to make it understandable to individuals who were not already involved in the government's operation.

Senior strongly encouraged me in this approach, and I was delighted to learn that Muñoz, also, was enthusiastic. He fully understood the necessity for starting from scratch and, after reviewing the materials, told me that not only was there too much detail to make the materials useful but there was not nearly enough forward thinking to provide key elements of Operation Bootstrap.

Muñoz was interested in the details of what I intended to write, and I was truly impressed with the scope of his understanding and intelligence. He urged me to continue meeting with him regularly to discuss the various facets of the program, as he wanted to use whatever materials I developed as quickly as possible and to have his own opportunity to have an input on what was being prepared. He made it clear, however, that it would be my report and that I could reject any of his ideas just as I would anybody else's. I was at first a bit skeptical about this but soon discovered that he meant every word that he said. He wanted fresh advice—not any playback of his own ideas as he often got from some of the governmental officials.

I explained it was my view that, if a development program was to be carefully planned over a substantial period of time, it would be essential to develop basic national statistics, including national product, income, balance of payments, and as much of the flow-of-funds data as could be organized meaningfully. He ordered all elements of the government involved in data collection to cooperate fully with me—in fact, to make the generation of such statistics a high-priority item.

I found through the really remarkable cooperation from the government agencies, together with a judicious use of the data made available to me in the briefing books, that I could make rapid progress. Soon I was able to make available drafts with individual sections covering the framework islandwide data and then a specific set of proposals on the various productive sectors (agriculture, manufacturing, services, etc.) as well as on trade.

When major sections of my report were completed, I would send them to Muñoz and key members of the cabinet. I invariably received very thoughtful comments on these segments, and I met quite frequently with Muñoz to discuss them, often in great detail.

With Muñoz's approval, I gave copies of the drafts to the head of the planning agency, Rafael Pico, who, I discovered, was much involved with almost every phase of islandwide planning, including the physical planning for each of the urban communities. This was a totally centralized operation but, given the lack of trained personnel, the paucity of resources in general, and the lack of a strong tradition of local government, centralized planning seemed logical at the time. Because of the scope of responsibility of the planning agency, I soon found myself involved with a multitude of issues, including such matters as the enlargement and modernization of the San Juan port, the location of industrial plants attracted through Operation Bootstrap, new tax incentives, needed improvements in the highway system, and possibilities for providing housing. Thus, as in Washington, I found myself working at several levels of government and learning more about the problems of achieving coherence among them.

An important example is a paper I wrote suggesting that the Island's budget was its most potent planning tool but that, in its existing form, it could not serve that function well. The budget was organized along traditional line items so that it was easy to know how much was spent for salaries and wages, purchases, and the other items. However, since functions spilled across departmental lines, it was difficult to know exactly how much was allocated for important functions, such as education, agriculture, industry, community development, and the like.

I suggested that the budget needed to be reorganized and, further, that the government needed to establish priorities among functions so that it could direct the budget to achieving its highest priority goals. I set out a listing of what such a priority ordering might look like, starting with education, going on to the support of the various producive activities, and ending with what I considered the less vital functions. I stressed that this was a suggested list only and that establishing such priorities should be the result of broad consultation and widely publicized adoption. It was important that every department and bureau not only prepare its own budget along functional lines but should also understand the logic of the priority system.

A few days after my report was distributed, Muñoz called late one evening asking if I would mind coming to his home to discuss the report. He had a modest but very pleasant house on a farm close to the area where my wife and I were living. We went over every phase of the report including exactly what needed to be done stage by stage in order to devise and implement the proposals. We talked on an open porch with the stars twinkling brightly in the clear sky.

After that, I spent quite a few evenings with Muñoz discussing issues that were of particular interest to him, including many which were outside my report. Munoz liked to bounce ideas against people, using conservations as a form of thinking aloud. I was completely captivated by the man and found the discussions a source of great delight.

I completed my reports by June of 1946. By then I had been successful in establishing a full-fledged national accounting system including income accounts, flow-of-funds, and the like. I had also succeeded in rearranging the budget and auditing accounts according to function. One of the most satisfactory aspects of my effort had been that not only the classification system but the actual priorities I had initially proposed were officially adopted and, in fact, were to remain for well over a decade. That is not to say that the priorities were fully adhered to by future administrations, but they had a perceptible influence on the shift of expenditures towards the educational and productive aspects of the society.

For me, a pragmatic approach to planning suggested that it was not enough to establish the centrality of planning as a rationale for decision making or for bringing knowledge to action. Certainly, rationality would be a logical goal if by

that we meant trying to choose the most appropriate means to the ends established seeking appropriateness in terms of both cost effectiveness and, for all
fair-minded people, enhancing the degree of equity and equality in the society.
But, to achieve this very logical objective, we needed information that was not
only accurate and timely but that permitted a reasonably accurate analysis of the
situation, the problems, and the kind of information pertinent to the design of
effective policies, programs, and plans.

I had been greatly impressed with the extent to which the creation of accurate and timely flow-of-funds accounts helped explain the major reasons behind
the sharp economic downturn of 1937, and in the preparation of compensatory
measures to offset the drawing down of governmental funds into the economy
through the new Social Security payouts. I also had good reason to believe that I
had made a major contribution to analysing Puerto Rico's problems by improving the social accounts and the reporting involved in their budgetary and accounting system. Thus, I had come to feel that planning could contribute at the
various government levels only if it could bring the kind of knowledge to action
that was in a form that made analysis and synthesis possible. Information rarely
came in this needed form, so that planning research had a big job ahead if it
were to make a genuine contribution to society.

Later I came to realize that I had had a dream assignment in Puerto Rico,
with the kind of impact that a consultant always hopes for but rarely achieves.
My stay in Puerto Rico was made even more memorable by the fact that it was
there that I met Rexford Guy Tugwell, the appointed Governor of Puerto Rico
from 1941 through most of 1946. He had resigned the governorship shortly
before I arrived on the Island, largely because he felt that his effectiveness in
Washington had been diminished and that the post should be turned over to
someone else.

Tugwell had stayed on to ease the transition to his successor's administration and to write a book on his experiences as governor, published in 1947 as the
Stricken Land. Tugwell had been a hero of mine from the time when I first read
about him as a member of Roosevelt's "Brain Trust" during the campaign of
1932 and as the builder of the greenbelt new towns.

Meeting him was a special treat, and soon my wife and I were spending
many hours with Tugwell and his wife, Grace, together with their two young
sons. Tugwell was quite interested in my work and provided valuable guidance
in what I was doing. In turn, it was a delight to hear his reminiscences and to
talk with him about the subject of great interest to both of us—planning.

Tugwell had a view of planning that placed it at the very center of decision
making; he called it a "fourth power." I found that hard to reconcile with my
own views of a strong unified executive power and a separate legislative and
judicial authority. His view was neither theoretically sound nor practically feasible, I felt, but I saw it as a distillation of his very wide experience and was more
than willing to discuss the issue in great detail. On most other subjects, we
found ourselves in substantial agreement, particularly because we both were
drawn to progressive politics and were concerned about issues of equity and
equality.

Some months after I met Tugwell, he told me that he had accepted the offer of a position to organize a new planning school at the University of Chicago. He told me about his plans for the school and asked me if I would be interested in joining him as a member of the faculty. I was much taken with his hopes for the school, and it seemed a logical next step in my career. I accepted with enthusiasm, and soon we were discussing the needed steps in the organization of the program beginning in the fall of 1947. Thus, the University of Chicago was to be the next station in my career.

THE PLANNING SCHOOL AT THE UNIVERSITY OF CHICAGO

Robert M. Hutchins, Chancellor of the University of Chicago, invited Tugwell to set up a "center of planning education." This invitation followed an initial proposal by Professor Louis Wirth, a highly regarded member of the Chicago school of urban sociology, who had worked on it closely with other interested faculty members in the division and with Walter Blucher, Executive Director of the American Society of Planning Officials (ASPO).

Wirth had argued that the very rapidly growing demand for persons with a planning background, as well as for knowledge of the planning field "widely being used by administrators, industrialists, and other practical vocations," justified the establishment of an institute of planning. Given the training required of planners, he suggested locating the institute in the University's social science division. He conceived of a planning education of great breadth that called on all of the social science disciplines in the division. In addition, he called for a cooperative arrangement in which the Illinois Institute of Technology would contribute its resources in architecture and engineering while the ASPO would provide consultative services and liaison with the planning profession. The proposal, he pointed out, had the support of not only these institutions but of the local chapter of the American Institute of Architects as well.

Blucher was not only anxious to promote "general, preprofessional, and guidance education for planners," but also the creation of refresher courses and the "retraining and supplementary planning education for members of allied professions and fields" at the University. He wrote, in a memorandum of May 26, 1945, to Louis Wirth, "We simply need more people who have been trained as planners."

The proposal inviting Tugwell to Chicago had been well received by the social sciences faculty so that Hutchins could invite him with enthusiasm. Tugwell readily accepted the invitation because he believed that the time had come to give up the governship of Puerto Rico. President Truman, however, had asked him to stay on, and he did so for another year; thus, it was not until the fall of 1947 that Tugwell took on the task of establishing a new planning school in Chicago.

Tugwell had invited me to join the faculty of the new school while we were still in Puerto Rico. Later he invited Melville Branch on the recommendation of G. Holmes Perkins, Chairman of the Harvard Planning Program where Branch had been enrolled. He could finish his Ph.D. work at Chicago and, in fact, received the first doctorate awarded at Harvard in the field of planning. He had

had training in architecture at Princeton University and had served as Administrative Aid to the Director of the U.S. National Resources Planning Board during 1939–1941. He had also been Director of the Princeton University Bureau of Urban Research during 1941–1943. The other initial member of the staff was William L. Ludlow. Ludlow had done research for the National Association of Housing Officials and had worked for the Resettlement Administration, the National Resources Committee, the Tennessee Valley Authority (TVA), and the New Jersey Planning Board. He had written on housing, urban densities, and land values and zoning. In addition to these full-time members of the staff, Blucher gave a course in planning practice; and Herman Finer, Professor of Political Science, who had written a critique of Hayek's *Road to Serfdom*, offered a course in "Comparative National Planning." The following year, Edward C. Banfield, Jr., Martin Meyerson, and Julius Margolis joined the faculty, and Richard L. Meier replaced Ludlow in 1950.

Banfield had been invited to join the staff because Tugwell had found his research on a cooperative farm, started during Tugwell's tenure at the Department of Agriculture, to be unusually insightful. He had served as Secretary of the New Hampshire Farm Bureau Federation and had worked in the public relations school while getting a Ph.D. Degree in political science. Banfield early displayed a questioning, critical approach to most subjects and, while he coauthored a book with Tugwell, he had an idiosyncratic approach to planning and social development.

Meyerson had come to the planning program shortly after he finished his work for the Master's Degree in City Planning at Harvard; but he had already had experience as a staff member of the ASPO in Chicago, the Philadelphia City Planning Commission, and the Michael Reese Hospital in Chicago. Thus, with Branch, he brought to the program some of the approaches and skills of the traditional design-oriented planner. His approach to planning, however, was anything but traditional. He, again like Branch, provided leadership in the effort to broaden physical planning through the social sciences without losing the central focus on improving the human environment.

Margolis was invited to join the planning program at my suggestion. He had been a student of mine at City College of New York and served at the Federal Reserve Board with me. His commitment to social problem solving through the application of some of the advanced techniques of economics, particularly choice theory, social accounting, and techniques for the evaluation of public expenditures, seemed particularly appropriate for the Chicago planning school. He was with the program from 1948 to 1951.

Meier was the last member to join the core faculty. As Executive Secretary of the Federation of Atomic Scientists, he had visited Tugwell to discuss their mutual preoccupation with the dangers of the atomic bomb. Tugwell had found his wide-ranging intelligence to be truly striking and suggested to the faculty that he would be a valuable member of a program as experimental as ours. Meier had a Ph.D. in chemistry but had schooled himself in the other sciences, and came very close to being a scientific generalist. His knowledge of the social impacts of technology suggested that he would fill an important gap in our program. Almost immediately, he found that the program—and planning in general—provided an appropriate setting for his broad-ranging interests. He was soon to carve out for himself a special niche in the planning field, pointing out in many cases how technological change posed significant problems for planning but, also unique opportunities for solving societal problems.

The planning program at the University of Chicago was started at a significant time in American history. The decade-long Depression and World War II each had a profound impact on planning thought and planning practice. The limitations of traditional design-oriented physical planning in coping with environmental problems—no less the broader social problems—had become increasingy apparent and a matter of great concern to leaders of the planning movement.

There was almost unanimous agreement that the training of planners had to encompass knowledge in social and economic matters as well as law and design. At the same time, the highly publicized efforts of the New Deal to evolve a planned approach to business cycle management and to wartime policy, as well as to such broad areas as river basin development, had ignited a debate on the proper place of planning in society in general. Tugwell represented one extreme in the planning spectrum, suggesting that planning should be an overriding guiding force in societal action directed by a scientifically trained elite. Frederick Hayek was at the other extreme, opposing any and all forms of planning. There were many positions in between these extremes.

The group that had pressed for the establishment of planning at the University of Chicago had not really tried to resolve any of the philosophical issues but came together simply because of the need for a school of planning. Each seemingly assumed that his approach would somehow ultimately dominate.

Louis Wirth saw planning as an applied social science strongly associated with research and in a sense doing for all of the social sciences what his group in urban sociology had been carrying forward. Also, as a community activist, he was very interested in what was coming to be known as action research, that is, research that could be applied directly to immediate social problems. Charles Merriam, a key figure in the Department of Political Science and who had been one of the members of the National Resources Planning Board (NRPB) and its predecessor agencies, saw the program essentially as carrying forward the NRPB's work of providing a social intelligence to problems at the national, regional, and local levels. Like Robert Walker, he saw planning as a staff activity and planning thought as largely applied to political science and administration.

Blucher, from his position as Executive Director of the ASPO, saw the school as providing the necessary high-level planners who were so badly needed in the field, given its apparent rapid growth. He felt that combined strength of the University's social science division and the architectural and engineering capacity of the Illinois Institute of Technology would permit the planning field to achieve the necessary broadening from its too limited design base. The latter objective was also important to the leaders of the local chapter of the American Institute of Architects.

There were actually other strongly held views on what planning was all about and what was needed at that period of time. Thus, given the total lack of agreement among its initial sponsors, the full-time staff of the Chicago School was essentially on its own. But the members of the staff were themselves bring-ing to the endeavor a very wide variety of backgrounds and views of planning so that the effort was essentially one of diverse approaches. It must be remembered that this was the first effort to base planning in the social sciences and every-thing was, in fact, invention.

One factor had a profound impact on the direction of the school: it turned out to be impossible to combine forces with the Illinois Institute of Technology. Their program, under the leadership of Ludwig Hilberseimer, was narrowly focused on the traditional design approach. Hilberseimer's overriding interests in developing high-rise linear cities made any possibility of cooperation impossi-ble—in fact, ludicrous. Thus, the easy dream of joining the architectural and engineering capabilities of the Institute with the social science strength of Chi-cago was totally shattered. If a cooperative program had been feasible, it is entirely likely that the Chicago program would have focused on the training of city planners and on providing a much broader philosophical base for such training than existed up to that point. Mel Branch stood almost alone in examin-ing the physical factors in planning. As it was, the urban planning portion of the Chicago effort was the weakest link in the whole setup and, when Branch and Meyerson left in 1951, training in urban planning was further weakened.

When the faculty of the planning school came together, it was generally agreed than an intellectual basis for planning had to be provided because none existed and the main thrust of the program demanded it. It was logical and, indeed, inevitable that Tugwell's theories on planning would be the starting point. None of the other faculty members had, in fact, thought much or had written about planning theory. But it was soon the essential focus for the pro-gram. In fact, a centralized approach to planning, then, seemed logical enough as did the stress on comprehensiveness and rationality in planning. Thus, not only did Tugwell teach and write on these core features of planning, but Ban-field was to join with Tugwell in a series of articles advancing this approach, and Banfield and Meyerson wrote a highly regarded book in which the rational approach to decision making was declared to be the center of any planning endeavor.

I was more comfortable with a more pragmatic approach to planning and tended to focus greater attention on ways of democratizing the planning pro-cess. In this, I was joined by Branch, Ludlow, Margolis, and, to varying degrees, other members of the faculty. Interestingly, the school's announcements de-scribing the approach of the program were, in the first instances, toned-down versions of the Tugwellian ideas on planning. Increasingly, over the years, they reflected a greater and greater interest in the more pragmatic approaches and the limitations on, as well as the uses of, planning.

After two years in which he had taken an active role in the development of the program, Tugwell left for a year's leave to teach at the London School of Economics. When he returned, he devoted almost all of his attention to writing books and articles, many of them on his New Deal experience. He had few contacts with the students, although his name, of course, remained a force until the very end.

THE WATER RESOURCES POLICY COMMISSION

I was invited to serve as a consultant to the President's Water Resources Policy Commission in Washington, D.C., during 1950. The invitation was a direct result of the pamphlet I wrote with Alvin Hansen in 1942, "Regional Resource Development," in which we had proposed a major planned program of river basin development following the lead of the TVA. The Commission was clearly interested in our proposal, and I was invited, in a sense, to make the case for the planned development of our extensive and rich river basins.

I soon discovered, through close contact with the able members of the Commission under the leadership of Morris L. Cooke, that, although our intuition about the broad outlines of a planned river basin development program were quite good, there were highly important issues surrounding the development of each of the basins that required much deeper probing than was provided in 1942. Fortunately, the Commission was able to provide such in-depth studies including a very extensive volume on "Ten Rivers in America's Future." The Commission also did a detailed study on water resources law. Its main proposals were presented in a first volume, "A Water Policy for the American People," which had an important impact on both federal and state policy in the years to come.

It was satisfying to discover, as in this experience, that I could continue to build on earlier work and to have at least some small influence on the policy decisions being taken on matters of great importance to the nation's future. During the 1950s and 1960s, the United States undertook a substantial program of river basin development. These projects were multipurpose—following the lead of the TVA and probably encouraged by the findings of the President's Water Resources Policy Commission—yet continuous regional planning (including careful review of the economic, demographic, and social issues in each of the regions) was not part of the picture. In a few regions, such as the Columbia, because of local traditions and a relatively strong regional agency, certain aspects of regionwide planning were incorporated into river basin development. With hindsight, it is possible to point to some of the factors that played a role in keeping regional planning to a limited scale, including the jealousies of the state planning agencies (coupled with their inherent weaknesses), the jealousies of the state and local area development agencies, and possibly the history of the political attacks on the TVA using the comprehensiveness of their regional planning as an indication that "they wanted to take over everything." On the positive side, the great strength of the multipurpose concept of river basin development produced a very broad type of resources planning far beyond what had taken place in the earlier history of the nation.

AN ECONOMIC UNIT WITHIN THE PUERTO RICAN PLANNING BOARD

During a summer stay in Washington, I used the detailed comments I had received on my Puerto Rican reports to prepare a book entitled *Puerto Rico's*

Economic Future (1950). I sent the manuscript to Puerto Rico when I left for the University of Chicago, and it was circulated among all the government offices. Munoz invited me back to the Island in September, 1949, for an in-depth discussion of my various proposals. These had been in the hands of the key members of the government for some time, but Muñoz was now governor and anxious to revitalize the Development Program Office. The governor devoted three days to the sessions held in La Fortaleza, the governor's palace, and my suggestions were reviewed in minute detail. At the end of the session, Muñoz named a seven-member committee to "implement a program for Puerto Rico's economic future" which was to follow the guidelines laid out in my report and in my discussions.

I had recommended establishing an economic unit within the Puerto Rican Planning Board because economics was the weakest aspect of what was otherwise a high-level planning operation. The governor and Pico asked me to set up such a unit and to train the people who would then take it over. I took a leave of absence from the University of Chicago in 1950 to establish the unit because I felt that this would be an excellent way of bringing into operation some of the ideas I had been propounding at the University. I was given a totally free hand as to staff and as to the work of the unit itself. It seemed to me logical that, instead of following the pattern established by the Council of Economic Advisers of focusing on an annual report, for Puerto Rico it was more appropriate to combine an annual report with a ten-year overview as guidance for governmental policy.

My first appointee was Candido Oliveras, an able agricultural economist whom I had come to know during my earlier stay in Puerto Rico. It was clear from the first day that he would take over the unit and that my stay was temporary. In addition to other Puerto Rican staff, I invited several economists from the mainland who had had Latin American experience or who had needed skills that were not then available in Puerto Rico: Alexander Ganz and Joseph Grunwald, both with broad experience in developing areas, as well as Britton Harris and Stephen Axilrod, both of whom had demonstrated an unusual capacity for statistics and mathematics.

In eight months, we produced the first report, "Economic Development in Puerto Rico, 1940–1950, 1951–1960." The report showed what the Island had experienced during the past decade and laid out a program of economic development for the decade to come. It covered trends in the United States economy and showed how they impacted on Puerto Rico; suggested targets for the Puerto Rican economy specifically for 1950 and 1960; and, finally, outlined "a program of accelerated economic development," including priorities for public expenditures; programs for manufacturing and agricultural development, education and vocational training; the provision of physical facilities, labor and employment policies; and, finally, financing the development programs. The report also summarized some new concepts being developed at the University of Chicago that I could apply here with substantial logic.

I saw a pragmatic approach to planning as involving the invention of appropriate designs for the future with effective strategies, policies, and programs. I saw my creation of a budget-by-priorities approach to governmental expenditures in Puerto Rico as providing one of the most important planning tools the

Island now possesses. I had also been impressed from my reading of city planning history with the fact that a tremendous amount of inventiveness was involved in those projects that had substantial impacts (as in Burnham's Chicago plan). These ideas were central to the professional planning activities I undertook while at the University of Chicago and were, in turn, reinforced and deepened by these experiences.

In the report that the unit prepared, the ten-year look backward and the ten-year look forward were based, to a large extent, on the use of the accounts which, in my earlier stay in Puerto Rico, I had felt necesarry either to create or to strengthen. The compelling data that we were able to bring together—often joint relationships among the key factors involved—turned out to be important in generating detailed debates among the cabinet members and legislature as well as in the newspaper reports.

As with my earlier report, I had kept the key members of the government informed about our findings at every stage so that, when Muñoz Marín called a series of meetings to discuss a newly available report, there had already been intense discussion, and disagreements had already surfaced. Implementation ran into normal political hassles but, on the whole, Puerto Rico was to continue with its program of planned economic development for many years to come.

Some of my most cherished ideas had been roundly defeated. These included a number of proposals in education, manpower training, intensification of some areas of agriculture, changes in the approaches to tourism (it seemed to me that the strong emphasis on the Miami/gambling type of tourism was socially unfortunate), and a number of other matters. However, the positives far exceeded the negatives. Also, my Puerto Rican experience had made it possible to produce one of the very earliest texts in the important field of planned economic development, and that was more than an adequate payoff.

TURKEY AND ISRAEL

As a result of the work I had done in Puerto Rico, the United Nations Office of Economic Development invited me to join a high-level mission to set up an "economic intelligence unit" in the government of Turkey to help guide its economic policy in developmental programs. It was described as one of the strongest missions the United Nations had launched because of the perceived importance of Turkey as a possible model for other developing areas. I saw this as an opportunity to advance the techniques of planned development in poor countries and was attracted by the U. N. description of this as an opportunity to establish a unit of the caliber that could serve as a prototype to other developing nations.

It turned out that the initial request for assistance from the U. N. had come from the head of Turkey's statistical unit. He had come to the conclusion that the reams of data the statistical unit was collecting and publishing did not provide a very effective base for decision making on economic matters. He saw the unit, to be established with the help of the U.N. mission, as providing the information needed for governmental decision makers. The team, in addition to myself, included two top U. N. officials as well as a British general economist and an American agricultural economist. We discovered immediately upon arrival that the request for the mission had come as a total surprise to the President of the country and his powerful Foreign Minister. The president, Menderez, we were soon to learn, even though the head of the so-called Democratic Party, was anything but democratic and corrupt to boot. These characteristics were true of the foreign minister, Zorlu, as well. Evidently, the president had decided that he was going to milk the U. S. "financial aid cow" as much as he could, given the strategic importance of Turkey. Turkish economic policy under Menderez was largely a matter of saving the agricultural oligarchy, the most important group supporting Menderez politically. Fortunately, I could learn a great deal about what was going on through a friend of mine who held a top post at the U.S. Embassy in Ankara. Thus, none of the events came as a shock to me as they did to the other members on the team. We were shunted aside—if with a certain amount of ceremony—and asked to contribute to establishing an economic intelligence unit by devoting ourselves to the training of Turkish economists who could take on the task. Actually, Turkey had an adequate number of economists who could readily have fit into such a unit and taken over after the U. N. team left.

The two U. N. members of the team started back to New York in anger while the three others remained behind to give a few lectures and prepare a report that might be useful to any future group attempting to set up an economic intelligence unit under more auspicious circumstances. In addition, we took advantage of our stay in Turkey to see something of the country firsthand. This turned out to be a delightful experience with an absolutely fascinating mix of the very old and the quite new in a unique Turkish amalgam.

In the midst of my travels, I received an unexpected call from the U. N. informing me that the government of Israel had requested my assistance. As almost two months remained before I had to return to Chicago, I grabbed the opportunity to revisit the country I had seen in such a dramatic way 18 years earlier in its new reincarnation as Israel. My experience was almost the exact opposite of that in Turkey. From the moment I arrived almost to the moment I left, I found myself working 10 to 12 hours a day and having the attentive interest of the governmental officials involved. The government had asked me to suggest how the Israeli planning activities might be strengthened and made more pertinent.

My invitation to Israel had been triggered by a recent event, the "firing" of an American economic consulting team organized earlier under the leadership of an able economist named Oscar Gass. Bertram Gross, who had been a key member of the U. S. Council of Economic Advisors during its earliest years, served as a member of the Gass group. This economic advisory group had made what turned out to be unforgivable political gaffs, challenging on economic grounds some of the most important military decisions and questioning the government's subsidies for certain food items, particularly bread. The government evidently felt that such policy matters were forbidden territory not to be entered by an outside group. With the departure of the very strong Gass team, Israel's economic intelligence was left in disarray.

I spent my first few weeks in Israel carefully reviewing various planning and economic intelligence operations and, through rather delicate interviewing of some key figures, got an impression of what was politically feasible at the time. The budget unit seemed the best equipped, under existing circumstances, to take on significant information and planning functions. I wrote a report to this effect that evidently had some impact on later reorganization. I also worked rather intensively with the regional planning units engaged in building new towns for recent arrivals. Particularly important were the ways that decisions on location, size, and public facilities would determine the viability of the new communities. This was a new learning experience for me, and I had the feeling that I probably took away more than I left behind, although my Israeli hosts were appreciative of what they considered to be valuable advice.

Again and again in Israel, I discovered the importance of pertinent, focused information on the complex issues with which they were dealing. It was disturbing, of course, to learn that, although both analysis and new approaches to the future were in themselves important, the former could only give the most general kind of guidelines to what needed to be done. Experimentation and risks seemed to be essential ingredients for moving ahead. After my Puerto Rican and Israeli experiences, I could never doubt the almost separate importance of each. It seemed that in planning, as in science, breakthroughs came almost by accident.

THE UNIVERSITY OF CHICAGO, 1951–1955

I had an equally vivid and instructive professional experience back home in Chicago. In fact, I had become well aware of the neighborhood problems emerging around the University of Chicago area during my early years in the program but it was not until after returning from Puerto Rico at the end of 1950 that I threw myself into the struggle to cope with the rapidly accelerating problems of decline and social tension.

The black population was increasing rapidly on the southside where the University of Chicago was located. Earlier, the University administration had joined forces with the community in trying to keep black families out through the use of restrictive covenants—an unexpected and shameful policy for a university administration. When the Supreme Court of the United States declared such covenants unconstitutional, the University looked about desperately to find other means to maintain the "viability" of the area. It had quite legitimate interests in maintaining the area as a good place for faculty and students as well as other university-oriented residents. Unfortunately, the admistration, backed by the Trustees, was not prepared to cope with the complexities of a declining and changing inner city. The individual the University had appointed to lead the way in its effort to cope with the neighborhood problems had a narrow "fortress" mentality. He was even able to convince the administration to follow a policy that, I thought, verged on the idiotic. The policy limited all new University building to one street, 61st Street, which would then serve as a barrier against the immigration of blacks and of the urban problems they brought with them. What happened, of course, was that everything south of 61st Street quickly deteriorated.

Both Louis Wirth and I became deeply involved with neighborhood affairs and argued from an early stage that improvements could come only through the commitment of the various neighborhoods surrounding the University so that all the residents became workers in a cause for improvement. Only neighborhood action could resist the predator speculators who rushed in wherever possible to turn houses into tenements. It meant a vigilant neighborhood insistance on the enforcement of building and zoning regulations.

I joined forces with our neighbors in creating the Hyde Park-Kenwood Association, which became one of the city's strongest neighborhood groups. By contrast, on the northside of the University, the University organized an association that turned out to be inherently ineffective, and the neighborhood deteriorated at a breathtaking pace, becoming a center of crime, drug dealing, and other well-known city ills.

A redevelopment project had been proposed for the center of the Hyde Park area where physical deterioration had set in. The University administration was to take an active part in the development of a local program under the new Housing Act of 1949, which provided federal money for urban renewal in cities where slums and blight had reached high levels. Its objective was to "upgrade" the area by bringing in upper middle-class families to replace the area's economically more marginal families and businesses. This policy seemed to be a mistake; rather, the effort should have been directed maintaining the present residents in the community and, at the same time, enhancing the University orientation of the neighborhood.

I urged a maximum amount of rehabilitation and a minimum amount of clearance and new building. In addition, where the new building was to take place, it should not be of the type priced beyond the means of the faculty and students as well as other University-oriented families. That would help to create a lively, attractive center of activities.

I laid out a plan to serve as an alternative to the one proposed. It was based on mixed-use development, with recreational facilities in an urban park setting (including an ice skating and roller skating rink) and shops geared to the needs of a university area (with careful selection of tenants). Such a mixed-use development in a lighted center could provide the neighborhood with an attractive core used both day and night. The architectural designs were carried out by a friend, Bertram Goldberg, who was later to design Marina City and other distinguished buildings in Chicago.

Unfortunately, the plan had little impact on the developer or the University Administration. Instead, a typically bland, suburb-like housing project that did very little for the University community was built in the redevelopment area.

Of the various proposals I had made, only the lighted center became a reality, and this through the efforts of the neighbors themselves rather than the developer. This was the basis for what later became a more extensive proposal for the creation of "new towns intown" that was incorporated into the Housing Act of 1970.

Although my proposals for the University of Chicago area were to see the light of day in only a limited way, I felt that this experience provided for me the richest kind of learning about the problems of the inner city. It also underlined the importance of both analysis and invention in creating new situations, whether physical, economic, or social.

In 1951, the University ran into financial difficulties, and Hutchins gave up the chancellorship and left. The financial problems were to plague the program from that point on until its demise in 1956. Although interest in planning among the individual members of the social science faculty remained strong and, in fact, an increasing number of courses in planning were provided by newly arrived faculty members (such as Ed Ackerman and Harold Mayer in the Geography Department), the individual departments saw the dissolution of an interdepartmental program as a logical way to preserve their own funds. Thus, in 1953, the Executive Committee recommended that the planning program end as of 1956 and that student admissions should be managed accordingly. I had been asked in 1951 to take over the leadership of the program, and I was just young enough and optimistic enough to try to keep a sinking ship afloat. I gave up the battle in 1955 when I was invited to join Resources for the Future, a research foundation in Washington, D. C. Ackerman had recently joined RFF and found that the organization offered a remarkably attractive environment for social science research.

Actually, in spite of the severe financial problems from 1951 to 1955, the program was able to continue to attract outstandingly able students and to turn out original and significant research. It was, I suppose, a not infrequent case of outstanding work being done under severe pressures. To its last day, the University of Chicago planning program remained a significant force in the field. It had launched planning into a new era where the central contribution of the social sciences was widely acknowledged and where the importance of evolving new approaches to planning at every level of government came to be better understood. Still, one has to recognize that the impact of the school was much greater at the intellectual level than at the practical level. It was not until some years later that city planning practitioners really began to employ the concepts and methods developed at Chicago and at some other intellectually advanced schools.

RESOURCES FOR THE FUTURE, 1955–1968

I received an invitation to join the staff of Resources for the Future (RFF) in Washington, D. C., in 1955, some time after the decision had been made to close down the planning program at Chicago. The President of RFF, Reuben G. Gustavson (who had formerly been Vice Chancellor of the University of Chicago and Chancellor of the University of Nebraska) asked me to set up a new division of regional and urban studies. I learned that the invitation had been due to two friends of long standing, Joseph L. Fisher, a fellow student at the London School of Economics, and Edward Ackerman, with whom I had worked closely at Chicago and on the President's Water Resources Policy Commission. I felt that I was being offered a dream position: I could give the regional-urban division any direction I thought appropriate; I could do whatever research interested me the most; and, because the organization was established as a foundation, I would be in a position to make grants to encourage the types of urban and regional studies that I thought would be most valuable. With an offer like that, I probably would have been attracted away from the University anyway, but it was particularly welcome given the circumstances at Chicago.

RFF had been established two years earlier with Ford Foundation funds in response to suggestions by a number of distinguished individuals interested in research that would improve national policies on resources use, development, and conservation. William Paley, who had headed up a Presidential Commission on the future of United States resources, was particularly influential. The form of a resource cum foundation was a powerful innovative move and contributed to the tremendous impact that RFF was to have on both United States policy and the strengthening of the environmental movement.

Gustavson and Fisher, the latter soon to take over as RFF's President, both knew of my interest in planning and strongly encouraged it, because the environment and resources were central interests to the organization as the two of them conceived it. It seemed appropriate to be concerned with the urban environment and with planned regional development as much as with the more usual direct approach to natural resources. There was, also, quite general support for my early effort to show that urban amenities were an important component of the resources and environmental wealth of the nation and that the amenity resources deserved the same attention through research and careful planning in use, development, and conservation as in all other natural resources. I was to write on this theme a number of times during my stay at RFF.

My first research effort at RFF, however, was directed toward summarizing my thoughts on planning education resulting from experiences at the University of Chicago and elsewhere. This research culminated in a book, *Education for Planning: State and Regional.*

In keeping with my strong belief that a solid basis of research and information was essential in improving the quality of policy and planning in urban and regional matters at all levels of government, I launched a number of interrelated activities. The first was a survey of regionally oriented research and education activities at U. S. universities. The survey was designed to provide an information base for RFF's activities as well as to permit scholars working in these fields to get a sense of what was going on in their fields at other institutions. A questionnaire was sent to all the United States educational institutions granting Master's and Ph.D. degrees (with a response of more than 85 percent). It showed some 80 universities carrying on research work, as well as education, in these fields.

The results of the survey, *Regional Studies at U. S. Universities* (1957), revealed that, whereas many different kinds of departments were involved in different kinds of urban and regional studies, most of the work was sponsored by schools of planning and departments of geography. Studies in departments of economics and business schools were largely limited to local economic surveys and real estate studies. In only a few instances were broader urban and regional economic studies underway. The survey turned out to be extremely useful in guiding the work of my section in various ways: by indicating the kind of research that we, ourselves, might undertake that could make a unique contribution to knowledge; by suggesting grants that might be made to advance urban and regional studies along the most promising avenues; and, finally, by indicating organizational efforts to fill critical gaps.

Lowdon Wingo, a student of mine who had impressed me with his intelligence and breadth of outlook and who had had substantial city planning experience in Texas, and Edgar Dunn, whose work on location theory I had greatly admired, joined my staff. Somewhat later, Irving Hoch, an able economist from the University of California, Berkeley, also became a member of the unit.

For our own research at RFF, it seemed logical to undertake a substantial, in-depth study trying to get at the underlying factors in relative regional economic growth and considering this element as key to urban and regional policy and general community improvement efforts. To help me with this major study, I invited three economists of proven ability: Edgar Dunn, from the University of Florida; Richard Muth, from the University of Chicago; and Eric Lampard, an economic historian from the University of Wisconsin. This research was a great learning experience for me, and I believe it was for others because, in addition to the individual work the four of us did, we held a continuous seminar on national, regional, and urban growth. These seminars included carefully selected outsiders who helped us to deepen our own analysis, to improve the method we were using, and to spot at least some of the errors in logic and interpretation that are inevitable in any major research. The product of this study, *Regions, Resources, and Economic Growth* (1960), was well received and widely used across the country and popularized some of the analytical methods we had employed.

UCLA, SINCE 1968

When I was invited to take over the deanship of the School of Architecture and Urban Planning at UCLA in 1968, I saw it as an opportunity to fulfill a long-standing ambition and, in the process, overcome some long-standing frustrations. All my experiences had convinced me that I wanted to devote my life to education and research—to help train new generations of students who were concerned about the problems of society and dedicated to creating a better future. I had long ago concluded that urban problems were too complex to understand and overcome without using a broad array of disciplines. But I had been running into all sorts of frustrations in trying to work out a really effective multidisciplinary approach to urban and regional problems and to planning for the future.

At Chicago, we were remarkably successful in introducing the social sciences into planning education and research, but we had much less success in finding effective ways of combining the physical considerations with the social science ones. During our unsuccessful attempts to redevelop the Hyde Park neighborhood, I came to realize that, while the University of Chicago Planning School was doing a fine job in leading the way to a much more profound and appropriate use of the social sciences in planning, it had not devoted enough attention to the significant architectural and urban design features that were so important to city development and redevelopment.

Again, at RFF, although some remarkably good things were accomplished, there remained areas of strong frustration. One was in trying to get urban analysis and urban planning focused on the three-dimensional city and away from the flat, two-dimensional city where simple-minded land use was the dominant consideration. The nation's urban stock (its buildings and infrastructure), which accounts for a large proportion of the national wealth, is located in the three-dimensional city. Hoch, who joined me in working on this theme, wrote some excellent papers on the subject, but RFF was not a good platform for launching a long-range, broad-based development of the concept.

I felt some frustration, also, in trying to direct attention to the close interrelationships among the natural environment, the focal point of RFF activities, and the built environment. I did write about urban amenities as the "new resources in an advanced urban society," and Lowdon Wingo and I published a number of papers on the importance of amenity resources to location decisions and the special characteristics of urban recreation. Here, too, RFF was not an ideal base of furthering this concept. It could be more logically developed in a professional school.

Thus, both the Chicago and RFF experiences, although wonderful in many ways, left areas of frustration. Much of this centered on the large gap I perceived between the idea level—where provocative and valuable concepts were being projected—and the world of actual practice. I felt a strong urge to get back to the university where education, research, and practice could be combined. All three elements had to work closely together. If practice did not reflect both the understanding that was developed in education and the dreams that were created there as well as the results of the most advanced research, it would be a pit of nonprogress. Against that background, I saw the invitation to create a school of architecture and urban planning as the fulfillment of a dream.

Bibliography

BOOKS

Modern Budget Policies, Unpublished Ph.D. Dissertation, Harvard University, 1939.

State and Local Finance in the National Economy, with Alvin H. Hansen, New York: W. W. Norton, 1944.

Puerto Rico's Economic Future. Chicago: The University of Chicago Press, 1950.

Education for Planning: City, State, and Regional. Baltimore: The Johns Hopkins Press, 1957.

Regions, Resources, and Economic Growth, with Edgar S. Dunn, Jr., Eric E. Lampard, and Richard F. Muth. Baltimore: The Johns Hopkins Press, 1960.

Planning and the Urban Community (Ed.). Pittsburgh: Carnegie Institute of Technology and the University of Pittsburgh Press, 1961.

How a Region Grows: Area Development in the U. S. Economy, a Supplementary Paper. New York: Committee for Economic Development, March 1963.

Revenue Sharing and the City (Ed. with Richard P. Nathan). Baltimore: The Johns Hopkins Press, 1968.

Issues in Urban Economics (Ed. with Lowdon Wingo, Jr.). Baltimore: The Johns Hopkins Press, 1968.

The Quality of the Urban Environment: "New Resources" in an Urban Age (Ed.) Baltimore: Johns Hopkins Press, 1969.

Alliance for Progress: A Social Invention in the Making. Baltimore: Johns Hopkins Press, 1969.

The Future of the U.S. Government: Toward the Year 2000 (Ed.). New York: Braziller, 1971.

New Towns: Why—and for Whom? (Ed. with Neil C. Sandberg). New York: Praeger Publishers, 1973.

Modernizing the Central City: New Towns Intown . . . and Beyond, with Thomas Berg, Robert Fountain, David Vetter, and John Weld. Cambridge, Mass.: Ballinger Publishing Company, 1975.

Agenda for the New Urban Era: Second Generation National Policy (Ed.). Chicago: American Society of Planning Officials, 1975.

The Arts in the Economic Life of the City. New York: The American Council for the Arts, 1980.

Planning the Post-Industrial City. Chicago: American Planning Association, 1980.

MONOGRAPHS AND REPORTS

Regional Resource Development (with Alvin H. Hansen). Washington, D.C.: National Planning Association, 1942.

Economic Development of Puerto Rico, 1940–1950 and 1951–1960: Report to the Puerto Rico Planning Board. San Juan, P.R.: Government Service Office, 1951.

Definition and Measurement of Standards of Living, Report of a Conference of U.S. Experts. Chicago: Public Administration Clearing House, 1953.

The University of Chicago and the Surrounding Community. Chicago: Program of Education and Research in Planning, 1953.

The Organization of Economic Intelligence with Special Reference to Turkey (with A. Dollinger and G. D. N. Worsick). United Nations: Technical Assistance Program, 1954.

Urban Renewal in a Chicago Neighborhood: An Appraisal of the Hyde Park–Kenwood Renewal Program. Chicago: Hyde Park Herald, 1955.

Regional Studies at U.S. University: A Survey of Regionally Oriented Research and Graduate Activities. Washington, D.C.: Resources for the Future, Inc., 1957.

The Urban Administrator: Education for Service in Metropolitan Communities, College Park, Md.: Bureau of Government Research, College of Business and Public Administration, University of Maryland, 1958.

A National Program of Research in Housing and Urban Development: The Major Requirements and a Suggested Approach. Washington, D.C.: Resources for the Future, Inc., September 1961.

"Urban Growth and the Planning of Outdoor Recreation," *Trends in American Living and Outdoor Recreation,* Report to the Outdoor Recreation Review Commission (with Lowdon Wingo, Jr.). Washington, D.C.: U.S. Government Printing Office, 1962.

Urban Research and Education in the New York Metropolitan Region: A Report to the Regional Plan Association (with Henry Cohen). New York: Regional Plan Association, 1965.

The White House Conference on International Cooperation: Report of the Committee on Urban Development. Washington, D.C.: U.S. Government Printing Office, 1965.

Design for a Worldwide Study of Regional Development. Washington, D.C.: Resources for the Future, Inc., 1966.

Prototype State-of-the-Region Report for Los Angeles County. Los Angeles: University of California, School of Architecture and Urban Planning, 1973.

Central City Modernization: A New Town Intown Approach. 5 vols. Report Prepared for the Department of Housing and Urban Development. Los Angeles: University of California, School of Architecture and Urban Planning, 1974.

JOURNAL ARTICLES, BOOK CHAPTERS, AND PAPERS

"Budgetary Symbolism." *Public Policy* 2, 1941: 36–63.

"Should Congress Vote a Sales Tax to Finance the War?" *The Saturday Evening Post* 214, June 20, 1942.

"Financial Preparation for Postwar Public Works." *Proceedings of a Symposium on Wartime Problems of State and Local Finance,* 1943, 164–177.

"Fiscal Policy at the State and Local Levels." In *Postwar Economic Problems,* edited by Seymour E. Harris, 221–38. New York: McGraw-Hill, 1943.

"Taxes are Good for You." *Survey Graphic* 23 (March 1943).

"Dynamic Elements in a Full Employment Program." In *Income, Employment and Public Policy: Essays in Honor of Alvin H. Hansen,* 199–217. New York: W. W. Norton, 1948.

"Unfinished Business in Puerto Rico." *Carribbean Commission Monthly Information Bulletin* 5 (November 1951): 123–27.

"The United States and the Economic Development of Puerto Rico." *Journal of Economic History* 12 (Winter 1952): 45–59.

"How Shall We Train the Planners We Need?" *Planning 1951,* Proceedings of the Annual National Planning Conference, American Society of Planning Officials, 1951, 13–22.

"The Requirements of an Effective Point Four Program." *Economic Development and Cultural Change* 1 No. 3 (October 1952): 209–215.

"Transforming the Economy." *Puerto Rico: A Study in Democratic Development, Annals of the American Academy of Political and Social Science* 285 (January 1953): 48–54.

"Knowledge Needed for Comprehensive Planning." In *Needed Urban and Metropolitan Research* edited by Donald J. Budge, 4–6. Oxford, Ohio: Scripps Foundation, 1953.

"Planning Concepts and Regional Research." *Social Forces* 32 (December 1953): 173–177.

"Training of Planners in Less Developed Countries." *United Nations Seminar on Training for Town and Country Planning,* Puerto Rico (March 1956).

"Education of City Planners: Past, Present and Future." *Journal of the American Institute of Planners* 22 (Fall 1956):186–216.

"Problems of Assessing Regional Economic Progress." Pp. 37–62 in *Regional Income*. Vol. 21. *Studies in Income and Wealth*. National Bureau of Economic Research. Princeton: Princeton University Press, 1957.

"Interrelations of State Income and Industrial Structure." *Review of Economics and Statistics*, 39 (May 1957).

Training for Town and Country Planning, pp. 66–70. New York: United Nations, Department of Economic and Social Affairs, 1957.

"Key Factors in Regional Economic Development." *Papers Presented at The Governor's Commission on Economic Trends in Iowa*. Iowa City: Institute of Public Affairs, State University of Iowa, 1958.

"Regional Research and Highway Planning." *Urban Research in Highway Planning*, Highway Research Board Bulletin 190. Washington, D.C.: National Academy of Sciences, National Research Council, 1958.

_____ and John Friedmann. "Education and Research in Planning: A Review of the University of Chicago Experiment." (translated by H. Kawakani), *City Planning Review* 28 (1959).

_____ and Lowdon Wingo, Jr. "Natural Resource Endowment and Regional Economic Growth." In *Natural Resources and Economic Growth*, edited by Joseph J. Spengler. Washington: Resources for the Future, Inc., 1961.

"Regional Economic Growth in the U.S.: Past, Present and Future." *Proceedings of the First Southwest Seminar in Public Responsibility*. Wagoner, Okla.: University of Okalhoma, 1960.

"Trends in Regional Economic Development," *Proceedings of the First Southwest Seminar in Public Responsibility*. Wagoner, Okla.: University of Oklahoma, 1960.

"Development and Its Implications." *Proceedings of the First Southwest Seminar in Public Responsibility*. Wagoner, Okla: University of Oklahoma, 1960.

"Lagging Sectors and Regions of the American Economy." *Papers and Proceedings of The American Economic Association*, Vol. 1 (May 1960): 223–230.

"Population Growth: Threat or Opportunity." *Jersey Plans* 12 (Summer 1961).

"Relative Regional Economic Growth: An Approach to Regional Accounts." In *Design of Regional Accounts*, edited by Werner Hochwald. Baltimore: The Johns Hopkins Press, 1961.

"National Planning and Multinational Planning Under the Alliance for Progress." *Organization, Planning and Programming for Economic Development*, Vol. 8 of *U.S. Papers prepared for the United Nations Conference on the Application of Science and Technology for the Benefit of the Less Developed Areas*. Washington, D.C.: U.S. Government Printing Office, 1962.

"A National System of Metropolitan Information and Analysis." *Papers and Proceedings of The American Economic Association* (May 1962): 356–364.

_____ and Raúl Saez. "Planificación Nacional y Multinacional en la Alianza para el Progreso." United Nations Conference Paper, 1963.

"Social Planning in the Metropolis." In *The Urban Condition: People and Policy in the Metropolis*, edited by Leonard J. Duhl. New York: Basic Books, 1963.

_____, G. Colm, and I. Fox. "Organizazione Statale per lo Sviluppo Economico Negli Stati Uniti d' America." *La Scuola in Azione* 14 (April 29, 1963).

"Organizational Requirements for Growth of Stability." *Papers of the Conference on Inflation and Growth in Latin America*, Rio de Janeiro (January 1963).

_____ and Rômulo Almeida. "Regional Economic Integration in the Development of Latin America." *Economía Latinoamericana* 1, 2 (November 1963).

"Process and Method in Social Planning" with Thomas Sherrard, and "New Directions in Planning: A Model for Social Planning" in *Social Progress Through Social Planning: The Role of Social Work*. Report of the United States Committee to the 12th International Conference on Social Work, Athens, Greece, New York, 1964.

_____ and Charles L. Leven. "Towards an Integrated System of Regional Accounts: Stocks, Flows and the Analysis of the Public Sector." In *Elements of Regional Accounts*, edited by Werner Z. Hirsch. Baltimore: The Johns Hopkins Press, 1964.

"Economic and Technological Trends: Implications." Paper presented at conference, *The Metropolitan Future: California and The Challenge of Growth*, Berkeley, California, September 26–27, 1963. Berkeley: University of California Press, 1965, 115–120.

"Planeamiento Educativo y su Relación con Los Planes Generales de Desarrollo." *Reuniones Técnicas Sobre Planeamiento Educativo*, 1965; abstracted in *SIAP* (Sociedad Interamericana de Planificación *Newsletter* (July–August 1965).

"Common Goals and the Linking of Physical and Social Planning." *Planning 1965*, 1965.

"Slums and Squatter Settlements," *White House Conference on the International Cooperation Year*, November 30, 1965.

"New Directions in Social Planning," *Journal of the American Institute of Planners* 31 (November 1965).

"Towards the Developmental-Servicing City," *Ekistics* 21 (February 1966).

"New Towns Intown," *Journal of the American Institute of Planners* 32, 3 (May 1966).

"New Resources in an Urban Age," *Papers, Symposium of American Cement Corporation and Urban America/ACTION*, January 5, 1966.

————— and Felipe Pazos. "Economic Policy Problems in Sub-National and Multi-National Regions," *Conference of Society for Inter-American Planning*, November 1966.

"Physical Planning and Social Objectives" (in Hebrew). *The Economic Quarterly* 12 (February 1966).

"Approaches to a Theory of Regional Planning." *Papers of a Conference on Regional Development Planning*. University of Puerto Rico/Cornell University, March 30, 1967.

————— and Royce Hanson. "The Inner City and A New Urban Politics." *Urban America: Goals and Problems*, Subcommittee on Urban Affairs of the Joint Economic Committee, Washington, D.C.: U.S. Government Printing Office, August 1967.

"Modernizing Urban Development." *Daedalus* (Toward the Year 2000: Work in Progress) 26, 3 (Summer 1967); 789–800.

————— and Felipe Pazos. "Los Problemas de la Economia en Regiones Subnacionales y Multinacionales." *Hacia una Política de Integración para el Desarrollo de la America Latina* (June 1967).

"Key Features of Regional Planning." *Journal of the American Institute of Planners* 34 (May 1968).

"Les Villes Americaines de l'an 2000." *Chronique Sociale de France* (July 1968): 88 ff.

"Regional Planning in Less-developed Countries." in Maynard M. Hufschmidt (Ed.), *Regional Planning: Challenge and Prospects*, 324–31. New York: Frederick A. Praeger, 1969.

"What Economic Future for the Inner City Ghetto?" *Science and Technology and the Cities, a compilation of papers for the tenth meeting of the Science and Technology Committee, U.S. House of Representatives, Washington, D.C.* U.S. Government Printing Office, 1969, 89 ff.

"As principais caracteristicas do planeamento regional," *Urbanização* 4, 1 (March 1969): 57–68.

"Urban Imperatives." *Modulus* (May 1969).

"A Framework for Dealing with the Urban Environment: Introductory Statement." In *The Quality of the Urban Environment*, edited by Harvey S. Perloff, 3–25. Baltimore: Johns Hopkins Press, 1969.

"Making Our Cities Livable." *World Books 1972*, Yearbook Transvision.

"Environmental Indicators: An Overview." *Proceedings of the Environmental Design Research Association*, 1972.

"National Urban Policy: Stage I: Building the Foundation." In *Spatial, Regional and Population Economics: Essays in Honor of Edgar M. Hoover*, edited by Mark Perlman, Charles J. Leven, and Benjamin Chinitz. New York: Gordon & Breach, 1972.

"Life Styles and Environment—The Future Planning Game?" *Planning, The ASPO Magazine* (June 1973).

————— and Marion Clawson. "Alternatives for Future Urban Land Policy." In *Modernizing Urban Land Policy*, edited by Marion Clawson. Baltimore: Johns Hopkins Press, 1973.

"The Development of Urban Economics in the United States." *Urban Studies* 10, 3 (October 1973).

————— and Kathleen M. Connell. "Subsidiary Transportation: Its Role in Regional Planning." *Journal of the American Institute of Planners* 41, 3 (May 1975): 170–183.

"Knowledge to Action: Creating an Undergraduate Problem-Solving Program." *American Behavioral Scientist* 18, 2 (November–December, 1974).

————— with Frank Klett. "The Evolution of Planning Education." In *Planning in America: Learning from Turbulence,* edited by David R. Godschalk, 161–180. Washington, D.C.: The American Institute of Planners, 1974.

————— and Daniel J. Flaming. "Approaches to the Future in U.S. Urban Transportation Planning." *Transportation* 5 (1976): 153–173.

"The Central City in the Postindustrial Age." In *The Mature Metropolis,* edited by Charles L. Leven, 108–129. Lexington, Mass.: Lexington Books, 1978.

"The Future of Downtown." *L.A. Architect* (January 1979).

". . . As We Enter the 1980's: The Evolving Situation of the Planning Profession." *APA Magazine* (July 1979).

"Comprehensive Programs for Community Development in Industrialized Countries." *Papers and Proceedings of the 35th World Congress of the International Federation for Housing and Planning,* Jerusalem (November 1980).

Index